The National Archives

Portico of the National Archives

THE NATIONAL ARCHIVES
America's Ministry of Documents
1934–1968

BY
DONALD R. McCOY

THE UNIVERSITY OF NORTH CAROLINA PRESS
CHAPEL HILL

Both the initial research and the publication of this work were made possible in part through grants from the National Endowment for the Humanities, a federal agency whose mission is to award grants to support education, scholarship, media programming, libraries, and museums, in order to bring the results of cultural activities to a broad, general public.

Manufactured in the United States of America
ISBN 0-8078-1327-3
Library of Congress Catalog Card Number 78-2314

Library of Congress Cataloging in Publication Data

McCoy, Donald R
    The National Archives.

    Bibliography: p.
    Includes index.
    1. United States. National Archives and Records
Service.   I. Title.
CD3023. M25   027.573   78-2314
ISBN 0-8078-1327-3

CONTENTS

―――――

ILLUSTRATIONS

PREFACE

Few who climb the thirty-nine steps to the portico of the National Archives in Washington know that the building is the seat of a far-flung dominion of documents. Indeed, this instrumentality of the government of the United States manages more than twenty archival repositories, presidential libraries, and records centers. How that came about is no small story.

My goal is to recount and to evaluate the significant steps and controversies in the development between 1934 and 1968 of a unique American institution, the National Archives and its successor, the National Archives and Records Service. I chose 1934, the date of the National Archives Act, as the beginning because the story of the lengthy movement that led to the founding legislation could fill a volume in its own right. In fact, it has been the subject of many articles and a fine doctoral dissertation, whereas little scholarly research has been done on the history of the National Archives itself. This study ends basically with the retirement of the fourth archivist of the United States, Robert H. Bahmer, in 1968. This seems natural because it was at that point that a new generation of archivists assumed direction of NARS.

The National Archives has had considerable influence on archival, research, and even management and cultural affairs both in the United States and abroad. Moreover, it has been an inextricable part of the nation's recent administrative and political history. I hope, because of this, that my book will be helpful not only to archivists, records managers, and associated professional workers, but also to researchers, administrators, and elected officials who

vii

have interests in the management of archives and records. Perhaps the general reader, too, will find this study occasionally interesting.

I am indebted to a great number of people and organizations for help in preparing this work. The National Endowment for the Humanities and the University of Kansas were most generous in supplying financial support, and the *American Archivist* kindly gave permission to use almost unchanged an article of mine from their pages which became chapter 2. In the course of my research, it seemed as though most of the present and former members of the staff of the National Archives and Records Service assisted me in some way. In particular I want to thank George Ulibarri, who spared me no effort in guiding me through the records of NARS. Also of great help were Robert H. Bahmer, Philip C. Brooks, Frank Burke, John E. Byrne, Robert W. Krauskopf, Philip D. Lagerquist, Albert H. Leisinger, Richard Maxwell, John R. Nesbitt, Harold T. Pinkett, Daniel J. Reed, Fred Shelley, Jane F. Smith, William Stewart, Karl L. Trever, Helen Finneran Ulibarri, R. Reed Whitaker, W. D. White, and John Wickman. People elsewhere were very helpful, too, including Mrs. Wayne C. Grover; Ernst Posner of the American University; Marion Howey and John Nugent of the University of Kansas; Carolyn H. Sung of the Manuscript Division of the Library of Congress; Melvin Margerum of the Office of Management and Budget; Robert W. Richmond of the Kansas State Historical Society; H. G. Jones and Carolyn A. Wallace of the University of North Carolina; H. G. Connor, who allowed me to use his uncle's journal; and Francis C. Jameson, who gave me permission to use his father's papers. I am deeply grateful to Assistant Librarian of Congress Elizabeth Kegan and Archivist of the United States James B. Rhoads, who gave me encouragement and support at every stage of my study and writing. Dr. Rhoads read a draft of my manuscript; Deputy Archivist James R. O'Neill, as did former Deputy Archivist Herbert E. Angel; Walter Rundell Jr., of the University of Maryland; H. G. Jones of the University of North Carolina; Frank B. Evans of UNESCO; and Oliver W. Holmes, former Executive Director of the National Historical Publications Commission. For their valuable comments and other assistance, I owe them many thanks. They are not to blame for the opinions and flaws in this book; I must shoulder full responsibility for those.

Donald R. McCoy

THE NATIONAL ARCHIVES

1. *Establishment*

During its closing hours in 1934, the Seventy-third Congress passed the National Archives Act.[1] Neither the debate surrounding it nor its enactment elicited headlines, for the legislation was usually just one item listed in the press among the measures "also enacted" during the heyday of Franklin D. Roosevelt's New Deal. Seldom, however, had a federal law a longer gestation and more potential permanence.

In discussing the background of the National Archives Act, it is worth recalling that the word "archives" derives from the Greek word *archeion*, which meant both records and their storage place. The use of records as society's memory antedates ancient Greece, however, having been traced to the Sumerians at least during the period before 2,000 B.C. Thereafter every nation came to have records and some means of preserving them in order for its government to operate and for the protection of personal rights. A third function eventually developed, which was the use of older records to document a society's cultural heritage.[2]

With the emergence of the complex modern nation-state, more attention was given to the preservation of records of enduring value. This occurred in Spain as early as the sixteenth century with the formation of the Archivo General de Simancas. The foundations of models for modern national archives, however, were laid with the establishment of France's Archives Nationales in 1789 and England's Public Record Office in 1838. The impact of the archival establishments in Spain, France, and England was immense, because developments in those countries often not only were introduced into their numerous colonies but were copied by

3

other nations as well. For example, by 1900 most European countries had developed similar institutions, including the outstanding Dutch and German archives, and in Latin America twelve national archives had been established.[3]

The growth of archival institutions elsewhere, the rise of the modern national state, and the development of a professional guild of historians contributed to a movement for a national archives in the United States. The first, of course, set precedents and provided something by way of models; the second gave some indication of the needs of a nation, of which some Americans, caught up in building their own nation, took note; the third set precedents for American historians (indeed, a number of young Americans traveled to Europe, especially to Germany, during the nineteenth century to receive training in the rapidly developing, research-oriented "science" of history).[4]

Happenings at home, however, were more immediately important to the establishment of an archives. Occasionally, concern was voiced in the United States for the proper keeping of the nation's records. The Continental Congress chose a secretary, Charles Thomson, who functioned superbly during the Revolutionary and Confederation periods as the custodian of the records of Congress and the central government. As the federal government was established and grew, its departments and bureaus gave some attention to the preservation of their archives. Yet, since the amount of care varied considerably, disaster was sure to strike. During 1800 and 1801, fire seriously damaged the records of the War Office and the Treasury Department. And these were only the first of many disasters visited upon the government's records. Not only fire, but also water, theft, negligence, insects, rodents, chemicals, extreme cold or heat, and mold led to the loss of or damage to many federal records over the years. These problems resulted in some remedial action. In 1810 Congress authorized better housing for government records, although the law was only partially executed. The government also allowed, encouraged, or sponsored the publication of great collections of documents, most notably by Ebenezer Hazard in the 1790s and by Jared Sparks and Peter Force during the three decades before the Civil War. Nevertheless, the actions taken fell far short of providing for satisfactory preservation of official records and regularized access to the archives.[5]

The Civil War was something of a turning point. This was largely because of the increasing growth of the national government and correspondingly of its records. Indeed, between 1861 and 1916 the accumulated total of federal records soared from 108,000 to 1,031,000 cubic feet. After the war voices were raised in the government beseeching Congress to provide for disposal of useless records and proper storage of those worthy of retention. After fire destroyed part of the Department of the Interior building in 1877, sentiment grew in the executive and legislative branches for the construction of a fireproof general repository in which federal agencies could place and separately control their records. From then on, bill after bill was introduced for such a purpose, but they failed to be enacted until 1896. Then Congress agreed to direct the secretary of the treasury to submit plans for a general storage facility, a "hall of records," which he did in 1898. Another five years passed, however, before Congress appropriated funds to buy a site for a records repository. The government duly acquired a site, but what followed was more discussion, not construction. Finally, in 1926, Congress took decisive action. By then, the goal had become not storage for records to be still under the control of individual agencies, but construction of a building in which the federal government's records of permanent value, its archives, could be centrally and professionally preserved and administered. That came about because the question of what should be done about federal records had become a national issue, however minor, as first historians and archivists and then patriotic groups such as the American Legion and the Daughters of the American Revolution lobbied for a national archival institution in order to make the documentation of the history of the United States easily accessible.[6]

Crucial to the movement for a national archives were the organizing and lobbying efforts of J. Franklin Jameson, the bewhiskered, bespectacled, lean, and dignified-looking patriarch of Clio's tribe in the United States. This was as it should be, for Jameson in 1882 received one of the first two doctorates in history granted in the United States. He then proceeded to do everything a historian could do professionally, including teaching, research, writing, editing, and administration. For almost a quarter of a century, beginning in 1905, he directed the Bureau of Historical Research of the Carnegie Institution, from which position he initiated innumerable advances in the gathering and publication of historical evidence. Jameson served as editor of the *American Historical Review* as well as president of the American Historical Association, and for the rest of his life he was a great influence in the association's councils. He helped to found the AHA's Public Archives Commission and later its Conference of Archivists, both of which he used to spur not only the movement for a national archives but for state archival institutions as well. Jameson rounded out his career by heading the Manuscripts Division of the Library of Congress. Without his constant attention, the National Archives might not have been born, at least not until later and probably not in the form it took.[7]

Over the years Jameson put together an effective alliance of archivists, historians, and patriotic groups that eventually won the support of President Calvin Coolidge and a majority of senators and representatives. Congress in 1926 thus appropriated $1,000,000 toward "the construction of an extensible archives building and the acquisition of a site."[8] It also authorized the secretary of the treasury to enter into contracts for erecting the building. That, however, was only the beginning of the successful end of the movement for a national archives. Not only had a new site to be selected, but plans had to be drawn up for a large and rather complicated building and further appropriations to be secured. These were accomplished, but not speedily. It was not until September 1931 that ground was broken, and the cornerstone was not laid until February 1933.

The cornerstone laying was a happy event, even though it occurred during the depth of the Great Depression. Herbert Hoover, who was the leading participant in the ceremony, was even seen to smile, a phenomenon that was rare during his last year as president. On that occasion, he voiced high aspirations for the National Archives:

The building which is rising here will house the name and records of every patriot who bore arms for our country . . . , the most sacred documents of our history, the originals of the Declaration of Independence and of the Constitution of the United States. . . . The romance of our history will have living habitation here in the writings of statesmen, soldiers, and all the others, both men and women, who have builded the great structure of our national life. This temple of our history will appropriately be one of the most beautiful buildings in America, an expression of the American soul. It will be one of the most durable, an expression of the American character.[9]

President Hoover, however, was more certain about the functions of the National Archives than anyone had reason to be. Despite the decades of debate, despite the fact that the building was going up, Congress had yet to provide for the organization and operation of the National Archives. Until the legislators acted, the National Archives could be no more than an empty building.

During the crisis-laden year of 1933, the National Archives received little attention. It was sufficient that progress was being made on the edifice. Of course, bills to give structure and function to the projected new agency had been introduced from time to time beginning in 1930, and interested parties both inside and outside Congress had discussed what the character of the legislation should be. Few citizens, however, were excited about the archives in 1933, partly because of the press of depression-borne economic and governmental problems and partly because some people believed that the main issues about the National Archives had been settled in providing for its housing. Yet, as time passed, other questions became clear. Would the National Archives serve only to care for the most valuable older records of the federal government or would it have other functions? Would it be an independent government agency or would it be part of another federal office? Would it be staffed with the best professionals available or would it become a haven for patronage appointees?

There was some interest in placing the National Archives within an already existing agency. One aide in the Bureau of the Budget suggested that the Library of Congress would be the appropriate parent organization; and Secretary of the Interior Harold L. Ickes contended that the new operation should be a part of his department's National Park Service in order to avoid an overlap in functions and an unnecessary proliferation of federal agencies. Yet neither of these suggestions became government policy. The Senate clearly wanted the National Archives to be an independent agency. Moreover, scattered documentation in the files of the White House and the Budget Bureau indicates that that was also the inclination of President Franklin D. Roosevelt and the bureau.[10]

The deliberations of Congress on the establishment of the National Archives revolved around two bills. These were H.R. 8910, which Democratic Representative Sol Bloom of New York had introduced on 2 April 1934; and S. 3681, which Senator Kenneth McKellar, Democrat of Tennessee, had submitted on 24 March. The House passed the Bloom bill, which was inhospitable to independent agency status for the National Archives, on 16 April. The Senate Committee on the Library combined the two bills as H.R. 8910, which strengthened the archivist's power to acquire records and gave statutory standing to a National Historical Publications Commission. The committee reported favorably on the consolidated bill by 28 May. J. Franklin Jameson and other historians, including John C. Fitzpatrick, Dumas Malone, and Thomas P. Martin, were involved at various stages in the writing of the legislation. Their participation did not mean that matters proceeded fully to their satisfaction, but it did guarantee that the bill would be adequate when measured by their professional standards.

Senatorial inaction was the biggest problem after the bill was reported. On 10 June, Bloom, Jameson, newspaperman Gould Lincoln, and Chairman Kent E. Keller and Clerk John G. Bradley of the House Library Committee initiated publicity in the Washington press to try to force the passage of H.R. 8910 in the upper chamber. Bloom also visited Franklin D. Roosevelt. Subsequently, the president asked Alben Barkley, one of the Democratic floor leaders in the Senate, about the National Archives bill.

"Well, Mr. President," the Kentuckian replied, "we have been quite busy, as you know."

Roosevelt told him, "Senator, I am personally interested in

that bill, and want some action taken on it right away." Barkley gave him immediate results, for the following day, 13 June, the Senate passed the legislation.[11]

The House disagreed with the stronger Senate version of the National Archives bill; so the measure was sent to a conference committee of the two chambers. On 16 June the committee reported out a compromise, patterned largely on the Senate bill, that both houses approved. On 19 June, the day after Congress adjourned, President Roosevelt signed the act into law and approved an appropriation of $50,000 to begin the agency's work during fiscal year 1935. Thus, the National Archives was authorized as an agency of the government of the United States.[12]

The legislation generally gave the National Archives the scope and authority its proponents desired. The new organization was to be an independent agency of the federal government; it was to be headed by the presidentially appointed archivist of the United States, who was to draw an annual salary of $10,000, a handsome sum for the time. The archivist was given broad personnel powers, being authorized to appoint the employees of the National Archives "solely with reference to their fitness for their particular duties and without regard to civil-service law." The archivist had the power to "make rules and regulations for the government of the National Archives." Furthermore, that official had "immediate custody and control of the National Archives Building and other such buildings, grounds, and equipment as may . . . become a part of the National Archives Establishment . . . and their contents shall be vested in the Archivist."[13]

The powers of the National Archives with respect to the records of the federal government were also broad. The archivist and his deputies were authorized to inspect any and all federal records —executive, legislative, and judicial—wherever they were located and, with the approval of the National Archives Council, to requisition such materials for transfer to the National Archives. (The right of inspection was to be of great significance in gaining the knowledge necessary both to save records of permanent value and, later, to develop a federal records administration program.) After records were transferred to the National Archives, they were subject to the archivist's "authority to make regulations for [their] arrangement, custody, use, and withdrawal." The crucial limitation on this power was that the head of any federal agency could, for no longer than his or her tenure in office, "exempt from examination and consultation by officials, private individuals, or any other persons . . . confidential matter transferred from his department or office."[14] This provision turned out to be a serious problem. Although some agency heads exempted little or nothing from examination, others, particularly after the coming of World War II, relied heavily on this right. Another problem was that while the law enjoined all persons in charge of agency records to give "full cooperation" to the National Archives in the inspection of federal records, Congress failed to specify that they be equally cooperative in handing over the materials requisitioned by the National Archives. The result of that and the act's failure to define *records* was that the archivist often had to enter into long, tedious, and occasionally unsuccessful negotiations to effect the transfer of archives to his establishment.

The National Archives Act was also concerned with things other than traditional archival activities. Thanks to action by the conference committee, the new agency was empowered to acquire and preserve motion pictures and sound recordings "pertaining to and illustrative of historical activities in the United States." The act also created the National Historical Publications Commission, as a separate organization but with the archivist as chairman, to "make plans, estimates, and recommendations for such historical works and collections of sources as seem appropriate for publication and/or recording at the public expense." This was J. Franklin Jameson's idea, and he fought hard to get it incorporated into the National Archives Act. Unfortunately for him, the commission did little until after its reorganization in 1950. The provision for the acquisition of films and sound recordings, however, was of importance almost from the beginning. It had the advantage, as did the NHPC's work much later, of allowing the National Archives to expand into activities beyond the collection and care of official government records.

The legislation provided ample opportunity for the archivist to be in touch with government officials who could assist the operations of his agency. The president had to appoint and the Senate had to confirm the archivist as well as those on his staff with an annual salary of $5,000 or more. Although this posed some patronage problems, it did mean that the archivist would have access to the White House and the Senate. More important was that in the course of his duties the archivist, with his responsibility for inspecting the records and acquiring federal archives, would have many opportunities to make his agency and its work known. This was reinforced by the requirement in the act that the archivist render an annual report to Congress on what the National Archives and the NHPC had done as well as to transmit recommendations for the destruction, with congressional approval, of federal records "which appear to have no permanent value or historical interest."[15]

The National Archives Council also served to give the archivist widespread contacts in the government since its membership was composed of, in addition to the archivist, the secretaries of each executive department or their alternates, the chairmen of the House and Senate Library Committees, the librarian of Congress, and the secretary of the Smithsonian Institution. Its duties were to "define the classes of material which shall be transferred to the National Archives Building and establish regulations governing such transfer." Moreover, the council was to advise on regulations regarding the disposition and use of the records in the archivist's custody.[16] This body could have hampered the development of the National Archives. It turned out, however, to be generally amenable to the archivist's recommendations and of assistance in smoothing the way for the agency's work. To a much smaller degree, the composition of the NHPC served a similar purpose, with its membership of representatives from the Library of Congress, the departments of state, war, and the navy and the AHA.

Of course, this was in the future. The important thing was that by the end of June 1934 the statutory bases for the National Archives had been laid, and the building to house the new agency was taking shape in the heart of the nation's capital. The edifice was impressive, even monumental; the law gave promise of being at least adequate to handle the federal government's archival problems. Yet, given the legal powers of the archivist, how well the building and the law would be used depended largely upon whom was appointed to head the National Archives.

2. Appointment of the Archivist

The first archivist of the United States would be in an unrivaled position to decide not only what the National Archives would be, but indeed how the nation's archival profession would develop. Yet those were only two factors that contributed to making the choice of who should fill the post a prickly affair. Additionally there were numerous people who wanted the position, especially as good jobs were scarce in depression-ravaged America in 1934. There were also some politicians who viewed the National Archives as a rich source of patronage because of the many appointments that the archivist would control. And there was the fact that few people had suitable qualifications, for there was no archival training program in the country and not many Americans had worthwhile experience as archivists or historical administrators. Finally, it was obvious that the president and interested legislators knew almost nothing about what an archivist should be.[1]

Candidates for appointment to the archivist's job quickly appeared after the laying of the cornerstone of the National Archives building in February 1933. Many people urged J. Franklin Jameson, chief of the Manuscripts Division of the Library of Congress, to apply for or at least to sponsor a candidate for the position. This patriarch of American archivists and historians replied that because of his wishes, personality, and advanced age (seventy-three), he was not eligible. Moreover, he had no candidate for the post; all Jameson wanted was the appointment of a well-qualified person from among the several candidates on hand. William E. Dodd, professor at the University of Chicago and vice president of the American Historical Association, wrote in May of the many applicants for the archivist's job. He indicated to Secretary of State Cordell Hull that the AHA council was apprehensive lest the wrong person be appointed. Although the organization did not yet have a nominee, he told Hull, "I hope you agree with me that the American Historical Association is entitled to be consulted."[2]

Competition for the top post in the National Archives flagged as it became clear that Congress was not going to authorize the agency's establishment in 1933. Interest in the appointment soared again the following year as the National Archives bill made rapid progress on Capitol Hill. Fear also arose, however, among Jameson, Dodd (by then president of the AHA), and their associates that politicians would dictate the choice of the first archivist of the United States. There was the rumor that James A. Farley, the chairman of the Democratic National Committee, was pressing a nominee for the office. There was also the aggressive campaign spearheaded by Senator Pat Harrison of Mississippi on behalf of his state's pioneering archivist, Dunbar Rowland, who was not to Jameson's liking if only because of his age (seventy) and use of partisan politics to get the job for himself. Therefore, Jameson, Dodd, and other AHA leaders resolved, in Jameson's words, "to circumvent the spoilsmen."[3]

A word should be said here about the nature of the historical profession in the United States during the early 1930s. Then and for roughly a generation before the nation's archivists and historians worked within a tightly knit hierarchical framework, with J. Franklin Jameson serving as the chief distributor of fishes and loaves. He, his mentors, and his early colleagues had established the profession; and since the turn of the century he had usually been *primus inter pares* among the most influential historians. This was because of the many professional activities and groundbreaking endeavors in which Jameson had successfully engaged. He and his associates and disciples knew what they wanted, and they had been exceptionally able in pursuing their goals. Now that the National Archives (for which Jameson had been the chief agitator) was about to be born, they were not prepared to let others, whether dissenters in the ranks or mere politicians, choose the head of the new agency and thereby decide what course it should follow. It was not difficult for Jameson's circle to rally the faithful in the fight to determine who should be the archivist of the United States. After all, in the United States in 1934 there were only about 1,200 professionally active Ph.D.s in history and probably far fewer professionally influential B.A.s and M.A.s, most of whom had studied or worked with Jameson and the elite group that led the AHA.[4] These men and women, the country's professional historians and archivists, knew who the bosses were.

They had a good idea, thanks to Jameson's crusades over the past three decades, of what qualities would make an accepteble national archivist. As Solon J. Buck of the University of Pittsburgh volunteered to the AHA, that archivist had to be a good executive and administrator who appreciated both the administrative and historical importance of archives. He had to be able to work with administrators and scholars and be familiar with archival principles. Additionally, Buck implied, the archivist must not cater to the whims of politicians or fail to act in concert with his colleagues in the profession. As Jameson would undoubtedly have agreed, there are professional and gentlemanly, yet effective, ways to do things. Those are the ways by which the archivist would be chosen and the National Archives run if the historical profession had anything to say about it.[5]

And historians were to have much to say about the matter. Of course, Jameson was busy in Washington trying to steer the archives legislation on the right course. However, William E. Dodd, the AHA president and by then the American ambassador to Germany, had decided to lay the question of selecting the archivist before the association's executive committee at its meeting on 20 May 1934. Indeed, he had arranged to secure President Roosevelt's invitation to the executive committee to nominate someone for the job, although that was no guarantee that the administration would accept the AHA's advice.[6]

On 20 May the AHA executive committee met at Columbia University. The group included the association's executive secretary, Conyers Read; Sidney B. Fay; Dixon Ryan Fox; William E. Lingelbach; Constantine E. McGuire; and, as chairman, Charles A. Beard. It was a good cross section of the historical establishment in the United States. Solon Buck's views on the subject of the archivist of the United States were presented to the committee, and Dodd, in a letter, urged the group to nominate a candidate for the position. The names of a number of leading historians and archivists were discussed, but, not unexpectedly, there was no consensus. The committee asked Lingelbach and Read to confer with Jameson, as the senior member of the AHA council, to recommend nominees.[7]

Jameson's first choice was his chief disciple, Waldo Gifford Leland, the executive secretary of the American Council of Learned Societies. Yet there were, Jameson thought, several problems with Leland. First, he did not want the job, although he was willing to discuss it; second, Jameson wondered what would happen to the ACLS (or more probably to the influence of the historians within it) if Leland left; third, Leland was a regular Republican, which could cause difficulties with President Roosevelt and the Congress. Still, Jameson had an ace in the hole personified by Robert Digges Wimberly Connor, the head of the Department of History and Government at the University of North Carolina. In fact, Jameson not only had told Conyers Read about both Leland and Connor toward the end of May but also asked Connor if he would be interested in the AHA's nomination for archivist if Leland declined to be considered. Connor replied that he expected to be in Washington in two weeks and would prefer to discuss it with Jameson then.[8]

Connor was, as Jameson knew, a splendid possibility. He was a member of a prominent North Carolina family and, of course, a Democrat. That would ease the problem of securing political support, especially in view of the southern and Democratic congressional backing that Dunbar Rowland, Mississippi state archivist, could secure against a northerner and a Republican. Professionally, Connor occupied a position in North Carolina much like that which Jameson held nationally; and Connor had friends all over the country as well, including Jameson, Leland, and Dodd. Connor would be fifty-six years old that summer. He had been a schoolteacher and administrator as a young man, but in 1903 he had become secretary of the North Carolina Historical Commission. In that role he developed the state's outstanding Department of Archives and History, and he became a prolific writer of scholarly materials on North Carolina history as well. In 1921 Connor assumed the Kenan Professorship of History at the University of North Carolina, a position in which he exercised considerable influence on scholars of southern history.[9]

Jameson thought of Connor with good reason, given his diverse historical and academic activities, as "a man of affairs, who knows how to deal with politicians. He is, and makes the impression of being a man of power. He did a fine job in the organizing of the North Carolina Historical Commission and pushed its affairs forward with energy, skill and tact. . . . I think he has the necessary backbone to resist the pressure of office seekers and their senators and representatives, but would not do it unpleasantly."[10] Jameson was not wrong in any respect. Waldo G. Leland could not be talked into being the AHA's nominee for archivist, and it is possible that as Jameson considered the difficulties involved he did not try to hard to change Leland's mind. Therefore, increasingly, it seemed that Robert D. W. Connor would be the nominee. And why not, for he was all that Jameson thought him to be and more besides. He looked like an amiable buffalo and was in fact a courtly, honest, modest, and likable person who was thoughtful and could get things done with a minimum of fuss. Obviously, Connor could get along with a variety of people and persuade them to do things. A man of integrity and professional dedication, he would not allow himself to be pushed around.

By 1 June AHA President Dodd had instructed the executive committee to pick a nominee. Dodd clearly wanted the association to be ready to go into action as soon as the National Archives legislation was enacted. Moreover, since he was in Berlin attending to his duties as ambassador to Germany, he did not want any more time spent on the matter than necessary. On 5 June the executive committee laid the groundwork for its campaign. It urged President Roosevelt to appoint as "National Archivist" a person with administrative ability and tact in dealing with government departments, yet one "who will maintain an intelligent and informed sympathy" with research scholars, one who was "deeply interested in facilitating and promoting the study of American history." Simultaneously, Executive Secretary Conyers Read pressed Connor for a decision on whether he would accept the job of archivist were it offered to him.[11]

Matters were not to proceed expeditiously. It would have been unrealistic to expect the White House to rush into an appointment, especially when there were several contenders for the post of archivist. Moreover, Connor was not to be speeded into a decision to be the AHA's nominee, regardless of what Dodd, Jameson, and Read wanted. Connor replied to Read that he would discuss the matter during his visit to Washington late in the second week of June. When he did see Jameson and Read, he told them that he could not make a decision until he had read the National Archives Act and been in touch with the president of his university, Frank P. Graham.[12]

The National Archives legislation was passed and approved by 19 June. Jameson was not entirely satisfied with the law, largely because the staff of the new agency would not be under civil service. That made him all the more sensitive to the need to appoint a dedicated and able historical administrator as archivist of the United States. For him, Connor was the man, and Jameson was prepared to do whatever was needed to see him in the job. The AHA's executive committee was of the same mind and apparently tried to force Connor's hand. Its members were polled by mail, and on 21 June Read reported that the committee had unanimously decided upon Connor as the association's nominee for archivist. Jameson mailed a copy of the National Archives Act to Connor for his study; Read advised the North Carolinian of his nomination and urged him to decide to accept so that Ambassador Dodd could get the State Department behind Connor's appointment, a move that could carry considerable weight in view of the department's long-standing interest and responsibilities in archival matters.[13]

Of course, others in Washington were interested in the situation. Congressman Sol Bloom of New York, who considered himself the father of the National Archives Act, urged the president to take plenty of time before making the appointment, since the goal had to be to name "the best man available." Bloom averred that he did not know who that was, but he nevertheless asked for a meeting with Roosevelt to discuss the matter. Clerk John G. Bradley of the House Library Committee undertook to evaluate for Committee Chairman Kent E. Keller of Illinois a dozen probable candidates for archivist. On 22 June he advised Keller that only three men were available, capable, and not too old. They were Connor; John C. Fitzpatrick, editor of the George Washington Bicentennial; and Thomas P. Martin, assistant chief of the Manuscripts Division of the Library of Congress. A week later, Bradley, indicating Jameson's influence on him and perhaps trying to pave his way to employment in the National Archives, told Keller that Connor deserved their support. Of course, Jameson's commitment to Connor eliminated Martin, his deputy in the Manuscripts Division, from consideration; and the old gentleman ranked Connor over Fitzpatrick, even though Sol Bloom apparently favored the distinguished editor. What it meant, as Jameson wrote to Connor on 22 June, was not only that Keller and Bradley wanted Connor but also that Bloom probably would go along with them.[14]

While all this was going on, President Graham of the University of North Carolina was pressing Connor to stay there. This had a great deal of influence on the historian, for he loved both Chapel Hill and the university. Indeed, Connor informed Jameson and Read on 22 June that he could not accept the position of archivist because of his obligations to the university. He indicated to Graham that the provisions of the National Archives Act also contributed to his decision, though he did not specify what bothered him about the legislation. Jameson and Read immediately urged him to change his mind, and the latter sent a telegram that stated, "All our hopes were pinned on you and we hardly know which way to turn if you cannot be induced to reconsider."[15]

Communications were something of a problem at this time, for Connor was in Morgantown, teaching in the summer school of West Virginia University. Yet the letters and telegrams between the interested persons in Washington, Morgantown, Chapel Hill, and even Berlin were numerous. Jameson volunteered to drive to West Virginia to talk with Connor, but, out of deference to his age,

Connor agreed to meet with him in Cumberland, Maryland. On 24 June Jameson arrived there to confer with Connor. The result of the meeting was that the North Carolinian agreed to reconsider his position and to consult further with President Graham, although Connor emphasized that both he and the AHA must retain freedom of decision. Immediately, Jameson wrote Graham urging upon him the importance to scholarship of Connor being the AHA's nominee for archivist of the United States. He also indicated to Conyers Read that he was prepared to adopt a new candidate, John C. Fitzpatrick, in the event that Connor did not accept the AHA's nomination. Ambassador Dodd acted to place the secretary of state in a holding pattern. He cabled from Berlin to Cordell Hull, saying that "Connor cannot accept at once" and asking for a month's delay in the appointment process. Secretary Hull, who had already informed the president on 22 June of Dodd's interest in Connor, immediately conveyed the ambassador's cable to Roosevelt.[16]

Connor's colleagues at the University of North Carolina and his fellow historians placed great pressure on him, the former pleading with him to remain at the university, the latter exhorting him to head the National Archives. Their reasons were plain in both cases. On the one hand, Connor was a power within the university (indeed, he had been seriously considered for president there), and he was highly successful in appealing to the state's people and legislators for support of Chapel Hill's educational programs. On the other hand, historians and archivists from all over the country liked and respected him, and he was highly appreciated as one whose backing of historical projects always seemed to enhance their possibilities for success. Additionally, Connor, at least as much as any other prominent American historian, appeared to have the qualities that would assure his acceptance as archivist by historical administrators, researchers, and politicians.

The tug-of-war for Connor's favor was ferocious, and he felt it profoundly. President Graham wrote him on 30 June that he would abide by Connor's decision, though he made it clear that he wanted him to stay at Chapel Hill. Jameson apparently acted prematurely on 7 July, when he told William E. Lingelbach that

Connor was free to accept. Actually the North Carolinian had not yet made his decision, although his correspondence suggests that he was then inclined to accept the AHA's nomination for archivist. Graham took heroic actions to retain Connor's services, not only telegraphng on 8 July to beg him to stay, but also visiting with Jameson in the hope that he would release his hold on Connor. It was to no avail, however. By 9 July Connor decided to allow the AHA to submit his name to President Roosevelt as a candidate for archivist of the United States.[17]

Many factors contributed to Connor's reluctance to accept the nomination: his love of North Carolina; his dislike of leaving the university on such short notice; his anxiety that perhaps he was too old for a new, uncharted venture; and his fear that despite all he would not get the appointment and thus would be thought of "as an unsuccessful job-seeker!" Then, too, he "liked Fitzpatrick and thought that he would be a good man for the job."[18] However, Connor and the AHA were now committed to each other in the struggle for the archivist's post and control of the National Archives.

When word got out that Connor was the American Historical Association's official nominee, many of the other candidates withdrew. In fact, some of them, like Solon J. Buck, threw their support to Jameson's annointed. The result was that there was only one other strong contender for the position, Dunbar Rowland of Mississippi. Rowland had been questing for the job since early 1933 and had already gained much support among southern Democratic politicians and even considerable backing from educators. The battle between the supporters of the two pioneers of the state archives movement would rage for ten weeks during the summer of 1934. The differences between Connor and Rowland, however, were considerable. The former was a man of many experiences in the scholarly world, while the latter's life since 1900 had been largely devoted to historical administration; the North Carolinian's support was more national in nature, the Mississippian's more sectional; Connor was moderate in personality, Rowland was highly assertive.[19] The question was, Whose forces would make the greater impression on the president? The answer was Connor's, for they were better organized to court Roosevelt than were Rowland's.

J. Franklin Jameson and the AHA carried the main burden of the fight to have Connor appointed as archivist, but the nominee himself became increasingly involved. Connor's modesty was never dented by his experience. He was amazed by what was claimed on his behalf, including the myth that he had been thought of seriously as a contender for governor of North Carolina in 1932. As he put it, regarding his supporters, "None realized better than I that they exaggerated my qualifications." Yet, plunging into politics was not so bad as he had earlier believed, partly because he found that he had a number of valuable political contacts and partly because, as he inscribed in his journal, "Politicians are not so bad when they are on our side!" Of the members of the North Carolina congressional delegation, Connor knew only Senator Josiah W. Bailey and Representative William B. Umstead. Although he believed that the state's senators and representatives backed him only because they had no other candidate for the "fat job," Connor's brothers were prominent in legal circles and well acquainted with a number of members of Congress. Of course, their father had been one of the best known political figures of his time in North Carolina, so the Connor name was well established among the state's elite. Furthermore, Connor was an old friend of Governor John C. B. Ehringhaus and of Franklin D. Roosevelt's long-time chief in the Department of the Navy, Josephus Daniels, who was currently ambassador to Mexico. Both were very supportive of Connor's candidacy for archivist. Secretary of Commerce Daniel C. Roper was another friend. He had already endorsed Fitzpatrick, but he promised to do what he could to help Connor. Roper did talk to the president and reported that Roosevelt was impressed with Connor.[20]

Of those in the AHA leadership, Jameson made the greatest efforts on Connor's behalf. He worked unstintingly to halt or to undermine the campaigns of other contenders for the job; to rally the support of historians, archivists, and bureaucrats; and to persuade politicians that, for the good of all, a thoroughly professional man had to be appointed as archivist. He particularly worked to reach the White House, bombarding Franklin D. Roosevelt and his staff with messages. On 20 September, knowing that the time for decision was growing ripe, he pressed upon the presidential secretary Marvin McIntyre the proposition that the prompt appointment of the archivist would be very helpful in determining the final phases of the construction of the National Archives building. Jameson wrote to Roosevelt at the same time, asserting that the objectives of the National Archives Act called for the appointment of a man of "scholarship and breadth of view." He added that Connor was superior, by far, to the other candidates of whom he had heard.[21]

There were many things that could have led Roosevelt to make his decision. It may have been the incessant campaigning of Jameson and his associates; the kindly words on Connor's behalf by Daniels, Roper, and probably Hull; the pressure exerted by the North Carolina congressional delegation; Roosevelt's own long-standing interest in historical matters; or even the president's knowledge that he would forever get the blame or the credit for whatever the National Archives became, and he would prefer that it be credit. Indeed, it may have been all of these things and others besides, but it is not known now and probably never will be. What is important is that after Jameson's letters of 20 September reached Roosevelt, he decided to act quickly. He penciled a note to McIntyre on Jameson's letter, "*Mac* Thank him and send for Professor Connor." Accordingly, McIntyre wrote to Connor, inviting him to meet with the president on Wednesday, 3 October, at 11:15 a.m. There was no mention of the obvious matter that they were to chat about.[22]

Robert D. W. Connor was, of course, available to meet with Roosevelt. Connor arrived in Washington 2 October; that night he "slept some but not too much." The next morning, he saw Jameson first, and then he went to the White House where he was soon ushered in to see the president. In their unhurried conversation, Roosevelt and Connor began by talking a bit about North Carolina. Next came the real subject of the meeting. The president said, "As you know, I am required by an act of Congress to appoint an Archivist of the United States . . . and the man I am going to appoint must have two qualifications—he must be a good Democrat and he must have the endorsement of the historians of the country."

Connor replied, "I can meet the first requirement, Mr. President, but I don't know about the second."

"Well, I do," Roosevelt declared, "and I am going to appoint you."[23]

With that settled, the president launched into several related subjects. He was not reluctant to take credit for the establishment of the National Archives, asserting, "It is my baby, you know." He then alarmed Connor by saying that he favored Sol Bloom's idea for creating a separate hall of records for routine documentary materials, for he thought the National Archives should be the repository for only the great state papers such as the Declaration of Independence, the Constitution, treaties, and presidential proclamations. The North Carolinian forthrightly argued against a hall of records. He contended that "ordinary office files" were historically very valuable and were often related to the great documents. More to Connor's liking, Roosevelt went on to say that presidential papers, including those in the Library of Congress as well as his own, should be in the National Archives. The president then ended the interview by suggesting that Connor see Interior Secretary Harold L. Ickes immediately about the government's survey of historical records.[24] It should be noted that Connor would be significantly involved in all of these vital archival issues during his years in office.

On 10 October the president signed Connor's commission as archivist of the United States, and the White House issued a press release on his appointment. Roosevelt also took care to write to Senator Harrison about Dunbar Rowland. He said that Rowland stood "very high in everybody's estimation," but that he appointed Connor largely because he was the "unanimous choice of the American Historical Association." Connor received his commission as a recess appointee on 19 October, and the Senate confirmed him the following 20 March.[25]

The leadership of the AHA was overjoyed. On 14 October, Conyers Read told the executive committee of Connor's appointment. He reported, "They all with one accord burst into paeans of

Robert D. W. Connor, first archivist of the United States, 1934–1941

thanksgiving. Nothing, they felt, could be better,—nothing which the American Historical Association has helped to do in the interest of American historical scholarship, of greater moment." William E. Dodd cabled to Connor from Berlin, "You have one of the most important historical opportunitys [*sic*] of our time," that is, providing easy access to government records for qualified researchers. The ambassador reasoned that Connor would have a free hand with appointments as long as the people employed were "competent and fairly trained."[26]

President Roosevelt had chosen well. When he made the crucial decision, thanks to the guidance of Jameson and the AHA, scholarly rather than political criteria prevailed. Furthermore, Robert D. W. Connor proved that he was not only professional and fair, but energetic, experimental, and innovative as well. Of course, there were troubles and false starts. Connor, however, was to provide the new National Archives with a competent staff, and he began the arduous work of rescuing and making available for research a great variety of federal records. Under his direction, the National Archives would become a pioneer in, among other things, methods of the repair and preservation of archives. It would also play the leading role in establishing a recognized archival profession in the United States complete with training and publication programs and a professional organization. Before Connor returned to North Carolina in 1941, the first presidential library, Roosevelt's, would be built and the seeds of modern records management sown. The first archivist had begun, as he had wanted, something that could "truly be called a national institution."[27]

3. *Space, Status, and Staff*

The AHA leadership might have been jubilant as a result of Robert D. W. Connor's appointment as archivist of the United States, but that was not the immediate attitude of the man who had to fill the job. "I feel considerably depressed—for the Lord only knows what I'm in for," he told his wife. The National Archives building was not ready for occupancy; in fact, he had neither an office nor a staff. Connor was, moreover, inexperienced in the practices and procedures of the federal government. As he wrote later, "I had agreed to take over a big job about which I knew next to nothing."[1]

Connor's feelings began to change when he met with Interior Secretary Ickes and his administrative assistant, E. K. Burlew, the morning of 4 October 1934. Their conversation centered on the National Archives building, since Burlew had served on the committee that had drawn up the plans for its construction. Out of this discussion came two important results. First, Connor was put in touch with Louis A. Simon, the supervising architect of the Department of the Treasury, who was primarily in charge of erecting the building. As a consequence of the close relationship that developed between Connor and Simon, the remaining problems of housing the new agency were easily attacked. Second, Ickes, Burlew, and Connor found that they had a community of interest. Ickes, in his other role as public works administrator, had money to spend on high-quality building projects, and Connor needed funds to finish off the National Archives building properly.

The cement of their alliance to provide additional monies for the National Archives building was their opposition to the establishment of a hall of records, which President Roosevelt had discussed with Connor on 3 October. Connor's opposition to housing the "ordinary" older federal files in an inexpensive central storage unit under the control of the agencies that had created them was based on his fear that his agency would end up being a mausoleum that contained only the best-known documents of state. The obvious ramifications of such a situation would be that the National Archives could become neither a major research repository widening access to federal archives nor a force in the government's records preservation practices. The Interior Department officials sympathized with Connor's viewpoint, but they had their own reasons for opposing a hall of records. They identified themselves with the National Archives; Burlew took pride in being among those who had planned the National Archives building, and Ickes knew that his National Park Service would have the responsibility for maintaining the new structure. Moreover, Connor and Ickes were concerned with the waste of federal money and the lack of coordination in archival management that would probably result from the operation of two agencies to deal with the government's older records.[2]

This was not idle conjecture, for already, earlier in 1934, some federal agencies had pressed for a hall of records that would allow them to store their older files cheaply and yet maintain control over them and restrict access to them. The Bureau of the Budget referred the question to the Interior Department, which then had responsibility for the management of federal buildings. Ickes's office devised a counter-proposal. They observed that the large inner court of the archives building was an open space and therefore recommended that it be developed into part of the new structure. Roosevelt tentatively endorsed this proposal in June. Three months later he approved an allocation from the Public Works Administration to build a huge stack area in the inner court. The president, however, cautioned Ickes to "be sure that we are violating no law," since the archives building apparently was limited by law to containing "historic archives and cannot be used for ordinary government records and files." The secretary of the interior replied that his attorneys had indicated there was no legal problem. When Connor, in interviews with the president in October and November, ardently opposed a hall of records, Roosevelt, for the time being, laid aside the question of what should be in the National Archives.[3]

There was a fuss in the Washington press after it was announced that the PWA had earmarked $3,600,000 for building additional stack areas in the court of the National Archives. One newspaperman wrote, "There will be a louder roar when Congress convenes [for it] intended the Archives Building for the important state papers and historic documents of the Republic. . . . All this new money for new stacks has led to the belief that it is the intent of the bureaucrats to load the costly structure up with cart loads of dry-as-dust departmental papers, the usual trash that is wrapped up in the customary red tape." The predicted roar on Capitol Hill "never exceeded," as Connor said, "a whine." Nevertheless, the hall of records idea continued to be raised in Congress. Representative John J. Cochran of Missouri, the chairman of the House Committee on Expenditures in the Executive Departments, particularly pressed for it from 1935 through 1939, with support from the Treasury and War departments. Connor and Ickes scored their most notable victory on the issue during 1935 when they persuaded Roosevelt once and for all to refuse to endorse the establishment of a hall of records. This led Cochran to criticize the National Archives sharply in 1936 and 1937, but his attacks were to no avail as Connor's allies in Congress, especially Representative Clifton A. Woodrum of Virginia, effectively came to the rescue.[4]

There were several results of the conflict over what the National Archives should contain and whether there should be a hall of records. First, the new agency soon discovered who its friends were in Washington. Second, the issue led to the construction of stack areas in the inner court, which proved vital to the future programs of the National Archives. Third, the government better preserved its archives, and researchers had greater access to older federal records, because of the central administration of archives for research rather than for just storage purposes. Fourth, although the decision not to authorize a hall of records perhaps delayed the government in addressing its overall problem of records management, it increased the odds that one agency instead of two competing organizations would deal with federal records. Fifth, it ensured that professionally competent persons would be highly influential in the development of a program to manage federal records. Sixth, the decision not to establish a hall of records subjected the National Archives to increasing stress as the problem of what to do with the government's records became more pressing; indeed, it ultimately led to a considerable restructuring of the agency.[5]

After seeing Ickes and Burlew and getting acquainted with Supervising Architect Louis A. Simon, Connor returned to North Carolina to wind up his affairs. He took the oath of office there on 20 October. Two days later, he left Chapel Hill for Washington to inquire further into his duties. Burlew arranged office space for Connor in the new headquarters of the Department of Justice, located just west of the site on which the National Archives building was being erected. Simon gave him a lengthy tour of what had been completed of the structure; Connor nodded sagely in response to the architect's explanations, though the building looked like "chaos" to him. He went back to North Carolina for a few more days, but he returned to the capital on 30 October, fully prepared to work. The archivist immediately occupied his quarters in the Justice Department and soon he visited again with Simon and paid calls upon President Roosevelt and the two senators from North Carolina.[6]

Connor had learned quickly that he would have to deal with a multitude of problems. Completing and outfitting the archives building was one of the easiest, because so many of the decisions concerning those areas had already been made and because he would have highly competent assistance in accomplishing what remained to be done. Yet it was a fundamental problem, for the National Archives could not be effective until after its building was ready for occupancy, which, because the edifice was so complicated, would not be soon.

Thanks to generous congressional appropriations and additional assistance from the Public Works Administration, Connor had no serious worries about financing the completion of the National Archives building. An advisory committee had outlined the basic requirements of the structure in 1930. The government had then engaged one of America's most outstanding architects, John Russell Pope, to design the building, which he did in grand style. "This Archives," he wrote in 1933, "will be . . . one of the most interesting and most important monuments in our great Washington plan." This was not only because Pope thought the building, considering its historical functions, to be something of a monument itself, but also because of its prominent location halfway between the Treasury and the Capitol. Its prominence would be reinforced by building it, unlike other recently constructed government buildings in the area, "in classical style to harmonize with the Capitol, the White House, the Treasury Building, and the Lincoln Memorial."[7]

The site for the archives building was the ground bounded by Pennsylvania and Constitution avenues on the north and south and by Seventh and Ninth streets on the east and west, which roughly had been the location of Washington's famous old Center Market. A stream ran beneath the site. Originally it had been called Goose Creek, but, in keeping with America's occasional self-identification with ancient Rome, it had soon come to be called Tiber Canal or Tiber Creek. The classical design of so many federal buildings, including the National Archives, was consistent with that bit of national ego. In the fall of 1932 the government awarded the contract to erect the archives building to the George A. Fuller Company, with completion specified within 720 days.

The considerable length of time allocated to construct the National Archives building, and the even longer time the job actually took, was attributable to the many purposes the structure was to fulfill. In addition to offices, the archives was to include an intricate series of self-contained, artificially lighted stack areas and vaults for storing records as well as rooms for serving researchers and for receiving, cleaning, repairing, and reproducing documents. There were also a library, auditorium, and, in the exhibition hall, a grand museum. The structure had to be provided with a heating and air-conditioning system that ingeniously used water from the Tiber for its operation. Moreover, proper storage of archives re-

The National Archives Building under construction

quired humidity, fire, and chemical controls and the installation of equipment for a variety of technical purposes. No federal building until that time had been more complicated to build.[8]

The artistic aspects of the building also posed challenges. In a structure in the classical style 168 feet high, the Corinthian columns were not only many (seventy-two) but very tall, standing 52 feet. The bronze doors, opening from the Constitution Avenue side to the exhibition hall, were the largest ever built, weighing ten tons and measuring one by nine by thirty-five feet. The building's exterior faces were generously covered with sculptural decorations symbolizing such ideas as "Destiny" and "Achievement" and serving as the guardians of, among other things, "The Secrets of the Archives." There were also exterior medallions that represented the major parts of the government of the United States and gigantic inscriptions chiseled on the crown of the building to glorify history, the nation, and the purposes of the archives. What catch most eyes are the huge statues flanking the two public entrances. The two pedestal figures on the Pennsylvania Avenue side are a wise-looking old man who represents the past and sits above the inscribed Confucian injunction, "Study the Past"; and a contemplative young woman who represents the future and sits above Shakespeare's words, "What Is Past Is Prologue." On the Constitution Avenue side a formidable figure of a woman with a child expresses "Heritage" and an armed, watchful male statue symbolizes "Guardianship." The latter rises in granite over the words attributed to Thomas Jefferson, "Eternal Vigilance Is the Price of Liberty," while the former surmounts the inscription, "The Heritage of the Past Is the Seed That Brings Forth the Harvest of the Future." Among the

The completed exterior of the National Archives Building

artists who contributed to this external sculpture were Robert Aitken, James Earle Frazer, and Adolph Alexander Weinman.[9]

The exhibition hall was designed in monumental proportions, too, in keeping with the building's vast ornamental exterior. Entered through the huge bronze doors and a large gallery, the hall is semicircular in shape, crowned by a half dome, the top of which is seventy-five feet from the floor. Handsome stonework and gold trim abound in the area, including a semicircular gallery that runs in back of the hall. Barry Faulkner was commissioned to do the two murals in the hall. One is called "The Declaration of Independence" and portrays Thomas Jefferson and his associates submitting the declaration to John Hancock. The other mural, "The Constitution of the United States," shows James Madison presenting the final draft of the document to George Washington. Both works are crowded with historical figures: twenty-eight signers are depicted in the first and twenty-five delegates in the second. The painting of these murals in the exhibition hall left no doubt that this was intended to be the shrine in which the two foremost documents in the nation's history were to be permanently displayed.[10]

Much of the planning was done before Robert Connor assumed the duties of archivist. For example, late in spring of 1933 the procurement officer of the Treasury Department had gotten stone samples for facing that were not of the quality required by John Russell Pope. The architect protested to Frederic A. Delano, the chairman of the National Capital Park and Planning Commission and, incidentally, President Roosevelt's uncle. He also complained to L. W. Robert, the assistant secretary of the Treasury, that the limestone samples on hand did not meet the specifications. Delano sent to the president the letters that Pope had written to him and Robert. Although Delano believed the specifications were "excessively liberal," he suggested that Roosevelt get the National Bureau of Standards involved to make sure that the stone available for construction "*comes up to the specifications*," adding in pencil, "in every respect." Delano's intervention led to a satisfactory solution of the problem; thus, Pope achieved his objective of having the materials for the structure "selected with permanence as the paramount consideration" consonant with "the principle of expressing in architecture the significance and safety of the various records to be deposited in the Archives Building."[11]

Another controversy that swirled about the structure, in 1935, concerned the suggestion, apparently from the Treasury Department, that the government could get vastly more space for its investment if the building's roof were pitched much higher than required by Pope. That may have been true, but sketches of the building with such an extension make it look elephantine and thus ruinous to the goal of harmonizing the architecture of the government structures located between the Capitol and the White House. Once again Pope complained bitterly. Consequently, the Fine Arts Commission, which had jurisdiction over such matters, felt impelled to disapprove the proposal. President Roosevelt took it upon himself independently to tell the Treasury Department that he agreed with the commission's decision.[12]

Connor was little involved in the discussions over the architectural and artistic aspects of the archives building. He and Supervising Architect Simon did protest placing inscriptions on the pedestals on the Pennsylvania Avenue side. They thought that quotations would distract attention from the statues, but Pope, as usual, had his way, contending that the words and the statues were integral to the building's design. He was probably right, for most people who remember what flanks the Pennsylvania Avenue entrance seem to recall the figures *and* the words. One result of this sally was that Connor, along with Pope, Simon, the artists, and Chairman Charles Moore of the Fine Arts Commission, was involved in determining the pedestal inscriptions. Apparently, all concerned found the quotations that Pope wanted chiseled on the Pennsylvania Avenue pedestals acceptable. The designing architect, however, had no acceptable candidates for the words to match the Constitution Avenue statues. Finally, the group decided upon Jefferson's quotation and a contribution from the sculptor, James Earle Frazer, as modified by Moore and Connor. This committee approach to originality probably accounted for the length of this latter inscription.[13]

Connor was far more involved in the "tenant changes" in the plans for outfitting the structure. Of course, before he could give informed advice to Pope and Simon, he had to have a staff to examine the operating potential of the National Archives and its building. The archivist had assistance enough by December 1934 to begin a study that would lead to specific recommendations for completing the structure in utilitarian fashion. And it was just in time, for the building's interior was about ready for finishing. Surveys were made of archival repositories elsewhere and considerable time was devoted to innovative planning. Moreover for months there ensued conferences among the archivists, the architects, and representatives of the Procurement Division of the Treasury Department and the National Bureau of Standards. The resulting changes in the original plans were substantial. The need for more work space led to the conversion of locker rooms and lunchrooms into offices as well as the addition of nine new offices on the thirteenth stack level. This and the division of some planned offices into two or more additional spaces often required a different finishing of the rooms involved. Special cabinets had to be devised for proper protection of films, and better provisions had to be made to protect the building's contents against fire and burglary. Furthermore, plans had to be made for furnishing the various offices and research rooms as well as for installing appropriate equipment in the receiving, repair, preservation, and storage areas. Considering all this, it is fair to say in retrospect that the quality of work and cooperation in the construction of the archives building was very high.[14]

It is reflective of that quality that only the decision made on stack equipment turned out badly. The beautifully crafted steel containers were easily dented and therefore sometimes became difficult to use; in case of fire, the documents they contained would be baked to a crisp, even though the costly metal boxes themselves would probably survive nicely; archivists and researchers found that the sharp edges of the boxes could tear their clothing and flesh; and, since papers could be placed in the boxes only horizontally, getting at what one wanted, or refiling it, was difficult. Then, too, the manufacturer of these containers went out of business during World War II, and replacements could not be made. This development was fortunate, for it had become clear that the steel boxes were a poor choice in terms of both expense and utility. It was just as well that the stacks of the National Archives had yet to be completely outfitted, so that there was an incentive to develop a better, safer, and cheaper method of storing archives.[15]

The Treasury Department informed the archivist in October 1935 that the administrative offices of the archives building would soon be ready for occupancy. By 8 November the small staff of the National Archives had moved from the Justice Department to its permanent home. There was still a great deal to be done in readying the building to carry out its functions, for only the offices on the main floor were equipped, with the telephone switchboard operative and some photostat and duplicating machinery installed. Indeed, many of the recommendations for outfitting the structure had not yet been approved.

It was not until May 1936 that storage equipment was acceptably installed in some of the stack areas. That gave the National Archives sufficient space for its early operations, however, since it provided for roughly 10 percent of the building's intended document storage area. By 30 June 1938, 45 percent of the stack areas was fully or partially equipped. This space included the construction of the extension in the building's inner court, which more than doubled the stack area originally planned for the National Archives. Connor had pressed for work to be begun on it "as soon as possible." Therefore, the contract was let in December 1935, and the construction was finished in February 1937. Progress meanwhile was made in outfitting offices, the auditorium, and research and technical areas; and a fire-alarm system and watchman stations were installed throughout. The building itself was not finished until 1938. Even then, outfitting and adjustments went on for years more, with the cost of the archives structure totalling $12,250,794 by 1941.[16]

The organization of the National Archives as a government agency was slow, largely because it took so much time to complete and outfit the building. Another delaying factor, however, was the problem of personnel. There were several facets to this, but the most immediate one was that the new agency was an inviting target for patronage requests because the archivist's appointments

were exempt from civil-service regulations. Connor was determined to resist political patronage pressures; he was cognizant of
the fact that this was one of the reasons why the AHA had nominated him for his job. He was relatively successful in this with
respect to professional appointments because President Roosevelt
gave him a free hand. For example, when Representative Bloom
pressed Roosevelt for the appointment of John C. Fitzpatrick as
Connor's deputy, the president sent Bloom's letter to the archivist
with a covering note stating, "This is just for your information, as
I do not want to force anybody on you as a member of your staff.
That is your responsibility."[17]

Connor also felt under little pressure from the Democratic
National Committee. He advised the national committee that although he would let their headquarters know of what jobs were
open, he alone would make the appointments, and only on the
basis of a candidate's fitness for the job involved. Apparently he
made his intention clear, for Democratic National Chairman James
Farley never interfered in his appointments. In fact, on one occasion, when one of Farley's aides was seeking to block an appointment, Connor conferred with Farley, who concluded, "It's your
job and if you want this man it's O.K. with me."[18]

Yet there was pressure for appointments from another quarter, Connor's fellow historians. Executive Secretary Conyers Read
of the AHA suggested at least two people for jobs at the National
Archives, and there were other prominent historians who sought
positions for their students or friends. J. Franklin Jameson was,
not surprisingly, Clio's champion spoilsman. Indeed, he began
making recommendations immediately after the White House announced the archivist's appointment. It is impossible to determine
how many people Jameson nominated, but in one case Connor
appointed nine out of a group that he suggested for consideration.
This is not to say that Jameson, Read, and the others were mainly
interested in professional patronage. Although that was a factor,
especially during the Great Depression, their chief concern was to
call to Connor's attention those whom they thought were best qualified to staff the National Archives. Connor certainly welcomed
these recommendations, for, he wrote, "There existed no reservoir

of professional archivists upon which" he could draw. Therefore, he deemed the knowledge and judgment of men like Jameson invaluable.[19]

It was natural that the leading historians believed they should have much to say in the staffing of an agency that they thought would mainly serve their profession. There is little doubt, too, that historians, because of their training and interests, were then usually the best people available for archival jobs. Given the old boy job selection practices among scholars at the time, the appointments to the professional staff of the National Archives were generally of high quality. In the few cases where there was a partisan political tinge to them, it was probably because Connor regarded that as protective coloring for the new agency. Moreover, there is no evidence that the first archivist ever appointed anyone whom he deemed unqualified. One way in which he relieved the pressure for patronage appointment of professional staff members was by consulting with congressional offices in the hiring of nonprofessional personnel, and even there he had legions of politically acceptable, competent persons to choose from. In the case of professional positions, Connor customarily responded to political pressure either by refusing to act or by delaying action indefinitely. The first approach was illustrated in his relations with James Farley. An example of the second was his fending off pressures on behalf of Dunbar Rowland, saying either than no job was open or that whatever was available was unsuitable for such an experienced person. Another such example concerned President Roosevelt's request that the archivist consider appointing a black, as a "valuable gesture," to work on records pertinent to the history of American Negroes. Connor dismissed this as a lamentable lapse by the president in the realm of patronage. Resorting to his Fabian tactics, he replied, "I shall be glad to adopt this suggestion as soon as the organization of the staff justifies it."[20] Not surprisingly, that opportunity never arose while the North Carolinian headed the National Archives.

As a result of the Great Depression, Connor had a large pool of talented people to consider for appointments. J. Franklin Jameson wrote to Ambassador Dodd at the end of October 1934 that more than 100 people had already applied to the archivist for jobs.

Upon seeing this letter later, Connor commented, "Tut! tut!, Dr. Jameson, how could a man of your perspicacity so underrate the interest of your compatriots in the enchanting subject of archives!" The fact was that there was not just a shower, but a flood of job applications. By the middle of 1935, the National Archives had furnished 35,000 application forms to job-seekers, 15,000 of which were returned properly filled out. And all this for an agency that by then only had forty-two persons on the payroll.[21]

It was clear from the beginning that the archivist would have to give much time and thought to hiring a staff. Soon after he occupied his temporary offices in the Justice Department, Connor consulted with Jameson and Librarian of Congress Herbert Putnam about his problems. They asserted that he should, before making any appointments, give serious thought to how the National Archives should be organized. Fortunately for him, the slowness of construction of the archives building gave Connor time to plan; yet he had to have some staff assistance immediately. By December 1934 he had designated two of his principal assistants: Dorsey W. Hyde, Jr., as director of archival service and Collas G. Harris as executive officer. The other two principal deputies, Director of Publications Solon J. Buck and Administrative Secretary Thaddeus S. Page, were appointed by May 1935.

The selection of men with such diverse talents and temperaments was a result, partly, of the need to find persons who would meet the test of Senate confirmation (which came in July 1935). Hyde had been a successful librarian, researcher, and administrator who had been employed mainly by business organizations. A graduate of Cornell University, he had become an outstanding figure in the special libraries field and had some acquaintance with archives. Harris, the only young man in the group, had been graduated from Washington and Lee in 1931. Thanks to his brightness and his ability at making friends in Congress, he had stepped up from a routine job in the Agriculture Department to a key personnel position in the Federal Emergency Relief Administration before his appointment at the National Archives. Page, like Connor, had been educated at the University of North Carolina and had come from one of the state's most prominent families. He had been a businessman and served as secretary to Senator Bailey of North Carolina. Buck was the only scholar, archivist, and Ph.D. among the four chief assistants. Educated at Wisconsin and Harvard, he had headed the Minnesota State Historical Society from 1914 to 1931 and more recently had taught at the University of Pittsburgh and directed the Western Pennsylvania Historical Society. He was a prolific writer and was well known among his fellow historians.[22] Despite occasional jurisdictional disputes, these men worked reasonably well under Connor's supervision in setting the course of the National Archives. Buck and Hyde performed effectively as envoys to historians and librarians, and Harris and Page occasionally exerted useful political influence on behalf of the agency as did Connor himself.

Fleshing out the National Archives with personnel meant that decisions had to be made on how the new agency would be organized. Dorsey Hyde's first assignment was to prepare recommendations along this line. Within a few days after joining the staff, he presented Connor with a memorandum outlining a staff structure for the National Archives, which was influenced by J. Franklin Jameson and patterned considerably after the organization of the Library of Congress. Connor adopted Hyde's proposal, with few changes, in 1935. The archivist was at the apex of the organization, with the four assistants reporting to him. Administrative Secretary Page was to be responsible for authenticating copies of federal records, to serve as secretary of the National Archives Council, and to handle the general correspondence of the National Archives as well as its relations with the press and with other federal agencies. Director of Publications Solon Buck would serve as secretary of the National Historical Publications Commission, plan the publications of the National Archives, and work on a variety of historical projects. Director of Archival Service Dorsey Hyde, Jr., and Executive Officer Collas G. Harris would supervise most of the agency's employees. Hyde would be responsible for the management of the operating units, which included accessions, repair and preservation, classification, catalogue, reference, research, library, maps and charts, motion pictures and sound recordings, and, most important, custody of archives. Harris would oversee the business and internal service activities of the National Archives. These included purchase and supply, personnel and payroll, finance and accounts, photographic reproduction and research, central files, building and grounds, printing and binding, stenographic pool, mail room, messenger service, and telephone switchboard.[23]

This organization was elaborate and promised jurisdictional disputes, but the National Archives functioned satisfactorily under it during its early years. It would often require modification, especially to replace inapplicable library work processes with archival approaches, which were frequently developed afresh. Yet it was the people who populated the organization charts, not the charts themselves, that made the structure work. In this, Connor was quite capable in getting his deputies to do what had to be done; they in turn usually had able and enthusiastic people with whom to work.

The success of the National Archives, as is the case with any organization, depended basically on personnel of lesser rank. The clerical and lower administrative and technical staff who were often drawn from congressional lists of recommended persons were generally competent. This was because during the Great Depression congressmen had unusually large numbers of people on their patronage rosters for lesser jobs. This gave the archivist a variety of skilled applicants to choose from and had the advantage of allowing him to seem to be doing congressmen favors in filling lesser positions from their lists. If these appointees occasionally carried tales to their political sponsors, it is debatable that they did so more than did aggrieved regular civil servants in other federal agencies. Moreover, Connor's troubles in this respect were minor; at least, he had no cause célèbre to deal with.

The archivist rightly saw the professional staff as the heart of his organization, and he was to achieve great success because of his ability to appoint a large number of bright, well-educated men and women. Of course, many of them had to be politically cleared. This was largely a charade, for there was never any trouble finding a congressional sponsor, even though few of the appointees were involved in politics. Their professional sponsors were more important. Here Connor relied chiefly on the AHA worthies, especially

Jameson, and William E. Lingelbach and Conyers Read at the University of Pennsylvania, as well as his former colleagues in the South, and Harry M. Lydenberg of the New York Public Library. The result of this was that the appointees had degrees from a relatively small number of universities, which partly accounts for the professional staff's solidarity of purpose during the first decade of the National Archives.

The young people who came to the National Archives in its early days were often part of a circle, too. For example, after finishing his Ph.D. in 1934, Theodore R. Schellenberg went to Washington to take a job on a joint project of the American Council of Learned Societies and the Social Science Research Council. He then worked for the National Park Service for several months before being appointed to the staff of the National Archives. In his search for something more permanent with a greater professional future, he was frequently in touch with his professors at Pennsylvania and with Lydenberg. It was equally important that he got involved and exchanged information with other people who were interested in jobs at the National Archives, including Herman Kahn, Philip C. Brooks, Robert H. Bahmer, Philip Hamer, Dallas Irvine, and Vernon D. Tate, all of whom also rose to positions of leadership in the agency. It was no accident in the initiation of their archival careers that Irvine, Schellenberg, and Hamer were graduates of Pennsylvania, and Bahmer and Kahn of Minnesota. It is significant, too, that Bahmer had been secretary to a representative and Brooks was the son of a former member of Congress; that Tate and Schellenberg were protégés of Robert Binkley, the prophet of the use of technological devices in libraries and archives; and that Kahn and Schellenberg had worked for the National Park Service. They and others like them among the successful applicants plainly had the right contacts, especially within the academic elite, to open the door to jobs in the National Archives. Yet it must never be overlooked that their primary qualification was the fact that they were able and well-trained scholars.[24]

Because of the amount of time that was required to recruit suitable personnel, the staff of the National Archives expanded slowly. Connor, though, appointed a number of division chiefs before fiscal year 1935 ended on 30 June of that year. Most notable among them were Percy Scott Flippin, a prominent historian, who inaugurated the work of the Research Division; John G. Bradley, who came from the House Library Committee to head the motion pictures and sound recordings operation; Roscoe R. Hill, one of Jameson's protégés, who transferred from the Library of Congress to try to develop a classification scheme for the National Archives; Vernon D. Tate, who developed the photographic reproduction program; and Thomas M. Owen, Jr., the nephew of House Speaker William B. Bankhead and Senator John H. Bankhead, who left the Alabama Department of Archives and History to direct accessions. The following fiscal year saw the staff grow from 42 to 175 persons, with the number rising to 249 and 319, respectively, by the end of fiscal years 1937 and 1938. During fiscal year 1936 Arthur E. Kimberly began his distinguished career in the repair and preservation of archives, John R. Russell left the New York Public Library to direct cataloging, Philip M. Hamer came to head the library of the National Archives, and Arthur H. Leavitt and Fred W. Shipman became chiefs of the agency's first two archives divisions. The prominent geographer W. L. G. Joerg, in 1937, was appointed to head the Maps and Charts Division.[25]

In addition to the young staff members whom I have just mentioned, others who joined the staff were Wayne C. Grover, Herbert E. Angel, Oliver W. Holmes, Paul Lewinson, Marcus Price, G. Philip Bauer, W. Neil Franklin, Edward G. Campbell, Emmett Leahy, Elizabeth B. Drewry, Herman R. Friis, Carl L. Lokke, and Karl L. Trever. The future of the National Archives would rest with them and many of the original division chiefs, for collectively they would shape its development more than any single archivist of the United States.

4. Preparing for Work

Connor often referred to himself as an amateur archivist. The reasons were clear, applied not only to him, but also to his staff. Neither their training nor their experience was easily applied to the formation of an American national archives. Indeed, many of the problems they encountered were far different from those faced by established archival institutions in other countries. Among these were the fact that the National Archives had to deal with the greatest volume of records in the world; the unparalleled diversity of their origins, arrangement, and types; and their widely scattered locations in 1935. Connor and his associates believed that scholars and government officials expected them to bring that material under control quickly, while simultaneously organizing, staffing, and outfitting the infant archival agency and even inaugurating innovative services.[1] Plainly, getting ready for work was a monumental task in itself, especially in the free-swinging setting of American domestic politics.

Archivist Connor had many important decisions to make. Although he had developed a divisional organization for his agency by 1935, he also had to make sure that interunit chores could be performed. The National Archives, in the process, initially resembled an American university in both its horizontal and vertical organization. In order to cut across divisional lines, the archivist in 1935 first created an advisory council and an administrative conference to coordinate the activities of administrative officers and then a staff assembly for all employees. It is not too difficult to see in these the equivalents of a council of deans, a meeting of deans and department heads, and a faculty assembly. There was

45

also a variety of committees dealing with, for example, book purchases, assembly program, fire prevention, and publications. To complete the analogy between the National Archives and a university, one only need mention the titles used among the professional staff that paralleled the rungs in the academic ladder of promotions. One started in the agency as a junior archivist (or cataloger, classifier, etcetera) and might look forward to promotion to assistant archivist, then associate archivist, and later archivist. The chiefs of divisions were equivalent to university department heads, the top administrators to deans, and the archivist of the United States to a chancellor or president.[2]

Before the National Archives was ten years old, it had lost its organizational resemblance to a university. This was to be expected as its staff grew increasingly away from their academic backgrounds and became professional archivists and career civil servants. Yet the academic organization of the 1930s served its purpose. It gave the staff a comfortable vehicle for traveling from amateur to professional status in developing and operating the federal archival agency.

The fact that the staff was not initially under civil-service regulations also paralleled the situation in many academic institutions during the 1930s. Connor and his deputies liked it that way, for it gave them great flexibility in personnel matters. Apparently, they believed they needed that freedom in building a new agency; certainly, they used their power to hire rather well, and they were not ones to use their power to fire arbitrarily. When the National Archives came under civil-service procedures, the White House and Congress were responsible for the change. The arrival of civil-service coverage in 1938 caused, according to Connor, "some little disturbance in our ordinary routine," but it did not last long. A few of the staff were dropped because they could not pass the noncompetitive examinations provided for by law. More of a problem was the recruitment of new archivists, for there was no civil-service test for them, though the problem was partly solved by including one for junior archivists as an option in the junior professional assistant examination.[3]

The conduct of relations with Congress occupied a good deal of the archivist's time. Connor was fortunate in this respect to have on his staff several men who had good connections on Capitol Hill. These included Collas G. Harris, who had been a protégé of Congressman Clifton Woodrum of Virginia; Thaddeus Page, who had been Senator Josiah Bailey's aide; and John G. Bradley, whom the archivist dubbed "an Illinois spoilsman." Moreover, Connor himself had the qualities to become adept at dealing with senators and representatives. J. Franklin Jameson had early called his attention to the necessity for dealing with politicians, administrative ones as well as legislators. For the time being, however, the denizens of Capitol Hill were the ones with whom he mainly had to deal. Unlike some federal agency heads, Connor possessed patience, courtesy, and charm in abundance. He was also a reasonably good golfer and card-player, and he would not refuse a drink in the line of duty. His ability as a raconteur was of a high order. He used all of these attributes as well as his professional dedication to good advantage with members of Congress as well as with his staff, the White House, and later other agency heads.[4]

The archivist had good reason to keep a watchful eye on Congress, where there were not only people who sought patronage everywhere, but those who had plans for the National Archives that did not coincide with those of Connor and the historical profession. Moreover, there were the budget cutters who saw the archives as a luxury that could be readily whittled down, and there were senators and representatives who would seize upon anything as an election issue. Historian William E. Dodd, after his retirement as ambassador to Germany, voiced another fear. After the Office of the Historical Adviser in the State Department had been abolished in 1938, Dodd complained to Connor that that "shows how high officials dislike history. Congressmen simply can't stand to study the behavior of their predecessors. So many 'honor' Washington and Jefferson and violate the basic principles of both great men!" The former ambassador exaggerated, but there was some truth in what he said, for anything that had been concerned with culture had had its troubled days in Congress simply because it might have been embarrassing or because it was not practical.[5] Eternal vigilance had to be the archivist's as well as Jefferson's watchword.

The archivist's first spot of trouble with Congress came in getting the House of Representatives to approve his agency's budget request for fiscal year 1936. There was a critical debate in the House on the matter in March 1935, but thanks to the efforts of congressmen Keller, Woodrum, and Emanuel Celler of New York, the economizing forces trimmed the appropriation proposal of $550,000 by only some $75,000. The cut did not harm the work of the new agency since the request had been based on the expectation that the archives building would be completed earlier than it was. Woodrum and Celler did a fine job of trying to inform their colleagues of the nature of the National Archives, but Connor was disappointed with the misunderstanding in the House about his agency's functions. As he commented, "It was hard for congressmen, even friendly ones, to grasp the idea that the National Archives is something more than a sublimated historical society."[6] One of his most important tasks thereafter would be to educate members of Congress about the character and the needs of his agency.

That was particularly true in the House. There Connor had not only watchdogs of the Treasury like Republican John Taber of New York to contend with, but also John J. Cochran of Missouri, the chairman of the Committee on Expenditures in the Executive Departments, and James P. Buchanan of Texas, the chairman of the Committee on Appropriations. Clifton Woodrum, who was a member of the Appropriations Committee, told the archivist in November 1935 that Buchanan "had blood in his eye for your outfit last time" and warned him to pay his respects to the Texan. He also suggested that Connor give Buchanan a guided tour of the archives building, a technique which the archivist was to rely upon heavily in the future in dealing with members of the House and Senate. Whatever it was that Connor did, he seemed to compose his differences with Buchanan.[7]

Representative Cochran was not so easily dealt with. He was one of the proponents of the hall-of-records idea, which would have limited public access to federal documents, and he was unhappy with what the National Archives promised to become as a broad-gauged cultural agency. As he wrote in January 1936 to Cordell Hull, who was the chairman of the National Archives Council, "it was a grave mistake to construct" an archives that would cost $12,000,000. That was because only a small building was originally contemplated "to house a limited number of historical documents." Although Cochran wrote that this was "water over the dam," he was still critical of the majority in Congress for providing a larger establishment. He suggested to Secretary Hull that in order to save federal funds the National Archives Council should consider advising Congress to restrict the activities of the National Archives. The congressman probably sensed that his was a losing fight, for he also recommended ways in which the National Archives could be used "to get some benefit out of the money that has been spent." He urged the council to direct Connor "to immediately take over all of the dead files in the government departments" in order to release office space for other uses and to put his employees to work. Cochran further recommended that the council define a historical document so that the agency's staff would not "go far beyond the original thought in preserving documents."[8]

Cochran was important not so much for his ability to harass the archivist as for his misunderstanding of the work of the National Archives. He found it difficult to accept the agency as something that would do more than shelter a small number of state papers, and he had no idea of what was required to satisfy the needs of researchers. He was apparently unaware that some government agencies would resist relinquishing their older records (which was one reason why they favored a hall of records, where they could still control the use of their records). Certainly, Cochran showed no sign of knowing that archivists often had to engage in delicate maneuvers to get possession of records, and that it was an elaborate process to deal with them after they were acquired.

The National Archives Council acted in February 1936 to speed up the transfer of archives. Perhaps, in that way, Representative Cochran would be placated by seeing some federal office space released and the employees of the National Archives actually working with records. Robert Connor tried to appease Cochran by inviting him and the other members of the Committee on Expenditures in the Executive Departments to tour the archives building. Unfortunately for the archivist, the Missouri congressman snapped back that he should have invited the committee members individually. Although Cochran posed no great threat to the archival budget in 1936, he did urge the agency's merger with the Library of Congress. That sent tremors of fear through the National Archives, not only because it was another sign of Cochran's opposition to the agency, but because that would make the organization part of a legislative agency and therefore more under the control of men like Cochran.[9]

In 1937 Cochran attacked the National Archives on two separate fronts. One was his introduction of H.R. 138, which called for the establishment of a hall of records in order to move the older but still active federal records more rapidly out of expensive office space. The Department of War was the chief supporter of this bill as it was also the most resistant among government agencies to transferring its records to the National Archives. Undoubtedly, the War Department found most attractive in Cochran's bill the provision that each federal agency would retain control over its own records in the proposed hall of records. The other sector in which the Missouri congressman battled was appropriations, where he sought to cut the budget of the National Archives. He was rebuffed on both fronts and was thereafter no serious threat to the National Archives. That was because of its increasingly good record in saving the office space and funds of other agencies as a result of its growing accessions and because of its effectiveness in handling congressional and public relations. Thus, the appropriations for the agency rose from $477,000 in fiscal year 1936 to $615,579 in 1937 to $709,000 in 1938 and to $789,000 in 1939.[10]

This did not mean that after 1937 the National Archives faced no trouble in its quest for appropriations. Every year the archivist and his assistants had to press their case before the House and the Senate. Yet they now had more experience, and help, in doing so. President Roosevelt was increasingly friendly and impressed with the work of the National Archives, as were many members of Congress. For example, the fact that Representative Woodrum could quote the president in support of the agency at a meeting of the House Appropriations Committee contributed to Congress's agreeing to a budget increase of almost 12 percent for fiscal year 1939.[11] The important thing is that the National Archives felt reasonably well established by 1938 and therefore more confident of its ability to defend itself. Even John Cochran had played a significant role in this, for his attacks had forced the agency to reconsider its role and to improve its defenses against political marauders. He particularly helped the National Archives when he forced it to defend itself against the possible establishment of a hall of records by assisting other federal agencies in dealing with their records problems. Of course, the implications of this for the archives' cultural and scholarly functions were great, for there is little doubt that its growing involvement in the management of current records often clashed with them. It is debatable, however, whether the agency could have thrived solely as a cultural institution. As rough a companion as it sometimes was, the agency's developing practical side, records administration, provided important protection for the cultural and research-oriented activities of the National Archives.

One reason for the troubles encountered by Connor and his staff was that they did not know exactly what they were to do. They frequently had to improvise the answers to problems as they went along. No sooner did they have one problem under control than another one arose. The situation was nevertheless challenging. It was clear to the staff of the National Archives that they were pioneers, not only in establishing a federal archival agency, but in finding ways to deal with the unique aspects of American records. They were fortunate, too, that they had the funds available to take advantage of technological advances while they pioneered. Moreover, they had the temperament to experiment and to joust intellectually about what they were doing. The result was that the National Archives was rich in concepts and had the latitude to make occasional mistakes.

Central to all this was the lavish nature of the National Archives building. Connor and his aides did not have to seek the authorization of ways, chiefly air conditioning, to control the temperature, humidity, and chemical elements that can be so harmful to archives. Thanks to the farsightedness of the 1930 advisory committee for the building these had been built into the structure already, and provision had been made for the installation of special equipment for repair, preservation, and reproduction. The staff, of course, had to adjust some of this equipment and design some of the rest, but they rarely had to conceive of it. That allowed them to spend most of their time on the difficult business of obtaining the records and readying them for use.

The National Archives was unable to collect and process records immediately after Robert Connor took office in October 1934. The archivist, however, could address himself to some lesser tasks in the early days. For example, he quickly displayed his interest in procuring the original engrossed copies of the Declaration of Independence and the Constitution from the Library of Congress. He took seriously the comments of Herbert Hoover, in Hoover's address at the cornerstone laying, and of Franklin D. Roosevelt, in his initial interview with Connor, that the archives would be the home for these two illustrious documents. Therefore, early in 1935, Connor got in touch with officials of the Library of Congress to discover how that institution had gained custody of them. In August the archivist and the president again discussed the transfer, which they both seemed to favor. Connor waited for presidential action. Roosevelt, however, was never interested enough to seek the necessary legislation. The question of the transfer of the two prime state papers was a knotty one, and it came up repeatedly in Connor's writings and correspondence. He took pains to state that the president was the one who usually raised the subject in their conversations, and that, contrary to press reports, the National Archives was not engaged in a battle with the Library of Congress for possession of the Declaration of Independence and the Constitution. Be this as it may, the archivist was interested from the beginning in having the documents for the National Archives, even though he left it up to Roosevelt to initiate the necessary legislation. There are two probable reasons for Connor's caution. One is that he did not want to seek the legislation himself, for fear that would plunge the National Archives into a controversy with Congress that his agency could ill afford. The other reason is that he did not want to offend Librarian of Congress Herbert Putnam, who had been cooperative and friendly. The archivist, therefore, was willing to wait, though consequently the issue remained unresolved until after Roosevelt, Putnam, and Connor were dead.[12]

More important to the archivist's work was the placing of the new Federal Register Division in his agency in 1935. For several years, many attorneys and government officials had been pressing for a register of administrative law. A special committee of the American Bar Association declared in 1934 that "Rules, regulations and other exercises of legislative power by executive or administrative officials should be made easily and readily available at some central office." Chief Justice Charles Evans Hughes's opinion of January 1935 in *Panama Refining Company* v. *Ryan* gave dramatic support to that statement. In that case, Hughes pointed out that the litigation had reached the Supreme Court based on an assumption by all involved, including the lower courts, that the regulation at issue was still in effect. It was not, and the high bench noticed "the failure to give appropriate public notice of the change in the section." As important as that comment was, the federal government had already begun the process of preparing remedial legislation before the Panama opinion was delivered. In October 1934 a committee of the National Emergency Council recommended the creation of a publication, with the title *Federal Register*, that would print administrative rules and regulations. This recommendation then went to the Interdepartmental Legal Committee, an organization of the chief counsels of major federal agencies. That group drafted appropriate legislation, which in July 1935 Congress passed, with a few alterations, as the Federal Register Act.[13]

The reasons for locating the Federal Register Division within the National Archives are fairly obvious. It made sense to incorporate it into an agency that issued few regulations and therefore would have little self-interest in the substance of the division's work. Moreover, it was logical that the central repository for government records should have custody of the materials that the division would handle. These included "any presidential procla-mation or executive order and any order, regulation, rule, certifi-cate, code of fair competition, license, notice, or similar instrument issued, prescribed, or promulgated" by any federal executive agency. The responsibility of the National Archives was to receive the original and two copies of such documents. The original was to become part of the archives of the United States; one copy was to be retained by the Federal Register Division for public inspec-tion; the other copy was to be transmitted to the Government Printing Office for publication under the division's editorial direc-tion. Congress further stipulated that the government's adminis-trative regulations would have no legal force until they were made available for public inspection and published.[14]

Connor immediately acted to implement the mandate of Con-gress. A month after the law's enactment in July 1935, President Roosevelt appointed, from among those candidates the archivist had recommended, a highly reputable career government attorney, Bernard R. Kennedy, as director of the division. Although Con-gress had not yet appropriated funds for publication of the *Federal Register*, a great deal of work had to be done. The archivist mailed letters to 123 federal agencies telling them of the act and its re-quirements for filing documents; he also asked them for a list of offices that issued pertinent regulations and for the designation of liaison officers. Some agencies did not respond, so Connor had to solicit them again. Then followed seemingly interminable confer-ences between the Federal Register Division's staff and the various agency liaison officers to set in motion the flow of documents. Furthermore, it was necessary to keep in close touch with the White House, the Budget Bureau, and the Justice Department to smooth out legal technicalities and to decide what exactly should be grist for the division's mill. Then there was the work of setting up procedures for receiving and annotating the regulations and quickly making such documents available for public inspection and publishing them. The law also established a permanent ad-ministrative committee, composed of the archivist, as chairman; the public printer; and a representative of the attorney general to oversee the Federal Register Division's operations. This committee met first on 27 September and frequently thereafter.[15]

For the National Archives, the Federal Register Act meant the gift of a constant flow of important documents from executive agencies as well as contacts within those offices that were often valuable in negotiating for other records. It also meant a considerable amount of work. The National Archives quickly assembled a specialized staff for that labor, as Congress had directed that the division's activities begin within sixty days after the approval of the legislation and that executive agencies had to comply with the law within six months after its enactment. In less than a year Kennedy had two editors, six lawyers, and six clerks skillfully functioning. The permanent administrative committee had drafted an executive order regulating the mechanics of issuing administrative orders, which President Roosevelt signed in February 1936. The committee had also established a format for the *Federal Register*, set the annual sale price at ten dollars, and formulated regulations for implementing the provisions of the Federal Register Act. Meanwhile, Congress had moved to finance the publication of the *Federal Register*. Government agencies began filing their orders and regulations on 12 March; two days later, the division and the Government Printing Office produced the first issue of the daily *Federal Register*.[16]

The Federal Register Division had been well launched. During its first full fiscal year of operation (July 1936 through June 1937), the division received 5,078 documents, published 254 daily issues, and, by the year's end, was sending copies of the *Federal Register* to 5,500 federal officials and 2,123 paid subscribers. The permanent administrative committee meanwhile had persuaded Congress to authorize the codification of agency regulations currently in effect. The president approved this legislation in June 1937; thus executive agencies were required to file a codification of their regulations by 1 July 1938 and every five years thereafter. The editing of this turned out to be a huge task. Therefore, the last of the fifteen volumes of the *Code of Federal Regulations* was not off the press until fiscal year 1941, though the Federal Register Division had meanwhile published annual supplements to keep the code up-to-date. By 1941 there was no doubt that the division's work was essential not only to lawyers engaged in federal practice and to government agencies themselves, but also to citizens who needed knowledge of their rights and responsibilities under administrative law. And the Federal Register Act came none too soon, for with the thousands of federal regulations being issued every year, the alternative to the work of the Federal Register Division of the National Archives would have been administrative and judicial chaos. In short, the publication of administrative law allowed the fulfillment of everybody's right to know what it was.[17]

Another area of special concern in 1935 was the National Historical Publications Commission. The National Archives Act authorized this operation, though as one separate from the archives itself. By law, the archivist was the chairman of the commission, and it seemed implicit that the National Archives was to carry out the staff work for the NHPC. Connor initiated the commission's work soon after taking office. Franklin D. Roosevelt appointed Professor St. George L. Sioussat, of the University of Pennsylvania, and Dumas Malone, editor of the *Dictionary of American Biography*, to join the archivist and representatives of the Library of Congress and the historical units of the departments of State, War, and the Navy as members of the NHPC. They held their first meeting on 29 January 1935. Then they asked Connor to furnish the basis for an up-to-date edition of the 1908 survey of government documentary historical publications that had been done by a committee of historians appointed by President Theodore Roosevelt; the commission also discussed recommending to Congress "a documentary historical publication illustrative of the origins of the Constitution," as part of the forthcoming sesquicentennial celebration of the adoption of the Constitution.[18]

On the basis of staff work done by Solon J. Buck, who was the commission's secretary, the NHPC recommended to Congress in 1936 the publication of six volumes of documents on the ratification of the Constitution and its first ten amendments. The Office of Director of Publications of the National Archives, which Buck headed, also began work on a new survey of the government's documentary historical publications. Although the commission seemed off to an energetic start, the appearance was deceptive.

The survey of documentary publications was not pursued after 1936, because, as Buck put it in 1940, the "Pressure of work" had "prevented any progress being made." In 1939, Congress finally got around to considering the NHPC's recommendation for a documentary publication pertaining to the Constitution, but the legislators never acted favorably on it or on the commission's 1940 recommendation to publish documents relating to the explorations of Zebulon Pike. The NHPC held no meetings during the following decade. As Oliver W. Holmes, the commission's acting secretary, wrote in his report for fiscal year 1942, the body's dormancy was caused by "the preoccupation of the Archivist [now Solon Buck] and of most of the other members with duties arising out of emergency and war conditions." The original NHPC, in effect, was killed by Buck's failure to find time to do its bidding, by its members' loss of incentive after their promising start, and especially by the lack of enthusiasm of Congress about the commission's recommendations. World War II merely provided the coup de grace.[19] Five years would pass beyond the end of the war and a new archivist, Wayne C. Grover, would be serving before the National Historical Publications Commission was resurrected.

The National Archives had to initiate another highly specialized program in 1935. That was in accordance with the legislative provision that the agency was to receive not only government-made films and sound recordings but could also presumably accept any such privately produced material illustrative of the nation's history. John G. Bradley, the clerk of the House Library Committee, is generally credited with getting this audiovisual section added to the National Archives Act. Thus it was no surprise when Archivist Connor appointed him chief of the Motion Pictures and Sound Recordings Division in January. Bradley swung vigorously into his job. The most pressing problem facing him was the serious fire hazard then accompanying the storage and use of films. He soon met with a large number of people who were concerned with the problem, including producers, distributors, chemists, and engineers. It was obvious that they all wanted to have fire-resistant film and safe methods of storage; it was equally plain that they had made little progress there. Bradley, therefore, sought to achieve those goals for the National Archives and for all who were interested in motion picture films.

His constant question was, "How can motion picture films be preserved for one hundred years?" In his search for the answer, Bradley became a member of the National Research Council's advisory committee to the National Bureau of Standards and chairman of the film-preservation committee of the Society of Motion Picture Engineers. In cooperation with the Carnegie Foundation he was instrumental in setting up a research project in the National Bureau of Standards to investigate how films might be better preserved. He also became an apostle to the motion picture industry for the use of cellulose acetate film, which was far safer than nitrate film and would allow for preservation of motion pictures indefinitely. On its own, Bradley's division in 1935 and 1936 designed and installed externally vented fireproof cabinets for film storage in the archives building. This work won almost complete approval from interested parties, including the National Bureau of Standards. The Motion Pictures Division's experiments in preservation enlisted the active cooperation of other units within the National Archives, especially the Division of Photographic Reproduction and Research and the Division of Repair and Preservation, which had their own related pioneering projects in progress.[20]

Franklin D. Roosevelt was interested in the work on the storage and preservation of films; yet despite the advances achieved by Bradley's division, the president and even the archivist were properly skeptical that both film and paper records could be kept safely under the same roof. Roosevelt suggested in October 1935 that Connor consider the construction of "a series of fireproof vaults under Constitution Avenue" for film storage that in the event of fire could be flooded with water. In February 1938 Connor told the president that investigation indicated the placing of film vaults under Constitution Avenue to be questionable in terms of both safety and practicability. He recommended instead the construction of a separate building to store motion pictures, especially in view of the tremendous increase in the amount of government films being made. The immediate consequence of this was the planning for such a building to be constructed during the second five-year phase of the administration's building program. Although the National Archives procured temporary housing for films during World War II, the government never provided funds for a permanent structure. The agency was to handle its films in other ways. Indeed, out of necessity, the National Archives followed Bradley's recommendation of the use of safe storage methods and of acetate film.[21]

Bradley also sought to develop a national film library, based on the latitude that the law gave the National Archives in collecting motion pictures. As soon as the vaults were ready to receive materials in 1936, Bradley's division began accessioning motion pictures and sound recordings from government agencies. Bradley also tried to arrange acceptance of private donations. Will Hays, the so-called czar of the motion-picture industry, repeatedly offered to give films to the National Archives. Just as constantly, and finally successfully, Bradley sought definite authorization to accept them. All of the necessary procedures were worked out by 1938, and the division began receiving considerable quantities of material from both government and private sources. By 30 June 1939, the Division of Motion Pictures and Sound Recordings had custody of 1,546,241 running feet of film and 331 sound recordings. This clearly established the division as the government's historical film library.[22]

Organization, politics, and recruitment were essential to the life of the new government agency; and special programs were interesting and often important. The National Archives' central mission and most important work, however, was to appraise, accession, preserve, and make available for research the official records of enduring value. In preparation for that, and using the archivist's broad statutory power to inspect the records of any federal agency, the archives' staff had to find out where the government's records were located, their content, their condition, and their bulk.

By April 1935 Robert Connor was ready to gain the answers to those questions. He first sent letters to all agency heads in which he asked them to tell him what classes of their records were "permanently disposed of as useless papers," how they were disposed of, in what volume, how often, and under what authority. Because there was "misunderstanding in application of existing laws," he also requested their advice about what was the best way of determining and getting rid of useless records. This was a forerunner to his letter of September requesting each agency, in compliance with law, to send him a list of records that had no current or historical value, so that he could report to Congress by 1 January 1936 on what should be destroyed.[23] Through those letters, the archivist gained information and established contacts that would be valuable to his staff in finding out the state of the government's records.

While Connor was doing this, he also dispatched examiners to survey the records of executive agencies in Washington in order to get the facts needed to determine future accessions as well as to assist him in formulating his recommendations to Congress on the disposition of useless papers. These examiners worked on two different though not totally unrelated projects. The director of archival service supervised the four special examiners employed to deal with useless records; the nine deputy examiners who searched for permanently valuable government records in the District of Columbia operated out of the Division of Accessions.[24]

The work of the Accessions Division's deputy examiners began in May 1935, and it was a massive undertaking. This survey of federal archives in Washington (as the project was usually called) was made even more difficult by the condition in which the records were found. Almost half of them were in danger of damage or loss from mold, rain, sunlight, filth, theft, and vermin; more than one-third were subject to fire hazards; and about half of the materials were so located or arranged that they could not be easily used. The National Archives also reported that "many are so badly worn by constant use or so weakened from age or other causes that they could not be used without danger of further damage." The bulk of the archives survey in the District of Columbia was done in 1936, although, because of various complications, the National Archives was unable to declare this monumental project completed until fiscal year 1940. By then, the deputy examiners had found almost 3,000,000 cubic feet of federal records (in more than 6,500 rooms) as well as some 34,500,000 running feet of film and millions of

Government records stored in a garage, before removal to the National Archives

photographic negatives and maps. It was on the basis of this work that the National Archives could move quickly and effectively to bring the government's permanently valuable records under archival administration.[25]

As I have observed earlier, the identification of useless government records was separate from but not unrelated to the federal archives survey in Washington. The archivist was by law charged with recommending to Congress what records should be discarded. The disposition of such records was a matter of importance to both the government and the National Archives. For the government, it was a way of reducing the funds spent in maintaining records that served no useful purpose, and the money involved was mounting substantially given the great growth of federal activities during the Roosevelt administration. For the National Archives it was primarily a matter of preserving materials of value for research purposes. This meant that the agency had to separate the archival wheat from the chaff very quickly in order to give suitable care to the records of enduring usefulness.

The survey of useless records began in 1935, based on the

archivist's inquiries and the studies conducted by the special examiners, who were often helped by the archives survey deputy examiners. During fiscal year 1936 enough information came in as a result of Connor's inquiries that he was able to recommend to Congress the disposition of certain records from fifteen federal agencies. The accomplishments of the special examiners increased substantially during fiscal year 1937, but the task confronting them grew even larger. Although in 1936 they had studied 2,484 of the 9,178 series submitted by the agencies for disposition analyses, they were now asked to examine 27,873 records series, of which they were able to study only 3,237. They were obviously lagging far behind the demand for action.

The National Archives sought ways to cope with this intolerable situation. The agency authorized the assistant director of archival service to coordinate the work of the special examiners and the deputy examiners and to deal with the appraisals of useless records. The whole problem was complicated by the fact that a large proportion of the disposable records was located outside Washington. That led to studies of ways to simplify the examination of federal records, for example, through sampling. Additionally, the National Archives sought legislation to facilitate disposition of useless records. An important step forward was taken in February 1938, when the special examiners were transferred to the Division of Accessions to provide even better coordination of their work with that of the deputy examiners.[26]

The result of these changes and studies was a vigorous move forward in dealing with useless records. During fiscal year 1938 there were 31,888 series on hand to be analyzed, of which 25,424 were dealt with. The National Archives, as was to be expected, recommended for destruction most of the records that the agencies thought suitable for disposal. Yet the archivist and occasionally the agencies determined that 3 percent of them were worthy of retention. In all this, the hard-gained experience of the examiners during the early years of the useless records program was put to good use. Not only had they learned how to appraise records more efficiently, they had also helped make the disposition procedures and forms simpler for agencies to use.[27]

During fiscal year 1939 there were further refinements in the system. The records divisions of the National Archives had acquired enough staff and specialized knowledge to assume responsibility for the appraisal of disposition lists. The agency also completed the standardization of disposition forms, and methods were devised to reduce the amount of time needed to formulate the archivist's disposal recommendations for Congress. More important, in August 1939, Congress passed the Records Disposal Act, which empowered the archivist to authorize the disposition of useless records under certain circumstances when the legislators were not in session. Of considerable significance in this respect was that the law approved the development of schedules of disposable records so that records of the same kind that Congress had previously authorized for disposition could be so identified that they could be destroyed without legislative approval when Congress was not in session. Such schedules greatly simplified the records disposal activities of the National Archives; indeed, their application (although it came slowly) constituted a great contribution to archival science, one that later would be widely adopted in other jurisdictions both in the United States and abroad. Of course, the archivist had to report to Congress any dispositions made without its specific approval, and he could not authorize for disposal any records of an agency without that agency's consent. The Records Disposal Act of 1939 also remedied a deficiency of the National Archives Act by providing a definition of records. Under the new legislation, *records* were declared to be "originals or copies of motion-picture or other photographic records in any form whatsoever, sound recordings, correspondence, papers, indexes, maps, charts, plans, drawings, punch cards, tabulation sheets, pictures, and other kinds of records belonging to the United States Government."

In September 1940 Congress enacted related legislation. This Photographed Records Disposal Act authorized the early destruction of records, with the archivist's approval, that had been suitably photographed or microfilmed, if they were "of the same specific kind in the particular agency . . . previously authorized for disposition by Congress." The lawmakers also provided that such photographs or microphotographs would have the "same force and effect" in law as the original documents. In retrospect, it is plain that the legislation of 1939 and 1940 not only allowed the National Archives to pioneer further in handling federal records, but that it laid the basis for records management, which profession would devise revolutionary methods to cope with the rapidly growing volume of records. However advanced these laws were, they barely came in time, for it was becoming clear by 1940 that increasingly vigorous action had to be taken to keep the government and the National Archives itself from being flooded with records.[28]

Before 1940 the National Archives was abundantly occupied with discovering the location, nature, and condition of the federal government's records. Vital to this were not only the useless records program and the survey of archives in Washington, but also the survey of federal archives outside the District of Columbia. Obviously, something had to be done about government records located outside Washington, which were every bit as bulky and almost as important as those found in the capital. The problem was that the National Archives lacked the funds necessary to survey them. The Works Progress Administration was looking for relief projects for jobless white-collar workers, however, and Harry L. Hopkins, the agency's administrator, was favorably disposed toward programs that would deal with historical materials. Therefore, the National Archives proposed to the WPA a project that would survey federal archives in the states. The WPA and President Roosevelt approved this and, in December 1935, allocated $1,176,000 to the project through 30 June 1936. It was designated the Survey of Archives of the Federal Government outside the District of Columbia but was known less formally in the WPA as Sponsored Project No. 4 and in the National Archives as the Survey of Federal Archives. The National Archives was the project's cooperating sponsor and provided its managerial staff. Two deputy examiners from the Division of Accessions, Philip M. Hamer and Theodore R. Schellenberg, became director and assistant director, respectively, and Archivist Connor appointed an advisory committee composed of three of his chief aides, Dorsey W. Hyde, Jr., Solon J. Buck, and Marcus W. Price.

The purpose of the Survey of Federal Archives was "to ascertain the exact location, the volume, and the conditions of storage of such archives, to identify them as regards their contents, and to furnish other information which may be of assistance in the formulation of recommendations designed to insure their safe preservation and to facilitate their use by officials and students." The project's accomplishments by the end of fiscal year 1936 were impressive: the survey had devised and distributed instructions and forms to be used by its employees, and Hamer had appointed regional directors in thirty-five areas as well as a number of state advisory committees. The vast majority of workers came from the relief rolls, with a peak employment of 3,171 being reached in May 1936. By 30 June the inventorying of field records had been completed in 569 communities and was going forward in 488 others. The survey had thus far examined more than 2,000,000 linear feet of government records housed in about 16,000 rooms in some 5,000 buildings. The WPA funded the Survey of Federal Archives for fiscal year 1937 in the amount of $2,152,115, and again the project's accomplishments were impressive. During that year, the inventorying of field records was almost completed as the staff found their way into another 43,910 rooms in 17,814 buildings, where they studied and reported on 2,794,670 linear feet of materials.[29]

Separate funding for the Survey of Federal Archives ceased at the end of fiscal year 1937, but the WPA incorporated the project into its Historical Records Survey, which, under the direction of Luther H. Evans, was inventorying state, local, and even private historical materials. Philip M. Hamer continued, without pay, to supervise the activities of the Survey of Federal Archives while carrying on duties as an employee of the National Archives. This situation lasted until 1942, when the WPA was terminated. The emphasis of Hamer's program during those years was largely editorial. Overall, by 1942, the project had surveyed more than 5,000,000 linear feet of federal records outside the nation's capital and had compiled 506 published and 81 unpublished reports on the location and nature of those materials. This *Inventory of Federal Archives* constituted, along with the results of the survey of federal records in Washington and the Historical Records Survey, an unprecedented and remarkably rich inventory of historical materials that researchers have not exhausted to this day. Altogether, those three projects were invaluable to archivists all over the country in providing them with the information that they needed to demonstrate not only their ability to save America's archives for posterity, but also their potential to handle the nation's rapidly developing records problem. Moreover, the Survey of Federal Archives also served as an important training ground or practice area for historians and archivists. Among the former who graced the halls of higher learning were Ralph P. Bieber, William O. Lynch, Richard B. Morris, and James L. Sellers. Theodore C. Blegen, Jesse E. Boell, Christopher Crittenden, and William D. Overman were among the prominent archivists who were connected with the project. Also deserving of mention were three other archivists who came to the staff of the National Archives from the Survey of Federal Archives: Elizabeth (Edwards Hamer) Kegan, who later became assistant librarian of Congress, and G. Philip Bauer and Edward G. Campbell, both of whom became assistant archivists of the United States.[30]

If the surveys of federal records in Washington and the states were crucial to the National Archives becoming a functioning archival agency, the National Archives Council was essential in deciding what the agency should accession. Congress created that body, with representation from all the executive departments, to "define the classes of materials" that were to be transferred to the keeping of the archivist, to approve his recommendations regarding useless records, and to advise him as to the appropriate regulations "governing the disposition and use of the materials" that the National Archives accessioned. The leaders of the National Archives were keenly aware that they could not accomplish their objectives of obtaining historically valuable federal records and readying them for use until the council acted.[31]

The National Archives Council held an organizational meeting 27 December 1935. President Roosevelt gave the group a good send-off, and he even arranged to meet for a while with the council and to have it hold its session in the Cabinet Room of the White

House. The results of the meeting were the election of Secretary of State Cordell Hull as chairman, Archivist Connor as vice-chairman, and Archives Administrative Secretary Thaddeus Page as secretary of the council. The National Archives Council's second meeting, which was held on 10 February 1936 in the Archives building, was the crucial one in its history. With Hull presiding, Connor presented resolutions regarding the transfer of records to the National Archives. The significant resolution was that defining the classes of acceptable records, which would authorize the archivist to requisition materials for transfer to the National Archives falling in the following categories:

I. Any archives or records (a) which the head of the agency in custody of them may deem not to be necessary for use in the conduct of the regular current business of said agency; (b) which he may consider to be in such physical condition that they cannot be used without danger of damage to them; and (c) for which, in his opinion, he is unable to provide adequate or safe storage.

II. Any archives or records of any federal agency that has gone out of existence unless its functions have been transferred to the agency which has custody of its records.

III. Any other archives or records which the National Archives Council by special resolution, or which the head of the agency in custody of them for special reasons, may authorize to be transferred to the National Archives.

The council readily approved this, along with regulations dealing with the physical transfer of archives and the archivist's recommendations to Congress on useless papers.[32]

Although the archivist neither requested nor was given maximum latitude in acquiring records, still the National Archives Council's grant of authority was broad. Connor probably had three things foremost in mind in drawing up his resolution for the council's approval. One was to assuage whatever fears the departmental representatives on the council may have had that their agencies would lose all control over the disposition of their older records; a second was to encourage agency heads to offer a wide range of materials to the National Archives so that the residual movement for a hall of records would be undercut; and the third was to place a good deal of archival material into the National

Archives as soon as possible so that no one could contend that it was slow in getting down to work. Plainly, Connor's resolution did an excellent job of satisfying these criteria.

Would that this were the beginning of a distinguished history for the National Archives Council. That, however, was not the case. Indeed, the council's composition militated against this. It became impossible to gather the original council together again since ten of the group were cabinet members and two others were members of Congress, few of whom conceivably had a burning interest in archival matters. It also turned out that a meeting of council was rarely necessary to the operations of the National Archives. The resolutions of 10 February 1936 served admirably to unlock the agency's gates to a great influx of material; and, after all, the archivist could and did solicit advice from council members on recommendations to Congress for the disposition of useless records. Not until July 1942 did the council meet again, and that meeting was possible only through the liberal use of designated alternates for the heads of executive departments.[33]

It was enough that the council had taken the essential action of defining the classes of records that could be transferred to the National Archives. That meant that by early 1936 the agency was prepared to receive archival materials; it was also ready to learn how to take care of the federal government's records of enduring value.

5. Early Operations and Issues

Records began to arrive at the Archives building as early as December 1935 in anticipation of action by the National Archives Council. By 30 June 1936, ten executive agencies had transferred 58,794 cubic feet of records to the National Archives. The dates of those documents (1791–1935) covered almost the entire scope of the nation's history under the Constitution. During fiscal year 1937, the archivists accessioned another 29,911 cubic feet of paper records, which were transferred from twenty-one agencies, including the Senate and the United States District Court for the District of Columbia. The National Archives also received for the first time quantities of maps, atlases, sound recordings, photographs, and motion-picture film.

The holdings of the National Archives grew steadily larger during the next four years when the agency proved to most government offices that it could handle their archives responsibly and ably. Consequently by 30 June 1941 the National Archives had custody of records from seventy-two agencies. The only significant exceptions were the House of Representatives and most of the federal courts. In bulk, the archives building then held 302,114 cubic feet of records. Its map and atlas collection contained 77,513 items, and there were also on hand 4,557,013 running feet of film, 3,820 sound recordings, and 215,728 still photographs. This was an awesome and unprecedented archival accumulation for five-and-one-half years of work. Clearly, it made the National Archives the largest and potentially the most important center for historical research in the United States.[1]

This, of course, did not happen by chance. Many federal

Government records after removal to the National Archives

agencies were reluctant to give up their valuable older records without a good deal of persuasion, a job which consumed much of the archivist's time. Robert Connor and his professional staff were constantly in touch with key officials in other agencies. Thanks to the surveys of records both within and outside Washington these contacts were available for use, just as Connor and his deputies used the connections they had made through the National Archives Council, the National Historical Publications Commission, and the other committees on which they served. The staff also conducted tours of their building for various officials to show what the National Archives could do to safeguard records, and, as gestures of goodwill, the conference room and the auditorium were often made available to other agencies for meetings. The National Archives relied heavily upon public relations to carry the good news of its work. Newspapers all over the country carried stories on the agency, and occasionally popular magazines published articles on the National Archives. Connor and his aides even took to the radio to publicize the work and the potential of their agency.[2]

Yet issues arose that public relations alone could not resolve. One question was, Could the National Archives give the agencies that had originated the records satisfactory reference service? Another was, Could federal agencies withdraw records when the nature of their work so required it? The National Archives had to demonstrate its willingness and ability to do these things lest most agencies transfer only a small and insignificant portion of their older records, and it resolved these two questions rather easily. The archivist made it clear that originating agencies had the first priority on the use of their transferred records and that the National Archives would offer expert reference service. Indeed, within a short period of time, he was shown to be as good as his word. As for agencies checking out their records for use, Connor issued regulations in January 1937 that provided for any federal agency, upon application and subject to the archivist's approval, to withdraw material temporarily. The result of these policies was to boost the confidence of government offices in the ability of the National Archives to meet their needs and thereby to encourage further transfers of records to the archivist's custody.[3]

All this, however, led to another issue that would become a source of irritation. One must concede that the National Archives had to take steps to spur the transfer of older records to its care. Yet, as a result, occasions later arose when the needs of government offices kept materials from use by private citizens. The matter was complicated by the possibility that an agency might have questionable use for the records, or retain them longer than necessary, or even lose them. That led to arguments between public officials, who easily justified to themselves whatever their agencies did, and citizens who considered their interests at least equal to those of the federal officers who were supposedly their servants. These disputes were rarely significant until well after World War

II, but when they erupted the National Archives often found itself in a difficult postion between its citizen and official clients.

This situation was further aggravated by the insistence of a number of agencies that restrictions be placed on the use of their records. Connor decided to accept records on that basis. Indeed, this was and still is a frequent practice among archivists, founded on the theory that it is better to have custody of records with restrictions than to chance never having the materials at all. Such restrictions varied greatly all the way from reviewing researchers' notes to occasionally excluding all except the donor agency from using the material, but the limitations were bound to generate controversy. As early as 1937, the Treasury, Justice, and Commerce departments, the Export-Import Bank, the Veterans Administration, and the National Labor Relations Board had placed restrictions on the use of some of their records in the National Archives. Archivist Connor was farsighted enough to consider this a problem, especially if additional agencies restricted the use of their records, and he fought to modify the restrictions.[4] Unfortunately for the cause of allowing researchers freer access to the records, not only did significantly more agencies adopt restrictions during World War II, but the National Archives itself became less concerned with fighting the sacristans of secrecy. The departments of State and War posed the two most difficult problems in acquiring materials. With the State Department it was a matter of transferring few of its records. This troubled the archivist, for with Secretary of State Cordell Hull serving as chairman of the National Archives Council, this department should set a good example for the rest of the government. The problem was that Hull's alternate on the council, the eminent historical editor Hunter Miller, opposed relinquishing control of the best and the bulk of the State Department's archives, although he was highly sympathetic to all the other objectives of the National Archives. As it turned out, this problem was soon solved. Miller retired from government service during the summer of 1937, and the only obstacle to be overcome was Assistant Secretary of State George S. Messersmith, who had become the key official in making recommendations on the disposition of the department's historic records. Messersmith did not take his duty lightly, but neither did Robert Connor. The archivist talked and partied with the assistant secretary and later escorted him on a tour of the archives building. By November 1937, Messersmith was favorably impressed with what he had heard and seen, and he soon recommended that the Department of State transfer its older and historically most valuable records to the National Archives. The result was that by the middle of 1938 the amount of State Department records in the archives building had risen from 1,249 to 9,196 cubic feet.[5]

The resistance of the Department of War was more deep-seated. That department had transferred nothing to the National Archives during fiscal year 1936 and only 833 cubic feet of records during the following two years. Plainly, the War Department wanted to have absolute control over the bulk of its older records. The archivist was deeply concerned about this situation, partly because of the poor and even dangerous conditions under which many of the department's records were stored and partly because of the interest of a large number of researchers in military archives. Neither Connor's logic nor charm moved the War Department to cooperate with the National Archives. In desperation, in June 1937, he appealed to President Roosevelt, who had also been concerned about the problem of storing military records. He asked the president to try to persuade the War Department to release its older records such as the military records of the Confederacy that were of no value to the nation's defense. The archivist emphasized the inconsistency of the department in complaining about lack of space while refusing to transfer its historic records.[6]

Roosevelt soon acted. On 17 June he wrote Secretary of War Harry Woodring, saying that he had heard the Confederate war records were located in a motor vehicle garage on Virginia Avenue. The president asked if they could be transferred to the archivist's custody, since "he has room for them and it would take the cost of space and maintenance off the War Department." Woodring replied that the Confederate archives were intertwined with his department's records and that they received heavy use. Stating that the War Department was experienced in handling such records and asserting that it had a legal obligation to maintain them, the secretary suggested that the "sentimental value" of wartime records was an insufficient reason for transferring them to the National Archives. The way for them to be better housed, he added, was for the government to construct a hall of records.[7]

Secretary Woodring's letter was clever. Indeed, Roosevelt believed he had made "a pretty good case." The president, however, was not willing to give in, for he asked the archivist what they should do next. Connor answered with a point that he thought he had made plain to Roosevelt in the beginning: the National Archives would take all of the War Department's older records. He reinforced this by eloquently pointing out that those records were not necessary to current military need, that they were in poor physical condition, and that they were stored in extremely hazardous surroundings. The National Archives, he stressed, clearly had jurisdiction over historic military records, and it could repair them and provide them with a safe home far from gasoline pumps and lubricating vats.[8]

The president immediately wrote Woodring on 22 July trying to arrange a compromise satisfactory to the archivist and the War Department. He urged the secretary to visit the National Archives in order to see what that agency could do for the department's records. Roosevelt further suggested that departmental personnel could be detailed to the archives building to handle the records, which would not only allow the safeguarding of the material from both Connor's and Woodring's standpoints, but would also save the money then spent to rent storage space. After this presidential salvo, the War Department raised the white flag. Woodring conceded that the present storage facilities were unsuitable and that the prospects were poor for construction of either a new War Department building or a federal hall of records; he indicated his willingness to move the records to the National Archives and to detail fifty-four departmental civil servants to take care of them there. Connor and Woodring soon met to begin working out the details of Roosevelt's compromise solution. As a result of this and several other conferences, the volume of War Department records in the National Archives shot up to 23,839 cubic feet in fiscal year

1939. They then constituted the largest body of agency archives there except for those of the Veterans Administration.[9]

Yet, because the Department of War had retained legal custody of the material, researchers did not have ready access to those of its records in the National Archives. This soon resulted in a minor cause célèbre when Margaret Pulitzer Leech was denied use of Civil War records in working on her book *Reveille in Washington*. Both she and her publisher, Harper & Brothers, demanded that the government remove the restrictions imposed by an overly possessive War Department. In December 1938 Connor took advantage of the dispute to press the president for freer access to the records. He told Roosevelt that although the government's interest in the material was paramount, the need to limit private use of them declined as time passed. The archivist urged liberalization of the War Department's restrictions, emphasizing that historians believed the limitations were "unnecessarily stringent" and that the truth must be available to achieve legitimate educational ends. President Roosevelt told Secretary Woodring that he agreed with Connor regarding the Civil War records. "After all," he wrote, "seventy-five years have elapsed. I think the War Department should loosen up, don't you." The department yielded somewhat to presidential pressure. The results were, as Connor pointed out, "understandings . . . in making possible much freer use of the records" and additional transfers of War Department materials to the National Archives.[10] That did not solve the problem of access, for until after World War II military personnel continued to help administer the Army's older records in the archives building and restrictions on newer accessions led to fresh disputes. Yet the National Archives had made great progress in acquiring physical custody of the material.

Arranging the transfer of records to the National Archives was only the first part of the agency's job, and it was no small one. The National Archives and the transferring agencies not only had to carry on negotiations, which were sometimes difficult and lengthy, but they had to prepare accessioning inventories of the materials involved. Moreover, Connor's employees had to ship the records from the agency to the archives building as well as to check the material at each end of the trip and to arrange for temporary storage until the documents could be further processed.

After arrival at the archives building, accessions had to be cleaned and fumigated quickly and safely. This was, therefore, another area in which the National Archives could pioneer. Such work, along with the development of new repair and preservation techniques, took place under the innovative direction of Arthur E. Kimberly, the chief of the Division of Repair and Preservation. It was vital work, for the records usually arrived covered with dust and often infiltrated with grit, fungi, and vermin. Kimberly's division devised an instrument, the airbrush, that cleaned all newly arrived archives with a blast of air. The records were then placed in a large, closed tank where they were exposed for three hours to a fumigant composed of ethylene oxide and carbon dioxide. Many of the records had been folded for decades and thus also required flattening in order to be stored and used properly. Again, Kimberly's staff found a technique to do the job with large amounts of records. Documents made before 1840 rarely posed special problems, for the inks used then were not soluble in water and the quality of the paper was often excellent. Therefore, they could usually be flattened with a water process. Later records, however, required more delicate handling. It was decided that they could be moistened for an hour, then ironed flat in either a mangle or a hydraulic press, depending upon the degree of their resistance to the process.

When all this was done, the records were ready for the custodial divisions to handle. Yet, because many of the materials were damaged or exceedingly fragile, the work of the Division of Repair and Preservation was not necessarily finished. The traditional method of repairing archives was a tedious hand process (called *silking*) of applying crepeline with an aqueous adhesive to piece out or fortify paper or parchment. This was too expensive and time consuming in dealing with great amounts of material. Consequently, the National Archives and the National Bureau of Standards developed a laminating machine that could apply cellulose acetate foil quickly and safely to the vast majority of damaged and fragile records, thus preserving them for normal research use. Silking was restricted to only the most delicate documents. Of course, Kimberly's division was equipped to perform binding repair operations, since many older records were bound in volumes. The division also played a key role in regulating the temperature, fire and water controls, light, humidity, and chemical content of the air in the archives building.[11]

The units that had custody of the records were originally called archives divisions. There were two of them in the initial organization of the National Archives, but they multiplied as materials were received. By 1937 there were separate divisions for the historic records of the departments of State, Treasury, Justice, and Commerce as well as for maps and charts. A year later, the National Archives also included archives divisions for Congress; independent agencies; the departments of War, Post Office, Navy, Interior, Agriculture, and Labor; the Veterans Administration; and photographic materials. After records were cleaned and fumigated, they were sent to the appropriate archives division. There they were removed from their original containers for storage in specially constructed equipment. In doing this, the archivists took care to reproduce the original arrangement of the records, or at least to preserve whatever evidence there was of it so that they could be rearranged later. This sounds less important and easier to accomplish than it was and therefore deserves further comment.[12]

The National Archives felt bound to observe completely only one traditional principle of archival administration, which was to arrange records on the basis of how they were created. The foundation of this was the French rule of *respect des fonds*, developed early in the nineteenth century. This concept dictated that a group of records, usually those accumulated by a functioning office of a government agency, must not be mixed with other groups. Later in the century, German archivists added a complementary idea, *provenance*, which meant that the original order of records must be retained. The Dutch, in effect, soon combined the two concepts and made the result into a universal principle of archival administration.

The advantages of following the principles of *respect des fonds* and *provenance* were several. First, anybody examining records thus arranged would have a good idea not only of how a government office functioned and was organized, but also of when and in what relationships its decisions were made. Second, archivists and researchers could use whatever finding aids and cross-references the accumulating office developed. Third, archivists could save time in readying records for use by relying on an arrangement that was already there or that could usually be reconstructed. Fourth, the universality of this sytem of arrangement would be a basis of the archival professional everywhere and the concept should not be difficult for researchers to master. The chief disadvantages were that individual documents or files might be hard to find and that a subject-matter approach to materials would be impeded.

Although the National Archives tried to devise systems supplementary to the principles of *respect des fonds* and *provenance* to remedy these problems, it was early committed to the traditional concepts of arrangement. For example, in February 1936 Director of Archival Service Dorsey W. Hyde, Jr., wrote to Connor about the "final *arrangement* of the archives in accordance with the principle of provenance or respect des fonds." It was obviously official when the archivist stated in his annual report for 1937 that "In arranging records in their place of final deposit the governing principle is that of *respect des fonds*, or the principle of provenance." No one seriously challenged that during the first two decades of the agency, although in a few instances, because of the impossibility of determining the original order of records or because of their peculiarity, as was the case with maps, charts, atlases, motion pictures, sound recordings, and photographs, the principles could not be respected.[13]

Before proceeding to discuss what the archivists did after arranging the records, it is illuminating to consider three of the failures of the National Archives in its quest to solve problems. First, there was the occasional foolishness involved in seeking to devise a standard terminology. Because the United States was late in developing an archival profession, archivists used a variety of terms to describe like operations. There was, therefore, considerable interest in improving terminology and communication in the emerging archival profession. Many staff members of the National Archives and particularly Roscoe R. Hill tried to come to grips with this problem. Although they were successful in joining with other American archivists in standardizing terms such as *stack area*, *series*, *record group*, *provenance*, and *finding aid*, they sometimes belabored the obvious and occasionally made themselves targets for ridicule. Hill crusaded for the adoption of such words as *archive* (a repository), *archivology* (science of archives), *archivalia* (the mass of archival documents), and *archimon* (an archival unit, such as a file). Therefore, in this lexicon one could speak of archimons among the archivalia in an archive being subject to the application of archivology. It is not that Hill and his confreres were not dealing with a real question. The trouble was that their solutions too often turned out to be jargon of the worst kind. It is to the credit of the archival profession that it did not adopt ersatz phrases, while it did agree upon a sufficient number of ordinary terms to achieve a satisfactory level of professional communication. If any confusion continued in American archival terminology, it was largely because Hill and his small band of disciples insisted upon using jargon in their writings.[14]

Roscoe Hill was connected with another and more important false start. That was the work of the Classification Division, which he headed. Classification was an idea derived from librarians, who had had great success in applying it to books, and it appealed to some archivists as a way of overcoming the two great disadvantages of the principles of *respect des fonds* and *provenance*, which were the difficulties of tracking down specific documents or files and of studying records through a subject-matter approach. Hill's division did not try to replace the well established archival principles but instead attempted to devise a classification system that could be coordinated with them. In short, their idea was to break down the materials in the National Archives so that their components' organization and function could be readily identified by numerical and literal symbols. This would allow catalogers to establish a system of references and cross-references so that archivists and researchers could easily find individual items and effectively employ a subject-matter approach to research. It became clear by 1940 that, given the diverse mass of materials in the National Archives, classification demanded vastly more time and expense than the agency could afford. Despite the effort and ingenuity of Hill's people, their classification schemes covered only a small quantity of records, and even those classifications proved cumbersome to use. Archivist Connor therefore disbanded the Classification Division in March 1941 and spread its functions among other units of the National Archives. He reassigned Hill to be chief of the Division of State Department Archives, where his talents were put to excellent use.[15]

Cataloging was another experiment that demonstrated the extreme difficulty—indeed, in this case, the impossibility—of applying library techniques to archival administration. The archivist appointed John R. Russell of the New York Public Library to be chief of the Cataloging Division in 1935. The division's goals were to collect existing guides to the records of the various agencies of the government, to supplement those guides with cataloging work in the National Archives, to coordinate transferred archives with the records retained by the agencies, and to develop a central catalog that would facilitate the work of archivists and researchers in tracking down information. It soon became plain that carrying out these tasks was impossible because of their immensity. Therefore the division's mission was reduced to developing a central catalog to accessions, government records by office units, and series of records. Even this was a monumental task for a small operation, especially as it was to be coordinated with the work of the Classification Division. As that division failed to reach its objectives, the work of the catalogers lagged, except in the area of logging accessions. Cataloging by series was in effect abandoned by 1939, and the next year John Russell left to accept the directorship of libraries at the University of Rochester. As was true with classification, cataloging was worthy of consideration and experimentation, but it proved too expensive. It was also questionable whether either a great series of classification schemes or a detailed and comprehensive catalog would really have saved archivists and researchers time and inconvenience, given the great amount of time they would have had to spend with the classification system and catalog before they could work with the records.[16] If highly competent persons such as Hill and Russell could not overcome the problems of archival classification and cataloging, it is unlikely that anyone else could. The National Archives would travel other avenues in seeking to make its resources more accessible to researchers.

Returning to the early work of the archives divisions, they had by 1938 acquired a number of tasks. The divisions made most of the arrangements for the transfer of records to the National Archives; they consulted with those responsible for receiving, fumigating, cleaning, and repairing holdings as well as with the classification and cataloging staffs; upon receipt of records in their respective stack areas, they made and implemented the decisions for arranging and storing the materials and they weeded extraneous or useless items from them; and the archives divisions made some descriptive studies of the records in their custody.

As might be expected, the professionals and subprofessionals who staffed the archives divisions were not the most prestigious people in the National Archives. Administrative personnel almost always tend to underestimate their operational colleagues, and the National Archives was no exception to the rule. Indeed, the staffs of these divisions soon dubbed themselves "stack rats," partly as a token of pride and partly because it seemed to them that was how they were viewed by those who occupied the administrative offices. Yet, increasingly, the stack rats were the ones who made the National Archives a success. That was because of the many essential day-to-day functions they carried out and because the archives divisions often provided solutions to the problems generated by the agency's false starts.

Accessions, receiving, and reference are cases in point. The Accessions Division had not kept abreast of the identification and appraisal of the federal records that were eligible for transfer to the National Archives. Therefore, during the summer of 1938 the archivist abolished the division and transferred its duties to the archives divisions, which had the knowledge of the records to do the work quite well. At the same time, Connor divided the job of records reception and temporary storage, which the second assistant director of archival service had supervised, between the archives divisions and the Division of Repair and Preservation. He also abolished the second assistant directorship as an unnecessary position.[17]

The Division of Reference was a knottier matter. Its chief, Nelson Vance Russell, was a teacher of history who had come to the National Archives from Coe College. His division's mission was to serve the government agencies and private researchers who wanted to extract information from the records. In effect, the unit was an intermediary between the seekers of information and the custodians of the records. The basic problem was that Russell and his staff did not know enough about the records either to understand fully the questions posed by researchers or to pass the questions on satisfactorily to the stack rats. As an academician turned bureaucrat, his proposed solution was that his staff be allowed access to the archives divisions so that they could dig out the pertinent information or files to be supplied to researchers. The absurdity of this is obvious. Not only would it have interfered with the work of personnel in the archives divisions, but Russell's staff, dashing as they would have from one division to another, would never have acquired as much knowledge about the various records series as had the custodial specialists who were ensconced in the stacks. The eventual solution was to allow the stack rats to serve researchers directly, which would bring researchers in touch with those who could most expertly provide them with what they wanted as well as eliminate the extra time required to gain information through an intermediary. The first step in this direction came in June 1938 with the archivist's authorization of the archives divisions to take reference calls from the agencies whose records they had custody. Nelson Vance Russell, seeing his jurisdiction being pared away, left the staff to reenter academic life. Soon afterward, the Library Division and the Reference Division were merged, and together, gradually, they served mainly as a screening and gathering place for researchers and to provide general and bibliographical information.[18]

The abolition of the Division of Research in June 1938 resulted in another accretion of work for the archives divisions. This unit had been established to prepare materials that would guide researchers to related sources in different kinds of records, to conduct research in the records for government agencies, and to assemble lists of materials found in the states or in foreign countries that were pertinent to the history of the United States. This was an experiment that sounded reasonable at the time of its inauguration, but it turned out to be unnecessary. The Division of Research had neither the time nor the funds to compile lists of relevant materials elsewhere, other divisions of the National Archives did a more effective job of guiding researchers to the records, and federal agencies usually preferred to conduct their own research. Clearly, the division was superfluous. Connor, therefore, divided its duties among the archives divisions and the Office of the Director of Publications.[19]

It is obvious that in 1938 and 1939 the archivist had caused a major reorganization of his agency. There is no need to detail all the changes, but an overview is in order to demonstrate how wide ranging they were. The superstructure of the National Archives remained basically the same, except that Director of Publications Solon J. Buck acquired some new duties and the Division of the Federal Register was made directly responsible to the archivist. Some switching around of functions had been made in the administrative divisions that were under the direction of the executive officer, Collas G. Harris. The really great changes, however, were in the province of the professional divisions under the supervision of Director of Archival Service Dorsey W. Hyde, Jr. Here there had been the tremendous growth of the departmental archives divisions from two to thirteen and the addition of the Division of Photographic Archives on a par with the two other specialized divisions dealing with maps and with motion pictures. Accessions, Research, and Library had been abolished, with their functions assigned elsewhere; and there had been substantial changes in the duties assigned to the divisions of Classification, Cataloging, Reference, and Repair and Preservation.[20] Perhaps Connor had been slow in reorganizing the National Archives and undoubtedly other changes would have to come. The fact is, however, that by 1939 a considerable amount of redundant, uneconomical, and unneces-

Franklin D. Roosevelt Library, Hyde Park, New York, during the 1940s

sary activity had been eliminated. The agency was now far better prepared to serve researchers.

One other development in 1938 and 1939 contributed to the restructuring of the National Archives and later to providing new services for researchers. That was the creation of the Franklin D. Roosevelt Library. President Roosevelt's concern for what would happen to his papers went back at least to 1935, and by 1937 he was thinking of some kind of repository on the family estate at Hyde Park, New York. On 4 July 1938, he told Robert Connor that he had decided to build a repository there for his papers, which would be financed by private subscription. The president contemplated deeding over the structure and its contents to the federal government, with the institution to be under the control of the archivist. Roosevelt publicly announced his plans on 10 December and soon established an executive committee to advise him that included Connor; Samuel Eliot Morison of Harvard; Charles E. Clark of Yale; Randolph G. Adams of Michigan; Helen Taft Manning of Bryn Mawr; Stuart A. Rice of Pennsylvania; and, as the chairman, Waldo G. Leland of the American Council of Learned Societies.

Using the technical services of the archives and the Treasury Department's supervisory architect, Louis A. Simon, the executive committee moved rapidly to formulate plans for what would be called the Franklin D. Roosevelt Library. They were assisted by a national advisory committee, composed mostly of scholars, and a committee on ways and means, consisting of well-to-do persons. Raising funds turned out to be no problem, as some 28,000 citizens quickly rallied to donate the $400,000 needed. The only snag was the mishandling in the House of Representatives of the legislation that authorized the government to accept, operate, and maintain the library, so that the resolution had to be voted upon again after it was initially defeated. Nevertheless, the Senate quickly passed it and it was signed into law on 18 July 1939.

The Roosevelt family deeded over land at Hyde Park for the Library, and construction was soon begun. It advanced at such a pace that the building was ready to be turned over to the government on 4 July 1940. By then, Connor had persuaded Roosevelt to appoint a professional archivist, Fred W. Shipman, to direct the library's operations under the archivist's supervision. The Franklin D. Roosevelt Library opened its doors as a museum on 30 June 1941 and as a place for research on 1 May 1946. By fiscal year 1947, when more than 300,000 people visited it, the library was a well established tourist spot, and by the 1950s it had become the Mecca for serious students of the New Deal period.

The creation of the Franklin D. Roosevelt Library held significant implications for historical research. Although it lent additional support to the troublesome tradition that presidential papers are personal property, it did allow the unprecedentedly rapid collection and opening of a former president's papers and also of those of his associates who placed their papers in the repository. Moreover, the use of scholars in founding the library set something of an example for the development of other such institutions, which has helped keep political considerations from being paramount in their administration. This was even more true of Roosevelt's innovative idea of placing his papers in a repository financed by private donations but operated by the public, for his well-publicized concepts about giving private papers were not lost on archivists, researchers, and presidents or other donors. His example, in short, had tremendous influence during the following generation in making available for research more manuscripts more quickly.

And this was not all. Roosevelt's decision to place his materials in the hands of archivists for arrangement and administration spurred the development of professionalism in the management of the raw stuff of history. The founding of the library by a popular president made it fashionable, too, to concentrate materials for the study of a given administration in one institution and to set an example for dispersing outside Washington research materials belonging to the federal government. Moreover, the library's establishment was advantageous to the National Archives. It gave the fledgling agency a great deal of extra publicity and brought the archivist of the United States into close touch with a broader range of academic, scholarly, and political figures. The success of the Roosevelt Library also inspired the foundation of other presidential libraries and eventually led to the creation of one of the National Archives' most important units, the Office of Presidential Libraries.[21]

There were other, more immediately important tasks to which the National Archives addressed itself during the 1930s. One of these was calling attention to the availability of the records in the archives and to its services. One of the earliest things that Robert Connor did as archivist was to hold a luncheon at Washington's Cosmos Club with Harold G. Moulton of the Brookings Institution, Arnold B. Hall of the Social Science Research Council, and several other leading social scientists. Connor's object then, and throughout his tenure of office, was to whet the interest of economists, political scientists, and sociologists in the National Archives' potential for research. Of course, the historians were his biggest target. The American Historical Association held its 1934 meeting in Washington during December, and Connor was much in evidence as he held a reception at his home, spoke formally on his problems as archivist, and conducted a guided tour of the archives building for those attending the convention. Connor was but one of the officials of the National Archives who were to be active in the association's affairs.[22]

Increasingly, Connor and many others at the National Archives wrote articles that were published in scholarly and professional journals. Their object was to describe the agency's operations and resources; and those articles were aimed not only at historians, but also at archivists, librarians, genealogists, museum curators, and many other groups at home and even abroad. The staff of the National Archives was active in a variety of organizations in other ways. Philip M. Hamer, for example, was president of the Southern Historical Association in 1938, and in his presidential address he focused the attention of his listeners upon the use of records in research. In 1937 Solon J. Buck began his twenty years of service as treasurer of the AHA, which was the strongest contact of the National Archives with that association's governing body. Thomas M. Owen, Jr., was the national historian of the American Legion and did yeomanly work in keeping the political support of the country's largest organization of veterans behind the agency's operations. Buck, Vernon D. Tate, and Theodore R. Schellenberg were active in the organization of the new American Documentation Institute, and Tate was the founder and managing editor of the American Library Association's *Journal of Documentary Reproduction*.[23]

The staff's activity was also expressed in a large number of lectures to a variety of scholarly, professional, and patriotic groups. These included appearances by staff members before, among others, the American Historical Association, the National Association of State Libraries, the National Genealogical Society, the Daughters of the American Revolution, the Conference of Executives of Historical Agencies, the American Bar Association, the American Society of Photogrammetry, the National Research Council, the American Geophysical Union, and the American Institute of Chemists. Moreover, staff members talked to an incredible number of regional, state, and local professional societies as well as to civic clubs and over radio stations in various parts of the United States. And their themes concerned not only the services and resources of the National Archives; the message was also that the agency saved funds through its storage, reference, and disposal activities. The agency's more practical work was occasionally criticized, as, for example, by columnist Alfred Friendly who commented in the *Washington News* that the archivist was becoming the "trash collector extraordinary and plenipotentiary for the U.S. government." Yet public opinion, where it existed, generally supported the practical as well as the cultural aspects of the National Archives lest, as the *New York Times* put it, Washington some day "be as completely buried in archives as Pompeii was in ashes."[24]

The National Archives also encouraged visits to its building by not only government officials, but also by archivists, librarians, architects, scholars, and the public generally. Within less than eight months after the structure was occupied, 10,195 people had signed the register as visitors. The number rose to 26,460 during fiscal year 1937 and by 1940 to more than 48,000. Clearly, the National Archives had become something of a tourist stop as well as a place of interest to those who might make use of its contents.[25]

The important point is that the agency was adept at public

relations, which was profitable in enlisting public support and attracting researchers. Archivist Connor reported for fiscal year 1938 that 501 searchers visited the National Archives. Government personnel made up 172 of the searchers and 329 persons engaged in private inquiries accounted for the remainder. Those researchers came from twenty-eight states, the District of Columbia, Alaska, Canada, and Cuba. The National Archives, moreover, handled among its service requests 5,734 by telephone and 5,858 by mail. The topics of interest ranged from the early diplomacy of the United States to genealogy to the operations of the National Recovery Administration.[26] All this neither made the National Archives a major research center by 1938 nor did it place a great work load on the staff. Considering, however, the relatively small gathering of records in the building then, it was a good beginning.

The work of serving researchers mounted steadily during the next three years, with the total number of service items climbing from 18,054 in fiscal year 1938 to 30,244 in 1939, 51,907 in 1940, and 87,180 in 1941. Researchers in 1941 came from forty-four states, the District of Columbia, and Alaska as well as from seven foreign countries. The volume of reference service by mail and telephone increased too, with, for example, almost 11,000 letters written in response to inquiries for information in 1941. The archivists had not expected the bulk of service requests to be by telephone and mail, but that is the way it came, and for good reasons. Many private researchers could not afford to travel to Washington, and governmental inquiries concerned individual items that could be easily handled by correspondence or over the telephone. Another thing the National Archives did not anticipate was that so much of its service work would be with government offices. Indeed, by fiscal year 1941, 47 percent of the inquiries came from the agencies originating the archives and almost 13 percent came from other government agencies. The increase in the research service work of the National Archives is explicable in large part by good publicity and by the growth of the amount of records in the agency's custody.

The institution also helped its researchers and itself by publishing guides to its overall holdings. The first of these was a 58-

page appendix to the *Third Annual Report of the Archivist of the United States*, which was released early in 1938; a second, more elaborate finding aid was the *Guide to the Material in the National Archives*, a 303-page volume published in 1940, which indicated for all to see what could be found in the archives building. In any event, there was no doubt by 1941 that the National Archives had quickly become a major place for research, one that could only grow more important in the future.[27]

The National Archives rendered research service by other means than furnishing papers for examination and providing data by mail and telephone. The staff also ran motion pictures and played sound recordings for researchers and reproduced record materials for them. These activities would grow in importance over the years as researchers increasingly understood their significance as forms of documentation. This was most dramatically true of photographic reproductions of documents, especially microfilm, in which area the National Archives was an outstanding pioneer. Robert C. Binkley of Western Reserve University had done the spadework for this in his survey of ways of reproducing research materials that was sponsored by the Social Science Research Council and the American Council of Learned Societies. He began the project in 1930 and issued its final report in 1936 under the title *Manual on Methods of Reproducing Research Materials*.

This volume was highly influential among archivists and librarians. Its impact on the National Archives was amplified by the fact that Theodore R. Schellenberg, one of the archivists, had served as Binkley's executive officer on the project; and that Vernon D. Tate, who was a disciple of Binkley, had been appointed chief of the institution's Division of Photographic Reproduction and Research in 1935. Tate quickly forged ahead to become one of the country's leading experts, probably the best-known one, on the subject of microfilming. Without slighting his duties in the traditional areas of photography, Tate successfully applied microphotography to every relevant operation of the National Archives. He thereby persuaded Robert Connor and the agency's other top officials of the value of microphotography in the preservation and the reduction of bulk of archives as well as in their quick reproduction. During fiscal year 1941, a sign of the maturity of Tate's division was that it photostated, photographed, or microfilmed 75,253 pages of records for researchers. It also inaugurated then the file microcopy program of the National Archives, whereby historic records that researchers frequently requested for reproduction were microfilmed in negative prints so that positive copies could be supplied on demand from the retained master negatives. This pioneering program barely got out of the experimental stage during World War II because of the press of defense activities. After the war, however, it became one of the chief research service elements of the National Archives.[28]

The National Archives had stayed afloat and indeed prospered during its early years. If it had had floods of problems to meet, the agency had welcomed them as opportunities to show that its work was valuable and its methods practicable. Mistakes were made, but they were inevitable, given the facts that there were no trained archivists in the United States during the middle 1930s, that the experienced archivists were amateurs in handling federal records, and that European theory and practice were not very applicable to American problems. The only conceivable approach was to experiment. And that was a success, for by 1941 the National Archives, often by trailblazing, had devised ways to find, accession, and process immense quantities of diverse kinds of records. It was clear that the institution had also been able to make itself of practical use to other federal agencies in both supplying needed information and initiating attacks on the government's burgeoning records problems. Archivist Connor had in 1936 set as the prime goal for his agency "to become ... one of the great research institutions of the world," just as unique in its field as were the Library of Congress and England's Public Record Office.[29] By 1941 the National Archives was unique and obviously on the verge of becoming a great world research institution.

6. *Building an American Archival Profession*

Robert D. W. Connor lamented the fact that there was no archival profession in the United States. He said of the country's archivists, "Most of us are still amateurs at our jobs." He knew that the National Archives could not apply the highly systematized European practices and training programs to its work because American records were so highly diverse and recent in nature. In the United States, the archivist declared, "the organization of an archives for the preservation and administration of this material, therefore, must be determined by the structure and functions of the particular institution with whose archives it is concerned. Moreover, the purposes for which the records were created, the methods following in producing them, the forms in which they were issued, must all be taken into account in their administration." Although the National Archives could learn something from archivists abroad, that knowledge was far from sufficient to solve the problems of the new agency. It seemed that American archivists, both in Washington and in the states, could learn far more from each other.

Consequently, almost from the beginning, Connor and his top aides encouraged the creation of an American archival profession as an essential supplement to their agency's development. In this, they could use the staff of the National Archives and its newly found knowledge and continuing enthusiasm. The hoped-for result would be the establishment of the institution "as a model in respect to archival practices." To accomplish this, however, would require both learning and teaching on the part of the staff. It soon became clear that one of the best vehicles for this would be a national association of archivists.[1]

Archivists and historical administrators had been gathering since 1909 in a Conference of Archivists at the annual conventions of the American Historical Association. In recent years, however, many of them had come to believe that archivists needed a separate professional organization. A. R. Newsome, Connor's successor as secretary of the North Carolina Historical Commission, supplied the initiative for action, supported by the archivist. Indeed, he and Solon Buck arranged for a program to be held at the December 1935 AHA convention that would discuss the formation of an independent association of archivists. Buck persuaded Theodore C. Blegen, his successor as superintendent of the Minnesota Historical Society, to give an address that would lead to consideration of the "need for," as Buck termed it, "an American Institute of Archivists." The discussion at the meeting was highly favorable to the suggestion, and Newsome, as chairman of the Conference of Archivists, soon appointed a committee of ten to draft a constitution for a separate organization and to make arrangements for the group's establishment. Solon Buck served as chairman of this committee, which was broadly representative of archivists, historical administrators, and historians. During the course of the following year, the committee of ten wrote a constitution for the new Society of American Archivists, which was to meet in conjunction with the AHA at Providence, Rhode Island, in December 1936.[2]

Those attending the organizational meeting of the Society of American Archivists in Providence approved the constitution on 29 December. They also elected Newsome president, Luther H. Evans of the Historical Records Survey vice president, and Philip C. Brooks of the National Archives secretary; Buck was chosen to serve on the council. Within a day after its founding, the SAA had enlisted 124 persons as members, 53 of whom were employees of the National Archives. Then, as in the future, the National Archives, far more than any other single institution, played a leading role in SAA affairs.[3]

The tone and the style and even some of the problems of the

SAA were set to a considerable extent during its first year. It was to be broad gauged in that its members included archivists, manuscripts curators, and historical administrators as well as records survey people, historians, and librarians. This was not just a matter of common sense in order to garner a maximum amount of support for the objectives of archivists. It reflected the way archivists thought at that time, for most of them were concerned not only with archives, but also with manuscripts, records surveys, and even books and museums, and they considered themselves historians, too. Connor and Buck were excellent examples of how multifaceted archivists were during the 1930s. Indeed, it was good that this was so, both for the archivists and for their new association. Had they taken a narrower view of their profession, not only might they had had too few members to launch a successful organization, but they would also have lost invaluable opportunities to teach and to learn from each other. Another important aspect is that they interpreted the word *American* as encompassing the Western Hemisphere, so that Canadians and Latin Americans were always welcome to participate. Although it was only later that the SAA had a sizable Canadian membership and that relations with Latin Americans occasionally became significant in the organization's affairs, the fact that the door was open from the start encouraged those developments. In fact, this international aspect was highlighted at the dinner meeting of the SAA's first convention in June 1937 in Washington, where addresses were given by Ricardo J. Alfaro, the scholarly former president of Panama, and James F. Kenney, the acting Dominion archivist of Canada.[4]

The SAA's broad scope also led to problems. One was to determine what the word *archivist* meant in the United States, which was no small matter given the unfamiliarity of the term among Americans. An illustration of this was the glossy print of Robert Connor that one enterprising Washington news photographer distributed to his clients in 1934. It bore the caption, "He's U.S. Archivist," and underneath the legend, "No, dear children, an archivist is not a radical. He is one who preserves historical documents."[5] That was close enough for the public, but it would take a long time for the professionals to develop a suitably precise definition of what an archivist was and did.

Another major problem was the role of the National Archives in the new society. Obviously, it would be one of great influence. As Julian P. Boyd of the Historical Society of Pennsylvania put it, in his address to the SAA at Providence in 1936, "The National Archives Establishment at Washington serves as the focus of the dawn's early light."[6] After all, Connor and Buck played important roles in the SAA's establishment, and staff members of the National Archives saturated its membership list. They continued to take an important part in the organization's operation down through the years, and not only in the publication of articles in the society's quarterly, *The American Archivist*, and the presentation of papers at meetings. Of the SAA's twenty-three presidents to 1968, nine were members of the staff of the National Archives and another two had previously been employees. Moreover, although Theodore C. Pease of the University of Illinois (1938–46) and Margaret C. Norton of the Illinois State Archives (1946–49) were the first two editors of *The American Archivist*, from then on personnel of the National Archives edited the journal. The reason for this was clear. By the end of the 1940s, the task of publishing the quarterly had become too great for a professor of history or even an archivist of a medium-sized institution to handle. Only the National Archives could absorb the burden successfully.

All this meant that sooner or later there would be unhappiness in the SAA over the massive participation and influence of the National Archives. Although rarely put on record, resentment was often expressed in open meetings and private gatherings. The officials of the National Archives were sensitive to it, often going out of their way to restrict the number of their colleagues who presented papers at the SAA's meetings and served on the organization's committees. Even so, there was no way that the National Archives could not be highly visible in the society's affairs. This was largely because of the fact that no other archival agency, however splendid its contributions, had anywhere near the number of professional staff members or the resources or the reportable accomplishments. Fortunately for all archivists, the tact of the staff of the National Archives and the good sense of the other archivists in the SAA kept the assertiveness of the former and the resentments of the latter from getting out of hand. The result was that over the years the National Archives was able to help immeasurably in raising the degree of professionalism among all members of the society as well as to share the invaluable ideas and accomplishments that all had to give.[7]

Some of the staff of the National Archives immediately used the opportunities offered by the new association to teach. At the SAA's first convention in Washington there was the all but mandatory tour of the archives building. At the discussion meeting in 1935 preliminary to the society's organization, Vernon D. Tate gave a paper titled "Micro-filming as an Aid to Research," which was the first of many such SAA papers delivered or arranged by the staff of the National Archives. Then there were the articles in *The American Archivist*, including Arthur E. Kimberly's "Repair and Preservation in the National Archives" and Dorothy Arbaugh's "Motion Pictures and the Future Historian." And there was also committee service, where much of the instructional work of the National Archives took place.[8]

Yet learning was of equal concern to Connor and his aides as well as to other archivists all over the country. The SAA informally served that purpose through its meetings, committees, and journal. And the society did a notable job in encouraging archivists to share their knowledge and ideas and in tapping a variety of sources of information. Nevertheless, the SAA and the National Archives early recognized that formal training was also desirable. The quest for training came about slowly, however, because the SAA's activities as well as the conferences and committee work within the National Archives were thought capable of meeting the profession's most pressing needs for learning. Yet these were slow in becoming effective, and thus there was increasing interest in formal training. There was also a growing belief among archivists in the United States that more could be learned abroad than they had earlier thought. Indeed, the wish for formal training and the interest in exploring foreign sources of information tended to reinforce one another.

The important year with respect to both these developments was 1938. Eager for material, *The American Archivist* looked to foreign sources to help fill its pages. It published in its first two issues, in 1938, a long article called "Manuscript Repair in European Archives," a major review of *A Manual of Archive Administration* by the English archivist Hilary Jenkinson, and what became a lengthy series of abstracts of European archival publications. That the National Archives was running along parallel lines was seen in 1938 in its first *Staff Information Circular*, a publication intended as a training device not only for its own staff but for American archivists in general. This twenty-one page pamphlet was a translation of Albert Brackmann's articles "Archival Training in Prussia," which was originally published in *Archivalische Zeitschrift*. It was not coincidental that *Staff Information Circular No. 2*, issued in February 1939, was a work by the Belgian archivist Joseph Cuvelier entitled, in translation, "Report on a Scientific Mission to German, Austrian, and Swiss Archives." It was about this time that Arthur H. Leavitt of the National Archives was engaged in translating into English Muller, Feith, and Fruin's *Manual for the Arrangement and Description of Archives*. Moreover, several members of the staff traveled abroad to find pertinent information, and SAA committees were seeking data from archivists in other nations. All this was just the beginning of the concern of archivists in the United States and particularly at the National Archives to find out about the archival experience of other countries.[9]

The National Archives had also given sporadic consideration to a program of in-service training. Until 1939 nothing effective was done except for the educational conferences that the Division of War Department Archives conducted for its employees. Solon J. Buck wanted to inaugurate a more formal training program within the National Archives, but that was no more than a hope stated in the annual report until fiscal year 1940. Then the agency sponsored 128 conferences in fifteen of its operating units as well as two general seminars for qualified staff members. The seminars' topics were "National Archives Correspondence and Report Writing" and "Federal Administrative History," and between them they drew fifty-four students. The National Archives offered similar courses in fiscal year 1941, but the coming of the war put an end to such programs. Once again the agency was forced to carry on in-service training in the informal, haphazard fashion of its first several years.[10]

The great training success of the National Archives was in the area of university-related courses. As early as December 1934 Professor Robert C. Binkley raised with Robert Connor the need for the formal training of archivists. Austin P. Evans of Columbia University, however, was the person who really pressed the matter. Between fall 1935 and spring 1937 he repeatedly brought it to the archivist's attention. Although officials of the National Archives occasionally chatted about a university-affiliated archives course, it took Evans to draw them out. In February 1936 Connor gave to Solon Buck the responsibility for considering the development of such a course. Buck wrote to Evans that the National Archives was interested in cooperating with Columbia in training people for archival work, but he did not rush into the matter. He settled down to tap the thoughts of various people and to think about the construction of an archival training course.[11]

Meanwhile, Dean Ernest S. Griffith of the American University in Washington asked Buck to teach a course called "Historiography, Methodology, and Materials for Research in American History" during 1937–38. This he did, with the assistance of Philip C. Brooks, and it gave him a splendid opportunity to test some ideas that would be of value in a course on archival administration. The reasons for the delay in launching an archival course are fairly obvious. In addition to fulfilling his obligations at the National Archives, Buck required time to plan and to gather materials for a trailblazing course. He also had to wrestle with the problem of whether a course was the proper approach to training archivists instead of, as many archivists and historians contended, a full-scale graduate degree program. Buck realistically concluded that if the latter were desirable, it might not be viable in terms of enrollments; and even if it were, it would take a great amount of time and effort to inaugurate it. He decided to develop a two-semester course, which clearly would be better than nothing.[12]

Thus did Solon Buck come to pioneer university training of archivists in the United States. Columbia University arranged for him to teach the course during the fall and spring semesters of 1938–39 on Saturday mornings. By then he had gathered an impressive amount of pertinent material and had developed an effective approach to the subject. He had toured Europe during the summer of 1938 in search of further material and ideas, visiting among other places the Archives Nationale of France, the League of Nations Registry Office, the Archives d'État of Geneva, and the Federal Archives at Berne. He had also been Connor's representative at the meeting of the Archivists' Commission of the International Committee of Historical Sciences.[13]

Buck's course in New York, which was called "Archives and Historical Manuscripts," was an invaluable experience for him and for others who would later offer archival training courses. Columbia University, however, concluded that the enrollment of fourteen students was insufficient to justify continuing the course. (Similarly, its experiment with a summer archives course, taught by Margaret Norton in 1940, was not repeated.) Buck was sure that his course was worthwhile, and he looked closer to home to establish it. Because of his connections with the American University, he asked that institution to sponsor the course, which, now entitled "The History and Administration of Archives," was offered there at night during the academic year 1939–40.[14]

As at Columbia, the course at the American University evenly divided attention between surveying the development of archival institutions and practices in the United States and abroad. The biggest change was that Ernst M. Posner joined Buck in teaching the course. Posner, who was a refugee from Nazi oppression, had had a distinguished career as an archivist and teacher at the Privy State Archives of Prussia. After spending six weeks in a concentration camp, he had fled Germany in 1938 and emigrated to the United States, settling in Washington during the summer of 1939. Posner played Mendoza to Buck's Cortez. Where Buck was the pioneer of archival training in the United States, Posner was the one who established it as a fixture on the American academic scene, for by 1941 Buck's mounting obligations at the National Archives made it impossible for him to devote the requisite time to the course.

At least eighteen students, including fifteen from the National Archives, took the course at the American University during the fall semester. These people included such future leaders of the archival profession as Herbert E. Angel; Philip C. Brooks; Helen L. Chatfield; Sherrod East; Elizabeth (Edwards Hamer) Kegan; Philip M. Hamer; Emmett Leahy; Fred Shipman; Karl L. Trever; and, as an auditor, Oliver W. Holmes. The course was considered a success, and Buck and Posner offered it again the following year.[15]

By the beginning of 1939, it occurred to Buck that an integrated program of archival courses might be developed at the American University. The university and the National Archives together moved rapidly toward developing an archival training program. During the academic year 1940–41, the American University offered a group of courses deemed to be of value to students generally and especially to enrollees from the National Archives and other federal agencies. In addition to "The History and Administration of Archives," this package included: Posner's courses "Introduction to the Study of History," "Materials for Research in Modern History," and "Comparative Administrative History"; Professor Louis C. Hunter's "Historical Backgrounds of the Federal Administrative System"; and two courses by Helen L. Chatfield, the Treasury Department's archivist, entitled "The Role of Records in Public Administration" and "Principles of Record Administration." The Carnegie Corporation, through the American Council of Learned Societies, agreed to underwrite five of these courses over a three-year period. The result was that a university-affiliated training program was established not only for the National Archives, but also for archivists and records managers from other government agencies. Moreover, the American University benefited from this in the successful expansion of its courses for its growing clientele from federal offices.[16]

The heart of the program so far as federal archivists were

concerned was the course "The History and Administration of Archives." Posner drew not only on his experience as an archivist and a teacher of archivists in Europe, but also on the available American and foreign literature to improve the course. He further sought to make the two-semester course as expert as possible by conducting it with the assistance of guest lecturers from the National Archives. Yet it was clear to him that however worthwhile the course was, it appealed essentially to archivists, particularly those in the Washington area. This was the pattern imposed by Buck, who believed that the course should be for people who were dealing with organized bodies of official documents and whose "first concern . . . is with the interests of the government." Obviously, only the nation's capital had the concentration of such persons sufficient to sustain an archival course. It was also clear that the course, as Buck saw it, did not cater to manuscript curators, for however much their work patterns coincided with those of archivists, the curator's first concern was not the government. Moreover, curators usually worked with collections of manuscripts instead of organized bodies of records. Buck's narrow professional definition served only to exacerbate the differences between archivists and manuscript curators, just as the course, because of its two-semester format, effectively excluded enrollments from outside the Washington area.[17]

This is not to say that Solon Buck was rigid in his view. He believed that universities in other parts of the country could offer pertinent courses that could ameliorate the situation. This would come in time, of course, but Ernst Posner thought that something should be done meanwhile. That was the development of a summer course that would serve the needs of archivists and even manuscript curators from all over the country. The result was the launching of the American University's intensive summer archival institute in 1945, to be held at the National Archives with a field trip to the Maryland Hall of Records. Posner directed the course and made use of guest lecturers from the National Archives and the Maryland Hall of Records. Later, in 1949, the Manuscripts Division of the Library of Congress offered its resources to enrich this "Institute in the Preservation and Administration of Archives."

The summer course was an immediate success, and over the decades its enrollment included archivists, manuscript curators, historical administrators, and historians from all over the United States and from many other countries. Indeed, its success spurred the university to establish a summer "Institute of Genealogical Research" in 1950 and an "Institute in Records Management" in 1954. The National Archives played a central role in the institutes as it had in the development of the American University's regular archival and records-management courses. Not only did the agency help found the institutes and supply guest lecturers and laboratory facilities, it also provided the directors of the genealogical and records-management institutes as well as of the archives institute by the middle 1950s, as Theodore R. Schellenberg, Oliver W. Holmes, and Frank B. Evans successively replaced Posner as its director. The archival institute became the best-known fount of knowledge for a generation of archivists and manuscripts curators, and attending it became the mark of professionalism. H. G. Jones wrote in 1968, "No other formal training activity has equaled these summer institutes in influencing archivists in the United States."[18] The quality of instruction was superior, and the institutes allowed for a remarkable exchange of data and ideas among enrollees from diverse places. The result was an impressive cross-fertilization of the profession in the United States and abroad as well as the forging of enduring professional relationships.

Although the National Archives and Records Service assumed complete responsibility for offering the archival and genealogical courses during the 1970s, the training programs have suffered no loss of continuity or of value. More than a thousand people have enrolled for archival instruction alone over the years. Moreover, other colleges and universities have offered archival, genealogical, or records-management courses that were at least encouraged by the curriculum evolved by the American University and the National Archives. This development started after World War II, and during the following thirty years the University of Michigan, New York University, the University of Denver, Meredith College, North Carolina State University, Wayne State University, the University of Wisconsin, Radcliffe College, the University of California at Los Angeles, Northwestern University, the University of Texas, and the University of Illinois have been among those successfully offering such courses or summer institutes.[19]

It is not fashionable among most archivists to give great credit to the National Archives for its role in the development of their profession. Yet the record is clear: the National Archives played the leading role in the establishment and maintenance of both the Society of American Archivists and training in archival and related work. As William D. Overman of the Firestone Library and Archives said in his 1958 presidential address to the SAA, American archival institutions during the 1930s were "starting from scratch, in establishing a set of standards and uniform archival practices." He credited the National Archives with quickly moving in on the problem, in addition to its pioneer work in records management and in spurring interest in specialized archives. Other SAA presidents also gave due credit to the National Archives. In 1948 Christopher Crittenden of North Carolina declared that "before 1936 the United States was woefully backward in the archival field." The National Archives, however, assumed leadership "and a number of states have followed" in the quest to know "how suitably to house records, how to give them physical protection, how to bring them under control, and how to make them available for use." Mary Givens Bryan of Georgia said in 1960 that archival work was "primitive indeed" before the advent of the National Archives. In praising the accomplishments of that agency and the SAA, she graphically described the earlier situation:

> There were no training courses for archivists. For restoration of manuscripts, the old silking process was being used. There were no developed systems and procedures for collecting and controlling archives. Manuscripts were being catalogued as if they were library books. Laminating and microfilming of records were untried processes. There was no Society of American Archivists to turn to for guidance. . . . Some states had no archival agencies at all. . . . There was little archival literature and there were no American manuals on archival practice. . . . On the part of state administrators there was little interest in archives and records, and that little was vague. Few could even pronounce the word "archives,"

and those who could thought that it meant only ancient records. . . .
Times began to change in 1934 with the establishment of the National
Archives.[20]

There can be no doubt that the National Archives dominated
the development of the archival profession in the United States.
Indeed, the very establishment of the agency lent prestige to the
archival movement all over the country. The fact that the National
Archives had the resources and the enthusiasm for a great deal of
innovation put the agency in a position where other archivists,
manuscript curators, and historical administrators would have to
observe its activities and learn from them. The coming of the SAA
and training courses gave the agency the means to teach as well as
to learn from similar institutions at home and abroad. Equally
significant is that the bases for all this were laid during the first five
years of Robert Connor's tenure as archivist of the United States.
This is not to say that there were not remarkably able contributors
to archival progress elsewhere in the nation, for there were many.
The plain fact is, however, that the National Archives had the
prestige, resources, visibility, and energy to lead; and it took advantage of this in the movement to establish an American archival
profession. The results were impressive for all concerned.[21]

7. Toward New Archival Standards

The National Archives was far from being a finished institution in 1940. The agency was in many ways a successful functioning organization, but its staff members were keenly aware that they faced many unsolved problems, particularly in the areas of records identification, appraisal, and disposal. They were also becoming alert to the fact that American involvement in the new world war would make the solution of some of those problems more urgent and would raise pressing new questions.

In dealing with old as well as prospective problems, two important activities of the National Archives were to search out the origins of federal record-keeping practices and to study the administrative history of various government agencies. These were essential tasks for the archivists so that they could better prepare themselves to appraise and arrange the materials in their custody. Their effort to acquire this information had been going on for some time, but it blossomed during the early 1940s both in manuscript histories for staff use and in the publication of a number of useful articles.[1]

More wide ranging in impact was the search to find better ways to identify the records than those developed by the Classification and Cataloging divisions. As has been observed, the classification and cataloging approaches had become mired in the awesome number of items that had to be brought under control. Many archivists had had reservations about these approaches from the beginning of the establishment of the National Archives, and those doubts grew as time passed, for it was becoming plain that the agency had to devise simpler and less expensive ways to identify and describe archives. With Solon J. Buck's visit to Europe in 1938, Ernst M. Posner's arrival in the United States, and the publication of pamphlets on European archival practices, the bases were laid to sidetrack the library-influenced methods of archival classification and cataloging. The crucial point was reached on 1 March 1940, when Archivist Connor established a committee to review the matter of finding aids.[2]

Solon Buck was the leading spirit in the work of this Finding Mediums Committee. It was not a one-person show, for many others contributed profoundly, including Martin P. Claussen; Theodore R. Schellenberg; Marion L. Rice; Carl L. Lokke; and, from outside the staff of the National Archives, Ernst Posner. The committee filed its report on 15 January 1941. On the basis of the report the archivist issued a directive on 28 February, which had far-reaching effects on archival practices.

Connor's directive required that the archives divisions—instead of the Classification and Cataloging divisions—would draft finding aids, under the supervision of the Office of the Director of Archival Service. In line with the agency's policy of being of maximum use to the people (which in itself was a revolutionary doctrine among many archivists), the finding aids would eventually be made available to the public. The required pattern of controlling archives would be to identify tentatively and to register "record groups"; to prepare preliminary checklists of the contents of those groups; later, to compile preliminary inventories, which would be basic finding aids to each group; and to prepare a final inventory after each record group was determined to be completely identified and arranged. In order to satisfy those who were concerned with a subject-matter approach to materials, the archivist also provided that special lists might be developed as the need arose. He declared, however, that the usual basis for description would be the record group, which he defined as "a major archival unit established somewhat arbitrarily with due regard to the principle of provenance and to the desirability of making the unit of convenient size and character for the work of arrangement and description and for the publication of inventories." Incidentally, on 3 March, Connor took the obvious step of abolishing the divisions of Classification and Cataloging.[3]

The impact of these decisions was great. With the establishment of the record group and the new order of controlling and describing records, the National Archives had found two of its basic and indeed unique operating devices. The record group would be a workable concept that staff members could use at every step from the appraisal of archives to reference work. Of course, it was based on the French idea of *fonds*, but it was easily adaptable to great quantities of materials in that it grouped together closely related series, usually the archives of a bureau of government. A record group was thus generally neither small enough, as a series is, to lead to an archival institution having a ridiculously large number of records units to handle, nor big enough to be too large for an archivist or researcher to command. Moreover, it fitted in well with the new procedure of description, for it was conveniently sized for a manageable but significant inventory. Special lists, of course, could fill in the chinks in the descriptive process. The chief problem was the slowness of the National Archives in sorting out the difference in form between a preliminary and a final inventory. This was done at first by deferring final inventories and then later by dropping the concept (until it was revived in the 1970s) so that descriptive efforts could be focused upon producing preliminary inventories. The use of registrations and checklists, plus whatever finding aids might have been developed by the agency of origin, kept the records under adequate control until a preliminary inventory could be prepared.

The impact of the record group and inventory concepts gradually spread beyond the walls of the National Archives, as many archival and manuscript repositories in the United States and even abroad employed them. The record-group idea was later adapted to the operations of federal records centers as they developed as a way to tie in the holdings of the centers with related archives in Washington. The preliminary inventory, as well as the comprehensive *Guide to the National Archives*, set a good example for repositories elsewhere in making finding aids available to researchers.

Of course, the National Archives did not invent archival finding aids; they had appeared here and there in diverse forms and degrees of usefulness in years past. What the agency did was to set standards for systematized guides and to become a mighty advocate of the need for the archivist and the researcher to know what a repository contained. Its role in this respect was all the more valuable as the holdings of archival institutions and manuscript collections rapidly expanded after World War II.

Serious discussions about exactly what record groups and systematized finding aids should be abounded in the National Archives during the early 1940s. There was no great trouble there, thanks to the deliberations of the Advisory Committee on Finding Mediums, the work of the archivist and his chief aides, and the experience of staff members generally. As director of research and records description, Oliver W. Holmes was responsible for coordinating the identification and registration of records and the editing of finding aids, a job he handled ably. His work in determining and numbering record groups was done, as Archivist Connor had suggested, "somewhat arbitrarily," since there was no scientific way to identify a "unit of convenient size and character." Thus record groups varied in size from a few cubic feet to tens of thousands because the job of deciding what they were was based largely upon the principle of *provenance*, that is, by identifying series of records with a suitable agency of origin. Not unexpectedly, questions would be raised years later about revamping the system by breaking up some of the largest groups and consolidating the smallest ones.[4] The system worked, however. If its pragmatism sometimes led to inconsistencies of categorization, that was the cost of pioneering. The real question for the future was whether it was worth paying an even higher price to smooth off the edges of a functioning system by redefining hundreds of record groups and preparing new inventories.

The coming of World War II forced the finding aids program to develop differently than had been anticipated. The archivists rushed the first preliminary inventory into print in May 1941. A sign of the times, it was a guide to the records of the War Industries Board. The National Archives produced few other inventories during the war, and those too were geared to the nation's defense efforts. The agency did process many special lists and guides and reference information circulars as well as numerous preliminary checklists. Nevertheless, the bulk of the archives lacked detailed descriptions by the end of the war, because the needs of war curtailed the amount of time that could be spent on such projects. For its own purposes of records control, the National Archives had directed most of its descriptive efforts toward completing by 1945 the registration of the 215 record groups then on hand. Everything else in the area of description had to be deferred until the postwar period.[5]

The year 1940 was also rich for progress in dealing with the vexing problem of appraising records. As the surveys of federal records went forward from 1935, it quickly became evident that the decisions as to what to transfer to the archives building had to be based on rather sophisticated criteria. This was no surprise, of course, for as early as 1910 the International Congress of Librarians and Archivists at Brussels had recognized the disposition of records as "certainement la question la plus grave qui puisse se poser." Now Americans were acquiring the experience with massive amounts of records to realize how serious the issue was. The National Archives had considered, from the start, its appraisal standards to be experimental and subject to frequent revision. By 1940 some American archivists had formulated some significant answers to questions of appraisal and disposal, just in time to be refined during the great inundation of records produced during the Second World War.[6]

The January 1940 issue of the *American Archivist* carried Emmett J. Leahy's brilliant article on the reduction of records. Leahy was an employee of the National Archives and chairman of the Committee on the Reduction of Archival Material of the Society of American Archivists, so he had given much thought to the question. The winnowing of records, he declared, was essential to preventing the loss of valuable archives. In considering making records and archives manageable, he recommended not only the expenditure of more effort in determining what records could safely be destroyed, but also "continuing authorizations for destructions" of such materials and even the further reduction of the bulk of valuable records by microfilming them and then disposing of the original documents. Leahy believed that sampling, summaries, tabulations, and transfers of certain records to other interested institutions were additional ways to keep the size of materials manageable. He suggested that useless records be disposed of at the agency of possession instead of wasting effort by taking them to an archival agency for destruction. He further advocated that archivists should advise government agencies as to what records could be dispensed with in order to promote economy and efficiency. The National Archives and the SAA were championing these ideas and a few agencies were implementing them, but that was a piecemeal operation. What Leahy wanted was no less than a comprehensive system of the management of records and archives.[7]

Nine months later, in the *American Archivist*, Philip C. Brooks of the National Archives reinforced Leahy's comments. He was less concerned with reduction techniques and more with appraisal standards, but his message was essentially the same: many records have to be eliminated and done so as cheaply and as efficiently as possible. Brooks wrote, "The earlier in the life history of the documents the selection process begins, the better for all concerned." Certainly, by considering the functions of records from their birth to either their immortalization or death, archivists could save themselves, the agencies of origin, and researchers a lot of unnecessary work, clutter, and expense. In order to take an effective view of the useful life of records, he urged archivists to use many different criteria for selection and to do so more astutely.[8]

The ideas of Leahy and Brooks would lead to diverging emphases and careers. Leahy's great concern and contribution would be in the area of reducing records and systematizing their management. Indeed, he would become the man usually considered to be the father of records management. Brooks would continue to have a diversified career, making noteworthy contributions to the development of records management and the presidential libraries system as well as to the continued sharpening of appraisal standards in the interests of economy and preservation. This last idea caught hold quickly, for as G. Philip Bauer indicated in 1944 in a widely endorsed statement, some records of potential value to researchers might have to be eliminated so that archivists would be able to save material of greater and surer value. However difficult the decisions, "Values must be weighed against cost." There was no way that everything could be preserved.[9]

More tangible, though less important for the immediate future of the National Archives, was an enactment of 1941. For some time the archivist had felt the need of a vehicle to receive financial gifts that could be used to underwrite activities for which there were no appropriations. He must have envied the congressional authorization of 1939 that permitted the Roosevelt Library to accept funds from outside sources. In May 1941 Congressman Robert T. Secrest of Ohio introduced such a bill on behalf of the National Archives. The House and the Senate passed the measure establishing the National Archives Trust Fund Board in June and President Roosevelt signed it on 9 July. Although for years the board received little money, it served as a useful device to allow the National Archives to add some fillips to its overall program and after the 1950s to undertake even bigger projects.[10]

All these things were significant in the development of the agency, and they showed that it had become anything but static by 1940 and 1941. Yet during Robert Connor's remaining time as archivist of the United States, the shock waves of the war in Europe were to affect increasingly the National Archives and to spur its flexibility. Within weeks after the invasion of Poland in September 1939, Dallas Irvine, the chief of the War Department Archives Division, alerted his colleagues to the perils and burdens that American involvement in the war might bring to the agency. The archivist, therefore, asked all custodial division chiefs and the Accessions Advisory Committee to study the needs of federal agencies to shift records to the National Archives and the meaning of such requirements "in terms of space, equipment, personnel, and funds."[11]

It was not until after Germany conquered France in June 1940 that the emergency had considerable impact on the archivists. Then, as the United States prepared its defenses, various federal agencies began looking to the National Archives for information on what the government had done during the First World War.

Government agencies also became increasingly interested in transferring records to the archives building in order to free space for their defense activities. Connor could gloat when, in October, the secretary of war sought the rapid transfer of his department's records to the National Archives. The result of this scramble to clear out records was that during the war years the National Archives accessioned most military and naval documents dated before 1939. Even though the War and Navy departments serviced them with their own personnel, Connor's battle for the safekeeping of those records was won thanks to the exigencies of a new war. Another nice twist was that although the War Department had not abandoned the idea of a hall of records, it did propose that if such an intermediate repository were established it be under the archivist's jurisdiction. [12]

Yet the National Archives and the archival profession were far from prepared in 1940 to meet the demands war would place upon them. Waldo G. Leland called upon them to ready themselves by better organizing their methods of administration, training, and description. The archivists did not need much urging from Leland to act, for most of them were already seeking solutions to the problems he discussed. Certainly the SAA, of which Leland was then president, acted quickly, setting up three pertinent committees. One, headed by Connor, dealt with the protection of archives against the hazards of war; another, with Collas G. Harris as chairman, was concerned with the emergency storage of records; the third, presided over by Solon J. Buck, investigated the history and organization of emergency agencies. Altogether these committees compiled and disseminated a considerable amount of information for the benefit of American archival institutions. [13]

The Committee on the Conservation of Cultural Resources was a related effort. The National Resources Planning Board established this committee in March 1941, at President Roosevelt's request, to "prepare plans for the protection of material of cultural, scientific, or historical importance in the possession of agencies of the federal government." The committee included representatives from the National Archives, the Library of Congress, and various other federal and private organizations concerned with cultural affairs or national defense. The particular contributions of the National Archives were a thirty-six page bulletin, *The Care of Records in a National Emergency*, of which the CCCR distributed ten thousand copies, and the "Tentative Bibliography on the Conservation of Cultural Resources in Times of War." As the CCCR came to serve the entire nation, both of these publications can be presumed to have had impact on not only archivists and records administrators but also on the preservation of cultural resources generally.[14]

Obviously, the staff of the National Archives was giving considerable thought to safeguards against fire and theft as well as to their plans for the emergency removal and storage of holdings. The archivist directed the shifting of the most valuable records to the innermost parts of the archives building and had flammable nitrate film removed for storage at a military post outside Washington. His organization also intensified its efforts in preparing administrative histories of federal agencies, especially those with defense responsibilities, and in giving reference service to such offices. The defense emergency and the later involvement of the United States in the war greatly spurred the National Archives to meet a variety of problems with which it had already been trying to cope. The result was that if the agency were not fully ready for the outbreak of hostilities in December 1941, at least it was far better prepared than it otherwise would have been.[15]

In the midst of these hectic activities, change came to the top leadership of the National Archives. The University of North Carolina had not been happy to let Robert D. W. Connor go to become archivist of the United States in 1934, and it had been after him for several years to return. Chapel Hill looked ever more inviting as Connor's wife's health began to suffer and the complexities of his job increased. When the university offered him the Craige Professorship of Jurisprudence and History in 1941, Connor decided to return to his home state. It was a good time to leave, for the National Archives' answers to the major problems of the defense period had been provided or seemed well on the way to being so.

Moreover, the major new addition to the agency, the Franklin D. Roosevelt Library, had been opened to the public at the end of June. In a conference with the president on 17 July, Connor submitted his resignation. Roosevelt asked him to recommend a candidate to be the new archivist, and he named Solon Buck. That probably was not a difficult decision for him. From the beginning Buck had been the leading source of new ideas at the National Archives. He was the one who was thought of primarily in connection with the development of training programs, the revolutionary change in records control and description, the progress made in preparing administrative histories, and the agency's relations with a variety of scholarly societies. Beyond a doubt, Buck stood second only to Connor in terms of reputation among archivists and academics.[16]

On 21 July the president asked one of his aides, James Rowe, Jr., to inquire into the possibility of appointing Buck. Rowe in turn got in touch with the librarian of Congress, Archibald MacLeish, who thought Buck was "very sound and thorough." (Rowe also concluded that there would be no political pressure on behalf of other candidates for "this sort of technical job.") Apparently Rowe's other checks on Buck confirmed MacLeish's opinion of him, for on 28 July Roosevelt wrote another of his aides, Rudolf Forster, that he expected to appoint Buck as archivist of the United States effective the date of Connor's departure, 15 September.[17]

The fact that the White House did not anticipate a tussle for the post of archivist did not mean that others were unprepared to begin one. Campaigns were started on behalf of former Congresswoman Ruth Bryan Rohde; Bernard R. Kennedy, the director of the Federal Register Division; and Joseph Broadman, the founder of New York's Broadman Library of World War and Post-Wardom. Moreover, Thomas M. Owen, Jr., the chief of the Division of Veterans Administration Archives and the American Legion worthy on the staff of the National Archives, actually applied for the job and received a considerable number of political and educational endorsements. By 7 August Connor became edgy. He wrote Executive Secretary Guy Stanton Ford of the American Historical

Solon J. Buck, second archivist of the United States, 1941–1948

Association that it would be "unwise" to exert much pressure on behalf of Buck, in view of the good favor in which he stood with the White House. "Nevertheless," the archivist added, "as certain other candidates are getting ready to do this very thing, I think it might be well for a few of Buck's friends to make their wishes known to the President." Therefore, he suggested that Ford, an old Minnesota acquaintance of Buck, ask ten or a dozen friends to write, and "at once."[18]

Although the campaign launched by Connor and Ford was nothing like that which the AHA had conducted in 1934, it was sufficient to show the White House that Solon Buck was the association's candidate as well as Connor's. It also gave the impression that the AHA had the prime right of nomination for the archivist's job. The endorsement letters came almost exclusively from historians and archivists such as Theodore C. Blegen, Herbert E. Bolton, Herbert A. Keller, Samuel Eliot Morison, and Arthur M. Schlesinger. Most interesting were the letters from Congressman Clifton A. Woodrum, the only politician to write on Buck's behalf, and Waldo Gifford Leland of the American Council of Learned Societies. Woodrum urged that there be no political appointment to the post and added that Buck was the man for the job. Leland recalled, not as correctly as impressively, that Buck was second only to Connor in the deliberations of the AHA Council in 1934 when the archivist's position was first filled.[19]

Whether or not this campaign was necessary, the president did not change his mind about Buck. Roosevelt nominated him on 15 September, and that was that. Solon Buck would turn out to be quite a different archivist than Robert Connor. They were both thoroughly professional and impressive in their dignity and large size, but their attitudes were dissimilar. Connor was open to change, while Buck was eager for it. Although Buck was probably more profound and certainly more somber, Connor was more likely to view things in a broader context. The new archivist had a more advanced grasp of what administration was, but he was less sensitive to human factors. Connor was the better politician of the two in dealing with the staff, other executive agencies, and congressmen. Buck's brilliance and even audacity stood him in good stead in advancing the scope of the archival movement, but his habit of lecturing people, even members of Congress, and his authoritarianism tarnished his qualities and led him into fights that Connor probably would have avoided. Buck's interests also sometimes differed from Connor's. For example, Buck was uninterested in pursuing the possession of the Declaration of Independence and the Constitution. It was not that Buck had no idiosyncrasies. Indeed, one was his preoccupation with imposing a numerical classification system on Connor's official files (the usefulness of that experiment has baffled any researcher).[20]

Yet if Connor during his years as archivist of the United States was probably the right person for that position, the same could be said of Buck. The new archivist had the abundance of energy, knowledge, profundity, and self-confidence to meet most of the difficult demands that would be placed upon him and the National Archives during the crisis-laden years of World War II.

8. War at the Archives

If, by September 1941, the United States was preparing for war on two fronts, so was the new archivist. Solon J. Buck was determined to recast his agency along lines that he deemed professionally more effective and efficient; he was also resolved to make the National Archives of use to America's defense effort, partly for the sake of service and partly to reduce the agency's vulnerability to cutbacks in budget and personnel. In Buck's eyes, the two goals could be pursued together, for the achievement of the first would support the effort to attain the second.

The National Archives since 1939 had become increasingly sensitive to what demands might be made upon it with the coming of war. The organization had decided, even before Buck became the archivist, to request status as a defense agency in order to facilitate its work. Soon after he took office, Buck gave thought to how the National Archives could best contribute to defense preparations both by positive assistance and by cutting back on unessential work. Some things were fairly easily done, at least initially. One was to ready more stack areas so that additional records could be transferred to the archives building and thus release more office space in other government offices. Another was to use acid-free cardboard boxes instead of steel document containers. Some of the staff resisted this, and in November 1941 this led to the type of explosion from the archivist that his subordinates would become accustomed to. "There are limits to my endurance," he wrote. "We are *not* going to request the purchase of *steel* boxes while there is a shortage of steel for defense purposes." He demanded advice about the best kind of cardboard container, not "further arguments against them."[1] Buck got his way, and the boxes were soon on their way. As it turned out, they became standard archival equipment thereafter throughout the country because they proved to be not only less expensive than steel containers, but easier to handle and at least as protective of records.

On 17 October 1941, Buck wrote to the chairman of the Civil Service Commission in support of the National Archives' bid for defense status. He pointed up his agency's "widespread defense responsibilities." Among these were (1) that the National Archives had prime control and knowledge of the government's records, which made it vital in providing knowledge needed by defense offices, in advising them on the administration of records, in transferring valuable records to storage space, and in identifying and disposing of useless records; (2) the value of the National Archives' technical services to defense agencies regarding such things as maps, sound recordings, film, photographs, and records preservation and rehabilitation; and (3) the importance of the *Federal Register* as "an official gazette . . . essential in the daily activity of Government officials and others concerned with the defense effort." Buck's case was effective, and on 30 October the government gave the National Archives status as a defense agency.[2]

This was well enough, but the organization did not rush into either defense work or the curtailment of its regular activities. Early in October, Executive Officer Collas G. Harris advised the Bureau of the Budget that the National Archives could make no staff cuts during the current fiscal year, although it was "willing" to lose fourteen positions in fiscal year 1943. Toward the end of October, Buck sought the Budget Bureau's advice on a reorganization of his agency that would lead to its better administration. That resulted in changes at the beginning of 1942 that gave the executive officer entire responsibility for budgetary affairs and the administrative secretary, Thaddeus Page, responsibility for the information and publications programs of the National Archives except for the Federal Register Division. The archivist abolished the positions of director of archival services and director of publications. Yet Buck made one net addition to the agency's second administrative echelon, with the establishment of three new directorates. These were Reference Service, in recognition of the increased reference load; Records Accessioning and Preservation, which had the responsibility for coordinating the activities of the archives custodial divisions and the work of repair and preservation of records; and Research and Records Description, which was responsible for research and description projects as well as for the library. To strengthen his own office, Buck appointed a special assistant and an assistant to himself to serve as planning and studies officers.[3]

This was only the first of several reorganizations during Buck's years as archivist. I shall not attempt to examine blade by blade these changes in the jungle of bureaucracy. The next high point came after Collas G. Harris left to join the Army Air Forces in October 1942. In a splitting up and augmentation of the abolished post of executive officer, there emerged a director of operations and an administrative assistant to the archivist. Operations was in charge of all professional divisions except for the Federal Register Division and the Roosevelt Library, which continued under the archivist's personal supervision. The administrative assistant served as budget officer and director of the National Archives' business-service divisions.

During fiscal year 1944 Buck carried out another major reorganization so that the administrative structure little resembled what it had been in Robert D. W. Connor's days. The archivist then abolished the positions of administrative assistant, director of records accessioning and preservation, director of research and records descriptions, and director of reference service. The office of the archivist now contained the administrative secretary (the only original second-echelon title left), budget officer, management officer (to coordinate the formulation of administrative regulations and directives), and program adviser (to help draw up plans for new activities). Consequently, the archivist's office now directly supervised the Federal Register Division, the National Archives Library, the Roosevelt Library, two business-service divisions, and statistical and documentation units. The work of Director of Operations Dan Lacy, who had been Collas Harris's assistant, was strengthened by gaining more direct management of the archives divisions, which had been reduced from sixteen to fourteen in number, and of three business-service divisions. Lacy's office was also fortified by giving it better control over preservation activities, accessioning and disposal operations, reference tasks and records description, and the agency's developing records management work.[4]

The archivist offered weighty justifications for the changes. One was that the organization of a young and unique agency like the National Archives was necessarily experimental; therefore, alterations would have to go on until the right combination for efficiency and effectiveness was found. Even then, the right combination could easily be upset by changes in society and in the agency's role and resources. These changes certainly had been tremendous since the National Archives was established in 1934. Buck was also much concerned with running the agency according to the best precepts, as he understood them, of the emerging discipline of public administration. Yet the archivist had another, less well known reason for what he did. When Collas Harris sympathetically wrote him in November 1944 that perhaps the latest reorganization would suffice to accomplish the archivist's goals, Buck bristled. He replied that it would not "be the last one. Anything that is static in this rapidly changing world might as well be dead and, as long as I am Archivist, whenever it appears to me that the functioning of the National Archives can be improved by changes in organization such changes will be made."[5]

There was much, of course, besides the worship of the fickle goddess of change to support Buck's reorganizations. The demands of the nation during a time of war placed new and great burdens upon the National Archives. For example, the number of services rendered by the agency rose from 132,772 in fiscal year 1941 to 206,485 in 1942; 223,704 in 1943; 254,712 in 1944; and then declined a bit to 237,757 in 1945. The volume of records housed in the archives building soared even more markedly, from 302,183 cubic feet in fiscal year 1941 to 459,932 in 1942; 542,242 in 1943; 632,572 in 1944; and 672,336 in 1945. And along with these were significant increases in appraisal, disposal, and related activities.[6]

Buck was also justified in concluding that administration in the National Archives could be improved. The archivist, by consolidating some of the operating divisions and by fostering more businesslike procedures, undoubtedly made progress toward effectiveness, efficiency, and responsibility. Yet there was a price to be paid. The reorganizations of the Buck years did not always work, and they sometimes created unnecessary confusion and even resentment among staff members. It is impossible to determine precisely to what extent Buck's failures were caused by his rearrangements, his personality, or by staff infighting and factors beyond his control. It is important, however, that no surviving staff member recalls his reorganizations with joy.

Numerous employees of the National Archives have commented that not only did they worry about their own positions under Buck, they often did not know from week to week who was in favor, or indeed who was doing what and under whose supervision. Many were vexed by the rapid growth of administrative staff, some of whom were introduced from outside the agency, at a time when the number of operating personnel was declining and work loads were vastly increasing. Moreover, administrators issued directives markedly more often, which sometimes added to the confusion. The stack rats, and even some personnel in the front offices, often questioned whether public administration was yet the science the archivist took it to be. Some also had doubts whether the National Archives should take on new programs when it had fewer staff and more duties. Even the expansion of the work week to forty-four hours could not make up for that.

Buck's personality tended to be authoritarian. Sometimes when people offered him assistance he refused it curtly, as though the archivist of the United States were divinely inspired to need no help or to do no wrong. Administrative Secretary Thaddeus Page commented that his work with Congress had been easier under Connor, for Buck "was anything but a diplomat when it came to dealing with politicians." Another respected member of the staff, Vernon Tate, the chief of the Photographic Archives Division, evaluated the archivist highly but added that he had problems "in dealing with people," occasionally lecturing his subordinates on petty things such as the use of paper clips and the proper way to fold letters in envelopes.[7]

Yet many of the agency's problems were not of Solon Buck's making. Some of them were structural (for example, the large number of divisions that he had to coordinate), and some involved difficult staff personalities. The two often combined to provoke intense fights among the various units of the National Archives that were protecting their interests. Certainly, the agency had a number of people with strong and even parochial views. And there were some who would run for help to a political protector at the appearance of anything new.

Moreover, the institution lost some stability as its numbers of employees fluctuated considerably during the war years. Its vastly increased work load and its designation as a defense agency did not save the National Archives from sharp staff reductions. Although the agency's personnel rose from 438 at the end of fiscal year 1941 to 502 a year later, it dropped precipitously to 345 by the close of fiscal year 1943, climbing only to 354 a year later and dropping again to 337 by the end of fiscal year 1945. This situation did not require firings, happily, for during the war years 187 employees joined the military services and many others were attracted to jobs elsewhere. Indeed there were so many separations that a new wave of civil servants was employed, which posed a serious problem of on-the-job seasoning so that they could adequately replace the old hands. To say the least, the high wartime turnover rate among employees caused much extra work as well as further confusion within the agency.[8]

Although Buck moved to align the National Archives closer to defense needs soon after he took office, the coming of war in December 1941 speeded things up. The archivist hoped to avoid curtailing services during the war, but he and his staff were alert to the possibility that that might be necessary. Indeed on 29 December Assistant Director of Archival Service Marcus W. Price notified the chiefs of the archives divisions and the Reference Division that in case services were curtailed the needs of government agencies would have priority over those of private citizens and organizations. Within those groupings war-related inquiries would have priority over those that would not contribute to the nation's war effort. Price's statement also discussed the need to consider simplifying service procedures, providing round-the-clock service to war agencies, and establishing security arrangements for the holdings and personnel of the National Archives.[9]

The pressures for change were becoming increasingly clear. As early as 3 December Executive Officer Collas Harris urged Buck to consider suspending "all work not directly concerned with the defense program" except as it was essential to prevent the deterioration of nondefense-related materials. Congress and the Budget Bureau talked of investigations of federal agencies to make sure that the waging of war was their priority task. That led Harris on 13 February 1942 to press the archivist to "resurvey" immediately the work of the National Archives "to see if any activities which are not directly contributing to the effective prosecution of the war could be suspended, and the personnel now assigned to such duties transferred to other activities."[10]

By 16 February Buck was ready to move. He held a meeting then of the heads of operating units to review the steps taken by the National Archives to meet the nation's needs during the emergency and to discuss "completing the conversion of the National Archives to a war basis." Warning that curtailment of services would probably be necessary, he expressed his disappointment with the efforts made to find ways of reducing operations to essential ones. The archivist urged his staff to consider their work from the standpoint of contributing to the war effort instead of from that of "saving funds or the staff of the National Archives." Therefore, he ordered a thorough and immediate examination of the agency's activities and he requested suggestions on how the National Archives could better serve the needs of the nation at war.[11]

This meeting served its purpose, for a flood of suggestions soon arrived in Buck's office. The staff's responses were motivated in part by patriotic fervor and in part by a wish to justify the agency's existence during the war. Director of Personnel Robert D. Hubbard commented with some truth, "The National Archives is looked upon generally . . . as an organization of 'parasites' of no value in the present war efforts." He warned that the agency's staff might be cut by at least 50 percent. That this was on everybody's mind was seen in the suggestions sent to the archivist, for none of them proposed reductions in staff.

Collas Harris submitted a good summary of the suggestions as to how the agency could "take a more aggressive part in the war effort, revitalize our present program, and also be thinking in terms of the post-war period." These included making archivists into experts on the information contained in the records with which they worked so that relevant agencies could use their knowledge. Some of the archivists could conduct formal research on historical problems that might keep the government from repeating the mistakes of World War I and its aftermath, and other personnel could assist federal agencies in avoiding repetition of the loss of war documents that occurred after 1918. Still other employees could work to expand records administration in government offices and to facilitate the proper disposition of federal records. Such ideas plainly influenced the archivist. On 2 March he urged the staff to determine what various government agencies wanted and to prepare themselves to meet those wants and to offer their services. The preparation included involvement in research studies, with priority given to "war-related activities." He also prodded his staff to "streamline" their operations in order to gain greater efficiency. [12]

Streamlining meant not only reorganization, but also the disapproval of various projects. The previous December John G. Bradley of the Division of Motion Pictures and Sound Recordings had suggested that the National Archives make sound recordings of important events and speeches. Buck vetoed this in March 1942. The following month he decided that the National Archives would not request additional stack equipment because of the persisting steel shortage; the agency would, if necessary, find alternative ways to use unequipped stack areas for the storage of records. The archivist also began detailing staff members as records officers to other federal agencies, partly to assist them with their mounting records problems and partly to spread the developing gospel of records administration. In this Buck was especially farsighted, for it contributed considerably to keeping the government from being suffocated by its own paper work and it gave the National Archives better odds in keeping abreast of its own obligations for acquiring and preserving federal records.[13]

Along with other federal offices, the National Archives had to respond to pressures to hire blacks. The agency's record in hiring them for unskilled work was not bad, but it had no record when it came to hiring them for advanced positions. The government's establishment of the Committee on Fair Employment Practices in 1941 changed that somewhat. On 1 September 1941, the National Archives employed blacks as 10.25 percent of its staff, all in unskilled jobs. Thanks to the work of the FEPC, they composed 13.48 percent of the staff on 31 March 1942, including one subprofessional employee and another in the clerical-administrative-fiscal category. The next day the National Archives engaged Harold T. Pinkett as its first black professional staff member. By 31 August 1942 its rosters showed that 68 out of 478 employees were Negroes, including 59 unskilled, 3 CAFs, 5 subprofessionals, and 1 professional.[14] It would be nice to say that the agency made aggressive moves to recruit a higher percentage of blacks in its skilled, clerical, and professional ranks during the next two decades, but that was not the case. Until the 1960s, Pinkett rarely had more than two fellow black professionals, and the proportion of blacks in skilled, clerical, and semiprofessional jobs grew only slowly until then. The situation was never scandalous, for it was generally conceded that once on the staff blacks were treated decently. The agency, however, would earn no awards for its recruitment and promotion among minority groups for responsible positions. As with most other sectors of the federal government, the situation with respect to women was only relatively better.

Congress and the Bureau of the Budget constantly posed problems in the never-ceasing battle for money. Despite Buck's efforts to contribute to the war effort, they cut his agency's funds. The National Archives' appropriations declined from $1,065,822 to $934,400 between fiscal years 1942 and 1944. The personnel situation was even worse, dropping from 502 to 354 during these years. To maintain even its modest position among federal agencies, the National Archives had to struggle to retain its designation as a war agency. When government offices were ranked in 1942, the archives was on the magic list, but it was at the bottom as a class 5 war agency. Buck asked that it be given class 3 status because it was in effect a "Federal Records Office" vital to the work of other war agencies. His protest met with some success as the government moved the National Archives up to class 4 status.[15]

The period between 1 July 1941 and 30 June 1942 was a critical year in the operations of the National Archives. Fortunately for the agency, it had on hand an unusually large staff since the number of employees had increased from 438 to 502 during that time. Buck took full advantage of it, knowing that there would soon be a sharp cut in personnel. His organization, therefore, was able during fiscal year 1942 to accommodate the increasing pressure to accession older federal records. The results were stunning as the records in the archives building then grew from 302,183 to 459,932 cubic feet, an increase of more than 50 percent. This marked a substantial contribution to the war effort by freeing critical and expensive office space and employee time for other uses, and it represented a windfall of treasures for future scholarly research. The National Archives also made impressive acquisitions of maps and atlases, its holdings of which during fiscal year 1942 mounted from 77,513 items to 114,609, and of still pictures that expanded in number from 215,728 to 567,235.

The archives building would keep filling up, though at a lesser rate, until, by the middle of 1945, 672,336 cubic feet of records, 405,240 maps and atlases, and more than 1,200,000 photographs were on hand. Moreover, between June 1941 and June 1945 the holdings of motion pictures and sound recordings grew, respectively, from some 4,500,000 running feet to 7,500,000 and from 3,820 items to about 95,000. The work of appraising and describing records remained heavy throughout the war years as did reference service; the National Archives also met fairly well the challenges of cleaning, shelving, and arranging the vastly increased number of records it acquired, though some shortcuts were devised in order to use its reduced staff most effectively during fiscal years 1943, 1944, and 1945. What it all meant was that with considerable effort and ingenuity the agency met its greatly expanding responsibilities while its staff was not only reduced but was in great flux. Of course, the National Archives had to curtail some of its activities, such as the repair and rehabilitation of documents and the development of more sophisticated finding aids, which would pose problems after the war. Occasionally the agency had to limit service to private researchers.[16]

Yet the National Archives successfully became involved in a number of war-related programs, the most important being records administration, which I shall discuss in a later chapter. Another activity blossomed in December 1941 with the issuance of two valuable publications, a 100-page *Manual of Information about the National Archives for Government Officials* and a 43-page *List of Federal World War Agencies, 1914–1920*. Both of those and the 1943 follow-up, *Handbook of Federal War Agencies and Their Records, 1917–1921*, were designed to assist federal war agencies to make maximum use of the institution's resources. They were later joined by a wide variety of other publications of the National Archives, including circulars and processed documents on records administration, reference information circulars, special lists, a few preliminary inventories on materials that might be of interest to war-related offices, and information on archival practices and repositories in enemy and occupied countries.[17]

The war assured that the National Archives would remain in the vanguard of the use of microphotography by the federal government. No less a person than President Roosevelt gave impetus to that. After his election to honorary membership in the Society of American Archivists, he asked archivists early in 1942 to help develop public sentiment for the microfilmed duplication of valuable records as a form of insurance against the hazards of war. The National Archives took this as a signal to shout "Open, Sesame" in its quest to expand microphotographic operations. In April Solon Buck issued a press release urging the extensive microfilming of records of intermediate value in order to reduce the space occupied by them by up to 95 percent. Vernon Tate followed this up in June when, in an address to the American Library Association, he called microphotography a technique ranking "in importance with any military weapon thus far disclosed." He went on to review the value of microfilming not only in preserving documents and books, but also in facilitating more efficient and economical distribution of information.[18]

Action was a consequence of all the talk about microphotography. As the war went on, government agencies microfilmed an increasing volume of records. Economy in terms of space, weight, and use of personnel was one of the chief factors involved. In spurring this and providing technical assistance and advice on microphotography, the National Archives thus made one of its most important contributions not only to the war effort, but also to public administration. Much microreproduced material, of course, would find its way into the archives building by the war's end, and the agency was fully prepared to handle such documentation. The National Archives also took advantage of the president's interest in microphotographic preservation to justify forwarding its file microcopy program during the war. Consequently, hundreds of thousands of pages of highly valuable research documents (400,000 in fiscal year 1943 alone) were reproduced in microfilm negatives as a security precaution. Thus one of the National Archives' most innovative reference efforts was kept alive during World War II.[19]

Of course, the agency had its hands full with requests from war administrators for information, first on the organization of defense agencies and then on specific problems, such as the control of the production of raw materials and the use of maps and photographs to illustrate bombing targets. The National Archives' development of technical processes was also important to the war effort. These included a better method of mounting and lacquering maps, the transferring of type from old to new paper, and the conversion of early movie prints into films that could be projected on currently available machines.[20]

During the war, by public screenings of movies, the agency occasionally made interesting use of its film holdings and contacts with the motion-picture industry. The rationale was to contribute to morale and some vague concept of propaganda. The result of this was the presentation of a motion-picture festival with an international theme from 25–30 December 1942. The films shown in the auditorium of the archives building included Walt Disney's "Saludos Amigos," Warner Brothers' "The Life of Emile Zola," and Paramount's "Ruggles of Red Gap." The National Archives did not repeat this kind of extravaganza, probably for fear that it would be considered frivolous, although it did from time to time show government-produced films. This activity, however, did set a precedent for the future. After the war the agency again screened films for the public, for example, the Signal Corps' Academy Award-winning documentary, "Seeds of Destiny," in 1947 and a series of historic and historical motion pictures in 1953.[21] All this, of course, was a prologue to the popular continuing series of instructive older films shown by the National Archives beginning in 1970.

Technically motion pictures had been a problem for the agency from the beginning because of the flammable quality of cellulose nitrate films. This led to the only significant evacuation measure that the National Archives took during World War II when such material was transferred to Fort Hunt in Virginia. Even as an emergency measure, this proved less than satisfactory because the heat and humidity there speeded the decomposition of the film. Thus before the end of the war the archivist had the material returned to the air-conditioned vaults of the archives building. That did not solve the problem of the chemical instability of nitrate film and the dangers of fire and explosion that it posed, despite the strenuous efforts of the staff to reduce this. Therefore, the National Archives by 1945 was pressing for the authorization of a specially constructed building that could contain such materials safely.[22] The government never approved this, which in retrospect was just as well, for the solution to the problem was the much less expensive alternative of transferring the cellulose nitrate film to safe and sturdy cellulose acetate stock beginning in the 1950s. Until then the officials of the National Archives lived in constant terror that their film holdings would either decompose or, even worse, go up in flames along with other records.

Other problems nagged the archivist and his aides during the war years. As early as 1940 they began to consider placing restrictions on persons entering and materials being taken out of the building, which eventually led to the imposition of security controls. Then, as the agency's staff level declined, the National Archives temporarily had to make room for elements of the departments of War and the Navy and the Office of Strategic Services. That led to a number of time-consuming incidents over the use of facilities. There was also a hue and cry at one time in 1943 over sixty-nine missing gasoline rationing coupons, an episode not without parallel to Captain Queeg's famous search for the ship's missing stores of strawberries. More serious was the drying up of the Tiber Canal that same year when the flow from Washington's Tidal Basin was temporarily cut off because of the construction of the Jefferson Memorial. The result was the ineffective operation of the archives building's air-conditioning system, which was so important to the preservation of documents, and the hurried switching over to a city water main to put things right again.[23]

More important were the strains that the great increase in the services offered by the National Archives placed upon its staff and facilities. Of course, the agency performed these services mainly for the government. Private researchers, however, still provided the archivists with considerable work, and there was an upswing in calls from citizens who needed to prove their citizenship, dates of birth, military service, or eligibility for social security. Requests from government agencies to borrow records constituted one of the most vexing problems. Not only did this eat directly into staff time, but it also led to trouble in two other respects. One was that lent records were unavailable to other government offices that might need them; the other was that some of the borrowers lost the records. The situation became so bad that by July 1943 more than 4,000 items had been out on loan for periods in excess of one year. Yet it took ten months of discussion before the agency tightened up its policy and required other federal offices to make strong cases for borrowing archives. This and better methods of keeping track of lent materials were helpful, but they did not make up for records that had already been lost by borrowers.[24]

The National Archives had to struggle to prepare its building for the flood of accessions that arrived during the war years. This was hampered by shortages of materials and funds. As the building began to fill up, Buck and his colleagues became increasingly worried about the unequipped stack areas, which numbered forty-five in September 1942. By October the archivist believed that the situation would become so serious (his agency's holdings had increased by 50 percent during the past ten months) that he decided to request authorization to equip the vacant stack area with wooden shelving. The government did not approve this expedient, but fortunately the rate of acquisitions fell to a level that the National Archives could accommodate during the rest of the war. That, of course, involved making better use of space for shelving purposes, constructing a storage house for oil and other dangerous materials in the moat surrounding the building, and leaving accessions in their original steel containers.[25] Not until after the war and indeed until after the appointment of a new archivist of the United States would the stack areas be fully equipped.

Shelving and, of course, an adequate number of personnel were not all that the National Archives did not get. With the support of various federal officials, Buck asked President Roosevelt in July 1942 to authorize the weekly publication of an "interdepartmental issue" of the *Federal Register* that would contain all the circulars, orders, notices, and directives of executive agencies. The idea was that this would be a more orderly and economical way to distribute such information. On the advice of the Budget Bureau, the president decided in December to disapprove the archivist's proposal basically because "the time is inopportune for launching new ventures in the absence of impelling reasons." Indeed that same month Congress acted to suspend some of the codification activities of the Division of the Federal Register for the duration of the war, obviously as an economy measure to relieve other federal agencies of their share of this burden.[26]

One of the most significant issues in which the National Archives was involved during the war attracted little attention then. That was the penchant of many officials to impose security classifications on documents, a situation to which Buck initially gave little thought. It became increasingly clear, however, that this would in time become an important problem. Nevertheless, the archivist was reluctant to intercede on behalf of individual researchers in their efforts to gain access to restricted records.[27] This was largely for fear of offending officials in other agencies who might decide to be less agreeable to transferring records to the National Archives. But it was also partly because Buck and his aides thought the best way to deal with restrictions was to peel them off after the war.

An illustration of the National Archives' attitude is found in its relations with the Department of State during the war. The archivist was eager to acquire the records of the War Trade Board, which in 1942 were stored at some hazard in a garage. In 1943 the State Department consented to their transfer but made restrictions on the use of the records, including one stating that the archivist could make no public announcement of the accession. Buck's only demurrer in this case, which he successfully carried, was that he was required to refer to the transfer in his published annual report to Congress. In 1944 the State Department was similarly secretive about records concerning applications for visas for the period 1933–40. The archivist did not object to those records being used only with the department's permission, but he now more strenuously refused to be gagged in making known their presence in his agency. As he wrote, "I conceive it to be one of the principal responsibilities of an archival agency to make known to other governmental agencies and to the public the records it has in its custody that may be useful to them in the conduct of their affairs or the protection of their rights. As a matter of general policy, therefore, I will ordinarily not accept the custody of records under conditions that restrict my freedom to make such statements concerning them as seem to me appropriate in the discharge of my official responsibilities." Buck had his way, and the visa applications were transferred to his custody. Later in 1944 he acquiesced to the State Department's demand that its records in the archives building not be made available for research when they were dated after 1913 and that access be completely barred to documents relating to passports and unsettled claims of financial interest to the United States government or its citizens. He did, however, encourage the department to establish after the war a restricted period of no more than twenty-five years.[28]

This is not to say that the National Archives never argued during the war for easing or removing restrictions on records less than fifty years old, but this seldom occurred, partly because as a member of the bureaucratic club the agency was sympathetic to a degree of restrictiveness. Probably more important was the fear that if it went far in arguing against restrictions it would jeopardize further acquisitions of important records and might even incur the enmity of those who could threaten its continued existence. Furthermore, the archivists assumed that things would ease up after the war.[29] All this is understandable, given the time, for the National Archives was treading a narrow path in balancing the conflicting interests of researchers and federal officials. Yet it is clear in retrospect that the archivist and his chief advisers should have been more concerned with what the saturnalia of secrecy during World War II might lead to. They should also have been more interested in explaining what excessive restrictions on federal records would mean to the public and even to the government itself in terms of constricting access to the information necessary to the making of decisions in a republic, let alone the development of sound scholarly inquiry. Of course, the National Archives probably could not have cured the government's hush-hush syndrome. By trying to, however, the agency might better have prepared itself and the nation to deal with that disease later on. The cost of overclassification of records would be high, particularly in widespread suspicion of the government's integrity. A later generation would pay the bill with compound interest.

More to its credit, the National Archives contributed to the cooperative efforts to save and make prompt use of materials documenting the country's participation in World War II. This proceeded in part from Buck's close relationship with the American Historical Association, of which he was the treasurer, and his encouragement of the interest of the Social Science Research Council in preserving "social data." Of course, many people and institutions were interested in recording the nation's wartime experience. Among them was the Bureau of the Budget, which called in political scientist Pendleton Herring of Harvard University to organize its records for use in documenting its wartime activities.

Herring worked closely with Buck and Guy Stanton Ford, the AHA's executive secretary, in carrying out his duties. Out of their cooperation came a conference sponsored by Ford on 18 February 1942 of the scholars and government officials most interested in recording the nation's war effort. Word of this meeting reached President Roosevelt, who enthusiastically requested the Budget Bureau on 4 March to establish a "committee on records of war administration" with representatives from scholarly societies and federal agencies. Roosevelt hoped that such a committee would strengthen the Budget Bureau's endeavors both in improving public administration and in "preserving for those who come after us an accurate and objective account of our present experience." He also urged war agency officials to cooperate in this venture and to keep their records systematically. Within a few weeks the Budget Bureau formed the committee, with Waldo G. Leland of the American Council of Learned Societies as chairman and Herring as executive secretary. The other members included Buck, Ford, and representatives of the Library of Congress, the American Political Science Association, the American Society of Public Administration, and the SSRC. This Committee on Records of War Administration had two major goals: to encourage federal agencies to "maintain records of how they are discharging their wartime duties" and to advise the Budget Bureau "in the making of current analyses of administrative problems in major policy fields of the war effort."[30]

The accomplishments of the committee and its small staff were significant. By the end of 1943 twenty-nine federal agencies had established historical units and Fred W. Shipman of the Roosevelt Library was working at the White House to complete documentation on the most significant wartime presidential activities. The work varied from agency to agency, of course, with some only putting their records in order but with others writing accounts of their war efforts. Despite this variety, it was plain that the results would benefit the National Archives, making it the ultimate repository for the materials, and thus benefit scholarship as well.[31]

The early successes of the Committee on Records of War Administration led the groups it represented to seek even more.

The SSRC and the archivist discussed holding a conference on war records in 1942 that would make recommendations on the handling of such material as a national resource. Buck took it up with Pendleton Herring and President Roosevelt, who was "keenly interested." Apparently the SSRC decided not to fund this conference, so the idea was dropped. Agreement was reached, however, on an alternative activity in which the archivist was the moving force. That was the drive for establishment of a national war history commission. The basis for this was a conference held at the National Archives on 29 December. Financed by the ACLS and the SSRC, this meeting met with a highly favorable reaction. Buck thus suggested to the American Historical Association that it propose the federal government establish a national war history commission. The AHA adopted the idea and appointed a steering committee to carry it through. The objective was that the commission would collect, preserve, and arrange for microfilm publication of sources as well as encourage the writing of war histories. Despite the AHA's enthusiasm, this action proved "nothing but talk, talk, talk," as Dallas Irvine of the National Archives had predicted. The director of the Budget would not accept any of the several versions of the war history commission that were proposed, apparently because he saw it as rivaling the work of his agency's Committee on Records of War Administration. The result was that the SSRC in September 1943 established its own Committee on War Studies to plan research on the nation's war effort. In August the Committee on Records of War Administration also had taken independent action by urging government agencies to write "first narratives" of their wartime activities and by encouraging state governments, scholars, industries, and others to write histories of the war effort in the United States.

Clearly, the interests of the two committees overlapped. In October, therefore, they associated themselves in forming an Advisory Committee on War History, under the chairmanship of Guy Stanton Ford, in order to achieve the goals set for the war history commission. The advisory committee operated to advise and to provide a liaison between government researchers and private scholars. In February 1944 President Roosevelt heartily encouraged its work as a way to expedite the writing of histories of the war.[32]

The results of all this were impressive. Some forty government offices ultimately pursued historical projects, which meant that the volume of conscious documentation of the nation's World War II activities vastly exceeded that of earlier wars in which the United States had participated. The AHA was pleased with the war history projects even though, as Executive Secretary Ford recognized, the "product will be uneven, the outcomes uncertain because of the turnover in staffs." As he predicted, the military services produced the highest quality works, such as the vast series the *United States Army in World War II* and Samuel Eliot Morison's series the *History of United States Naval Operations in World War II*. There were, however, others of quality, both in print and manuscript, as well as a great outpouring of documentary publications. Moreover, there has been a continuing interest to the present time in officially sponsored historical activities.

Equally important, a large amount of documentary materials was made available for archivists to process and increasingly for scholars, private and official, to use. This justified the effort that the National Archives invested in cooperative endeavors with the ACLS, AHA, Budget Bureau, SSRC, and other learned societies and federal agencies in encouraging improvements in the keeping of documentation and the writing of war history. The National Archives' work also allowed for some scholarly cross-fertilization, including the discussions between the agency and the SSRC about encouraging the employment of specialists in the National Archives who could assist social scientists in using relevant records, the provision of time for archivists to conduct their own research, fellowships attached to the agency, and the expanded utilization of microfilm and of records management functions for archivists. All of these would in one way or another at least be experimented with before the 1970s.[33] Ironically, they had little to do with social science research, for social scientists increasingly moved away from expert use of government records, to the intellectual impoverishment of themselves and archivists.

It was only natural that during a world war the interests of the National Archives reached beyond the borders of the United States. Of course, this was not completely a new situation, for foreigners had visited the building before the war and several members of the staff, including Solon Buck, had traveled abroad. Buck had been highly impressed by what he had seen and heard in Europe, and his regard was reinforced by his close relationship with Ernst Posner after Posner's arrival in the United States in 1939. It is not surprising that when the pressures of the early months of the war let up a bit the archivist would seek a role in international affairs for his agency.

Buck's first effort was to ask Secretary of State Cordell Hull in 1942 for representation on the Interdepartmental Committee on Cooperation with the American Republics in order to facilitate an exchange of information about archives and history. The State Department approved this and appointed Almon R. Wright of the National Archives to the committee. He was soon succeeded by Roscoe R. Hill, who encouraged further contacts between archivists in the United States and Latin America. Indeed, Hill was of assistance in the development of Cuba's new national archive building, which opened in the fall of 1944. The National Archives also facilitated the visits of archivists from Latin America and Canada for training in the United States. This was just the beginning of larger and broader-ranging international archival training programs that the agency sponsored after the war.[34]

More complicated was the National Archives' interest in the preservation of the records in areas occupied by American troops and of the records of those forces themselves. Early there had been concern in various quarters for saving cultural materials abroad from war damage. In January 1943 that led the ACLS to form the Committee on the Protection of Cultural Treasures in War Areas, a group usually called the Dinsmoor Committee after its chairman, archaeologist William Bell Dinsmoor of Columbia University. A talk delivered by Ernst Posner in Washington on 5 May sparked the government to make the committee into an effective force for the protection of records. This paper, entitled "Public Records Under Military Occupation," showed how historically the records of occupied territories had been an important tool of control for the conquering forces. The National Archives processed the paper as a publication and it was later carried as an article in the *American Historical Review*. More immediately important, the director of the Roosevelt Library, Fred Shipman, heard the talk and called it to the attention of President Roosevelt, who discussed it at the cabinet meeting of 8 May and asked the department heads to arrange for the protection of records in war zones.[35]

In June 1943 the Dinsmoor Committee, of which Buck was a member, and the National Archives really began their work with respect to the protection of archives and other historical treasures in Europe. The immediate goal was the making of lists of cultural institutions, monuments, and treasures for the military so they could aid in their protection. Upon the recommendation of the National Archives, Posner was engaged to compose the lists of archival institutions. The Dinsmoor Committee and the military used this and other pertinent information in devising municipal maps and national atlases for air forces, army field headquarters, and military government units. The National Archives hectographed Posner's lists, which included considerable information not used by the Dinsmoor Committee, for distribution to interested government agencies. The Military Government Division of the Provost Marshal General found them particularly useful and encouraged the compilation of such lists for all enemy and enemy-occupied countries in all theaters of war. The result was that Posner's lists, by the time the last was processed in June 1945, made available information on some 1,700 archival agencies in Europe and Asia. Other National Archives projects enhanced the value of the lists for occupation forces; these included the translation into English of Italy's archival law of 1939 and contributions to the preparation of War Department pamphlets titled *Field Protection of Objects of Art and Archives* and *Information on German Records*.[36]

The National Archives moved more slowly in the attaching of archivists to overseas army headquarters. Here Allied headquarters in Algiers took the initiative in November 1943 by requesting the services of an archivist. Solon Buck nominated Fred Shipman.

Because of the slowness of communication and the need to clear the matter with President Roosevelt, Shipman did not reach the Mediterranean theater of operations until March 1944. He found when he arrived in Italy that the eminent English archivist, Hilary Jenkinson, had preceded him. The two of them worked effectively together, which was well, for Shipman could stay only a couple of months. Yet they furthered the knowledge and use of Italian archives by the Allied occupation authorities. They also persuaded the military to add an archivist to the Monuments, Fine Arts, and Archives Subcommittee of the Allied Control Commission for Italy and to assign archivists to Allied armies in the Mediterranean theater. Although an American archivist, Captain William D. McCain, was delayed in reporting for duty until September 1944, British archivists were on hand to continue Jenkinson's and Shipman's work.[37]

The National Archives was also slow in dealing with the area of military operations that opened in France in June 1944. Fortunately, Major Mason Hammond, a historian, made plans for archival work in the Supreme Headquarters, Allied Expeditionary Force. Archivist Buck in July asked that Shipman be sent to assist SHAEF. Again red tape interfered so that the Roosevelt Library director and his aide, Captain Asa Thornton, did not leave for Europe until September. Despite Shipman's connection with the president, his new mission was far from successful. He made some impression on General Eisenhower's staff and gained some useful knowledge; but his proposal to attach Thornton permanently to SHAEF fell through, and the captain was assigned instead to the First Army. Moreover, SHAEF's agreement to place an archivist with each of the American armies went unfulfilled despite the urgings of Shipman and the National Archives. Even worse, Thornton soon had to return to the United States because of illness. The officers assigned to the armies to protect monuments did the best they could with archives, but Oliver W. Holmes later correctly judged the attempt to operate through SHAEF to preserve and use records in occupied areas as a "failure at a critical time."[38]

The National Archives picked up the pieces as best it could. The government approved the agency's recommendation that Sargent B. Child, who was formerly director of the Historical Records Survey, be made archivist to the United States Group of the Control Council for Germany and also to SHAEF until the control council took up its military government duties. Child arrived in Europe in April 1945. During his year overseas, he helped to establish collection centers for "homeless archives, records, and books" in Berlin and several locations in western Germany. Captain (later Major) Lester K. Born was Child's chief assistant and successor; other American archivists attached to the operation by 1946 included Jesse Boell, Edgar Breitenbach, Harold J. Clem, Seymour Pomrenze, and Paul Vanderbilt. With assistance from army personnel and German archivists, this group had considerable success in organizing records for use by the military government and, when appropriate, for return to their original owners. Born spearheaded the drive to persuade the American military government to reconstitute professional German archival organizations and was of great assistance in reestablishing Germany's archives and libraries. If American archivists had been tardy in paying attention to the prosecution of the war in Europe and to postwar military government, theirs ultimately was a good record, at least the equal of what any other American scholarly group did.[39]

This record, however, was not matched in the Far East. The National Archives did not look in that direction until February 1945. Then Solon Buck recommended sending Major Arthur E. Kimberly to Manila "to initiate and supervise first-aid measures." Kimberly arrived in June and did what he could to assist the government of the Philippines in reconstructing its archives. Captain Collas G. Harris later served as archival adviser to the military government in Japan. The truth is that neither the military nor the National Archives gave as much attention to archival matters in the Far East as they did in Europe.[40]

Things might have been a bit different had it not been for the Posner affair. Ernst Posner had been invaluable to the National Archives from his position on the faculty of the American University. In his teaching and writing he had successfully joined European archival theory and experience to American experimentation, which had had a salutary influence on American archivists. He had also had impact on his adopted country's war effort as a result of his paper "Public Records Under Military Occupation" and his privately sponsored work in compiling information on archives in enemy and enemy-occupied lands. Yet this did not keep him and the National Archives from being victimized by one of the seigneurs of the United States Senate, Kenneth McKellar of Tennessee.

When Archivist Buck appeared before McKellar's Senate Appropriations Subcommittee in February 1944 to discuss his agency's budget, he ran into the fight of his life. Senator McKellar had read *National Archives Staff Information Circular No. 11*, which included Ernst Posner's piece, "The Role of Records in Administration: In German Administration." The thrust of the article was to demonstrate the importance of records in efficient government management in Germany. During the budget hearings, McKellar labeled the paper as "German propaganda" aimed at converting the United States to totalitarian tactics, and he implied that Posner was behind the use of cardboard document containers that he seemed convinced would render American records more vulnerable to damage. Buck and his aides valiantly tried to set the record straight: Posner had nothing to do with the adoption of the cardboard containers; he was not a German propagandist; his work in compiling information regarding archives elsewhere was not designed only to protect the records of other governments, but also to assist America's armed forces; the National Archives was not being Germanized. Senator Gerald P. Nye tried to help by asking questions that showed Posner was neither a Nazi nor a Communist but had been a victim of Nazi oppression. The testimony made no difference to McKellar, for he continued his tantrum not only against Posner, but also Buck, to whom he said, "I think you ought to put in your resignation as soon as possible."[41]

The archivist believed, probably correctly, that a disgruntled former employee of the National Archives had put Senator McKellar up to his ill-informed crusade. And the matter did have repercussions. The American Commission for the Protection and Salvage of Artistic and Historic Monuments in Europe had given

Ernst Posner a key staff position. He had only been on the job five days, however, when the commission decided to press for his resignation. Thus did the commission lose the services of the person who was best prepared to undertake its work with respect to archives and archival institutions. This reflected poorly on the courage and integrity of the commission. Buck did maintain his honor, protesting vigorously to the commission and rallying people such as Guy Stanton Ford of the AIIA, Waldo G. Leland of the ACLS, and Librarian of Congress Archibald MacLeish to Posner's cause. It was to no avail, however, for McKellar and bullyragging won the day. By the end of February Posner resigned, and Buck, protesting to the end, quit the commission's subcommittee on archives and libraries.[42]

The National Archives remained in trouble with McKellar, manifested by the senator's lack of support for the agency's struggle to have restored the budget cuts made by the House of Representatives. McKellar wrote Buck on 1 June asking if Posner still had a desk in the archives building in connection with his archival courses. The archivist answered that Professor Posner had not had such space since February, although, of course, for his research he had used tables in the public search rooms. Even that, the main effect of which was to cramp Posner's efforts on behalf of his students on the National Archives' staff and his research for the military services, did not put an end to the matter.

In January 1945 Administrative Secretary Thaddeus Page sought Senator McKellar's support for amendments to the National Archives Act that would facilitate the transfer of certain categories of records to the archivist's custody. McKellar bridled, making it clear that he would not introduce the amendments because he believed that a German alien should not have had a desk in the archives building and access to the records. Page answered forthrightly. He defended the amendments as necessary to help release further office space in war agencies. He also defended Buck, himself, and their colleagues for their testimony before the McKellar subcommittee the previous February. As for Ernst Posner, Page defended the teaching of his course in the archives building, an arrangement dating back to Robert Connor's days as archivist, as a convenience for students who were employees of the National Archives. He further stated that Posner was now an American citizen, that he was not (as he had never been) an employee of the National Archives, and that he had only the privileges that any other private researcher had. It is not surprising that Kenneth McKellar had learned nothing from Page and Buck, for he still viewed Posner as a dangerous enemy alien. Roared the senator, "As long as Dr. Posner is a member of the Archives, . . . I shall never interest myself in it. It seems to me that Dr. Posner is running the Archives and not Dr. Buck." Regarding the War Department's use of Posner's privately compiled lists, McKellar declared, "It is certainly remarkable that the War Department has taken him over and I suppose . . . he will probably have some position in the Navy Department or be giving advice to the Navy before long." Clearly, McKellar, who thought of himself as the father of the National Archives, would support neither the agency's quest for increased appropriations nor its proposed amendments to the National Archives Act. Just as plainly, McKellar did not care to know the facts about the relationship between Posner and the National Archives.[43]

As for Posner, the War Department seriously considered him to be its chief adviser on archives in war areas, an appointment that apparently was scheduled to be made in March 1945. It did not come about, probably because McKellar's renewed interest in Posner caused the department to fear what congressional reaction would be. Indeed, even the Dinsmoor Committee on the Protection of Cultural Treasures in War Areas quavered before the senator's wrath, for Dinsmoor himself insisted upon severing the committee's connection with Posner. Buck stood by Posner to the end. It was plain, however, that he would receive no appointment either in the government or in private organizations that did work for the government. Their loss was the gain of the archival and historical professions, both in the United States and abroad. Operating from the American University, Posner became a teacher, scholar, and archival adviser of world renown.[44]

In a sense, the last round of the battle over Ernst Posner marked the end of World War II for the National Archives, just as

Solon J. Buck's appointment as archivist of the United States had marked the war's beginning for the agency. The years in between had been turbulent and had led to changes for both better and worse. The agency had undergone a series of far-reaching reorganizations that had contributed to the growth of institutional effectiveness as well as to a degree of confusion and even resentment. Its budget was $1,110,840 for fiscal year 1945, only $29,000 higher than in 1942.[45] Wartime inflation had substantially eaten into the funds of the National Archives; this was reflected in the drop of personnel by about one-third between those years. Yet by mounting efficiency and hard work and curtailment of some regular activities, the agency was able not only to meet the great demands of the war upon it, but also to generate new programs and to expand its influence. This was a remarkable achievement, however much it meant that the archivists would have to struggle in the future to make up for their wartime losses and to capitalize on their wartime gains.

9. *Another Kind of Archivist*

"It is almost inconceivable," Wayne C. Grover said in 1953, "that the federal government, in the twenty-two years from 1930 to 1952, should have created more than seven times as many records as it did during its previous 155 years of history." That was the reason, according to the then archivist of the United States, why federal archivists "began to go beserk—frightened at birth, one might say—by a very real monster." That is also what spurred their participation, roughly beginning upon the eve of World War II, in the development of what has come to be known as records management.[1]

Records administration was of increasing concern to the National Archives during the war. As Solon J. Buck pointed out, many people agreed—titteringly—with Jerry Klutz of the *Washington Post* that "an archivist is a dead file clerk." Archivist Buck's objective was to have his agency counter that impression, particularly by coping with the threat that "society be overwhelmed by an unmanageable mass of records." So that they could be more than just custodians of discarded documents, he urged his staff to interest themselves in everything about records from their creation to their destruction or preservation. The National Archives thus could increasingly make itself valuable to governmental administration as well as to research. Not only could it contribute substantially to the saving of expenditures on space, equipment, and personnel, the agency could also save the government from an inundation of paper by making its record-keeping practices more efficient and useful.[2]

The Records Disposal Act of 1939 enabled the National Archives to assist federal agencies in facilitating the disposition of their useless records. It was only a beginning, however, for the agencies, which were insufficiently aware of the mounting records problem, legally remained the initiators in the process. In 1940 the National Archives took another step forward by joining with the Civil Service Commission to sponsor gatherings of government employees in Washington who were interested in records matters. These meetings evolved into the Interagency Records Administration Conference by the end of 1942. It held monthly meetings in the capital during the war and issued the transcripts of more than twenty conferences. Although the National Archives became the guiding force in the IRAC, after the war Buck moved to have the organization run by its own elected steering committee. IRAC's activities expanded and broadened over the years, matching the development of records management in the federal government. Since 1950 counterparts of the Washington IRAC have sprung up in a number of other cities under the auspices of the National Archives and Records Service. IRAC (later named the Information and Records Administration Conference) has been a vital force in encouraging the development of effective records administration and in keeping archivists and records officers in step with one another.[3]

The National Archives also worked in conjunction with the Society of American Archivists in advancing records management. Emmett J. Leahy served as chairman of the SAA's Committee on Reduction of Archival Material (in 1941 this title became the Committee on Records Administration). Philip C. Brooks, another leading records administration expert in the National Archives, succeeded Leahy as chairman of the committee in 1944. Between the two of them, and with abundant encouragement from archivists Connor and Buck, they skillfully spurred the committee to develop standards for coping with records problems.

Late in 1941 the National Archives established its own records administration program so that it could more directly foster the adoption of improved filing and appraisal practices in other federal agencies. The objective was to facilitate the proper handling of records in the agencies and the transfer of appropriate documents to the archives building in the interrelated causes of economy, effectiveness, efficiency, and preservation of essential data. The National Archives supplemented this program by encouraging the employment of archivists by other federal offices (for example, the Tennessee Valley Authority, the War Production Board, and the Navy Department) and by cooperating with pioneer records officers like Helen L. Chatfield of the Department of the Treasury. Working with various government agencies, the National Archives also conducted detailed surveys of the location, amount, and nature of federal records so that records administration could be better geared to workaday reality.[4]

By 1942 it was plain that more attention had to be given to the records of federal offices located outside the nation's capital. The goal was, using the archivist's right of inspection, to identify the volume and nature of the records so that useless materials could be disposed of eventually and valuable documents preserved. The National Archives lacked funds to establish branches of its own, but it did dispatch a few archivists to various places to work as best they could. In spring of 1942 Forrest R. Holdcamper went to the West Coast; later Gaston L. Litton visited the Panama Canal Zone, Puerto Rico, the Virgin Islands, and New York City; and Theodore R. Schellenberg went to New Orleans. Although they made some progress, they were too few to bring the field records under control. The National Archives also attempted to instruct the home offices of the problem so that they could spread the principles of good records management to their field offices. Another expedient was to appoint some state archivists, including Christopher Crittenden of North Carolina, Margaret C. Norton of Illinois, and Leon de Valinger of Delaware, as part-time consultants to tackle selected records problems in federal field agencies. Nevertheless, sufficient personnel was never available during the war to cope satisfactorily with field records. As Oliver W. Holmes suggested in 1943, a solution would probably require the construction of records repositories in various parts of the nation.[5]

Clearly, the National Archives recognized that the rapidly growing accumulation of federal records was often unnecessarily costing the government funds, space, equipment, and staff as well as clogging channels of communication. The agency also recognized that unless something was done about this, it would have increasing difficulty in carrying out its tasks of identifying and preserving records of enduring value. On a piecemeal basis, the archivists had done what they could to keep the patient functioning, but they had not yet developed a cure for his disorder. This would be slow in coming. Indeed, the National Archives and others interested in bringing the records glut under control were dashing off in many directions in trying to deal with the problem.

It was not until April 1942 that Emmett J. Leahy, the chairman of the SAA's Records Administration Committee, submitted a report that set in motion a train of events that led to an overall policy. His report proposed the appointment of records officers in the major federal agencies and the establishment of a council of records administration in the Bureau of the Budget to coordinate their activities. Endorsing Leahy's statement in principle, Solon Buck transmitted it to the Budget Bureau for the SAA. The archivist, however, suggested that something more was needed, particularly that the National Archives should be granted the authority to make a greater contribution toward solving the government's records problems.[6]

The Budget Bureau immediately showed interest in Leahy's report and Buck's observations. In June its representatives and those of the National Archives met to consider drafting an appropriate executive order. This turned out to be more a battleground than a conference, for the Budget Bureau's representatives agreed neither among themselves nor with the archivists. John Keddy, who was the bureau's prime liaison man with the National Archives, raised the main issue, which was the substitution of a federal records council for the National Archives Council. Not without reason, Buck considered this to be an attempt by Keddy to gain greater control over the National Archives by rearing in his bureau a council that would have more power over the archivist than either the National Archives Council or Leahy's proposed council on records administration. The matter went no further because of Buck's opposition to Keddy and the refusal of some of Keddy's colleagues in the Budget Bureau to go along with him.[7]

The National Archives quickly resumed the initiative that summer. By July, in consultation with a number of government records officers, it had drafted a federal records disposal bill. After winning the approval of the National Archives Council, Solon Buck forwarded the proposed legislation to Harold D. Smith, the director of the Bureau of the Budget, in August. The archivist and his staff were prepared to fight hard to gain the bureau's approval, such was their concern for coping with the government's records problems and with expanding their agency's usefulness. One of Buck's aides, Dan Lacy, compared the records administration offensive and other National Archives' programs to the expansion over the years of the Library of Congress's services, without which the United States "would have lost one of its most valuable and useful institutions." Certainly, the drafting of the records disposal bill documented his comment, for the National Archives had put the legislation together well and speedily and had presented it forcefully. The assertiveness of the archivists and Director Smith's keen interest in records administration resulted in a quick and generally favorable reaction from the Budget Bureau to the proposal. The bureau's assistant director, F. J. Bailey, conveyed his agency's response to Buck on 22 September. He wrote that the bureau would approve introduction of the legislation in Congress subject to three changes. These were to submit the National Archives Council's regulations for the disposition of records to the approval of the president, which was in line with the tightening up of his and the Budget Bureau's authority over executive agencies; to give agency heads more authority to dispose of records of the same nature as those already approved for disposition by Congress and as those of little value that had been preserved by photoreproduction; and to relieve the archivist of the responsibility to report to Congress that such records had been authorized for disposal.[8]

In view of the Budget Bureau's general agreeableness, Buck's resistance to its suggestions was probably surprising. He objected to presidential approval of the National Archives Council's records disposal regulations because that requirement would delay implementation of the act after its passage. He added that the council, composed as it was chiefly of presidential appointees or their alternates, could "be depended upon to draft appropriate and workable regulations." Yet the archivist indicated that if the bureau insisted, he would accept its instruction on this. He completely opposed, however, the Budget Bureau's other two counterproposals. He emphasized that they could lead to indiscriminate destruction of records because many earlier congressional authorizations for disposal had been vague and not based on professional advice; many records that had been photoreproduced could be of greater value than estimated by agency heads; and they might not have been photoreproduced properly. Buck reminded the bureau that the primary objective of the bill was "to prevent the disposal of records that might be valuable to the Government or the people" and not just to clean house.[9]

While the National Archives and the Budget Bureau thrashed out the proposed records disposal act, Buck went ahead as far as possible in records administration without new legislation. Encouragement for the appointment of records officers in federal agencies continued as did attempts to get them to train themselves and to coordinate their activities. Philip C. Brooks and Buck promoted the development of training literature, which, beginning in December 1942, led the National Archives to issue a series of pertinent publications, including Brooks's *The Function of Records Officers in the Federal Government* and a symposium entitled *Current Aspects of Records Administration*. The National Archives also facilitated the use of its personnel as file consultants by agencies that lacked records officers. Furthermore, archivists acted to extend their agency's influence in the federal government with respect to records programs. Brooks noted, for example, that his colleague Thomas Owen, Jr., "gets things done in Veterans [Administration] by talking to 'the General' [Administrator Frank T. Hines] at cocktail parties." These activities were not a one-man operation, for comment was invited from the staff of the National Archives and sharp discussion ensued. The response led to some changes in tactics, but it did not alter the agency's goal of finding ways to bring federal records under orderly control throughout their lifespan.[10]

What Buck and Brooks were trying to do cost money. Thus in

September 1942 the archivist asked the Budget Bureau to approve twenty-three new positions so that the National Archives could further assist federal agencies in preventing the creation of unnecessary records, promoting efficient record-keeping practices, releasing space, and disposing properly of currently unneeded materials. Buck must have felt pressed, being involved in this and so many other activities. As he wrote a former aide on 4 November, "Life at The National Archives is still one damn thing after another . . . , but we are managing to keep our heads above water."[11] Within the week, however, Buck undoubtedly concluded that this was an optimistic assessment of his situation.

On 5 November the Budget Bureau called the president's attention to the records administration activities of the National Archives. Budget Director Smith informed Roosevelt that the agency was requesting funds and following policies that would, "contrary to the intent of Congress," transform it "into a gigantic central files for current records of the entire Federal Government." He recommended that the archivist be instructed to halt accessioning active and semiactive records and "that the cost of reference service on active records be financed through reimbursement by the agencies requesting such service." If followed, these suggestions would permit the government to pare the National Archives' appropriations for fiscal year 1944 well below the estimate that the Budget Bureau had previously approved.[12]

This led the president to send a letter on 10 November 1942, which must have jolted Buck. Roosevelt wrote that continuation of the policy of accepting active and semiactive files was "contrary to the original concept of the National Archives." He went on to say,

After careful consideration of this matter, I am satisfied that the present trend in policy must be discontinued and the original policy of housing only the inactive records of permanent value and historical interest be reinstated. Moreover, a plan should be formulated for financing the cost of reference service through reimbursement by the departments or agencies requesting such service on the active records now in your custody pending the appropriate return of these records to the agency of origin.

Roosevelt added that he looked forward to savings in the use of funds by the National Archives during the current fiscal year and cuts in estimates for fiscal year 1944.[13]

There was much agitation in the National Archives over the president's letter because it was as severe a reprimand as the chief executive was likely to send to a federal agency. Several staff members correctly assumed that the letter was drafted by someone in the Bureau of the Budget. Certainly, it was clear that the faction in the Budget Bureau that opposed the archivists's records concepts and tactics had scored a point, despite the fact that many of the bureau's employees were interested in using the National Archives in the struggle to solve the government's records problems.[14]

Buck moved quickly to deal with the president's letter. The National Archives directed the chiefs of the records divisions not to recommend for transfer to the agency materials on which reference service requests might run more than five weekly per 1,000 cubic feet unless there was extraordinary justification. On 23 November the archivist replied to the president, vowing that he would strictly observe the policy of accepting only the inactive records of permanent historical value. The only records outside that category that had been housed in the archives building were those awaiting destruction pending authorization by Congress. He added, "A few groups of records of permanent value and historical interest that are still somewhat active have been taken in, either because they were rapidly disintegrating and the agency that had the custody of them had no facilities for giving them adequate care, or because the agency insisted that it must have the space occupied by the records for important war work." The agencies involved in these instances gave at least partial reimbursement for reference service. The National Archives, Buck told Roosevelt, was studying the records in its custody to determine which were "administratively active or semi-active. As each such group is identified, the agency from which it was received will be asked to remove it or to provide complete reimbursement . . . for the cost of servicing the records."[15]

Plainly, Buck had turned the president's letter somewhat to his agency's advantage by casting doubt on the knowledge of whoever had drafted it. He had particularly indicated in his reply that there was little money to be saved by adhering more firmly to the policy that Roosevelt had outlined. Indeed, the unobligated balance of the National Archives for fiscal year 1943 totaled only $13,943 and the agency's original appropriations for the following fiscal year were $892,000, which was but slightly below the $900,000 estimate that Budget Director Smith had talked about slashing considerably.[16] The archivist knew it was unlikely that whoever had initiated this exchange was going to follow it up, for that person's knowledge of the National Archives was not such to court the embarrassment of being proved largely wrong.

The president's letter nevertheless had an adverse impact, for the agency's hopes for a 20 percent increase in its fiscal year 1944 budget were dashed. Moreover, the tightening up of the bases for transfer recommendations reduced the National Archives' chances of gaining custody of some records it had wanted either for their own sake or because of the value of other materials that might be transferred with them as part of a quid pro quo agreement. That problem, however, was minimal, for there were not—and indeed still are not—statutory definitions of *active* and *inactive* records. Thus Buck, using Reference Service Director Hamer's suggestion, could equate *inactive* with *noncurrent* records. In other words, the archivist decided that transferred materials could be somewhat actively used, so long as they were not among the currently compiled records of the originating agency. This was not an evasion, because had he done otherwise very few valuable documents less than fifty years old would have come within the reach of archival care and been available for research.[17] There was a problem that Solon Buck never resolved. Roosevelt had not warmed to him as he had to Robert Connor; their exchange of letters in November 1942 indicated that it was improbable that he ever would. Given the archivist's lukewarm relations with the White House and his difficulties with Senator Kenneth McKellar, he was unlikely to gain significant support in his quest for additional funds.

Buck and his agency, however, still had friends as well as enemies in the Budget Bureau. Those friends helped bring the bureau and the National Archives to agreement on records disposal legislation by February 1943. Except for the bureau's insistence that the National Archives Council's regulations for the disposition of records be subject to presidential approval, the proposed law was essentially what Buck had taken up with Budget Director Smith in August 1942. This meant he had won his main point that the heads of agencies not be given more authority to dispose of records without strict guidelines that the archivist could enforce. Alfred J. Elliott, the chairman of the House Committee on the Disposition of Executive Papers, introduced the bill in Congress in February 1943. His committee favorably reported the legislation to the House of Representatives in June. During the debate on the floor, the House amended the bill to provide that records concerning accounts or claims in which the federal government was involved could not be disposed of without the comptroller general's permission before the settlement of those claims or accounts. The House approved the amended legislation unanimously on 28 June and the Senate did likewise on 1 July. Six days later, President Roosevelt signed it into law. [18]

This Act Concerning the Disposal of Records of 1943 marked a major step forward in the development of effective management of federal records. The measure gave a broader, more exact definition of what constituted records, which was

all books, papers, maps, photographs, or other documentary materials, regardless of physical form or characteristics, made or received by any agency of the United States Government in pursuance of Federal law or in connection with the transaction of public business and preserved or appropriate for preservation by that agency or its legitimate successor as evidence of the organization, functions, policies, decisions, procedures, operations, or other activities of the Government or because of the informational value of data contained therein.

The new law also established a broader criterion for the preservation of records by replacing the old standard phrase, "permanent value or historical interest to the federal government" with "sufficient administrative, legal, research, or other value to warrant their continued preservation." These definitions were better than those stated in earlier legislation, though as it turned out they failed to cover all situations that would arise in archival and records administration. Definition of *records* continues to be somewhat of a problem at present.

Yet the heart of the new legislation was the section that facilitated the preparation of schedules for the disposal, after certain periods of time had passed, of records of specified character or form. The eventual result of this was the saving of immense amounts of time and effort by both the National Archives and the agencies of origin because huge amounts of identifiably useless papers could now be destroyed automatically once Congress had approved the schedules. Other provisions established improved guidelines for getting rid of records constituting a menace to health, life, or property; emergency disposition, when necessary, in wartime of federal documents located outside the country; simplification of standards for the photoreproduction of records slated for destruction; and facilitation of the disposal of other useless records. Altogether this legislation not only promoted greater progress in eliminating useless records but did so in a way that could achieve substantial savings of funds, space, equipment, and personnel and gave promise of speeding up the transfer of permanently valuable records to the custody of the archivist of the United States.[19]

Incidentally, the new law's requirement that the National Archives Council's regulations for the disposal of records be approved by the president posed no problem. The council met on 14 July, a week after the act was signed, and formally passed the regulations. They were: (1) agencies would submit schedules to the archivist, in accordance with his instructions, accompanied by samples of the items proposed for disposal; (2) after Congress, upon the archivist's recommendation, had authorized destruction, the head of the agency involved would cause the indicated records "to be sold as waste paper," "to be destroyed," or "to be transferred" to any other government unit or "appropriate educational institution, library, museum, or historical, research, or patriotic organization" within the United States; (3) photographic reproduction of records would be done according to technical standards approved by the National Bureau of Standards and so that the usability and "integrity of the files will be preserved." On 20 July, without making any changes, President Roosevelt approved those regulations.[20]

The Act Concerning the Disposal of Records led to no records revolution, however, for neither the National Archives nor other federal agencies had the personnel to take full advantage of the legislation. Indeed, by November 1944 disposal schedules had been prepared for only twenty-six agencies and significant numbers of records were involved in only six. Solon Buck desperately sought an additional congressional remedy for this "wasteful and uneconomical" situation. He requested the Budget Bureau's approval for legislation that would speed up the scheduling of records for disposition. This involved preparation of schedules that would cover "housekeeping" records of limited usefulness that were commonly created by several or all federal agencies such as those dealing with routine personnel, property, and fiscal affairs. These "general schedules," as they were called, not only could facilitate the disposition of records for destruction, transfer to the archives building, sale, or gift, but they could encourage greater cooperation from other federal agencies since they would largely be prepared by the staff of the National Archives. The general schedules could also apply to the records of discontinued agencies, which were papers that had been in limbo so far as disposition was concerned. The Budget Bureau speedily assented, making only a few minor changes, and the legislation was introduced into Congress in January 1945. It became law on 7 July as a series of amendments to the 1943 records disposal legislation.

The National Archives did not invent the concept of disposal schedules, for it had turned up earlier in professional literature and occasionally in the practice of governments in the United States and elsewhere, though never before with such broad applicability. The idea of a general schedule, however, that would cover the common records of two or more or all agencies of a government, was not only new but awesome in scope when applied to a government as large as that of the United States. Its potential for savings was great, as was its promise for effectively earmarking material of archival quality. Of course, it would take time to realize the potential and to reap the promise, thanks to the large mass of records involved and the parsimony of the government in implementing general scheduling. But it would come. Even if general

schedules had to be revised more often than was originally anticipated, it was worth the effort. The other goal of the 1945 records
disposal amendments was important, too. From the beginning the
matter of handling the records of the dozens of terminated federal
agencies had been a perplexing one at the National Archives. The
archivist could not legally take such materials into full custody;
even when Congress had designated successor agencies, those agencies had no legal right to dispose of the records that they had
inherited. The 1945 amendments ameliorated the problem by authorizing the archivist and the successor agencies to arrange for
the disposition of the records of discontinued offices.[21] Thus, it
was possible to solve a knotty problem, although negotiations
between the National Archives and the successor agencies sometimes proved sticky.

However important the Act Concerning the Disposal of Records and its amendments would ultimately prove to be, they were
only part of the program of the National Archives in 1943–45 to
deal with the costly problems posed by the government's 16,000,000
cubic feet of records and their annual growth of about 1,000,000
cubic feet. The agency had been crusading for the appointment of
departmental records officers, for the development and distribution of knowledge to help them, and for channels through which
they could exchange information and ideas. By 1943 those approaches had made a dent in federal records problems. The rein-
vigoration of the National Archives Council and its conversion
into something of a records council further contributed to the
coordination of the records administration programs of various
agencies. That was done not only by using the alternates of the
council's members to attend meetings, beginning in July 1942, but
also by making sure that some of these delegates were departmental records or historical officers. By then these alternates included
Helen L. Chatfield of the Treasury Department, Emmett J. Leahy
of the Navy Department, E. Wilder Spaulding of the State Department, and Thomas W. Spaulding of the War Department. These
and other delegates who later joined them on the council helped
considerably to simplify regulations pertaining to the transfer of
materials to the archivist's custody; the council also struck a blow

for principle by declaring that "any archives or records that have been in existence for more than fifty years" be transferred to the archives building unless the head of the agency involved certified that they were needed for the conduct of current work. Equally important, the National Archives Council helped to frame the 1943 records disposal legislation and its amendments, and it generally advised the archivist about records problems.[22]

Philip C. Brooks spearheaded the records administration activities of the National Archives during the war. He worked under several titles, first as assistant director of records accessioning and preservation, then as assistant director of operations, and finally as records appraisal officer. Brooks basically developed the "life-span" concept of records administration, as we have seen, and he constantly publicized the idea that records could be made more functional and less expensive to maintain through well-planned records administration programs. He promoted the appointment of records officers in federal agencies. In this he emphasized that such officers, for economy's sake, should have "either direct supervision over, or the authority to coordinate, line activities in the preparation of documents, handling of mail, filing, servicing the files, and the retirement of records." Brooks also contended that the work of agency historical officers should be coordinated with that of records officers so that between them the identification and preservation of records of archival quality could be enhanced.[23]

Brooks spurred his colleagues in the National Archives to become part of his and Buck's crusade for improved management of records in the federal government. He recognized that some archivists were reluctant to involve themselves because they "link missionary work with lunatic fringe activities" or because they "hesitate to spread our restricted resources too thinly over too broad a field." His answer was "that selling the agencies good records administration now will save us costly weeding and other wasteful processes in the future." Brooks conceded that the management of records in the agencies would most often be carried out according to their definition of a good program instead of that of the National Archives. The important thing, however, was to get records administration programs going, "hammer the main principles," give more "concrete advice" on what constituted a good overall program, and "try to reconcile the differences" in approaches. To do otherwise would be to risk losing the battle to paper. Buck fully backed Brooks in his efforts. In September 1943 he established a conference on records administration within his agency. Its goal was to encourage the members of his staff to pool their intellectual resources so that they could improve their ability to cope with the government's records problems. The archivist constantly urged the staff members of the National Archives to contact personnel of other agencies in order to promote good records-administration programs and practices. To Buck's way of thinking, one could not go too far in making archivists conscious of the need to "pay attention to the whole spectrum of records."[24]

One of the archivist's special concerns was to make official Washington immediately aware that the termination of emergency agencies after the war would present "unmanageable" problems, not only because of the mammoth size of their records, but also because it was questionable who would see that such materials were adequately administered. By August 1944 Buck believed that he had made the Budget Bureau aware of this situation. He was probably premature in his assessment of its understanding, for in September the Budget Bureau asked the National Archives, as it did other executive agencies, for its plans to reduce postwar operations to "a peace footing." One can imagine the archivist fuming over the sending of this letter to any agency whose personnel had been dangerously cut back as a consequence of the war. Nevertheless Buck exploited the requirement to reply in order to state a strong case for the National Archives' need to expand as soon as possible to meet peacetime needs. He pointed out to Budget Director Smith in October that the quantity of federal records had more than doubled during the past eight years, and that it would be expensive to handle them effectively. The alternative to their proper administration would be even more costly. Indeed about $6,000,000 alone would be needed annually for the bare maintenance of the orphaned records of the some eighty temporary wartime agencies. Buck declared that the National Archives, with fewer personnel available than five years before, was handling a work load 325 percent greater. Without additional funds there was no way that his agency could continue what it was doing, catch up on its ever increasing backlog, and deal with the anticipated growth in its postwar functions.[25]

The Budget Bureau asked the archivist to elaborate on his statement. That he did in December. He recalled the fate of the records of the government's World War I emergency agencies, which had been dispersed throughout various successor offices and later reassembled only with great labor so that they could be of value during World War II. "Every effort possible should be exerted to prevent a recurrence of that unfortunate experience with respect to the records of this war." That, he asserted, would conform "to the apparent intention of Congress and to the expressed policy of the President." Having been discouraged by the Budget Bureau from expecting significantly higher appropriations, Buck therefore emphasized that legislative remedies would be useful, referring to what was to become the 1945 amendments to the records-disposal legislation of 1943.[26] It was plain that he was forced to look for promissory notes instead of coin.

Despite the obstacles placed in his way, Buck was not discouraged. The National Archives vigorously pursued the preservation of archival material and the improvement of records administration during 1944 and 1945. The agency undertook, in various ways, to prevent overzealous civil servants from contributing unassessed records to wartime scrap paper drives. The archivists also dealt rather effectively with the records of agencies that would be terminated at war's end, partly through legislation and partly through negotiations with the officials of such offices and of the Budget Bureau. All this, of course, was in addition to the National Archives' continuing efforts to advise federal agencies on systematic records administration and to provide pertinent literature such as its fifty-page publication of 1945, *How to Dispose of Records: A Manual for Federal Officials*.[27]

Any assessment of the role of the National Archives in forwarding effective records-administration programs for the federal government would have to be both encouraging and discouraging. Plainly, the agency played the central part in starting such programs. The National Archives also aided considerably in the emergence of another profession dealing with documentary materials, that of records management. Considering the agency's small budget and the fact that records problems were already out of hand before the war began, these were weighty contributions. The National Archives, however, rarely was able to serve beyond being the consultant at large and the promoter par excellence. Therefore, the agency could not direct what it had set in motion. The results were bound to be some confusion and waste during the early years of federal records administration. In one way this was just as well: by fathering another kind of archivist, the records manager, the National Archives would learn as much as it taught. It was only fair that the agency's erstwhile archival amateurs, who had accomplished so much because they had been unfettered by dogma, did not dictate to those in the new profession of records management.

One cannot end the early story of the National Archives and records management without looking more closely at what records officers did. In many cases this resulted from the concern of agency records managers to share what knowledge there was with each other and with the National Archives. This was most notably seen in the activities of Helen L. Chatfield, the archivist and records officer of the Department of the Treasury, who inaugurated and for many years taught the American University's courses on records management. Thanks to the volume and quality of her teaching, writing, and talks, her influence was tremendous. Chatfield never saw herself as the exclusive fount of wisdom, so she also constantly sought information and ideas from others in a one-woman quest to stimulate action, reaction, and interaction among archivists and records officers. Other persons who particularly deserve mention are Colonel Thomas M. Spaulding, who imaginatively coordinated the records activities of the Army; John S. Lucas, who pioneered various practices in files and records management in the Department of Agriculture; and his successor, Linwood E. Donaldson. These men, like Chatfield, were eager to share their experiences and to receive in return ideas from others in the rapidly expanding field of records administration.[28]

The work of National Archives personnel who took positions in records administration with other federal agencies was also highly significant. Emmett J. Leahy was the ranking figure here as indeed he was in the overall early development of records management. In September 1941 he accepted a commission in the Navy. He recruited a top-notch team of aides, including Herbert E. Angel, Robert H. Bahmer, and Everett O. Alldredge from the National Archives; and, with their help, he developed a signally successful records program in that service. Leahy's contribution went far beyond that, however, as he took every opportunity to spread his ideas around government and even business circles. He hit hard at the need to release expensive office space through the implementation of records-administration programs that would promptly eliminate useless records, reduce the bulk of many other records through the use of microphotography, and achieve space and personnel economies through more efficient use, shelving, and boxing patterns. The Adjutant General's Office in the War Department was but inches behind Lieutenant Commander Leahy and his crew in pioneering and adapting various records-management techniques. Although Colonel Spaulding was not an archival or records expert, he was an excellent administrator who learned quickly. One thing that marked him for distinction was his recruitment of an excellent staff that included Wayne C. Grover of the National Archives, who would succeed him, and later Robert H. Bahmer, who could employ his experiences from the Navy and the National Archives.[29]

The records center was the pioneering venture of the Navy and Army programs that probably had the greatest impact. The two military services, however, did not originate the concept of establishing an intermediate repository where aging records could be housed. Credit for that idea, or at least its dissemination, apparently belongs to the Belgian archivist Joseph Cuvelier, who discussed it as early as 1923. In the United States, historian Richard B. Morris deserves credit for publicizing the idea. He suggested a regional archival depository for the New York City area in 1937, and three years later, before the American Historical Association, Morris pleaded for "the rescue of tons of archival

material from the 'Stukas'" through decentralized housing and
the increased application of microphotography. There were also
those who, early in the war, had progressed from thinking about a
national hall of records to considering the establishment of a records center to take care of semiactive files. President Roosevelt
was among them, for he mentioned this to Robert D. W. Connor
in September 1941 as something that might develop under the
archivist's supervision, although not as an integral part of the
National Archives. Interestingly, the president was toying with the
idea of making the Pentagon building into a records center after
the war, a thought that seems whimsical in retrospect.[30]

It was the Navy, however, not the National Archives, that
established the first federal records center. That occurred in February 1942 after Leahy asked and received permission to find a
place to store semiactive naval records. His superiors told him to
examine a former brewery that the Navy was using for storage
purposes in Rosslyn, Virginia. It had insufficient room, however,
so he also acquired space in a Baltimore warehouse. During the
summer of 1942 Leahy's operations moved into a vacant garage in
Alexandria, Virginia. Cleaned up to insure the safety of the records,
the garage became a center for experimentation in how to shelve,
box, and administer large quantities of semiactive files until it was
replaced by better quarters in December 1943. The Army followed
with its own records center soon afterward as well as with its own
trailblazing records-management experiments. The results of the
Navy and Army programs were widely known throughout government because of the close relations between Leahy, Grover, the
National Archives, and records officers in other agencies. As for the
Navy and Army records centers, they were not exactly what Cuvelier or Morris or the proponents of a federal hall of records had in
mind. Leahy and Grover adapted such ideas to their agencies'
immediate needs. The results were, first, repositories for semiactive
records that could therein be handled efficiently and economically
with due regard for the intermediate preservation of material of
archival quality; and, second, repositories that could serve the
government's needs in various regions of the nation. Obviously,
the Navy and Army had established repositories that combined

the Belgian archivist's idea of an economical center for the storage of records of marginal value, the American historian's concept of regional archival repositories, and the hall-of-records approach of inexpensively dealing with semiactive records.

Other federal agencies adopted what the Navy and Army had pioneered, and by the war's end scores of government records centers were in operation. This development posed problems. The lack of overall supervision of such facilities led to widespread and often wasteful variations in management practices. Those centers, however, usually served to keep the government's growing mountains of records under better control than would otherwise have been true. As Bahmer later wrote, the rise of agency records centers, however trendy, made possible "a return to that excellent idea . . . that accessions should be planned" as well as to the idea of decentralizing research materials that were chiefly of regional or local value.[31]

The National Archives was caught up, too, in the records-center idea. The administrative staff frequently discussed it in one context or another. Executive Officer Collas G. Harris strongly supported the development of "a system of regional depositories" in 1942, declaring that planning should start on the type of building to be used. While Richard B. Morris was further urging in 1943 the establishment of regional records repositories, Program Officer Oliver W. Holmes of the National Archives proposed building centers in various areas to house some federal field office records. Indeed, he suggested the construction of regional repositories to contain federal and state records. Later that year Holmes proposed, at the annual convention of the American Historical Association, the establishment of a joint federal-state-local "archives center" in New York City.[32]

Holmes's public comments mirrored Buck's keen interest in area centers. When the National Archives' experiment with field representatives began in 1942, he had kept in mind the eventuality of some regional repositories. The press of business, insufficient appropriations, and dwindling staff, however, kept him from seeking such a program until the fall of 1944. Buck believed by then that it was "definitely desirable to open branches at several strategic locations that can serve as records retirement centers for the records of field offices of the various war agencies." That way those materials would not have to be brought to Washington for disposal, which would save on shipping costs and on space in the nation's capital. He also anticipated that area centers would become permanent repositories for records that would be needed in the regions. Knowing that a system of area centers could not spring to life full blown, the archivist contemplated the establishment of a repository on an "experimental basis" in New York City, in the hope that Congress would soon authorize funds for six to nine regional centers.[33]

As it turned out, Buck got encouragement for neither nine nor six centers nor for even one in New York City. He immediately changed his tactics and proposed acquiring an inexpensive building just outside of Washington to house noncurrent but semiactive federal records, of which he estimated there would be two million cubic feet by the end of the war. This proposal, too, was unsuccessful.[34] In short, the archivist had insufficient political capital left by the end of 1944. His squabble with Senator McKellar and his inability to establish rapport with President Roosevelt contributed to this situation. Then too, however rapidly agency records managers were growing as an element in governmental administration, they were not yet enough of a force to be helpful, and some of them undoubtedly believed that federal records centers should be under their control, not the archivist's. Probably most crucial to Buck's failure was that although many people in the Budget Bureau were interested in records administration, their ideas were not uniform. Moreover, there was a force in the bureau, largely in the person of Dr. John Keddy, that was unsympathetic to the National Archives having anything to do with semiactive records. Since Keddy was the budget officer chiefly in charge of matters concerning the National Archives, he was in a splendid position to block the development of that agency's budget and programs. Whatever the reason, records centers and indeed a more direct role in the management of federal records were several years away for the National Archives.

Edward G. Campbell was right when he wrote in 1944, "The

history of the National Archives has been one of experimental growth against a background of rapid expansion and alteration of government structure and function designed to meet the immediate needs of successive emergencies. Definitive orientation of the agency in its relations to scholarship and to the rest of the government has been impossible."[35] During World War II this was best seen in the efforts of the National Archives to make itself useful to the prosecution of the war and especially to stimulate the growth of records management in the federal government. As for the first, the agency did its bit; as for the second, despite overloads, backlogs, misunderstandings, and shortages of funds, the National Archives contributed importantly to keeping the government's records problem from growing completely out of hand. Like the constable of yore, the agency "saw its duty and it done it!" Duty done during the war, however, did not result in a cessation of emergencies for the National Archives in the future.

10. *Brave One World*

During the 1940s the National Archives was committed to keeping in close touch not only with people at home but also increasingly with those abroad who were concerned with the operations of research repositories. In the United States its relations with scholarly organizations remained intimate, and the agency found time to encourage the development of a new group, the American Association for State and Local History. The National Archives was also interested in assisting the development of archives. Therefore, correspondence between it and other archival agencies in the United States grew steadily from 1944 on.[1]

Moreover, the National Archives gave advice to a variety of Americans. These included the state archivist who wanted to know how to deal with flammable film, the publisher who had to cope with fungi in newsprint, the motor company that wanted to establish an archives, the historical society that had a problem with water-damaged newspapers, the architects who were interested in records fumigation facilities, the register of deeds who was concerned with records photography, and the private collector who wanted to laminate his manuscript collection. For these and hundreds of other inquirers, the agency had become the clearinghouse for a variety of information.[2] This kind of activity, as well as cooperation with scholarly organizations and other archivists, was an integral part of the work of the National Archives during the 1940s, and it would continue to be so. The vision of Robert Connor, Solon Buck, and others that their agency would be the grand leader in American archival affairs was being fulfilled.

A nagging concern, dating back to the prewar period, that

scholars would not make full use of the materials in the archives building, persisted, though. In 1943 Special Assistant Dorsey Hyde, Jr., suggested that the National Archives could guide researchers to certain valuable subjects that could be richly documented, for example, histories of federal agencies, efforts to reorganize the government, key industries, and federal-state relations. Later that year Dan Lacy went a step further, arguing that traditional historical approaches were inadequate in dealing with the masses of archival material available and in exploring broad and significant topics. He thought that the solution was for archivists "to work out a sound methodology for the use of modern records in research and demonstrate it to other social scientists." Buck agreed enthusiastically.[3]

It was plain, despite Buck's enthusiasm, that the National Archives could not do such things until after the war. Yet even then the agency was unable to initiate any new departure in research techniques. Whatever was done to stimulate the use of federal archives was along lines that had been charted before the war. In other words, archivists continued to publicize the materials in their custody and occasionally to recommend topics for research. These ways fell short of what archival administrators wanted, but they generated good publicity for the National Archives.[4]

Private scholars also assisted this work. W. Turrentine Jackson, for example, chided historians for making little use of the agency's vast resources concerning the Great Plains and the Far West. In a survey of historical journals, he found that "less than seventy-five studies based on federal government records . . . relating to the Trans-Mississippi West have been published since 1934 in the national historical review and in regional journals." Those came from the pens of fewer than twenty-five contributors.[5]

The National Archives never gave up trying to make American scholars more oriented toward research. The most important of its efforts after the war was the 684-page *Guide to the Records in the National Archives* (1948), which was published with the goal of giving researchers a better idea of the holdings in the archives building. Yet after 1948 the staff less frequently wrote articles on the materials in their custody. To spread the word of their holdings they came to rely more on lists of accessions in scholarly journals and the agency's own bulletin, *National Archives Accessions*, which by 1954 also began to carry articles reflecting the applicability of government records. The end of the war also permitted the National Archives to turn out additional guides to the records in its custody, including preliminary inventories, special lists, and reference information circulars. These proved to be of considerable assistance to both staff and researchers. Whatever the cause, the use of federal archives rose substantially during the postwar years. The number of reference services furnished by the National Archives mounted from 237,757 to 473,658 between fiscal years 1945 and 1953, and private researchers accounted for even more of this increase than did government inquirers. Although reference services declined for several years after 1953, they never fell anywhere close to the peak figure of the 1940s, which was 377,135 registered in 1949.[6]

The coming of peace also allowed the National Archives to play a highly significant role in international archival affairs. By 1945, for example, government-supported fellowships were being offered to Latin Americans for in-service archival training in the United States. Within a few years a number of Latin Americans had used these fellowships, and archivists from other lands, including Canada, China, and India, had received similar training on a nonfellowship basis. Moreover, with the end of hostilities requests from abroad for publications of the National Archives greatly expanded and archivists began to come from all over the world to visit the agency for tours of inspection.[7]

Like so many other Americans, Solon J. Buck had become enamored of the idea of international cooperation. The archivist's first step, taken in conjunction with Program Adviser Oliver W. Holmes, was to propose the establishment of an archives for the United Nations. As they saw it, such an agency could serve not only as the repository for documentation of existing international organizations, but also for the archives of defunct international offices and for "other records of international interest and importance that cannot logically be placed in the permanent custody of any one national government."[8]

Buck and Holmes presented their proposal on behalf of the National Archives to the State Department in October. The department forwarded it to the American delegation to the United Nations Assembly, which in turn brought it to the attention of the international organization's secretariat. Meanwhile, the United Nations was developing an archives unit under the interim direction of Arvid Pardo. The proposal, the follow-up efforts of the National Archives, and Pardo's work impressed various officials of the secretariat who recognized their need for a professional archival operation. The result was that in fall of 1946 the United Nations formally established its archives and Robert Claus went from the National Archives to direct it. Although the United Nations Archives did not become the wide-ranging repository that Buck and Holmes had envisioned, it quickly developed into a highly competent and influential archival agency.[9]

During 1946 the National Archives became involved in a variety of projects abroad. These included encouragement of studies of the best ways to protect records from the ravages of war; contacts with archivists in occupied lands, especially Germany; and Roscoe Hill's tour of Latin American archives. The archivist's chief effort, however, was reserved for his presidential address, "The Archivist's One World," to the Society of American Archivists in Washington in October. There Buck repeated his plea for the establishment of an agency to preserve the archives of all international organizations, but he took a giant step further. He contended that "civilization rests squarely on documents and that its preservation and improvement depends in large part on the preservation, improvement, and effective utilization of man's cultural heritage of documents." Therefore, government archivists everywhere should be concerned with the integrated preservation of the "archives of mankind." This could be best facilitated, Buck declared, by an international association of archivists. Such a society could foster not only better care of government archives on all levels, but better service to all users of official records.[10]

Buck's idea of an international association of archivists was not new. There had been attempts in that direction before World War I, but, as Sir Hilary Jenkinson said, they were neither "very successful" nor "sufficiently representative." Efforts to promote international archival cooperation during the 1930s had been more promising, but the coming of World War II put an end to them. What Buck did was to provide the initiative to renew that cooperation on a more highly organized basis and with a rationale that placed greater emphasis on freedom of access for researchers. The beginning of this work, of course, had been the National Archives' proposal of October 1945 to establish a United Nations archives. As time passed, Buck became certain that more could be achieved, for archivists badly needed information on how to rehabilitate war-damaged archives, to deal with rapidly mounting quantities of records, and to employ new technical approaches in their work. He and his American colleagues believed that such data could best be exchanged through an international professional association.[11]

With all this in mind, the National Archives, with the support of the SAA and the Library of Congress, had already prepared a proposal to follow up on Buck's October 1946 address to the society. This document was entitled *A Proposed Archives Program for the United Nations Educational, Scientific, and Cultural Organization*, which UNESCO considered in Paris at its first general conference in November and December 1946. The proposal called upon UNESCO not only to establish an archives for its own records but also, more importantly, to sponsor an international archival association and to call a world congress of archivists for 1947. UNESCO responded favorably to this proposal.[12]

The formation of what would be called the International Council on Archives moved fairly expeditiously. After a visit from Edward J. Carter of UNESCO, Solon Buck agreed to canvass by summer of 1947 leading archivists in various countries as to what should be the new association's purpose, basis of membership and representation, and organizing procedure. Buck used the replies to his inquiries to make preparations for a small organizational meeting of archivists in Paris under UNESCO's auspices. The archivist; the SAA's International Affairs Committee, of which Oliver W. Holmes was chairman; and Colorado State Archivist Herbert O. Brayer, who was UNESCO's archival consultant, were instrumental in preparing a draft constitution for the new association. The organizational meeting took place 9–11 June 1948. It was technically a convocation of a prewar archival liaison group, the Committee of Experts, and included representatives from Czechoslovakia, France, Great Britain, Italy, Mexico, the Netherlands, Norway, and the United States. Australia, UNESCO, and military occupation authorities in Germany had observers on hand. The Committee of Experts quickly founded the International Council on Archives and spent most of their time discussing the draft constitution. That document was adopted largely as originally written, although amendments were carried that restricted the membership chiefly to top administrative officers of governmental archival institutions and established voting rights by national representatives only. Thus was formed a vehicle for exchanges of information and opinions among the world's archivists with the aims of improving the preservation of archives and facilitating their use.[13]

During the next two years the ICA's leadership was mainly occupied with making preparations for the First International Congress of Archivists. That meeting took place in Paris, 21–26 August 1950, and was attended by some 350 archivists from thirty countries. The representation from the United States was small but conspicuous, including Buck; his successor as archivist of the United States, Wayne C. Grover; Oliver W. Holmes; and Illinois State Archivist Margaret C. Norton. They succeeded in expanding the ICA's voting basis, so that important repositories in addition to national archival agencies were enfranchised. The Americans were less successful with their substantive resolutions. Even though the congress established a special committee to study the preservation of archives during times of war, it failed to set up a committee to formulate standards to allow scholars greater access to archives, although the delegates approved the idea in principle. Principle was not enough, however, for researchers rarely saw any loosening of restrictions during the 1950s.

The 1950 congress discussed three other subjects close to the hearts of Americans: microphotography, the control of the creation of records, and the establishment of repositories for semicurrent records. And discussion was all that happened then, for most repositories were either unable or unwilling to make rapid advances in those areas. In retrospect, however, talk represented progress. After all, archivists elsewhere had first to educate themselves in such matters and then to work out the ramifications in terms of their agencies' individual missions and resources. The Americans would have been unrealistic and unreasonable if they had expected their colleagues abroad to have plunged into those things without giving them considerable thought.[14]

The Americans had contributed much, however. The International Council on Archives would grow into an effective organization for the exchange of ideas and information. Not only would there be the quadrennial archival congresses and the more frequent meetings of the executive board, but, in 1951, the ICA and UNESCO would launch a valuable annual publication, *Archivum, Revue Internationale des Archives*. The ICA would also within a few years sponsor the Round Table on Archives in order to provide an annual forum for archivists. The results of these activities were impressive. During the two decades following the ICA's founding, most archival institutions, with its encouragement, advanced significantly in the areas of preservation, disposal, reproduction, space utilization, and even preparation of guides. The ICA successfully pressed the compilation of bibliographies on archival administration and lists of repositories, and it promoted the availability of technical literature. All this, as well as the organization's meetings, was particularly helpful in the development of archival agencies in the many new nations founded after the end of World War II.[15]

It is not surprising that the development of the Cold War affected the ICA as well as the national antagonists involved. The second edition of the *Great Soviet Encyclopedia*, published in 1950, attacked the National Archives as the creature of "monopolistic capital" to help strengthen the bourgeois state. As for the ICA, it was viewed as an imperialistic American tool. Americans rarely had sharp words for archivists and historians in Communist countries, but they were reluctant to cooperate with them. Nevertheless, detente developed among Communist and non-Communist archivists more quickly than it did in most other sectors of human endeavor. Therefore, as early as the meeting of the Third International Congress of Archivists, held in Florence in September 1956, representatives of the Soviet Union and most of its allies in Europe were in attendance. Indeed, by 1961, when the ICA's Round Table met in Warsaw, it was clear that the organization was not ideological in scope and composition.[16]

Ironically, as the Communist nations began to take their place in the ICA, countries in the Western Hemisphere, including the United States, were becoming less of a factor. Americans served as officers, and they continued to make proposals for international archival activity, to cooperate in ICA projects, and to publish in *Archivum*. The big problem was that archivists from the Western Hemisphere often could not find funds to attend the meetings of the ICA, which were held almost exclusively in Europe. For example, it was not until 1961 that a representative from the United States, Ernst Posner, attended a meeting of the ICA Round Table. The Round Table also presented another problem. That was that its official language was French, which few American archivists spoke with any degree of proficiency.[17] Nevertheless, the influence of Americans and especially of the National Archives was still felt in the ICA and among other archivists in the world. This was partly because American innovations could not be ignored elsewhere and partly because of other international activities of archivists in the United States.

The UN and UNESCO were not the only international organizations affected by the National Archives. Two of the American agency's employees, Arthur Leavitt and Henry Edmunds, became, respectively, archivist of the United Nations Relief and Rehabilitation Administration and chief of the records division of the International Monetary Fund. The National Archives also maintained liaison with both American and German archival authorities in occupied Germany. Solon Buck was highly active in Latin American affairs in 1947 and 1948. This included his work as a member of the new Inter-American Committee on Archives and his tour of archival and other cultural institutions in Cuba, the Dominican Republic, and Haiti.[18]

During the late 1940s and early 1950s the National Archives received an increasing number of inquiries as well as visits from people from other countries. The requests were far from routine. An Australian business firm wanted to know about the effects of ozone on paper, and a Scotsman needed information about dealing with illegible documents. The most dramatic inquiry was from Israel, concerning "disinfecting soiled and blood stained documents, and . . . exterminating all kinds of insects in the Army archives." (The National Archives sent the Israelis a suitable reply, although someone placed the correspondence in the domestic section of the files, probably on the same principle that led to the filing of Puerto Rican matters in the foreign category.) There was also keen interest abroad in the SAA's quarterly, the *American Archivist*. By 1951 119 foreign members and subscribers received the journal; by 1970 the number of foreign memberships had risen to 370 in some fifty-six countries. Since 1949, when Karl L. Trever became the editor, members of the National Archives' staff edited the *American Archivist*. Thus there was no question of the quarterly's importance as a channel of international as well as national communication for the National Archives and other American repositories. And communication went not just one way internationally, for after World War II the *American Archivist* listed large numbers of foreign publications and foreign archivists occasionally contributed articles and book reviews.[19]

The international influence of the *American Archivist* was based largely on its position as a showcase for the most varied and technically advanced professional information. This was also true of archival education in the United States in the decade after the war. And archival education then meant the courses offered under the supervision of Ernst Posner by the American University. Other educational institutions entered the field, but at this time they were either copies of the American University's offerings or they catered largely to local clienteles. What was important about American's courses was that they quickly incorporated new advances in archival administration and related areas and that they took advantage of the unparalleled facilities of the National Archives, the Manuscripts Division of the Library of Congress, and the Maryland Hall of Records. Thus this program became the Mecca for those who wanted training in the most up-to-date archival operations. The significant contributions of the National Archives to this program made it another channel of communication for the agency with archival institutions all over the world. Thanks to his inestimable abilities, Professor Posner became a linchpin between the National Archives and archivists in various other nations. He left all with whom he came in touch the better for the meeting. And this applied especially to the National Archives, which could count upon him to serve with distinction in the separate roles of its unofficial ambassador to others and the resident commissioner of others to itself.

The National Archives' growing influence in the archival world thus was exerted through its staff's publications, the SAA, personal and postal contact, the ICA, training programs, and by example. The results were manifold. In some cases, as in Ghana and India, they were seen in the adoption of the name *National Archives*. American influence in the early volumes of the new international journal *Indian Archives* was also considerable.[20] Such influence and indeed its growing mutual character was seen particularly in Canada.

Canadian archivists shared many attitudes with their cousins to the south. Because of that and a rising level of government support, the Public Archives of Canada was well prepared to implement selected ideas germinated in the United States as well as to foster constructive criticism. This sharing proceeded slowly until the appointment of William Kaye Lamb as dominion archivist in 1948. Within two years Canada had authorized the construction of a federal records center, which was completed in 1955. This Public Archives Records Centre operated basically along American lines as an intermediary repository designed to begin systematic transfer of records of limited value and to earmark materials for permanent preservation. Yet the PARC also managed its affairs with adjustments to national conditions and with improvements devised by Canadians. While it was under construction, other developments took place in the Public Archives of Canada, borrowing heavily upon American experience. Preliminary inventories gradually replaced calendars as basic finding aids. Moreover, archives and manuscripts were reorganized into record groups "somewhat after the pattern adopted by the National Archives of the United States," as Archivist Lamb wrote. Further steps were taken by 1957 to implement a records-management program by the development of retention schedules for federal records. Finally, nine years later, an Order in Council gave the dominion archivist full authority over the scheduling of records for transfer, retention, and destruction; the appraisal of agency records management practices; and over the establishment of guides, standards, and training. Canada had in a mere score of years gained an integrated records and archives program that became the envy of most other nations, including in some respects the United States.[21]

In building its archival system, Canada had consciously rejected most British and French influences. And make no mistake, there was competition for world archival leadership among England, France, and the United States. American archivists were keenly aware of the differences between their system and those of England and France. France rested largely on its laurels, quietly trying to preserve its prewar archival eminence. England, under the leadership of Sir Hilary Jenkinson, was more aggressive, but it lost much of its influence because it was archivally less systematized than France. Fervently, the Americans sought to forge ahead with their many new ideas and techniques. The times were right for their success; new nations needed help in establishing their archival systems and older countries were struggling to keep abreast of their mounting quantity of records.

American archivists were sure that the more traditional techniques of English and French archivists and those elsewhere who followed their leadership would fail to meet modern needs. Philip C. Brooks, in a review of Hilary Jenkinson's *111th Report of the Deputy Keeper of Records*, indicated this. Brooks's praise of the professionalism of English archivists did not obscure his essential question: Could they meet the needs of scholarship and government by remaining largely aloof from responsibility for how public agencies managed their records?[22] It seemed obvious that the English position led not only to tardiness in transferring records to archival care, but it also ensured that too many records would be badly handled and even lost before archivists took custody of them.

A more trenchant critic was Director of Archival Services Theodore R. Schellenberg of the National Archives. He had risen through the ranks to head, beginning in 1949, the agency's strictly archival operations. In that position he had had considerable success in reorganizing the archives branches so that they could recover the ground lost during the financial stringency of the 1940s. By 1954 Schellenberg was ready to seek other pastures, and his first venture was in Australia. The Australians had for some time been concerned with developing a system of their own instead of adapting English ideas. This had led to the creation of the Commonwealth Archives Commission in 1942, which had increasingly looked to the United States for inspiration, particularly in dealing with the problem of semicurrent records for which Jenkinson and his disciples had no solution. This interest led Australians to request that an American be dispatched to deliver lectures on archival topics. Schellenberg was chosen for the task, and he arrived in 1954 to spend several months supported by Fulbright funds speaking to and with Australian archivists, civil servants, librarians, and scholars. He also found time to visit New Zealand and several Asian and European nations. He consciously avoided parading American archival practices as being better than those of other countries, and he tried to learn as much as he was teaching. What Schellenberg emphasized was that ways had to be found to take care of the problems posed by the nature and frightening proliferation of modern records. He also pointed up the American view that administrators and archivists had to know the values of proper records management and to keep in mind the need for research access to records in devising new programs.[23]

The impact of Schellenberg's visit was tremendous. The archivist of the University of Sydney, David S. MacMillan, described the visit as the "single most important event in the recent history of archival development in Australia." There is no doubt of the truth of that statement, particularly in view of Australia's greater concern for the use of American records management methods and the detaching of archives from libraries. The Australians, however, were not uncritical in considering those ideas. Indeed they were to become among the most searchingly constructive critics of American practices. It is also possible that Schellenberg's sidetrip to New Zealand was connected with that nation's decision in 1955 to rename its archival establishment the National Archives. Yet American influence had preceded him there, for in 1953 New Zealand issued its first preliminary inventory, which basically followed the form of those of the National Archives of the United States.[24]

Schellenberg's time in Australia had much broader impact, however, because of his subsequent activities. Early during his stay there, he wrote to a friend, "I'm tired of having an old fossil cited to me as an authority in archival matters. I refer to Sir Hilary Jenkinson . . . who wrote a book that is not only unreadable but that has given the Australians a wrong start in their archival work." A person of consuming passions throughout his career, Schellenberg now added another one. He would use his Australian lecture drafts and seminar statements as the basis for a book that would replace Jenkinson's *Manual of Archive Administration* as the seminal work on the subject in the English language. The result was Schellenberg's *Modern Archives: Principles and Techniques*, which was published in 1956 in Australia and the United States.[25]

It is a matter of personal opinion whether Jenkinson's book or Schellenberg's is the less readable. It is certain, however, that neither would be a contender for even a local literary prize. That is a shame, for the Englishman could write charmingly and the American passionately upon less technical matters. Be that as it may, Schellenberg's *Modern Archives* became the chief work on archival administration during his generation, not only in English-speaking lands but in many other countries, too, as it was translated into several other languages. The reasons for its success are easily discovered. Schellenberg provided not only a history of the development of modern national archival institutions, but he also formulated a model for how a modern archival agency should operate regardless of whether it followed the European registry system or pragmatic policies like those of the Americans. His concern was how to meet current challenges on the basis of present practices and resources, not starting over again from scratch. Indirectly, and sometimes directly, Schellenberg sharply criticized the ideas of European archivists and especially those of Jenkinson. It could not be assumed, he emphasized, that administrators would make correct decisions as to what records had enduring value to all who might be concerned. Archivists had to establish appraisal standards and they had to be concerned with the entire process of the keeping of records from their creation to either their destruction or preservation.

Schellenberg was trying to encourage archivists to be more than people who sat in their repositories awaiting the next shipment of old records for processing and then waiting again until a researcher asked them if they had X, Y, or Z on hand. Archivists had to take a role in the entire business of records management in order to ensure that archives would be preserved; they had to use the most up-to-date methods of appraising, preserving, and arranging records of enduring value; they had to make sure that the archives were effectively made available to researchers. All of this called for new, expanded, and vigorous methods of operation. It also required additional resources, which archivists should not be reluctant to seek if they were to serve many publics and to keep themselves and their clients from being swamped by superfluous paper. Schellenberg further endeavored in *Modern Archives* to perk up the pride of archivists. He was aware that many of them suffered from doubts that they were appreciated, that scholars often viewed them as third-rate historians, that librarians saw them as fellow librarians of very limited scope, and that government officials considered them as a kind of file clerk. This he tried to counter by showing archivists a world in which they combined the skills of exacting scholars, reference specialists, efficiency experts, and administrators in the quest to keep the circulatory systems of scholarship, government, and society itself functioning.[26] He may not have been entirely successful in curing the inferiority complexes of some archivists, but he did bolster their faith in themselves and in the significance of their profession.

Schellenberg's trip to Australia was just one of the first by an employee of the National Archives and Records Service seeking to spread American archival views abroad through teaching. In 1955 John P. Harrison carried on some of this during his nine-month tour of Latin America. There were also the trips of Herbert E. Angel and Arthur E. Young of the Records Management Division and Philip C. Brooks of the San Francisco Federal Records Center in 1954. From January to July Brooks taught a course to government employees at the University of Panama, and he gave other lectures there and advised Panamanians on many archival and records management questions. Thomas J. Pugliese, the records officer of the Atomic Energy Commission, served for three months in 1954 in a similar capacity in the Philippines, being succeeded by Arthur E. Young of the Records Management Division of NARS. The director of that division, Angel, spent the fall in Iran lecturing to graduate students and records personnel. All were enthusiastic about the results of their trips, which collectively represented a considerable American effort to strengthen public administration elsewhere.[27]

Schellenberg, as the theoretician-in-chief, had much to say about such undertakings. He stressed that America's archival ambassadors had to keep in mind that foreign systems were different from those at home. Whereas records in the United States were kept on the basis of diverse filing methods, most other countries used the registry system whereby documents were kept in numbered units with name indices keyed to the numbers. Backgrounds also varied greatly, for whereas archivists elsewhere often had much training in handling very old documents, Americans were more skilled in appraisal work and in dealing with modern records in bulk. Schellenberg saw American archivists and records managers as the wave of the future because of those things and because of their comparative liberality in allowing researchers access to materials. Yet, he cautioned, the American "is likely to learn as much as he is able to teach, and he should certainly learn before he ventures to teach."[28]

The activities of 1954 and 1955 were the beginning of an expanded program of teaching and learning by NARS officials. This included more visits abroad, clinics for foreign officials, and increased mailing of instructional materials and answers to specific technical questions. NARS also received considerable numbers of foreign visitors every year. For example, between August 1964 and May 1965, they came from Argentina, Australia, the British West Indies, France, Germany, Mexico, and Upper Volta; and, reflecting the archival detente between East and West, Czechoslovakia and Russia. The results of all this were varied. By 1960 Brazil's Arquivo Nacional had translated and published nine publications from the National Archives and the *American Archivist.* The Nigerian National Archives looked to the United States as well as to England and Southern Rhodesia for advice in constructing its new building. Moreover, the National Archives of Rhodesia and Nyasaland had established records centers and adopted a program of records management.[29]

Because of its proximity and possibly because the National Archives and President Roosevelt's Good Neighbor Policy had emerged at about the same time, Latin America had early drawn the attention of archivists in the United States. Roscoe Hill, John Harrison, Solon Buck, and Philip Brooks, among others, had served to conduct a Good Neighbor program for the National Archives. And the results were not negligible. During the 1940s and 1950s four Latin American nations had constructed modern archival buildings, the archivists of the Western Hemisphere had achieved closer relations, and Latin Americans had adopted a variety of North American techniques in dealing with documents. Yet many archivists in the Americas were not satisfied that the United States had done enough to help their colleagues to the south.[30]

Out of this came a visit by Schellenberg to Brazil in 1960, at the invitation of the archivist of that country, to study the situation there and to make appropriate recommendations. This stretched out to a three-month tour that included six other South American countries as well as Brazil. It was a busy trip for Schellenberg, for he delivered twenty-six lectures, visited forty-three cultural institutions, distributed archival literature that had been translated into Portuguese and Spanish (including his own *Modern Archives*), and offered advice freely, all in the cause of arousing sentiment for good archival and records management programs. He also promoted the Inter-American Archival Seminar that was to be held in Washington in 1961. In short, his trip had all the hallmarks of an archival tour à la Billy Graham.[31]

The Inter-American Archival Seminar was a considerable success. Sponsored by NARS, the State Department, the Pan American

Union, and the Rockefeller Foundation, it met from 9 to 27 October 1961, drawing forty-three archivists and historians from seventeen Latin American countries. The seminar also served to found the Inter-American Technical Council on Archives that promoted the establishment of archival associations, training programs, the publication of guides to archives, and a quarterly, *Boletín Informativo*.[32] Although the council was a promising program to spur further archival development in Latin America, it began to collapse after Schellenberg retired from the National Archives late in 1963. It was a worthwhile venture, however, for it forwarded a number of excellent projects that added to the education and professionalism of archivists throughout the Western Hemisphere.

Yankees are an impatient people, and this includes the archivists among them. Certainly, many American archivists in the postwar period expected that other nations would quickly adopt the ways and wares that they believed were needed everywhere. This did not happen, predictably so, given the pride, prejudices, principles, problems, and procedures of other peoples. Yet the Americans, however frustrated they felt in selling their ideas, however long it took them to perceive the problems of other people and the limitations of their own concepts, did not sour on trying to convince others. After a generation, the results were significant. Not only had a strong world organization of archivists been established but also substantial progress had been made in forwarding the use of new methods, particularly in terms of reproduction and preservation. And it was plain that many countries had adapted ideas from the United States about appraisal, guides, organization, and records management.

How interrelated much of this was is documented by Robert H. Bahmer's statement about the Third International Congress of Archivists. He wrote in 1957, "Almost everyone subscribed to the theory that the archivist should have a commanding voice in the matter of disposal. Many frowned on the present British proposal to allow administrators a free hand to discard records of no administrative interest after 5 years. Practically everyone uses some form of the record schedule or disposal list. Many have record centers." Even England showed signs of yielding. Soon after Sir

Hilary Jenkinson's retirement in 1954, the chancellor of the exchequer presented recommendations on records keeping to Parliament. This so-called Grigg Report suggested that there should be a high-level records administration officer in the Public Record Office. Although the office would have no central authority over departmental records, the report recommended that its records administration staff should work with other governmental units in dealing with records problems and that there should be records management officers in those agencies. The government largely implemented the Grigg Report in 1958 and thus provided some definition of records and the professional management of them. This action also set the standard of transferring documents to the Public Record Office normally thirty years after their creation. Although the new system increased the care of records, the British still, by the 1970s, had a long way to go in tightening up appraisal and disposition programs and in preparing to establish records centers.[33]

France was also something of an exception. Its highly complex, centralized, and multifunctional archival system had resisted most American ideas, although in one area, the photoreproduction of documents, France had as much claim to pioneering as did the United States. Nevertheless, the proliferation of records caused France's Directorate of the Archives in 1962 to begin the establishment of a huge records center in the *cité interministérielle*. New Zealand and West Germany also set up such centers, adapted from American models, to deal with the overflow of records and to provide better appraisal for materials that might be of archival quality. It was about these and similar developments elsewhere that the Dominion archivist of Canada, Wilfred I. Smith, wrote in 1972. He observed that the contribution of records management "to governmental and corporate efficiency and economy is now taken for granted in North America and is gradually being recognized in Europe." Spurred by such successes, American archivists and records managers, especially those from NARS, continued to reach out.[34]

Additional proof of their impact was that archivists in other countries felt increasingly free not only to make modifications in

American practices and concepts, but also to criticize them. Early they had doubts about using microfilm to preserve documents while destroying the originals. It was, as Robert W. S. Turner of the Central African Archives wrote, a "grave step," since one could not be sure how long the master negatives would last. Turner also pointed up some of the problems with lamination regarding flexibility and discoloration. NARS personnel conceded the validity of these questions but answered that they were giving them constant consideration. Peter J. Scott of Australia questioned the feasibility of the record group concept, especially since a given series could have been in and out of several agencies during its active lifetime.[35] Such discussion was a healthy sign, for it demonstrated the emergence of "One World" of archivists who shared concepts drawn from many nations and who were able to evaluate and debate new ideas professionally.

This world profession was by no means agreed on everything, nor should it have been. Many of the new ideas, whether from the United States or elsewhere, needed testing, and not all of them fitted everyone's needs anymore than everyone had the facilities and resources to utilize them. Yet the evaluation and discussion went on, to a considerable extent because American archivists pressed a variety of issues upon their colleagues in other lands. An example of this was the Extraordinary Congress of the International Council of Archivists held in Washington in 1966.

There is little doubt that Americans felt a bit left out of the ICA, which they considered their child. With this in mind, the archivist of the United States, Wayne C. Grover, sought in 1964 to have the next ICA congress held in Washington. When that proved impossible because the ICA had agreed that its 1968 congress would be held in Spain, Grover proposed a special congress in Washington for 1966. The ICA approved that. Soon, therefore, an organizing committee consisting of Archivist Grover, Librarian of Congress L. Quincy Mumford, Canadian Dominion Archivist W. Kaye Lamb, Kenneth W. Munden of NARS, and Morris Rieger of the National Historical Publications Commission began to prepare for the extraordinary congress.[36]

Some 175 delegates attended, representing fifty-three countries as well as UNESCO, the United Nations, the International Association for the Development of Libraries in Africa, and the Pan American Institute of Geography and History. The sessions lasted from 9 through 13 May. Lyman H. Butterfield, the editor of the Adams Papers series, led off the proceedings with an address in which he pressed for increased publication and photoduplication of archives and manuscripts with an attendant dropping of barriers to research access. W. Kaye Lamb followed with a report that was a survey of the widely different practices of archival institutions with respect to accessibility. The Dominion archivist recommended greater use of microfilming in order to safeguard original documents and to place more material at the disposal of scholars, and he suggested that restrictions on access be reviewed with the goal of their liberalization. Morris Rieger later recommended (1) the resumption and advancement of ICA's efforts to serve as a clearinghouse for finding aids and the publications of archives; (2) the expansion of cooperative international finding aids projects; (3) the creation by ICA of a cooperative program for microfilm publication of important series of documents then in various national custodies; and (4) the expansion of the UNESCO and ICA program of technical assistance for the training of archivists in Africa, Asia, and Latin America. All these Rieger saw as ways to promote increased research access to documents. Oliver W. Holmes, the director of the NHPC, and Albert H. Leisinger of NARS added remarks about publication and microreproduction practices.[37]

Although Americans and Canadians were proud of these comparatively liberal access policies and their advanced programs of documentary photoduplication and publication, it was surprising that they did not participate more in the discussions at Washington. Probably it was because they knew that archivists from other nations were sensitive in these matters, especially accessibility, and could raise a variety of reasons as to why greater progress could not be made in those directions. Thus the North Americans used the soft sell, and with some effect. The extraordinary congress went on record favoring liberalization of research access to archives and of equal access by researchers "irrespective of nationality." Moreover, the delegates expressed the wishes that the preparation of finding aids be accelerated, that microfilm and publication programs be promoted, and that technical archival assistance be advanced in developing nations.[38]

If the delegates did not ardently throw themselves into breaking down the barriers to access to research materials, they at least showed their recognition of the problem and their willingness to discuss it. UNESCO, under pressure from the ICA, additionally supported raising the standards of archival work in less developed lands. The ICA itself established committees on microfilming and on liberalization of access. The Microphotography Committee promoted the use of microreproduction in numerous ways, including the publication in 1968 of Albert H. Leisinger's *Microphotography for Archives*. Interestingly, a survey by the committee showed that of the fifty-six countries responding, archives in all but ten were prepared to do microfilming. Of the fifty responding as to the equal availability of microfilm copies of records to scholars and institutions, forty-three did so affirmatively. The Committee on Liberalization cautiously reported that progress was being made in increasing the access of archives to researchers.[39]

In 1968 the International Congress of Archives in Madrid moved to further progress in matters of accessibility and photo-reproduction. The delegates resolved that proposals should be made in the various nations to remove "all unjustified restrictions with the object of adapting the system of archival access to the needs of scholarly research." The congress also urged that microfilmed series be available for purchase as an additional way of promoting greater access; another resolution showing the influence of American experience and concern authorized a committee "to study, with respect to current records, problems of classification and filing and of appraisal for retirement." No one expected that these proposals would lead to great changes immediately, but it was clear that the currents of change were affecting archivists all over the world.[40]

Americans were cautious in assessing the results of the Washington extraordinary congress. As Morris Rieger wrote, much depended upon adequate financial support. He suggested, however, that since representatives of higher rank and from more nations attended that congress than any previous international archival meeting, what was discussed there might have considerable impact. Whatever the reason, archivists from many nations moved forward, however slowly, toward providing greater access to research materials, more use of microphotography, and the employment of records management in their operations. Some of this was attributable to additional funding from UNESCO and other sources and some to pressures from scholars. No small part of it, however, was attributable to the willingness of archivists to broaden their thinking as to their functions and methods.[41]

There is no doubt that the ICA facilitated these and other worldwide archival advances. The initiatives of the National Archives, which led to the organization's founding, had paid off for all concerned. After twenty years Solon J. Buck's "Archivist's One World" had largely been achieved. Charles Kecskeméti, the ICA's secretary, observed in 1969 that the number of countries represented in the organization had grown from thirty in 1950 to almost eighty. He added that the council's activities had become not only global but also livelier. As Archivist Robert Claus of the UN remarked, the ICA had gone a long way toward developing an "international community spirit among archivists," where "the barriers of distance, language, nationality, and ideology have all but disappeared."[42] No better sign of this could be found than the assignment, respectively, of Moscow and Washington as the sites for the world archival congresses of 1972 and 1976.

11. *Time of Troubles*

As World War II approached its conclusion, the staff of the National Archives brimmed over with ideas as to how to handle the many tasks confronting them. That reflected not so much innovativeness as the fact that their agency had fallen behind, thanks to wartime exigencies. It was unsurprising, therefore, the staff leaders argued, that advances had to be made in a great number of areas. These included records analysis and description, records management, preservation, packing, shelving, rehabilitation, and staff training as well as such long-range projects as documentary publication, file microcopies, establishment of a research journal, research in archival and records management. Archivist Buck brought his aides back to earth by stating that the agency was confronted with "an economy of scarcity." The question was, he declared, "What modifications . . . do we consider to be desirable even though we realize that an increase of one function means a necessary decrease elsewhere?"[1]

To be sure, 1945 to 1948, Solon Buck's remaining years as archivist of the United States, was a time of troubles. He was, however, a bit too dour in viewing what could be accomplished then. With skillful use of its personnel, the National Archives advanced along several fronts without always making equivalent retreats elsewhere. One of the areas in which the agency excelled was in keeping its existence known to the public. For example, as a result of its attractive exhibitions, the visitors to the National Archives numbered 77,000 in fiscal year 1945 and swelled to 154,000 the following year. Exhibits from the National Archives also took to the road with the displays in the Victory Loan Tour late in 1945, which were seen by almost 250,000 Americans; and more than 3,500,000 people viewed the documents on board the Freedom Train in 1947 and 1948. Supplementing the exhibits was the inauguration of the National Archives' popular program to sell facsimiles of historic documents such as the Bill of Rights, George Washington's oath of allegiance, and Mathew Brady's photographs.[2]

Another way in which the agency strove to maintain its visibility was through the works of its Federal Register Division. The division took on further responsibilities such as publishing for most federal agencies descriptions of their organization, procedure, and delegations of authority (beginning in 1946); and assuming two years later the publication of the *United States Government Manual*. Preparations were also made to issue a new *Code of Federal Regulations* in 1949, a task made more important by the Supreme Court's decision in 1947 that the administrative rules and regulations appearing in the daily *Federal Register* were legally binding. Administrative law was here to stay, and the Federal Register Division played a central role in sorting it out. However, the number of people affected by administrative law diminished after the war. Consequently, the paid circulation and thus the division's financial basis sharply declined from 13,631 to 5,300 between 1945 and 1948. Congress assumed the printing costs, but the National Archives had to supply from its own slender resources the staff needed to shoulder the division's continuing and additional responsibilities.[3]

Despite the war the file microcopy program had inched forward and by the end of fiscal year 1946 some 1,600 negative microfilm rolls of frequently requested documents existed. The National Archives, however, was unable to meet the demand for purchasing copies of them. Although another 530 rolls were added to the stock the following year, the agency was unable to fill all orders. A major change occurred in 1948 when Dallas D. Irvine led a successful campaign to procure $20,000 of support from the Rockefeller Foundation. With those funds and the publication of the *List of File Microcopies*, the program quickly became successful, for file microcopies allowed many scholars to save time and money by doing much of their research at home instead of traveling to Washington.[4]

The accessioning of archives did not continue at the frantic pace of the period between fiscal years 1941 and 1945. Nevertheless, the volume of records in the National Archives rose from 689,195 to 855,925 cubic feet between 1945 and 1948. Particularly noteworthy among the accessions were the increases in motion-picture film from about 7,500,000 to 35,366,400 running feet and in sound recordings from 95,000 to 259,000 discs. Moreover, the number of maps on hand rose from 404,455 to 478,000 and of still pictures from 1,200,000 to 1,424,642.[5]

The need to keep up with new accessions and with growing reference service demands made it difficult for the National Archives to deal with its backlog in other areas of activity. Some progress was made in boxing archives, so that the backlog of unpacked materials, which amounted to 114,000 cubic feet in 1946, was cut to 64,000 cubic feet by 1948. Preservation, however, remained a critical problem. The agency strained its resources between 1945 and 1948 in trying to make progress in flattening, laminating, and otherwise rehabilitating records. The greatest problem was that the proportion of archives requiring such services had increased substantially, with the result that relatively little was accomplished. In short, preservation as well as analysis and description remained critical areas because of the agency's inability to procure enough personnel to eliminate the backlog and to meet pressing current demands.[6]

It was because of the growth of records management that the National Archives' problems were not worse. Admittedly, its records-management efforts absorbed the services of a number of employees, which contributed to the shortage of staff in dealing with other challenges. It was, however, an investment repaid manyfold in terms of reducing the demands upon the agency for accessioning and government reference service. During the immediate postwar period, records management required a three-pronged attack: first, the tightening up of appraisal and accessioning policies; second, the search for additional inexpensive storage space;

and third, advancing the efforts of federal agencies in coping with records problems. The impetus for this attack was that the bureaucracy was threatened with being drowned in a flood of paper of its own making. As the archivist wrote in 1946, "probably more than 10,000,000 cubic feet of records were accumulated during the war. Buildings to house them permanently would cost at least $75,000,000. . . . Moreover the most diligent work could not make so gargantuan a mass usable." The problem, therefore, was to find ways to select from that mass those records that should be preserved and then to arrange adequate housing and care for them. This could be done with the expansion of records management, the proper use of disposal schedules, and adequate financial support for the National Archives in its battle against the paper flood.[7]

At the end of the war, Solon Buck rushed to clarify his agency's accessioning policies in order to slow down the influx of records of marginal value. Therefore, on 22 August 1945, he issued an official circular defining the accessioning regulations. Buck distinguished between current records (those used by the agency creating them for the purposes they were originally accumulated) and active records (those used by anyone for any other official purpose). His point was that current records were ineligible for accessioning. Another criterion was that accessionable records had to be of enduring (though not necessarily permanent) value "for administrative, legal, research, scientific, or other purposes." Thus the archivist announced that the National Archives intended to take a greater role in judging the value of acquisitions.[8]

With Buck's official circular showing the way, his staff set out to sharpen the criteria for appraising records that might be transferred to the National Archives. The key factors they considered were the legal and research importance of records, significance of the operations documented, avoidance of duplication of documentation, usability, arrangement, confidentiality, and even cost and volume. This work was not done mindlessly, for appraisal standards came in for a great deal of examination. Indeed, refinement and discussion continued endlessly and deservedly so, given the many interests involved.[9]

Although the National Archives was accessioning fewer though higher quality records after the war, although Buck reported in 1946 that the "seemingly endless pyramiding of Government records . . . has come to a stop," it was clear that the agency's space would soon be exhausted. Additional housing had to be found to care properly for records lest they be lost or damaged. During the war the National Archives had sought such space, but with scant success. The agency continued immediately after the war to request appropriations for the establishment of "field records retirement centers." By December 1945, however, the archivist decided to withdraw the request. This was done in the vain hope that additional funds might be authorized instead for personnel to meet pressing demands in the archives building, and it was based on the mistaken idea that the need for such centers would soon lessen.[10]

Obviously, Buck's decision did not dispose of the issue, for other agencies continued to overflow with records. This led archivists to two revised conclusions. The first one, arrived at without enthusiasm, was to endorse the establishment of additional records centers by other federal agencies. The second aim was to find more room for the National Archives' own operations. By late 1946 forty-three of its stack areas were still unequipped, but that did not stop the staff from storing archives there in whatever containers were available. Moreover, the capacity of the archives building was expanded from 962,000 to 1,045,000 cubic feet by the conversion of some offices and corridors to records storage space, and the weeding out of redundant materials later made room for another 14,000 cubic feet of archives. Such actions, however, only postponed the crisis.[11]

At the suggestion of the Public Buildings Administration, the National Archives also requested space in Suitland, Maryland. That soon led to the assignment of part of Federal Office Building No. 4 there for the storage of records that would require relatively little service. Thus, in July 1947 an area of about 39,000 cubic feet was added to the agency's capacity. This did not solve the problem, but it did point the way, for with the acquisition of the Suitland facility the National Archives was on the path toward operating its own records centers.[12] Given the realities of the time, it was accepting either that or the loss of its central role in federal records administration.

As much as anything else, pressing forward with a federal records-management program absorbed the time and interest of Buck. He spurred the National Archives to take advantage of the legislation of July 1945 that authorized the use of general schedules to provide for the automatic disposal of useless records of a character common to two or more or all federal offices. This innovative approach to disposing of such records would allow the government to deal better with the flood of paper that threatened to engulf it. The National Archives, however, made progress slowly. Only three general schedules dealing with routine types of personnel, postal, fiscal, and accounting records had been drawn up and approved by Congress by 30 June 1947. This number grew to six during fiscal year 1948. Unfortunately, shortages of staff made it impossible for the National Archives to forward general scheduling during the following year. The promise of general scheduling in dealing with the government's records glut was obviously great, but it was a promise that would not be substantially realized until the 1950s.[13]

There were some archivists who feared that too much emphasis was being placed on records administration. Solon J. Buck, however, did everything he could to advance the cause of records management during the immediate postwar period. Although his relationship with President Harry S. Truman was formal and remote, he did take the liberty of pressing on him the value of reading the first five pages of the archivist's eleventh annual report when it came off the presses in February 1946. That would, he wrote to Truman, give "an idea of the tremendous undertaking it is to cope with the 18,000,000 cubic feet of federal records now in existence and of the importance of preserving the information in some of those records." There is no indication of whether or not the president read those pages, but somebody in the White House took note, for part of Buck's letter was sidescored in pencil, and it was not filed until almost six months after its receipt.[14]

This was probably tied in with the combined action of the

Bureau of the Budget and the National Archives to secure the issuance of an executive order aimed at forwarding records management in the federal government. President Truman signed that executive order, number 9784, on 25 September 1946. It directed that (1) each agency would operate "an active continuing program for the effective management and disposition of its records"; (2) only current records would be retained by the agencies; (3) useless records should be disposed of promptly; (4) those of enduring value should be transferred to the National Archives; (5) regulations regarding the transfer of records to any other agency would be tightened up in order to avoid losses and closure of nonconfidential material to other federal agencies and to the public; and (6) the Budget Director "with the advice and assistance of the National Archives" should carry out inspections, receive reports, and make rules necessary to implement the order's provisions.[15]

Encouragement of records-management programs in the various agencies was now less of a problem, for the appearance of E.O. 9784 and the role of the Budget Bureau in drafting and implementing it was a clear signal that such operations would be funded. Within a couple of years, many federal agencies had flourishing records-management programs in operation that resulted in considerable savings and more efficient use of records. Significant inroads were also made in the disposition of useless records, transfers of enduringly valuable documents were more smoothly made to the National Archives, and additional controls were established over the transfer of records from one agency to another. Although E.O. 9784 caused no revolution in the management of government paper, it was the most effective thing done to encourage federal records management until additional steps were taken during the 1950s. It was fortuitously supplemented by the action of the Public Buildings Administration in 1946 to see that government agencies cut in half the amount of space they rented for the storage of noncurrent records. More directly related, the National Archives spurred the professional development of records managers by broadening the activities and membership of the Interagency Records Administration Conference. The agency also revised its publication *How to Dispose of Records*, and it issued other booklets between 1945 and 1949 such as *Putting PAW to Bed: The Records Retirement Program of the Petroleum Administration for War* and *Disposition of Federal Records.*[16]

The National Archives took pride in the fact that because of its initiative the federal government was holding the dikes against the flood of paper. From scattered evidence, the agency concluded that federal offices, with its assistance, were doing a heroic job of coping with their records. There was, for example, the reduction of the records of the Office of Price Administration, the Office of Censorship, the Petroleum Administration for War, and the Civilian Production Administration of the War Production Board from 1,300,000 to 38,000 cubic feet. The National Archives took special joy in reporting in fiscal year 1948 that the OPA, the WPB, the Selective Service System, and the departments of the Army, Navy, and the Air Force had destroyed nearly 2,000,000 cubic feet of useless records. In this case alone, it seemed that more records were discarded than the entire government might have created that year. It appeared that the gospel of records management was not only improving the flow of valuable documents into the National Archives but also preventing the inundation of government in its own paper. It must be said in retrospect that miracles did occur. More were needed, however, for the government would soon show that it could produce larger amounts of paper than its records-management programs could cope with.[17]

During the war, the National Archives had participated in getting the government to document its war efforts. The result was, as Solon Buck wrote, that "however understandably sparse, incomplete, or ill-organized in places, the documentation of the war was in existence." The National Archives worked hard to preserve that documentation either through accessions or through promoting records-management programs in various government agencies. Its staff was not so large that they could think beyond that point. There were others, however, including President Truman, who were concerned with finding ways to make the mass of documentation more usable, and the task was placed in the hands of the National Archives. As the archivist saw it, the program required the compilation of a handbook of the government's wartime agencies and their records, inventories of the significant records, lists of pertinent published and unpublished writings, and an overall subject guide to the relevant documentation. President Truman approved Buck's recommendations as well as the transfer of $78,000 for fiscal year 1947 in order that the job "begin at once." Thus the World War II records project of the National Archives was operative by September 1946.[18]

It might have been just as well for the National Archives had the project never been undertaken, for the government's renewal of the funding of the task was tardy and niggardly. Nevertheless, the National Archives completed one records inventory and the handbook *Federal Records of World War II*, which appeared in 1950 and 1951 in two volumes. That publication constituted a magnificent overview of the documentation of the war effort, one that was of considerable reference value to both historians and the government. It was done, however, by further straining the slender resources of the National Archives.[19]

The restricted use of records was another problem, however mild, in the immediate postwar years. Security classification had become rampant in many federal agencies during the war, thanks in no small measure to the fetish that President Franklin D. Roosevelt had for secrecy. As he put it in a memorandum of 16 September 1943 to Secretary of State Cordell Hull, "Four people cannot be conversationally frank with each other if somebody is taking down notes for future publication. I feel very strongly about this." Roosevelt had a point, no doubt. The problem was that he stretched secrecy to include almost everything except that which would serve propaganda and political purposes. Worse yet, his subordinates in government all too often followed his example. The result was that large batches of documentation were unnecessarily restricted. Even worse, woefully inadequate procedures were established for the declassification of materials, and restrictions were often continued far beyond the time that they served any legitimate purpose of state. This is not to lay the responsibility for all this with Franklin D. Roosevelt. Given his deep interest in history, it is conceivable that had he survived the war, he might have arranged for rapid and effective downgrading of security restrictions. The fact of the matter is that his successor, Harry S. Truman, who was caught up in the Cold War, did not downgrade restrictions, and in turn his successors did little in that direction until Richard M. Nixon's term, and he did less than scholars and journalists requested.[20]

Under another archivist the National Archives might have had some influence in keeping government secrecy within reasonable bounds. Solon Buck, however, was not the person for that task. Seldom during the war did he or his aides make any gesture in that direction. On the contrary, with their concern for service to government above all, they were not oriented to combat the growing secrecy in federal record-keeping. For all practical purposes, they indeed became collaborators. There is a hint they may have believed that after the war restrictions would gradually vanish. That did not happen, however, and they infrequently showed concern about the situation.[21]

This is not to say that archivists tried to do nothing about the problem of overclassification after the war. They, along with government historians, sought to secure some declassification or downgrading of the classifications on records before their transfer to the National Archives. Moreover, the agency attempted to persuade the heads of other federal offices to delegate to the archivist their authority over restrictions on records in his custody. Few agencies, however, downgraded classifications or surrendered any power over the security classification of their records. Even when power over restrictions was delegated to him, the archivist seldom felt free to exercise it.[22]

In a way, this caution is understandable, for the archivist's first objective was to gather together the government's records of enduring value for preservation. He and his aides concluded that this could be done only if agency heads had confidence in the discretion as well as the technical effectiveness of the National Archives. Then there was fear that if archivists pressed the classification issue vigorously, retaliation would be taken at budget time. There was, moreover, the nettlesome possibility that if the archivist and his staff substituted their own judgment for that of an agency on questions of classification, they might be wrong and thus endanger national security. Finally, there was an issue of whether the rights of researchers might conflict with the right of privacy. As Herman Kahn wrote in 1953, the growth of governmental activities had "resulted in making an official record of many of those things in our lives that have hitherto been regarded as unassailably private in character." Although Congress had placed restrictions on much documentation of this nature, Kahn was correct in pointing out that archivists and others had not given this question proper consideration.[23]

Whatever the reason, the National Archives was timid in dealing with restrictions on the use of federal records. It is only fair to point out, however, that few scholars or officials were concerned by this state of affairs in the immediate postwar period. One of them was Army Chief of Staff Dwight D. Eisenhower, who declared in November 1947 that "the Army possesses no inherent right to conceal the history of its affairs behind a cloak of secrecy." In line with that statement, he charged army officers to facilitate the access of researchers to information of a historical nature and to achieve the maximum downgrading of such material except when it "would *in fact* endanger the security of the Nation." The postwar revisionist historians, sensitive to the fact that certain agencies favored a small group of scholars in granting access to their restricted records, also took up the cudgels in this matter. As Charles A. Beard asserted in 1947, archives must be open to "all citizens on equal terms, with special privileges for none."[24]

Eisenhower's directive led to no perceptible change in army secrecy, nor did the cries of the revisionists result in any easing of restrictions. Indeed, in 1948 Congress amended the National Archives Act so that agency heads could order the archivist to impose restrictions on their records when the documents were transferred to his custody; he was forbidden to remove or to relax such restrictions without the agreement of the agency head concerned or even in the event of the agency's termination. The archivist thus had even less leeway in dealing with classified records. Another section of the new legislation, in fact, stipulated that restrictions on the use of documents applied to him and his staff. Not only did these amendments make more work for the National Archives in terms of segregating restricted materials and in gaining staff security clearances, but they further discouraged archivists in struggling with excesses in classifications. Over the years, some archivists even became reluctant to volunteer information to researchers as to what classified records were in their custody. There was something to be said for historian Howard K. Beale's criticism in 1953 that not only government offices but also archivists were unreasonably secretive.[25]

Another part of the problem was that the National Archives was a bit laggard in recognizing the rapidly growing penchant of historians after World War II to work with recent records. Gone were the days when the historian who was interested in archives less than fifty years old was rare. As political scientists abandoned dealing with recent history, as large amounts of documentation of recent creation became available, as the interest of students and publishers in recent history grew, so would rise a new breed of historians who used their skills to get beneath the surface story that in the past had been accepted as recent history. The National Archives, of course, could pride itself on acquiring for researchers a great deal of documentation of recent years. The agency was also correct in its understanding that it was unrealistic to expect that all records would be open for research soon after they were created. After all, it was not the prime concern of government officials that documentation be made fully and quickly available to scholars. The United States, moreover, had a better record in this respect than almost any other nation.

It was, however, becoming clear to some researchers that many of the restrictions on records were questionable, that they served purposes other than protecting lives, preserving the privacy of citizens, or otherwise guarding the national interest. Indeed, it was slowly becoming obvious that restrictions too often merely protected public officials from embarrassment or catered to the concerns of security faddists. The National Archives in seldom challenging such restrictions did neither itself nor the citizenry a favor.[26] By lying low on this issue during the 1940s, the agency thought that it was protecting itself at a time when it had more than enough troubles. It is plain, however, that its timidity and its conviction that it was doing the right, patriotic thing led it into a poor habit that would continue into the latter half of the 1960s. Then the National Archives suddenly found itself, along with the ship of state, being a target for angry researchers who believed they were being dealt with shabbily as a result of the pyramiding problems created by the government's security classifications on documents.

During the postwar period, the National Archives neatly avoided criticism on a related issue. That was the hullabaloo of 1947 over the practice of high officials taking papers away with them upon their retirement from office. The National Archives had from its beginning been concerned with this problem and had hoped that its own existence, and also the example of President Roosevelt in establishing his library, would lessen if not solve it. The archivists further hoped that they could formulate acceptable legislation that would tighten up the definition of public records, so that all concerned would know which office files were records and which were personal papers. The issue was also a live one for the American Historical Association, which in December 1945 adopted a resolution urging that "chief executives" retire with only strictly personal correspondence in their possession. The hand of Archivist Buck was seen in the resolution's reference to the government's "admirable facilities" to care for presidential records.[27]

The issue burst forth upon the national scene in late January 1947 when Secretary of the Treasury John W. Snyder demanded that his predecessor, Henry J. Morgenthau, return his so-called diary of some 900 volumes to the government. Plainly, President Truman approved of this action. This was partly because of his irritation with many Roosevelt appointees for carrying off large amounts of papers that he considered essential governmental documentation, and it was partly to defuse possible attacks from the newly organized Republican Congress on the issue. Truman indicated that he would take no state papers with him when he left office. Moreover, he suggested that he would request legislation to restrict the personal use of federal records by former officials.[28]

This apparently took the National Archives by surprise. The agency was prepared, however, to give its advice. On 3 February, Assistant Archivist Dan Lacy wrote the Budget Bureau that there were two separate problems involved in the Morgenthau diary issue. One was the loss of records of value to the operation of the government and to historical research; the other was that official documents taken away by former federal officials might be used so as to affect national security adversely or to raise ethical questions as to their use for private purposes. The National Archives could legitimately be concerned with only the first problem, for issues regarding ethics and security regulations lay within the province of Congress and the agencies that had created the restrictions. Respecting the loss of federal records, Lacy pointed out that the government had the power to act, although public records needed to be defined more precisely. He urged legislation or an executive order that would require each head of a government agency to include among the agency's records at least one copy of every record pertaining to that agency's work that was received, made, or sent by him. Of course, confidential records could be put under seal and placed in the custody of the archivist for, say, ten years to prevent their use in politically embarrassing the parties involved.[29]

It did not take long for Congress to enter the discussion. The Senate War Investigating Committee, of which Owen Brewster of Maine was chairman, began making inquiries into the disposition of government records. On 11 February considerable debate took place in the Senate on the issues of better defining records and what penalties should be applied for their illegal removal. Although the results of the debate were inconclusive, Senator Homer Ferguson of Michigan urged that the government take action to compel the return of the Morgenthau materials. When, two days later, the former secretary of the treasury agreed to transfer any official documents in his possession to the government, much of the controversy subsided.[30]

The issue was far from dead, however. In March Senator Arthur Vandenberg of Michigan demanded to see the files in the Franklin Roosevelt papers on the Yalta agreements. The Senate War Investigating Committee, at the beginning of May, asked to see materials relating to negotiations about Arabian oil. President Truman and Roosevelt's executors rejected this. The committee, however, called Buck before it to have him explain why he did not hand over the relevant papers in his custody. He answered that he could not grant access partly because of restrictions imposed by Roosevelt and partly because the White House had authority over some of the material. Recognizing his limited responsibility, the committee did not press Buck immediately on the matter. The committee was also placated when toward the end of May Truman and the Roosevelt estate allowed it to see some of the pertinent Roosevelt papers.[31]

Hostilities, however, had ceased for only a short time. On 19 July the Senate War Investigating Committee subpoenaed papers from the Roosevelt estate, since it was unsatisfied with the material that it had been allowed to see. This action was followed two days later by a decision of the Dutchess County surrogate's court that the papers acquired by Roosevelt in the White House were, in accordance with the late president's will, federal property. That made the material subject to administrative decisions, so the committee's subpoena was forwarded to Buck. After consulting White House officials, the archivist located a variety of the papers demanded and declared them available for the committee's purposes. Thus, the immediate question was settled.[32]

The basic issue had not been resolved. The White House, with the advice of the National Archives, wrestled with the problem of keeping appointed officials from taking away records when they left office. President Truman gave serious thought to issuing a directive that would deal with this. He believed that government officials should see to it that a full record be made of their operations, that the record should not be destroyed, and that they should not take with them upon leaving office anything but personal papers and extra copies of unclassified and unrestricted documents. Moreover, Truman suggested that appointees had an obligation to preserve their personal papers and eventually to arrange for their deposit in an appropriate research institution.

The National Archives and the Budget Bureau collaborated with the White House staff in preparing a presidential directive along these lines. It was never issued, however, because of strenuous objections from the Justice Department. Appointed officials therefore continued to remove with impunity documents of more than a personal nature, which often included restricted material. Although the president was generally recognized as a separate case, he could have set a fitting example for appointed officials. Truman did not, however, for he—and his successors—claimed almost all White House records as personal property. There were some benefits in this otherwise deplorable situation. Most of the papers of the presidents from Herbert Hoover through Lyndon B. Johnson were deposited in presidential libraries. Moreover, large numbers of appointed officials sought a form of immortality by deeding their papers to appropriate repositories. Some others were generous enough to allow researchers access to such materials in their personal possession, which sometimes resulted in researchers being able to use documents that would otherwise have been caught up in the red tape of often questionable federal restrictions.[33]

The other unresolved question, of course, was that of security classifications. Although the Senate War Investigating Committee was finally permitted to see much of the material it had requested, the executive branch in that and similar later instances often made the process of gaining access inconvenient. Congress did not mount a large-scale offensive on this issue until the 1970s. The results then, however, were far from satisfactory. Rather than risk breaching what it considered national security, Congress settled for less than it could have gotten. Indeed, even the president and other high officials found it difficult to repress the coils of red tape to the extent that they were willing to go. Despite Richard Nixon's easing of security classifications in 1972 and the liberalization of the Freedom of Information Act in 1974, it was unlikely that all questionable restrictions on public and congressional access to federal records would be swept into the dustbin.

Given its many problems during the 1940s, the National Archives tried to follow a course that would offend neither Congress nor the executive branch. The agency, of course, had no choice but to obey legislation that bound it to enforce restrictions and security classifications imposed by the president and various federal offices. The archivists also found it politic to argue rarely for changes in such limitations; indeed, in case of doubt as to what the limitations were, they usually concluded that access should be restricted. The

most the National Archives would do for researchers who pressed
the issue was to ask for clarification from the agencies involved.
When the archivists checked back, they seldom questioned the
right, the logic, or the reasonableness of those who imposed restrictions upon records. Buck even protected his staff from doubt
in the event that legal process was served. In regulations of 19 September and 4 November 1947, he stated that only he could decide
how to respond to a subpoena for records in his agency's custody,
and that he could decline to produce subpoenaed material when
he determined that its disclosure was "contrary to law or would
prejudice the national interest or security of the United States."[34]
It was obvious that the National Archives operated in the interest
of the government first and of others afterward; yet it was also
plain that few researchers were unhappy with the situation. It
would have been expecting a great deal of the agency to be in
advance of its constituency and to have engaged in mortal combat
with the gladiators of red tape in the government.

The National Archives was having serious postwar problems
with a large backlog of work, new challenges, and the questions of
removal of records by retiring officials and security classification.
All those had to be met with a chief, Solon Buck, whose personality
often fomented unhappiness within the organization and seldom
enlisted political support from without. Yet these burdens were
light when compared with the postwar problems of reorganization
and economy that the National Archives had to face. Six changes
in the agency's structure had come, thanks to Buck's zeal, between
late 1941 and the middle of 1944. Thereafter, except for consolidation of the motion picture and photographic divisions into the
Photographic Records Office, the archivist had left well enough
alone. The wounds inflicted by organizational changes had begun
to heal.

Reorganization was in the wind again toward the end of 1945.
This time the impetus was from outside, specifically from the president and Congress who sought with the Reorganization Act of
December 1945 to foster greater efficiency and economy in the federal government. Immediately the National Archives considered
how it should respond to the inevitable request from the Budget

Bureau as to whether organizational change would lead to more economy and efficiency. Archivist Buck and his chief aides discussed several possibilities for their agency. They doubted that its merger with another organization would occur or was desirable. They believed that it would be most beneficial for the National Archives to retain its independent status, although the archivist was willing to transfer its function of dealing with private film and sound recordings to the Library of Congress. Interestingly, Buck said that if a merger were required, it should be with a group of administrative services because of the housekeeping functions of the National Archives as well as the probable closeness of such an organization to the president and its resultant budgetary advantages. Of course, that surmise was not passed on to the Budget Bureau. The archivist, not surprisingly, officially recommended that no changes be made in his agency's status, functions, or organization.[35]

Buck's recommendation was not the last word, for the Budget Bureau exerted pressure on the National Archives to consider reorganization. By June 1946 the archivist agreed with the bureau's liaison man, John L. Keddy, that "major revision" was needed. He disagreed, however, with many of Keddy's specifics. Buck put the matter of devising recommendations for reorganization into the hands of his assistant, Dan Lacy. The burden of Lacy's thinking was that the archivist's control over his agency's operations should be tightened up, the workload should be better distributed, and the number of operating units should be reduced. The archivist generally agreed with Lacy. Before the end of the year (partly because of John Keddy's transfer to the Smithsonian Institution in August) the National Archives' reorganization plan was completed, had won the Budget Bureau's favor, and was ready for implementation.[36]

Buck announced the reorganization on 31 December. It provided for the consolidation of thirteen records divisions into six records offices, which were those of general records, industrial records, legislative reference and records, natural resources records, photographic records, and war records. The functions of the eleven service units were consolidated into six service divisions, which were cleaning and rehabilitation, finance and accounts, exhibits and publications, personnel management, printing and processing, and property. The Federal Register and the Roosevelt Library remained separate operations, with the status of offices, directly responsible to the archivist. The property, finance and accounts, printing and processing, and cleaning and rehabilitation divisions were grouped together in a new Records Control Office that included the World War II records project, the library, and the general reference division. Operating directly out of the archivist's office were the newly created assistant archivist, who was to be the archivist's deputy, and the divisions of exhibits and publications and personnel management. Also established was the secretary's office, responsible to the archivist, which encompassed the operations of the management officer, records and communications, and miscellaneous other duties. Buck also phased out the National Archives' elaborate committee structure, which eliminated the last vestiges of the agency's original collegiate organization. Clearly, this sweeping reorganization reduced the number of levels of supervision, released a considerable amount of supervisory personnel for operational duties, tightened up the archivist's control of his agency, and afforded office directors greater scope in carrying out their planning and coordinating obligations. Although the Budget Bureau had shoved the National Archives toward a new reorganization, Buck and Lacy had taken to the idea and planned it with a flourish. Their handiwork saved little for the federal economy movement, but it certainly added to the efficiency of the National Archives in tackling its multitudinous chores.[37]

Unfortunately for Buck and new Assistant Archivist Lacy, the reorganization also caused much unhappiness among those whose supervisory responsibilities had been reduced or removed. The archivist and his deputy probably hoped that reorganization would improve staff morale at least by allowing archivists to make greater inroads on the agency's tremendous backlog of work. Moreover, Buck badgered Congress and the administration for more funds. He emphasized, correctly so, that while the number of the National Archives' employees had been cut by about one third since early in the war, its workload had risen substantially, in fact beyond the agency's ability to deal with it properly. Yet the archivist was bucking a strong tide of economy in Congress and the administration. He not only failed to get restoration of the staff to the 1942 level, he was even unable to retain the number of personnel authorizations he had had for the current fiscal year, 1947.[38]

To make matters worse, something of a bureaucratic mutiny broke out in the National Archives during the spring of 1947. It was, as Lacy put it, a "plot" among disaffected employees. These people supposedly believed that the most recent reorganization had downgraded them; they were allegedly in touch with elements on Capitol Hill in a maneuver to remove Buck, Lacy, and several other ranking staff members from their jobs. That something was afoot became clear during the hearings of the House Appropriations Subcommittee on Independent Agencies. On 16 May some committee members indicated to Buck that the National Archives had been victimized by his penchant for reorganization and for bringing in former employees of the Works Progress Administration at high salaries. He defended himself spiritedly, although he was on weak ground where the issue of excessive organizational changes was concerned. As word of the charges spread, the National Archives was plunged into turmoil because of the likely adverse consequences for Buck and his top aides and because congressional hostility could have chilling effects on the next year's budget. Lacy demanded that the plotters be disciplined and that the White House and the public be mobilized to support the archivist. As one of the targets of the disaffected, the thirty-three-year-old assistant archivist, however, declared that he could "take care of myself."[39] No one doubted that, given his rapid rise from an M.A. candidate at the University of North Carolina in 1935 to the assistant directorship of the WPA's Historical Records Survey by 1940 to the number-two spot in the National Archives by 1947.

The situation quickly became desperate in terms of morale and budget. The effects of the wartime cuts in funding had been serious, but the frustration of postwar expectations for fiscal improvement would make matters grave, coming while the workload rose more than had been anticipated. The number of available employees, which stood at 433 in fiscal year 1942, had dropped to 331 three years later and had risen to only some 363 by 1947. By 13 June 1947 it was obvious that the archivist had not only lost his battle to gain more positions, but that there would probably be fifteen to twenty fewer jobs on the staff the coming fiscal year. Things looked so dismal that Lacy told Buck, "We can't simply go on as we are."[40]

The assistant archivist was right; things got worse. Within a few days, the Independent Offices Appropriations Bill was amended to prohibit using appropriated funds to pay the salaries of National Archives' employees in grades P-4 and CAF-11 and above who originally had been appointed to the staff on a war-service basis and who were not war veterans or army reservists. That proviso had been carefully drafted to get rid of Lacy and six others who were regarded as the archivist's staunchest aides. Buck immediately protested the rider, and both he and Lacy wrote to friends asking for their help in eliminating this amendment. As Lacy said, it would "substantially wreck the present internal administration of the National Archives." Friends of a couple of the intended victims saved them by exerting enough influence to raise the cut level in the proviso to P-5. Yet, as Buck pointed out, that made the rider "even more objectionable" because it was now "more clearly aimed at specific people." On 25 June the *New York Times* condemned the amendment, which the House of Representatives had passed, as "a dangerous precedent." The newspaper urged the Senate to strike out the rider, for its only purpose was to inflict revenge upon the supporters of the reorganization of the National Archives.[41]

The protests were to no avail. By July it had become plain that Congress would not drop the proviso. Lacy therefore resigned as Buck's assistant to take a job with the Library of Congress, where by 1950 he had become the deputy chief assistant librarian. Another of the intended victims also resigned, one was demoted to fall below the cut level, and two others were given separation notices. Congress soon approved the rider and appropriations that left the National Archives with 20.3 fewer positions than those available the previous fiscal year. Buck's enemies within the National Archives had inflicted their toll. It was at a terrible price, however; one that made it even more difficult for the agency to meet its obligations and that demoralized its administrators and the many staff members loyal to them.[42]

Buck's first step toward putting his agency on the upward path was to seek a new assistant archivist who might be able to repair the fissures in the agency's staff and administrative structure and to improve relations with Congress. Buck was fortunate in his choice. He was Wayne C. Grover, a former employee of the National Archives, who had served since 1943 with distinction as the army's leading records management officer. Grover had also taken a Ph.D. degree in public administration from the American University, and it was significant that this forty-year-old Utahan was the son-in-law of one of his native state's United States senators, Elbert D. Thomas.[43]

The next several months was a nervous time for the National Archives. Pursuant to Congress's budgetary mandates, Buck and Grover had to formulate policies to implement the shrinkage of the staff. It was, as Grover said, "distasteful," but there was no alternative. With the reduced number of authorized positions, the staff level declined from 384 to 341 during fiscal year 1948. The consequence was that not only an equivalent number of employees had to resign or be terminated, but that within the agency there was much shuffling of duties to try to cover the work of those who departed. There were also budgetarily required demotions and those requested by some personnel so that they could qualify for classified civil-service status. The result was the largest number of demotions (fifty-one) that the National Archives has suffered as well as the highest number of forced separations.

Grover assumed most of the responsibility for carrying out those actions, since Buck was plagued by serious illness during the fall of 1947. "I am not fond of the role," the assistant archivist reported to his chief. And well he might not be, for not only did it cast him as the villain with many employees, but perhaps also with Buck, since Grover felt forced to make critical policy decisions during the archivist's hospitalization half a continent away without consulting him. He was right to do so, however, for his decisions were budgetarily and immediately necessary as well as politic in order to make the best impression upon Congress during the National Archives' preliminary budget hearings. Not only did it mean firing, demoting, and reassigning employees, but even a minor reorganization. Grover therefore decided that efficiency and economy required the elimination of the secretary's office, which was little missed, and the Division of Exhibits and Publications, which was a sore loss. Yet Grover took these actions smoothly and Buck endorsed them. The National Archives consequently got through fiscal year 1948 within its limited budget.[44] It was just as well that Wayne Grover made most of the budgetary and personnel decisions during fiscal year 1948. Even had Buck done so and had made exactly the same decisions, it is probable that he would not have carried them out as well. One can argue, indeed, that the archivist's frequent absences because of illness and travel allowed many of the wounds left by his series of fights with the staff and Congress to heal.

It was during the late fall or early winter that Buck decided to leave the National Archives. One cannot say whether his decision was based on the toll taken by his illness or because he had concluded that it would be in the agency's best interests. He did make the decision on his own, however, and not because of any dissatisfaction with him at the White House. In January 1948 he informed a presidential assistant, Donald S. Dawson, that he would resign by the end of the fiscal year. Buck suggested several men for consideration as his successor, including his old friend Dean Theodore C. Blegen of the University of Minnesota and Professor Thomas Cochran of New York University. He did not mention Wayne C. Grover.[45]

After Buck returned from an official tour of the Caribbean in April, he picked up the matters of resignation and succession again. He wrote Dawson indicating that he had worked out an agreement to take a position at the Library of Congress. More important, he had changed his mind about his successor. His first choice now was Grover, who he thought had done "a magnificent job under difficult circumstances" as acting archivist during Buck's most recent absence. On 28 April Librarian of Congress Luther H. Evans offered Buck the appointment as chief of the Manuscripts Division and incumbent in the Chair of American History. The archivist submitted his resignation two weeks later, effective the end of May. He gave as his reason his wish to be less involved in administration and to spend more time on "research in American history and the guidance and assistance of others in such research."[46]

Thus came to an end the tenure of the second archivist of the United States. After almost seven years in the job, Solon J. Buck could pride himself on his administration's accomplishments during times of severe shortages of personnel and equipment. He had plunged the National Archives into the work of records management, with the result that the government dealt with its burgeoning records problems with greater efficiency and economy. Not a small by-product of this was the agency's role in developing the records-management profession and in encouraging archivists to take a broader view of their functions. The National Archives had also played the leading part in laying the foundations for an international archival association while expanding the training and organization of archivists in the United States. Buck had implemented the concepts of organizing archives into record groups and the preparation of innovative guides to archives, especially the preliminary inventory. With considerable success he had carried on the programs of the Connor days, most notably the accessioning of older federal archives, the file microcopy program, and the Franklin D. Roosevelt Library. Buck's experiments with reorganization of the National Archives had had mixed results. Without a doubt the agency's operations had become more efficient under his leadership. That was, however, at the cost of some false starts and considerable staff unhappiness and even resistance. He had made the National Archives into a more effective servant of the state, but there too a price was paid, for the agency became too acquiescent to restrictions on the use of federal records. Buck's authoritarianism and abrasiveness certainly contributed to problems among his staff and with Congress. In effect, that led to his downfall and to jeopardizing the financial support necessary to carry on the operations of the National Archives. If it had not been for his imaginativeness and courage, however, the agency might not have become the many-faceted institution that it did. Buck's was a mixed legacy, but on balance his contributions to archival administration outweighed the detrimental aspects of his labors.

12. A New Leader, a Different Status

The retiring archivist and the White House kept word of his impending resignation secret at least until late April 1948. Solon Buck, moreover, had apparently smoothed the way for Wayne Grover's appointment with his fellow hierarchs in the American Historical Association. Consequently, Grover had no competition as Buck's successor. On 12 May, the date of Buck's letter of resignation, presidential aide Donald Dawson recommended Grover to President Harry S. Truman for appointment. The White House staff had by then cleared the assistant archivist with the Democratic National Committee, the Federal Bureau of Investigation, and the two senators from his home state of Utah, Democrat Elbert D. Thomas and Republican Arthur V. Watkins. Dawson suggested that the president play a little political game with Senator Thomas, who was Grover's father-in-law. The aide's idea was that Truman, before committing himself, would telephone Thomas, "saying something to the effect that Grover has been recommended to you and that you understand he is quite close to the Senator and wondered if his appointment would have the Senator's blessing, etc. etc." There is no sure evidence that the president played this game, obviously intended to suggest that a quid-pro-quo was expected; indeed, someone penciled in a question mark alongside this passage of Dawson's memorandum. Truman did telephone Senator Thomas, according to columnist Drew Pearson, but it was Elmer Thomas of Oklahoma, who had no son-in-law. If the president had intended to follow Dawson's advice, that blunder probably ruled it out, for

Wayne C. Grover, third archivist of the United States, 1948–1965

when he did get in touch with Elbert Thomas, he supposedly confessed that he "got mixed up on my Senator Thomases." Truman, in any event, nominated Grover to be archivist of the United States on 13 May, and the Senate confirmed his appointment on 3 June.[1]

Wayne Grover was a man of average height and rotund appearance, which was accentuated by his moon-shaped face. He was not yet forty-two, which was considerably younger than his two predecessors had been, when he assumed the post of archivist. If he was not courtly as Connor had been, he was far less abrasive than Buck. More important was Grover's quite different background.

Unlike his predecessors, he was neither a teacher nor a writer of history, nor did he have standing in any scholarly association. He had been a journalist and a congressional aide in earlier days, and he was a seasoned federal civil servant, having worked for the National Archives, the Office of Strategic Services, and the army. He was one of the first trained archivists in the United States and a pioneer in the records-management profession, whereas Connor and Buck had been groundbreakers in the state historical society movement. Grover received his doctorate in public administration only two years before he became the archivist. He was, in short, one of the new breed increasingly found in the federal government: a trained administrator. More than that, Grover was adept at politics, and he had a strong appreciation of the value of public relations and a great interest in history. All this would be revealed during his more than seventeen years as archivist of the United States.

Grover's first year in office did not promise much, struggle though he did to side-channel the ugly currents of the final period of Buck's tenure. He raided the army's records program to appoint his close friend Robert H. Bahmer as assistant archivist. Not only had they worked together in the adjutant general's office, but they had also come up through the ranks together in the early days of the National Archives. Bahmer, who held a Ph.D. in history from the University of Minnesota and had also worked as a congressional aide, would work hand-in-glove with Grover over the years. Together they were a remarkably well coordinated and effective leadership pair. Even in personality and appearance they complemented one another, Grover being diplomatic and pleasantly rounded in features, Bahmer being alternately tough and folksy in manner and imposingly rugged in appearance.[2]

The problems confronting Grover were much like those that Buck had faced. The new archivist continued the crusade to convince the Budget Bureau and Congress that his agency had to have additional funds and staff to deal with its backlog of tasks as well as with mounting new challenges. In this he had some success, for during fiscal year 1949 the funds available increased from $1,279,-634 to $1,481,740, and the number of the National Archives' personnel rose from 341 to 362. Acquisitions, however, also mounted significantly during that year, including 52,546 cubic feet of records. The archives' holdings of maps increased by 263,000 to a total of 741,000 and of still pictures by about 575,000 to some 2,000,000 items. Additions to motion pictures and sound recordings were more modest, although the net size of those collections grew, respectively, to some 37,000,000 running feet and 300,000 discs. The library of the National Archives contained 102,069 volumes and pamphlets, making it in itself an important historical collection.[3]

Like Buck, Grover was alarmed by the fact that the federal government was becoming increasingly mired in the problems of administering its records. The National Archives gave help and advice where it could. That, however, was inadequate to the task. In August 1948 the archivist queried government agencies to discover how many records they had on hand. The responses indicated that there were more federal records in existence than had previously been estimated, with some six million cubic feet in Washington and fourteen million in field offices. Moreover, the rate of the accumulation of the records was larger than had been anticipated, running almost one million cubic feet annually since the end of the war. The conclusion was obvious to Grover: the government was bursting at the seams with records, and unnecessarily so, since 70 percent of this material could be scheduled for destruction. It was important that the government provide funds for a more effective program to get rid of useless records, to shelter and administer materials of temporary value, and to preserve and administer federal archives.[4]

The space problem was part of the records crisis Grover was trying to handle against discouraging odds. Storage room in the National Archives building and its annex in Suitland was almost exhausted. Moreover, most federal agencies were spending unnecessarily large sums of money on staff and space to take care of their records, and even then many of them were not doing so efficiently for management or preservation purposes. It is no wonder that space, staff, and records management weighed heavily on the archivist's mind.[5]

Grover, of course, had many other administrative concerns. At most, the National Archives could undertake only emergency repair and rehabilitation of archives. The work of analyzing the records in its custody and then of describing them continued to lag behind. Although the file microcopy and document facsimile programs developed, the rate of progress was barely satisfactory. One program of great interest was the Freedom Train, the highly successful traveling exhibition of historical treasures in which the National Archives had played a great part in assembling. When the Freedom Train's much acclaimed sixteen-month tour of the country ended in January 1949, Attorney General Tom Clark proposed that the agency assume full responsibility for its continued operation. Congress soon authorized that, but it appropriated no funds. Thus the project was permanently sidetracked. The National Archives, however, with the cooperation of the American Heritage Foundation, exhibited the Freedom Train's contents in Washington from September 1949 through that city's sesquicentennial celebration in 1950.[6]

There were two areas in which the National Archives dared not falter. One was the Federal Register Division's preparation for publication of a new edition of the *Code of Federal Regulations*, which was ten years out of date and was vital to government operations. There was also reference service, the essential end product of archival work. To keep this current required the effort of an ever larger proportion of the staff, as reference services grew from 346,739 in fiscal year 1948 to 377,135 in 1949. What the National Archives could talk of in this respect also increased. Reference service requests from federal agencies encompassed, for example, documentation for the treason prosecutions of Axis Sally and Tokyo Rose. The archivists further served private citizens who were seeking support for their claims against the government or other citizens. Books appeared by well-known scholars, including James Truslow Adams, Samuel Flagg Bemis, and Stanley Vestal, who had done part of their research in the National Archives. Moreover, Edward R. Murrow and Fred W. Friendly drew in part on the agency's sound recordings for their famous album "I Can Hear It Now."[7]

Nevertheless, despite occasional glories and despite Buck's departure, the National Archives remained in serious trouble. Increased space and budget were desperately needed. Grover therefore had no choice but to assign himself two vital tasks. One was to find authorization for a records program that would keep the government and the National Archives from being swamped by paper; the other was to fill in the gap created by years of financial stringency. He rightly saw those as being equally crucial, for progress in one area would be limited without an advance in the other. Certainly if today's records were not properly dealt with, the survival of tomorrow's archives would be jeopardized; and if archives were not currently taken care of, one of the most important reasons for records management would be vitiated. The archivist thus wanted funds to expand the programs of drawing up and executing disposal schedules, to build centers to house records of intermediate and indeterminate value, and to encourage improved agency records programs. He also sought money to construct vaults for the safe storage of nitrate film as well as to provide additional room and care for archives. Indeed, the National Archives' space situation was so pressing that at one time Grover asked his aides for their opinion of whether some archives should be microfilmed so that the originals could be destroyed and whether other agencies should be encouraged to establish their own archival arms. There was little interest in the first and fierce opposition to the second.[8]

Another problem was that little had been done to keep the archives building in good condition since 1940. Consequently, money was needed for the repair and improvement of the fire and burglary protection systems, air conditioning, roof, stack area lighting, incinerator, stack elevators, and exhibit cases. The continuation of the government economy movement posed even more of a problem, threatening another round of staff reductions for federal agencies. Much of Grover's time was spent in trying to ward off that for the National Archives. By March 1949 the situation was so unpromising that the archivist and his chief aides discussed how to cope with congressionally proposed new cuts in the agency's budget for fiscal year 1950. Preliminarily, in December 1948, Grover had modified the responsibilities of a number of his agency's units.

The increasing possibility of reductions in force for the National Archives suggested that a full-scale reorganization might be necessary during fiscal year 1950.[9] The budget threat did not materialize, as it turned out. Indeed, what happened to the National Archives is a radically different development.

That story is tied in with developments in records management and overall governmental reorganization, which led to the creation of the General Services Administration, of which the National Archives became a part. That change in status resulted from the coming together in the postwar period of three concepts. They were the growing beliefs among political scientists and public officials that there were too many separate federal agencies for the achievement of efficient and economical administration, the government's scattered housekeeping services should be gathered together in a single superagency, and the administration of federal records should be better controlled. The first idea was the basis of the creation of the vehicle used to approach the other two objectives. Thus in July 1947 Congress unanimously passed and President Truman approved the establishment of the Commission on the Organization of the Executive Branch of the Government. Former President Herbert Hoover was the chairman of this body, which became popularly known as the Hoover Commission. Its mission was to recommend ways in which the units of and the operating methods in the federal government could be recast in order to achieve greater economy, efficiency, and public service. The commission was bipartisan in membership, and, in order to remove it further from the political arena, it was under orders to report after the 1948 elections. To facilitate its operations, the commission established twenty-four research groups, or task forces, composed of experts in the various areas under study.[10]

The problem of federal records was not originally on the commission's agenda. However, Emmett J. Leahy, now director of the privately organized National Records Management Council, Edward B. Wilber of the Budget Bureau, and Wayne Grover separately suggested to the Hoover Commission's staff early in 1948 that this was an appropriate item for investigation. Because, as Grover wrote, some 60,000 federal employees were involved in records management, "there are few areas of administration in which there are so great possibilities of economy and efficiency being effected as in this one." Largely on Grover's recommendation, the commission decided that this was well worth looking into, and in April it commissioned Leahy to study the federal government's records problems. Associated with him on the resultant Task Force on Records Management were Robert H. Bahmer; Herbert E. Angel of the Navy Department; Edward Wilber, now of the State Department; and Archivist Frank M. Root of the Westinghouse Electric Corporation. Grover was also appointed to the task force but left after he became archivist of the United States.[11]

Leahy's task force completed and transmitted its report to the Hoover Commission on 14 October, and it was published by the end of the year and publicly released in January 1949. According to the report, the making and keeping of records were the "greatest consumers of salaries, space, and equipment of all the housekeeping activities of the federal government." It was estimated that those records occupied 18,000,000 square feet at an annual cost of $27,000,000 for space and of at least $20,000,000 for operating and maintenance purposes. Federal records were, the task force declared, currently administered in an unnecessarily expensive way and done so far from efficiently as management tools. Leahy's group recommended two overall actions to remedy the situation: the establishment of a federal records administration, which would include the National Archives; and the enactment of a federal records management bill. The proposed new agency would operate centers in order to house and service the government's semicurrent records most economically and efficiently; develop standards and controls for the creation, administration, and disposition of federal records; and nurture the archival and historical functions of the National Archives. The legislation would establish a comprehensive legal basis for the thrifty and effective "creation, preservation, management, and disposal of records." Moreover, it would create a federal records council to make regulations for the administration of government records and archives, and the act would require each federal agency to have a records officer who would facilitate the carrying out of appropriate legislation and regulations. The task force stated that in those ways the government could not only better safeguard the record of its experience but also render improved service and save at least $32,000,000 yearly.[12]

The archivist and Assistant Archivist Bahmer were pleased with the innumerable contributions that the National Archives had made to the thought and data contained in the report of the Task Force on Records Management. Bahmer, with Grover's approval, had even agreed to the concept of a federal records administration. Although many members of their staff, fearing that their professional status would be compromised, were shocked by the proposal for a new agency, Grover believed that the situation was desperate regarding both the National Archives and federal records administration. Everything else, after all, that had been tried since 1942 to gain more room, more funds, more personnel, and better management of records had fallen short. The task force and the Hoover Commission seemed the best vehicles for enlisting support to carry out properly the stated functions of the National Archives and to control the government's steadily growing records problems. In January 1949 Grover prepared to exploit the momentum created by the task force's report. He then asked key members of his staff to discuss the nature of needed new records legislation, and he directed his legislative liaison officer, Thaddeus Page, to draft a bill for consideration by Congress when that body was ready to move in response to the Leahy report.

Originally, Grover had not expected the task-force approach to result in much beyond additional publicity and contacts that would enhance the National Archives' chances to attain its records-management objectives. It is clear that the archivist had reservations about the Leahy report after it was completed. Reading between the lines, it appears that even Grover was unhappy with the idea that a federal records administration should absorb his agency. Nevertheless, the National Archives had ample opportunity to contribute to the task force's report; certainly the agency was prepared to exploit it. The report, as it turned out, had an impact far beyond the archivist's expectations. It would considerably influence the thinking of the Hoover Commission, the Budget Bureau, and Congress. In particular, it would contribute to a radical alteration of the structure and functions of the National Archives.[13]

When one discusses how the National Archives lost its independent status as a government agency, it is usually only in connection with the Task Force on Records Management and the Hoover Commission. Yet the Bureau of the Budget was a force that had an equal amount of influence in this matter. That agency, which worked closely with the commission on questions of government reorganization, had ideas of its own about the National Archives. As early as April 1948 the Budget Bureau was considering a rudimentary Hoover Commission proposal for the establishment of a department of administrative services that would encompass the Executive Office of the President, the Civil Service Commission, the Bureau of Federal Supply, the Government of the District of Columbia, and the National Archives. Raymond C. Atkinson, the analyst responsible for reviewing this, was sharply critical of the proposed new department as being unwieldy. More to his liking was some office of government services that would include agencies dealing with building construction and maintenance, property disposal, procurement, and "perhaps archives."[14] As time passed, the Budget Bureau became wedded to this concept of a new consolidated agency and to the National Archives being part of it.

Clearly, the Budget Bureau was developing its own line of thought with respect to the National Archives and government reorganization, and it was to have its effect, just as the report of the Task Force on Records Management did. The Leahy report, when it appeared publicly in January 1949, drew much adverse response from the staff of the National Archives because of the recommendation that the agency become part of the proposed federal records administration. Of course, Grover and Bahmer did what they could to calm this reaction, explaining that the new agency was not necessarily going to be established. Indeed, on 28 January, Grover wrote Herbert Hoover to assert that the "excellent" records management functions that Leahy championed could better be implemented by the National Archives than by a new and larger office.[15] What the archivist did not know was that the great threat to his agency's independence would come from the recommendations of the Hoover Commission staff and the Budget Bureau, not the Leahy report.

The Leahy report unwittingly strengthened the ideas of the Budget Bureau and the consolidationist attitudes of the Hoover Commission staff by emphasizing the housekeeping functions of a new records agency. The assistant to the executive director of the Hoover Commission, John D. Millett, cast the die after reading Leahy's report in October 1948. Millett recommended, in a widely circulated statement, that a federal records administration could not, consonant with the Hoover Commission's goals, be an independent agency. He urged that it be placed in a "Department of General Administration" or a "Central Services Agency." The result was that when the commission reported to Congress on the organization of the housekeeping and cultural services of the government, it recommended the establishment of an office of general services, which would include a records-management bureau of which the National Archives would be a part. That was a neat combination of the ideas of the Task Force on Records Management and the Budget Bureau with the added concept that the Smithsonian Institution, the National Capital Park and Planning Commission, and the Fine Arts Commission be included in the new superagency. The Hoover Commission also endorsed the enactment of comprehensive records legislation and the creation of records-management programs in all federal agencies. The commission submitted this report to Congress on 12 February 1949, and bills were soon offered in the House of Representatives and the Senate authorizing the establishment of an office of general services, the abolition of the National Archives and the office of the archivist of the United States, and the transfer of their functions to the new agency.[16]

Now the archivist was as agitated as his staff. He called a special meeting of his chief aides for the morning of 15 February. Although the division directors and other key personnel had plenty to say, it was Grover and Bahmer who dominated the discussion. The tenor of the talk was that the National Archives had spread itself too thin and that a clear distinction had not been made between the functions of an archivist and a records manager. Consequently, those who would reorganize the government were confused about the nature of archival operations. The beginnings of a remedy lay in better defining the role of an archivist. That professional's fundamental concern was to evaluate records for their documentary value and then to work for the transfer, preservation, and research administration of those of archival value. In short, an archivist's task was to become especially expert in the content of enduringly valuable records, not in how the creating agencies filed and administered them. That did not mean abandoning interest in the retirement of records. Far from it, for an archivist had to play an active part in records retirement in order to insure that archives were preserved and made available for research. A records administrator, of course, was concerned with the management "aspects of records creation and maintenance." That the two types of officials should work in concert was obvious, but the confusion of their roles had to be eliminated. This confusion was the big problem with the Leahy report and with the Hoover Commission's recommendations. According to Grover and Bahmer, the National Archives' immediate missions were to study the commission's report and to devise "a positive program" in response to it.[17]

On 1 March 1949 the president asked the archivist for comments on the Hoover Commission's recommendations. Individually and as a group, Grover's chief aides researched and sifted ideas for his response. They obviously wanted the National Archives to retain important cultural and housekeeping functions as well as an independent or at least quasi-independent status. And this was not just to satisfy their own egos. The archivists understood that new and old tasks had to be accomplished, but they believed those could best be done by an agency that had both the professional competence and prestige that would be recognized among all three branches of government and over the nation. They were not trying to resist change; they were seeking to guide it along the most fruitful avenues.[18]

On 21 March the archivist sent his response to President Truman. Grover concurred wholeheartedly in the Hoover Commission's recommendations for a new records management law and for establishing adequate records administration programs in all executive branch agencies. He asserted, however, that the creation of a records-management bureau in the proposed office of general services was "unnecessary and ill-advised and . . . contrary to certain of the basic principles proposed by the Commission." For example, the creation of centrally administered intermediate centers for records that were still relatively active clashed with the commission's recommendation that the management of housekeeping services within departments be decentralized "to the greatest extent possible." This was not to argue against records centers, but against their transfer from operation by the agencies whose still-active records were in them to administration by an entirely different agency. Where the existing decentralized approach was not practical, as in the Washington area, the proper solution, Grover declared, would be to expand the National Archives' Suitland facilities for active records of enduring value and to provide space for agency records operations. The archives and the Public Buildings Administration could also assist other agencies to establish needed regional records centers economically. As for the Leahy report's recommendation that centralization was necessary for more effective records management, Grover went along for only part of the way. He suggested that the small professional staff of records analysts needed to establish standards and controls for the making and keeping of records in federal agencies did not require an additional bureau in the proposed office of general services. Such personnel could be attached to the Budget Bureau. As for overseeing the line operation of federal records activities, records officers in the various agencies could best do that. Even if that were not so, the task could be easily and effectively done by creating a records-management division in the Budget Bureau or the National Archives. (Clearly, the archivist was appealing to the Budget Bureau, which would analyze his response, for support in an area in which they were both very much interested.) Grover apparently thought his most strategic argument was that the proposed records-management bureau could not assume the roles of the archivist and the National Archives Council because of their archival functions with respect to the judicial and legislative branches of government, which were not powers vested in the president; the authority of Congress to dispose of records, which had been delegated to no one and which Congress had "jealously" guarded; and the archivist's special professional competence in evaluating records for protecting the vital core of the documentation of government operations and citizen rights.

Grover plainly hoped to show that while there were pressing reasons to provide better administration for federal records, the establishment of a records-management bureau was neither a desirable nor an economical way to do it. As he wrote his predecessor, Solon Buck, "I don't want to give anyone an excuse for establishing a new bureau if I can help it." Grover's was a closely reasoned argument, but it was not beyond debate. As is often true in such situations, he could both win and lose, and in unexpected ways. The Hoover Commission staff, in any event, remained unmoved, for it staunchly adhered to its original recommendation for a records-management bureau.[19]

The Budget Bureau reacted quickly, though not completely unfavorably to the archivist's response to President Truman. Raymond C. Atkinson quickly dismissed the suggestion that the proposed change might lead to the establishment of separate legislative and judicial archival offices and create problems with the approval of a new bureau as Congress's agent in records disposal, since the National Archives was already located in the executive branch. He thought, however, that another of Grover's arguments deserved "careful consideration." That was that a new bureau for records management was neither necessary nor desirable because it clashed with the concept of decentralization of line housekeeping functions and because the advising of government agencies on records management and disposal could well be done by the National Archives and the Budget Bureau. Atkinson was probably not far from the truth in an afterthought that he penned in on his analysis to the effect that "the Archivist is more disturbed by the recommendation for putting Archives in a Bureau of Records Management than for putting it in OGS." More important is that Atkinson's hunch led the Budget Bureau to underestimate the concern of the staff of the National Archives for maintaining their agency's independence. That interest was genuine enough, but so was the archivist's apparent intuition that in the whirlwind of reorganization his institution would lose its separate status. In that case, the National Archives would prefer to be under an office of general services, which would have more budgetary influence, than under a records management bureau or, worse yet, under such a bureau in such an office. It was also clear that, either as an independent agency or as a bureau within a general services organization, the National Archives would rather be *the* government records office than have a bureau created that might compete with or absorb it.[20]

The Budget Bureau acted rapidly. On 28 March Budget Director Frank Pace, Jr., sent President Truman his recommendation regarding an office of general services. He endorsed the Hoover Commission report in large part. The most significant difference was that he made no recommendation on establishing a records-management bureau. The National Archives, Pace asserted, could "exercise effective government-wide leadership" in records management within a general services agency. This would be particularly true since the Public Buildings Administration would be part of the new organization too and thus federal records-management and space programs could be better coordinated. Also important was that the Budget Bureau disagreed with the Hoover Commission on placing the Smithsonian Institution, the National Capital Park and Planning Commission, and the Fine Arts Commission under the general services organization. The Budget Bureau won out, and therefore the National Archives, as a cultural agency, was isolated from kindred institutions.[21]

The National Archives was inextricably caught in the swiftly moving currents of the time. Congress wanted to act as soon as possible in response to the Hoover Commission's recommendations, and the Truman administration was equally interested in gaining reorganization powers. Since the idea of a general services agency was among the most acceptable of the commission's reorganization proposals, congressional and administration leaders quickly compromised their few differences on it. A pending bill, H.R. 2781, to improve property management in the government, was rewritten as H.R. 4754 to become the vehicle for achieving both that goal and the objectives contemplated for a general services office. By late April it became obvious to Grover that he stood no chance to stop his agency's inclusion in the new organization.

There was not enough time to mobilize archivists and researchers in defense of an independent National Archives. Moreover, there was no sign that researchers were greatly interested, and certainly Grover and Bahmer were not well enough known among the scholarly associations to gain their support for maintaining a separate National Archives. It is understandable that the archivist and his assistant bent their efforts to oppose the establishment of a records-management bureau. Therefore, the National Archives had to settle for becoming the records-management and archival organization under the supervision of a general services administrator.[22]

The sponsors of H.R. 4754 and its Senate equivalent moved ahead speedily. Indeed there were no legislative hearings on these bills and little debate as well as little discussion in the White House, which bore out the archivist's estimation that there was insufficient time for a counterattack. Not only was "reorganization" the watchword, but rapid reorganization at that, largely because of the desire of Congress, the Hoover Commission, and the White House to achieve economy and efficiency quickly. Furthermore, certain legislation that these bills were partly designed to replace was scheduled to expire on 30 June. Grover strove to retain his authority to make direct recommendations to Congress on the disposal of records. Representatives of the Hoover Commission, however, succeeded in their zeal for consolidation in having this deleted from the legislation, so that all of the archivist's significant functions would be transferred to the head of the new general services agency in order to strengthen his records-management authority. Nevertheless, the bills did not contain provision for a records-management bureau. By 30 June 1949, the House and the Senate had passed and the president had signed the new Federal Property and Administrative Services Act. The legislation basically gathered together under one superagency, the new General Services Administration, five previously independent agencies: the Bureau of Federal Supply, the Federal Works Agency (including the Public Buildings Administration), the National Archives, the Office of Contract Settlement, and the War Assets Administration.[23]

A good case can be made that over the years the General Services Administration has largely accomplished its chief objective of providing more economical and efficient management of government supply and property functions. It is not my purpose in this study, however, to deal with the GSA except as it has affected the work of the National Archives. Many of the essential issues about the National Archives' new status were raised right at the beginning. Oliver W. Holmes, who then headed the agency's Natural Resources Records Division, pointed these up in an article written in 1949. He believed there should be no serious problem in the new relationship *if* the administrator of general services delegated to the archivist and held that official responsible for exercising the powers necessary to carry on a sound, professional program of archives and records management. Another delicate balance to be struck was that the cultural and scholarly functions of the National Archives could not be, in any way, "relegated to a lesser rôle." Looking to the future, Holmes also suggested that the pertinent scholarly and professional associations consider creating a committee to keep close watch over the situation and "to furnish advice and support." (The American Historical Association's Committee on the Historian and the Federal Goverment served this purpose to a small extent, but it was not until the latter half of the 1960s that the AHA, Organization of American Historians, and Society of American Archivists jointly initiated watchdog efforts.) Holmes and most senior federal archivists were particularly disturbed that the congressional delegation of power to the general services administrator to recommend disposal of records could lead to ill-advised and even politically motivated decisions on the destruction of such material. Yet Holmes also saw many potential advantages in the new arrangement. These included the development of a coordinated federal records-management program, with adequate funding for archival as well as records work; the centralized control of records centers (which then numbered about 100, operated in various ways under various conditions); better cooperation between the National Archives and the Public Buildings Administration in space utilization; and the spurring of the adoption of general disposal schedules. In short, the invigorated association between archives and records management could contribute not only to increased efficiency and economy, but also to achieving better the established research aims of archivists and historians.[24]

On 1 July 1949, the National Archives became part of the new General Services Administration. It had lost its status as an independent federal agency, though not under circumstances as discouraging as would have been the case if it had been placed within a records management bureau. Moreover, there was the promise of having more funds available, even though the National Archives was under a mandate to become a broader-gauged operation. The agency clearly was, as Holmes had written, "at a turn in the road." Only time would tell what lay ahead.

13. Records Service

On 30 June 1949, when President Truman signed the Federal Property and Administrative Services Act into law, he also named the head of the Federal Works Agency, Jess Larson, administrator of general services. The Senate confirmed Larson a week later. He was forty-five years old and a lawyer by profession. He had been active in politics in Oklahoma, and, like the president, he was a long-time member of the National Guard with the rank of colonel. He had seen service during World War II and had been wounded in action. After the war, Larson had joined the War Assets Administration, becoming its chief late in 1947. He had served as federal works administrator for only eight weeks before assuming his new and larger responsibilities with the General Services Administration.

Larson swung vigorously into his new job. For the time being, the agencies gathered together in GSA remained functioning as they had been. Larson, however, appointed committees composed of representatives from those bureaus to advise him on the structuring, integration, and operations of the new agency. He made it plain that changes would take place consonant with achieving the mission of management reform with which the president had charged him. He also made it clear that the establishment of a government-wide records-management program was vital to that mission. "Maximum service at minimum cost" was the reputation he aimed at for GSA.[1]

The months following Larson's appointment were, as Wayne C. Grover wrote in August, "a period of turmoil" for the National Archives. Since this was linked to the "reorganization growing out of the Hoover Commission recommendations," the archivist admitted that he had "no one to blame but myself" in view of his contributions to them. Gradually the administrator's office took over functions that the archives had previously exercised for itself, such as legislative liaison and legal, personnel, and procurement matters. On 11 December the agency was given a new name, that of National Archives and Records Service. Its organization was also soon altered, with four major divisions operating under the Office of the Archivist, namely, the National Archives, the Franklin D. Roosevelt Library, the Federal Register Division, and the newly created Records Management Division. This did nothing to reduce the turmoil of which Grover had written, any more than it brought about the identification he had urged among his staff as employees of GSA as well as of NARS. As late as October 1950, he complained of the "confusion and dissatisfaction" among NARS officials and particularly of their tendency to blame all problems on GSA.[2] Those problems declined as time passed, but they never disappeared, partly because of the understandable difficulty of personnel in the National Archives and the presidential libraries to identify their work with GSA's management missions. That situation seemed to bear out the occasional criticism from outside GSA that cultural and management agencies could not be completely or happily integrated.

Yet there were advantages for the National Archives in being incorporated into GSA. Although the new agency intruded a layer of bureaucracy between the archivists and the White House and Congress, it did assume administrative tasks that the archivists had often found onerous. It also made NARS more conscious of how to do things efficiently. Equally important, NARS would be generally better financed and better protected from the occasional wrath of Congress and the White House than had been the National Archives. Larson, moreover, set a good example for his successors. From the beginning job classifications were not adversely affected, and NARS fared rather well in its budget hearings with GSA.[3] There would be troubles, of course. The archivist would have problems getting everything for his organization that he believed it needed, and occasionally officials in GSA's central office would be overbearing, interfering, and even obtuse. They were, however,

ever so much more effective at getting program authorizations and funds for NARS than the National Archives had ever been.

The increase in NARS's budget was impressive, swelling from less than $1,300,000 in fiscal year 1949 to about $2,500,000 two years later. Although most of the rise was for records management, some of it went to other operations within NARS. Then there was the advantage of being part of the agency that controlled space and supplies for the government. That was especially true in finding room to move some of the questionably valuable records out of the archives building and in refusing records that were "unscreened, too recent, too active, or of dubious enduring value" now that space was becoming available in newly acquired records centers. That also allowed the archivists to resume working on other tasks that had been sidetracked. By November 1951 Grover thought things looked so rosy that he could say, "NARS was generally pretty well staffed," which was a far cry from the fiscal panic that had seized the agency during the year before the advent of GSA.[4]

The archivist worked diligently and successfully at developing the records-management functions of NARS. That aspect of his labors following GSA's creation came to fruition in two significant and related developments in 1950: the passage of a new federal records law and the establishment of the Division of Records Management. The origins of the Federal Records Act of 1950 predated GSA. As we have seen, the National Archives under Robert D. W. Connor and Solon J. Buck had sponsored legislation and programs that were designed to begin grappling with the government's records. Wayne C. Grover was moved to press the Hoover Commission to recommend further action regarding federal records problems, and the commission agreed that ways had to be found to deal efficiently with them. The Property and Administrative Services Act of 1949, however, was enacted so rapidly that it did little more than hint at the coming of a comprehensive records management program. Although the law authorized the administrator of general services to study records management practices and to promote their improvement, specific legislation was needed to cope better with the records problem.[5]

The National Archives had begun drafting a far-reaching records administration bill as early as January 1949. It was clear by June, however, that the property and administrative services bill might not contain adequate authorizations for launching an effective government-wide records management program. Then Chairman Chet Holifield of the House Subcommittee on Organization of the Legislative and Executive Branches indicated keen interest in comprehensive records legislation. Assistant Archivist Robert H. Bahmer sent a copy of the National Archives' draft records management bill to Holifield on 14 June. Before the end of the month an attempt was made in conference committee to add this draft to the property and administrative services legislation, but that failed because of the press of time. Yet the National Archives, the Budget Bureau, and the appropriate congressional committees recognized the probability that the new legislation would have to be amended in the future in order to deal effectively with federal records problems.[6]

Soon after Jess Larson became administrator of general services, Bahmer secured his approval to cooperate with Congressman Holifield's subcommittee in drafting a records management bill. The work was done, largely by the archives' staff, during the first half of July, for the subcommittee wanted the bill introduced soon so that it could be taken up immediately at the 1950 session of Congress. Grover pressed Larson for his approval of the new draft bill. Although Larson indicated on 10 August 1949 his continued interest in having such legislation passed in 1950, he thought there was too much detail in the draft. The archivist asserted that there was no more detail in it than there was in the property section of the Property and Administrative Services Act. What Grover sought was that GSA be given responsibilities with respect to the records of the entire federal government, not just the executive branch. He also wanted a better statutory basis within GSA for the established operations of the National Archives as well as for the anticipated new records management functions. Crucial to that was the authorization of a federal records council with broad powers to take the place of the National Archives Council. Moreover, the archivist was insistent that Congress retain the prerogative of approving the destruction of federal records upon the recommendation of NARS.

This was because he feared that federal agencies would feel less willing to abide by decisions made on a level lower than Congress, with the result that fewer useless records would be destroyed and other material would be destroyed prematurely. It was also clear that congressional approval of the destruction of records would relieve GSA and NARS of criticism if later the materials disposed of were wanted by House or Senate investigating committees.[7]

By the end of August the archivist had been excluded from some of the discussions in GSA of proposed records legislation. In fact Larson had come increasingly under the persuasion of the Budget Bureau, which believed that the draft bill espoused by NARS and the Holifield subcommittee was overly detailed. The bureau also disagreed with some of the bill's organizational provisions, particularly those relating to a federal records council. Grover continued working to influence Larson, but the results were not completely satisfactory. Indeed they had led to a gulf between GSA and the Holifield subcommittee by January 1950. By then, however, NARS had persuaded GSA to accept almost all of its draft. Grover's legislative adviser, Thaddeus Page, therefore recommended that NARS end its agitation, since Larson had accepted so much of what they wanted and "since we have to deal immediately with GSA."[8]

Representative Richard Bolling of Missouri by March 1950 introduced comprehensive records legislation, which he resubmitted on 8 May after all involved had come to agreement. That was by then a sizable company that included interested members of Congress, NARS, GSA, the Budget Bureau, the Society of American Archivists, the president, the Comptroller General's Office, records management expert Emmett J. Leahy, and (because of Leahy) the Citizens Committee for the Hoover Report. John L. McClellan of Arkansas offered similar legislation in the Senate in July. By 5 September the House and Senate unanimously passed the Federal Records Act as an amendment to the Property and Administrative Services Act, and President Truman approved the measure that day.[9]

The Federal Records Act of 1950 not only pulled together most of the previous legislation relating to the National Archives and applied it within the framework of GSA, but the new law also added considerably to the authority of GSA and NARS. The administrator of general services was charged with improving procedures, methods, and standards regarding the creation of records, their organization, maintenance, and use when current, and their disposition when they were no longer current. Moreover, he was specifically authorized to operate records centers. He inherited the archivist's powers to accept federal records for deposit in the National Archives (when the archivist judged them to be of enduring value) and to inspect and survey records in federal agencies. The general services administrator was also empowered to accept the personal papers, when offered for deposit, of the president and other high executive officials. Two other changes were the establishment of the Federal Records Council, although only advisory in nature, in place of the National Archives Council and the expansion of the membership and functions of the National Historical Publications Commission. The act directed heads of federal agencies to make and keep adequate records of all aspects of their organizations' operations and to run effective records-management programs. To foster the work of controlling the creation of records, their efficient administration while current, and their prompt and orderly retirement when no longer current, the law gave the general services administrator the power to inspect the agencies' records-management practices and to have agency heads use GSA-operated records centers for storage purposes whenever that was deemed most economical or efficient. Congress retained its authority to approve of the disposal of federal records.[10]

Thus had Grover and a growing company of officials who were interested in records management finally prepared the government to begin taking adequate care of its records, lest its various agencies be smothered in a blanket of paper of their own creation. The Federal Records Act of 1950 also had the desirable result of specifically restating the powers of the former National Archives and even in some cases expanding them. All this seemed to many to compensate for the loss of the National Archives' status as an independent federal agency, and all the more so as Jess Larson soon delegated to the archivist all of the archival and records functions that had by law been assigned to the general services administrator. The failure of the law (which continues to the present time with respect to the Supreme Court) to specify GSA's right to accept judicial records for deposit did not interrupt the flow of such documents into the archives. The fuzziness, however, of the agency's power under the new law to requisition the older records of the executive branch would be nettlesome until remedied later in the 1950s.[11]

Although fourteen months passed between the enactment of the Property and Administrative Services Act and the Federal Records Act, Wayne Grover used the miniscule records-management provisions of the former "to follow up as vigorously as possible on the objectives of the Leahy report."[12] The records work of NARS fell into four basic categories, which were securing necessary legislation and regulations, establishing the Records Management Division, creating records centers, and promoting records-administration programs in federal agencies.

I have already noted the campaign for a comprehensive records law, but also important was the promulgation of two sets of regulations. The first was readily prepared. This set concerned microphotographic standards that the National Archives Council issued in July 1949 and the president approved in August. The idea was to encourage the microphotographing of a larger number of records of intermediate value so that the originals could be destroyed, thus saving space, equipment, and staff time through the reduction of bulk. The second set of regulations was more far reaching and took NARS, with the advice of the Federal Records Council, until December 1951 to develop. Designed to establish standards for the implementation of records-management programs, this group was incorporated as part of the *Regulations of the General Services Administration*. The regulations dealt with agency records-control plans (which all executive agencies had to implement by the middle of 1954); general retention and disposal schedules; and other methods of and conditions for disposition, reproduction, and transfers of records to records centers, the National Archives, or other executive agencies. The aim of the regulations was to force federal agencies to develop records-management programs that would result in greater economy and operational efficiency, better documentation of operations, and a smoother flow of enduringly valuable records to the archives. Certainly, those regulations were to be central to the Records Management Division's struggle to cope with the government's records problems.[13]

Helping to stop the gap meanwhile was Theodore R. Schellenberg's forty-page booklet *The Disposition of Federal Records*, which the National Archives issued late in 1949. The pundits greeted it with derision. Caskie Stinnett suggested that "this be the first record disposed of," and William Knapp noted that it was distinguished by its "crabwise verbiage." Nevertheless, if Schellenberg failed to get his message across to the press, his work was technically excellent, and it was widely read by those who were gifted with the ability to translate the mysteries of federalese.[14]

The National Archives also fully informed Larson about the government's records problems and its recommended solutions to them. By 25 July 1949, the archives had processed a document for him pointing out that there were more than 20,000,000 cubic feet of federal records extant and that those materials were accumulating at the annual rate of about 1,000,000 cubic feet. Seventy percent of the government's records were in the field and at least three-quarters of them could be scheduled for periodic destruction; the remaining records were located in the Washington area and 60 percent of these could be disposed of within a reasonable time. According to the archivists, the problem of too many records could be dealt with by imposing "birth control" procedures on needlessly created records, promptly disposing of records when they became useless, using records centers and microfilm to store many records less expensively, improving methods of keeping records, and making sure that records did the essential tasks of documenting policy and of reference. The way to accomplish all this was to employ a specialized staff to make certain that it was carried out. Larson was impressed by the document and he used it as a basis for both GSA's program development and his public statements. He was certainly convinced that there was a grave records problem. As he said in one speech, using a favorite National Archives analogy, it requires the equivalent of six Pentagon buildings to store the government's records, and it costs well over a billion dollars yearly to make and keep federal records. What was needed, he declared, was a "lot of bonfires."[15]

Larson, despite his inflammatory rhetoric, followed the advice of the National Archives in principle, if not always in detail. In addition to supporting the movement for comprehensive records legislation, he authorized the establishment of the Records Management Division in NARS with money that he procured from the president's management improvement fund. NARS in January 1950 brought back two of its former staff members from the navy, where they had worked alongside Emmett J. Leahy in pioneering records-management programs. They were Herbert E. Angel, who was to head the new division, and Everett D. Alldredge, who was to be his deputy with particular responsibility for supervising records centers.[16]

Angel and Alldredge were a vigorous and imaginative pair of leaders. Starting from scratch, they had to put together a new bureaucratic structure that would satisfy the high aims of the archives, the general services administrator, the president, and Congress. Angel and Alldredge could not proceed in a leisurely fashion, and they did not. They steadily built a staff, recruiting experienced people when they could but often molding considerable numbers of persons with raw talent when they had to. They were very much in the same position that Robert Connor had been in when he became archivist of the United States in 1934, except that they did not have a building in the final stages of completion. Although Larson and Grover backed them as much as possible, there was seldom enough money. Angel indeed had to borrow staff from other divisions of NARS to make progress during the rest of fiscal year 1950.[17]

The main objective of the Records Management Division was to use the last half of fiscal year 1950 to prepare for the launching of a full-scale, government-wide program during the following year. By 30 June 1950 considerable progress was made. A pilot records center was opened in Brooklyn in the Naval Clothing Depot by 1 May, and within two months it had taken in 45,000 cubic feet of records, thus releasing 57,000 square feet of more valuable room. The net saving was $57,000 in space alone; it was estimated that avoidance of costs in buying new equipment would run almost $300,000. Negotiations were started for the establishment of centers in the three other urban areas of Washington, Chicago, and San Francisco where there was the largest concentration of federal records. Moreover, the division conducted a survey of some eighty government offices to see what components were included in their records-management programs. Only four of them contained all of the eleven elements (correspondence management, reports control, administrative issuances control, forms control, paperwork procedures control, microphotography, mail service, files operations, records-retirement programs, records storage and centers, and space and equipment clearance) considered minimal by Leahy's Hoover Commission Records Management Task Force. Clearly, a huge educational task lay ahead for the Records Management Division.

Angel also began surveys of the number of records held by federal agencies. This was only the beginning of such studies, but by June Angel knew enough to conclude that previous estimates of the amount of government records and what was being done about them were too optimistic. For example, only thirty-seven executive agencies had records-disposal schedules. It was discovered, too, that federal agencies not only operated 104 records centers of their own, but that they used 204 other storage locations for their accumulations of noncurrent records. This finding pointed to an area where considerable efficiency and economy could be achieved through the use of fewer, larger, better located, and more centrally administered centers.[18]

Congress financed the Records Management Division in fiscal year 1951 so that it could really move ahead. During the year its average number of employees was 109, which was almost a quarter of NARS's entire work force. In September 1950 a unit of the division was placed in each of GSA's ten regions to promote better records-management procedures in field agencies and to set up records centers to receive, service, protect, and screen for disposition records of intermediate value. That same month the Washington area center was established in several buildings that had previously constituted the Naval Torpedo Plant in Alexandria, Virginia. That facility, with 421,625 square feet of room, was the largest among the early federal records centers. By 30 June 1951, the New York City center had been enlarged, and the division had established federal records centers in Chicago and San Francisco. There were multitudinous problems, among them shortages of funds and equipment because of the requirements of the Korean War. Nevertheless, the four centers accomplished a great deal. They had received more than 550,000 cubic feet of records by the end of the fiscal year, thus allowing the release for other purposes of 520,000 square feet of more expensive office and storage space as well as an appreciable amount of office filing equipment. While the prime function of center personnel was the transferral of records, they were also able to dispose of 45,000 cubic feet of records, provide 69,000 reference services, and begin their program of microfilming and storing vital papers for security purposes. The division also operated similar, though smaller, establishments in the other six GSA regions. They were called GSA centers, to distinguish them from federal records centers, because they were smaller and located in temporary quarters. They accessioned about 50,000 cubic feet of records by the end of fiscal year 1951.[19]

By 1953 NARS's network of records centers had proved its worthiness, despite the setbacks encountered as a result of the Korean War. Federal records centers were now operating in eight of the ten GSA regions: Alexandria, Atlanta, Boston, Chicago, Denver, Fort Worth, New York City, and San Francisco. There was a special repository for federal civilian personnel records in St. Louis and the GSA centers in Kansas City and Seattle were scheduled to be designated federal records centers. Moreover, there were small records annexes located in Los Angeles, New Orleans, Philadelphia, and Portland, Oregon, and another would soon open in Honolulu. By 30 June 1953, the federal records centers contained 1,881,000 cubic feet of records; there had been 902,000 reference inquiries during the previous fiscal year and 88,000 cubic feet of records had been disposed of. GSA estimated the replacement cost of the equipment freed at $3,109,000 and the annual rental cost of the reassignable 669,000 square feet of released office and storage space at $1,054,000. In addition, Records Management Division personnel disposed of 200,300 cubic feet of records in the agencies holding them, and federal records center employees microfilmed almost 8,500,000 pages of vital records. The personnel records center at St. Louis held 317,000 cubic feet of material and received 518,000 inquiries during fiscal year 1953.[20]

There were numerous problems, of course, in getting Herbert Angel's paper empire into full operation. The shelving equipment on hand did not keep pace with the volume of records pouring into the centers, and although the amount of space available in the records centers continued to grow, it was not as fast as had been anticipated nor were the structures the most desirable for records-storage purposes. Then there were staff problems. Even though an average of 387 NARS employees worked in the records centers in fiscal year 1952, with dozens more authorized to be hired the following year, there were not enough of them, and too high a percentage were novices at records management. Grover commented upon this after a tour of several centers. He pointed out that the staff's preoccupation with "meeting accessioning quotas" and their inexperience in describing records gave him the impression that the disposal program was lagging.

There were special problems, too. The Kansas City flood of 1951 threw the development of the center there off schedule, as employees had to spend time on leveeing and then evacuation to another temporary site. Not until 1955 did the repository find a permanent location. The Honolulu records annex reported a unique situation. Mongooses, which years earlier had been brought to Hawaii to kill rats, roamed the building after hours, "chasing each other about and screaming shrilly." Since they were capable of damaging the building and the records, an operation was launched to exterminate the animals. The score in early 1955 stood at six mongooses caught; five were executed and one escaped.

Not the least of the Records Management Division's problems was political in nature. Agencies in Washington, for example, were reluctant to allow their field officers to deal directly with NARS's regional personnel, and it was not "going to be easy," as Wayne Grover wrote in 1951, "to loosen some of the Washington reins." By perseverance, however, in both the capital and the regions, the problem was fairly well solved by 1953. It should be observed that NARS was not creating a similar problem on its side. Although Grover and Angel constantly demanded greater field accomplishments, they allowed their regional supervisors and center managers considerable latitude in deciding how to achieve NARS's records-management objectives. This was wise, for theirs was a pioneering venture operating under varying conditions all over the United States. As one veteran center manager has said, it was a case of the central office using "the carrot and sometimes the stick, but never the axe." There was also politics in the traditional sense with which to contend, for GSA regional directors were invariably political appointees as were some of their deputies who supervised NARS field activities. Career records managers often found that they had to develop ingenious strategies to deal with the political machinations of their bosses. Fortunately for them as the years passed the NARS regional offices gained more autonomy and their directors (who by 1956 were called NARS regional directors) became chiefly career civil servants.[21]

There was, of course, more to the division's program than the centers. As soon as the Federal Records Act was passed, NARS pressed the general services administrator to establish the Federal Records Council. It took some time to get the council's members appointed and together, for its twelve members came from all three branches of the federal government. Their first meeting was finally held in June 1951. The Federal Records Council turned out to be a useful mix of political officials and senior civil servants, and it included several professional archivists and records managers such as Helen L. Chatfield of the Budget Bureau, Ollon D. McCool of the Defense Department, and Fred W. Shipman of the State Department. The council quickly developed into not only a good sounding board, but also into an effective channel of communication between NARS and other government agencies for archival and records-management programs.[22]

The Records Management Division's personnel throughout the country labored hard to achieve conformity in government agencies with the provisions of the Federal Records Act and the regulations issued pursuant to it. They sought to have each agency operate an effective records-management program and, especially, to adopt disposal schedules and to expedite the removal of non-current records to NARS facilities. They were also concerned with phasing out agency centers. By fiscal year 1953, fourteen general disposal schedules were in force, covering about 10 percent of all federal records. The division also formulated plans to issue pamphlets to instruct agency personnel in various phases of records management. The staff continued making surveys of the records holdings of government offices, which led to the disposal on the spot of a large amount of useless material. The 104 agency records centers had been reduced to 75 by the end of 1952. Although the exigencies of the Korean War hampered some aspects of the division's work, shortages also impelled other federal offices to be unanticipatedly cooperative in establishing their records-management programs and using NARS facilities. To take advantage of that, the division, whenever possible, gave technical assistance to the agencies. Its management staff had almost doubled during fiscal year 1952, so it was better able to do that kind of work. Technical assistance aimed particularly at increasing the number of records controlled by some sort of disposal schedule, and between fiscal years 1951 and 1954 the percentage of federal records remaining unscheduled dropped from 44 to 5. NARS records managers provided other services, such as assistance in preparing manuals, installing filing systems, and training records personnel. The Records Management Division also joined with the Federal Supply Service to keep agencies from ordering excessive amounts of filing equipment, with the result that the procurement of filing cabinets declined from 97,000 in 1951 to 32,000 in 1952.[23]

The records service had taken shape quite well by 1954. Although the number of federal records centers would change a bit in location and number during the ensuing years, the network was functioning effectively. The regulations for records management would change, too, but the basic rules had been well established. The Records Management Division had quickly gone to work to see that the regulations and the law upon which they were based were obeyed. The staff had done a great deal to help found or revise records programs in federal agencies, either through educational methods, distributing pamphlets, giving advice, or even going in and doing the task themselves. And they had contributed to improving standards for the use of filing equipment and microphotography in records management. NARS further expanded the work of the Interagency Records Administration Conference in Washington; it also sponsored similar educational programs for records personnel in Atlanta and Dallas. Moreover, studies and surveys continued, partly in order to monitor progress and partly to let individual agencies know how to improve their operations.[24]

In December 1953 Wayne Grover said, "Sometimes I reflect with anguish and a degree of personal mortification" that the federal government's archivists have "become known and acclaimed for the expert way in which they dispose of records." That kind of work, he believed, was not the heart of the archival profession. Yet the proliferation of government records had to be dealt with, not just to keep administration relatively unencumbered, but also to make sure that the documentation of the nation's heritage was preserved. He had no doubt that the great rate of records creation threatened a breakdown of the whole system. Certainly, despite the labors of archivists and records managers, the problem had not yet been solved, for while they had disposed of three million cubic feet of records during fiscal year 1953, four million had been made. "The net gain," the archivist wryly observed, "was thus happily reduced to only one new Archives building full each year." Clearly, the country could not afford to erect another such building every year.[25]

Yet the government was trying to face up to its records problem. If it had not been solved, a start had been made. And, thanks to NARS and particularly its Records Management Division, the government was becoming increasingly effective not only at containing the flood of paper, but at channeling it in ways that would better serve administration, scholarship, and the documentation of citizens' rights as well. NARS was also contributing to keeping down the concomitant costs in providing caretakers, filing equipment, space, paper, file folders, and all the other paraphernalia needed to produce and protect records.[26]

The struggle would sometimes take new avenues, but it would be ceaseless.

14. The National Archives Division

It was clear to Archivist Wayne Grover during the early 1950s that he had been involved in a series of decisions that would have a profound effect on the established operations of his organization. In the whirlwinds created by the proliferation of federal records and the work of the Hoover Commission, he had successfully championed keeping, as he wrote, "all the records activities of the federal government under the archivists' banner." When the question of whether the chief of a new records institution should be called commissioner of federal records or archivist of the United States was raised, he favored the latter in order "to keep the professional archivist on top of the heap." Not all appreciated Grover's wish to keep archival and records administration together. As he realized, his course placed a burden on archivists by asking them to combine a large-scale management program with their traditional scholarly functions. Yet, as the archivist saw it, the National Archives was the "very heart" of the National Archives and Records Service, and the work of the Records Management Division would achieve excellent results for it. Chief among those was to relieve the National Archives from receiving records of less than enduring value and from carrying out a number of records-management functions. The consequence would be to give the archivists time to clear marginal material out of the archives building; to apply stricter standards of appraisal to potential accessions; to begin to catch up on the backlog of repair, arranging, and description tasks; and to keep up with "the radical changes that are taking place in the of-

247

fices that produce archives." Moreover, according to Grover, the records service would operate to reduce further the loss or damage of records of enduring value before the National Archives accessioned them.[1]

When NARS was organized in December 1949, the National Archives, along with the new Records Management Division, became one of its two chief units. Grover, as archivist of the United States, headed the overall organization, with Robert H. Bahmer continuing as assistant archivist and Herbert E. Angel becoming director of records management. Theodore R. Schellenberg, as head of the National Archives Division, was Angel's counterpart. A member of the staff since 1935, Schellenberg had proved outstandingly able in a variety of jobs in the National Archives, most recently as program adviser. The title that he bore beginning in 1950 was director of archival management.

Schellenberg's division was very much like what the National Archives had been before it became the "very heart" of NARS. Of course, Grover's office handled supplementary services, such as property and finance, as well as the Roosevelt Library and the Federal Register Division; and the National Historical Publications Commission, under the archivist's chairmanship, theoretically remained separate from NARS. Within the new National Archives Division, the old divisions were downgraded to branches, and most of the former branches were downgraded to sections. Director of Archival Management Schellenberg thus was responsible for seven records branches: war, natural resources, industrial, legislative and veterans, general, audiovisual, and cartographic. Those branches conducted the basic work of appraisal, accessioning, arranging, preservation, description, and reference. There were, moreover, two service branches. The records-control branch handled the planning and coordination relating to finding aids, file microcopy work, and reference service, and it operated the central search rooms and the library. The preservation services branch was the authority on preservation policies; dealt with the internal security and use of the archives building; and carried out the physical transfer, cleaning, fumigating, and repair of records. An exhibits and publications officer attached to Schellenberg's office was concerned with exhibitive, instructional, and certain public-relations functions.[2]

Months before he placed Schellenberg in charge of the National Archives Division, Grover moved ahead with several programs of vital interest. One was to find a solution to the flammability and the high deterioration of nitrate-based film, problems that had long plagued the National Archives. Indeed, this was one of the first matters that the archivist had raised with the administrator of general services. Jess Larson was sympathetic but "doubted that there was anything we can do about it." He was probably correct so far as gaining millions of dollars from Congress for the construction of fireproof facilities. Grover, however, did not give up, although the solution was different from the one that had been anticipated originally. Marcus W. Price, the chief archivist of the audiovisual records branch, observed that funds might be granted to take advantage of technological developments that allowed nitrocellulose film to be copied onto nonflammable triacetate stock. This could be done at a fraction of the cost of building and maintaining safe motion-picture film vaults. Congress approved this new approach and in 1953 appropriated $200,000 to initiate it. The National Archives' photo-science laboratory, the Agriculture Department, and the Signal Corps did the work of converting the film then on hand to more permanent stock. The task was finished by 1958,[3] but new accessions of nitrate film made the conversion process a never-ending task.

Grover also successfully pressed the revival of the production of guides to the records of World War II. He saw that to be not only a project of intrinsic worth, but an opportunity for archivists to develop competence in subject matter so that they could give superior reference consultation and produce better finding aids to the records. The time was soon right to move in this direction. With the coming of the Korean War in June 1950, a variety of agencies demanded information from World War II files. The government thus allocated $100,000 to resurrect the World War II records description project. It helped to speed the completion of the two-volume guide, *Federal Records of World War II*, as well as the preparation of a number of inventories and detailed lists of wartime records. Consequently, the National Archives was better armed to answer the many inquiries from federal agencies that were directly involved in the Korean War. The emphasis, however, on the World War II work had led to the sidetracking of a number of other worthwhile description projects. Therefore, the archivist called it off in late 1951, partly because enough had been done to cope with pertinent reference requests and partly because it had upset the development of an orderly approach to meeting other goals of the National Archives.[4]

The third thing that Grover was most involved in before Schellenberg became director of archival management was the most important item of business: the space problem of the National Archives. In submitting legislative program estimates to Administrator Larson in 1949, the archivist asked not only for a new $5,125,000 structure to house nitrate film safely, but also for $3,100,000 to provide additional space in the archives building and $11,000,000 for construction of an annex to the building. Grover did not expect to receive much if any of those funds, but in making the request he was dramatically able to make the point that "Space in the National Archives building is virtually exhausted." As he emphasized, accessions had to be drastically limited during fiscal year 1950; he doubted "that any space in the building will be available for records after this year."[5]

NARS did not get funds for additional room for the archives, so another tack had to be taken that was basically to be determined by Schellenberg. His first task was to find out exactly what was happening in the operating units and what resources were at hand, and then to devise clear policies and procedures to achieve the division's essential aims. It was plain to him that several things had to be done quickly. These included making space for archival accessions by moving out records of less than enduring value; improving appraisal, arrangement, and descriptive standards; and making maximum use of the staff and facilities available. All this had to be done without disrupting reference service and indeed with a hoped-for increase in preservation work.[6]

Schellenberg and Grover resurrected the *Staff Information Circular* series, which had been a victim of World War II exigencies, in order to provide the staff with the best ideas available on various basic operations. Thus in 1950 and 1951 the National Archives issued pamphlets entitled "The Preparation of Preliminary Inventories," "The Control of Records at the Record Group Level," "The Rehabilitation of Paper Records," "The Preparation of Detailed Lists of Records," "Principles of Arrangement," and "The Preparation of Records for Publication on Microfilm." Although these circulars had considerable influence beyond the walls of the archives building, they were meant chiefly to meet the division's immediate problems. They served reasonably well in that capacity.[7]

The results of Schellenberg's new order were substantial despite a tightening of funds from GSA. His overall goal was the survival of the National Archives as a viable organization, and his approach penetrated every corner of the division in order to achieve that end. Thanks to the tighter appraisal and disposal standards outlined in Schellenberg's 1949 manual, *The Disposition of Federal Records*, for several years the division moved out more material from the archives building than it accessioned. By accepting less and disposing of more, the holdings dropped from 908,852 to 749,500 cubic feet between 1950 and 1955, when the reduction program was completed. The National Archives did not trust its own judgment completely in carrying out this massive project, so from time to time it called in consultants for their appraisals. Opinion was virtually unanimous that the application of Schellenberg's standards reduced bulk without jeopardizing the documentation essential for research, government operations, and the maintenance of citizens' rights. Of course, the growth of records centers was of great help in all this. They not only absorbed the records that the National Archives determined to be less than enduringly valuable, but they also served as depositories for incoming materials about which final decisions had to be made as to their archival quality.[8]

Schellenberg was concerned too with better organizing his division's holdings physically for the purposes of analysis, description, and reference. Therefore, in fiscal year 1952 he began planning to rearrange the location of archives. This program's aims were to provide the most valuable materials with the greatest amount of protection, to arrange records on the basis of accepted archival principles, and to consolidate empty stack space for better handling of future accessions. Because of shortages of personnel, equipment, and room, the division did not begin the relocation program until September 1953. It was a slow process, with only 82,000 cubic feet being rearranged by 30 June 1954. The work was speeded thereafter and was considered complete by July 1956 after a total of 555,000 cubic feet of archives had been moved. From then on, it was easier for the National Archives to keep current in arranging new accessions and to carry out its reference, analysis, and description duties.[9]

Schellenberg also ranked preservation and repair activities high on his list of priorities. The problems of the 1940s had made it impossible to keep up with needs in those areas, and the poor arrangement of archives had impaired the efficiency of whatever was done. Of course, the National Archives fumigated all newly received records, as was essential, and cleaned, packed, and shelved materials when necessary. That had left, for years, little time for repair. Fiscal year 1950, when only 168,000 sheets were rehabilitated, saw no change in this situation. During the next four years, the National Archives devoted more time to this, repairing some 2,625,000 sheets as well as a small amount of passenger lists, still-picture negatives, film, and bound volumes. That was not enough, however, for a survey taken in 1953 indicated that 8,000,000 items urgently needed repair and another 11,000,000 had to be attended to soon. And that did not include motion-picture film. Even the increasing use of microfilm to preserve brittle archives made little more than a dent in this problem. Higher congressional appropriations helped to step up rescue efforts, so that in fiscal year 1957, 1,054,000 items were microfilmed and another 416,000 otherwise saved from deterioration. That, however, was still not enough. Preservation and repair would continue to be a major problem for the National Archives.[10]

Analysis and description was another program spurred by Schellenberg. Originally, the National Archives Division emphasized spreading knowledge of its World War II records. By 1952, however, it could spend time on describing various other documents. The result during the following years was an adequate production of lists and other guides. And there were related developments. The *National Archives Accessions*, which had been published quarterly since 1940 to publicize recent acquisitions, was expanded in 1954 to include articles and pertinent news notes. Consequently, such excellent pieces of scholarship came to light as Carl L. Lokke's "The Continental Congress Papers: Their History, 1789–1952." The problem was that the publication was not issued regularly. Indeed, between June 1954 and December 1967 only ten issues appeared. The file microcopy program expanded substantially during the years immediately following the consolidation of the National Archives with GSA. Between fiscal years 1950 and 1955, the number of rolls available for purchase more than doubled to 5,800; and since 1948, when the program had been given a better financial basis, some 25,000 rolls had been sold.[11]

Reference service still commanded about one-half of the time of the staff of the National Archives. The statistics on use, however, varied considerably between fiscal years 1949 and 1956. The total number of inquiries handled stood at about 78,000 and 79,700, respectively, in those two years, but ran as high as almost 113,000 in 1952. The volume of records and reproductions furnished for research reached a peak of 372,900 in 1953 but numbered 299,000 in 1949 and 334,000 in 1956. Although much time was spent in trying to explain those fluctuations exactly, no one could do so. Apparently coming into play was the rising research use of records centers and of file microcopies. It also seemed that the proportion of complicated scholarly requests increased, which required more time to service. Yet the fact was that by the middle 1950s not as many people as had been anticipated were using the National Archives.[12]

The staff sought to publicize the National Archives' holdings and services further. This was partly the motive behind paying more attention to the preparation of guides to the records and to advising scholars and graduate students about worthwhile research topics. Also noteworthy in trying to generate interest were articles like Philip C. Brooks's "Archives and the Young Historian" and "The Historian's Stake in Federal Records," and Wayne Grover's "The National Archives and the Scholar." Historians and archivists outside NARS echoed concern about the use of archives. They indicated that historians were failing to make adequate use of the treasures awaiting them in repositories and that archivists had to do a better job of attracting scholarly researchers. More cooperation between them was plainly needed.[13] Fortunately for all concerned, a new time was coming. Soon, not only would the ranks of professional historians greatly increase, but there would be a higher proportion of those who were research-oriented among them.

If the National Archives worried about the fluctuations in archival research during the decade after World War II, it did not have to worry about the patronage of its facsimile and exhibits programs. Grover was very much interested in them as a way of boosting the service and public-relations aspects of his organization. He and Schellenberg employed to good effect Karl L. Trever, a veteran archivist, to reinvigorate those programs. Trever soon expanded the facsimiles to include handsome, inexpensive reproductions of fifteen great documents such as the Declaration of Independence and Abraham Lincoln's Emancipation Proclamation. Additionally, in 1952 there was the facsimile publication, reduced in size, of the Declaration of Independence, the Constitution, and the Bill of Rights in a handsome booklet entitled *Charters of Freedom*. That sold 165,000 copies in less than five years. The archives building's ever-changing exhibits on such things as the United Nations Charter, Korea, and Mathew Brady's photographs of the Civil War drew more and more visitors. Between 1949 and 1956 their annual number soared from 79,000 to 420,000. By 1956 NARS had also produced a color film, "Your National Archives," for popular viewing.[14]

Mentioning the *Charters of Freedom* indicates that at least one of the initial goals of the National Archives had been attained. Although the second archivist of the United States, Solon J. Buck, had been indifferent to the matter, Grover was as intensely concerned as their predecessor, Robert D. W. Connor, had been with acquiring "our heart's desire," the original engrossed copies of the Declaration of Independence and the Constitution as well as the records of the Continental Congress and the Constitutional Convention. The State Department had transferred most of these documents to the Library of Congress in 1922, although the National Archives had accessioned the rest of them, including the Bill of Rights, sixteen years later. In part, the archives building had been built to house the entire group, and presidents Hoover and Roosevelt had thought it the proper resting place for them. The Library of Congress in 1951 took precautions to provide better protection for its display of the Declaration of Independence and the Constitution. The library also sponsored a grand ceremony, with President Truman and Chief Justice Fred M. Vinson on hand, to celebrate their reincasement on 17 September 1951. That was too much for Grover. He directed that the matter be looked into discreetly but thoroughly. Thaddeus Page, his legislative expert, reported that legally the records of the Continental Congress were part of the government's archives. Arthur E. Kimberly of the preservation services branch observed that the Library of Congress had not taken adequate precautions against shock, bombing, fire, or temperature changes. The solution, Kimberly believed, was to move the Declaration and the Constitution to the National Archives' exhibition hall, which was designed to give them comprehensive protection.

The archivist believed he could try to requisition the papers of the Continental Congress as government archives. He decided, however, to avoid the nasty fight to which that could have led. After reviewing for Librarian of Congress Luther H. Evans the law, the present vulnerability of the documents, and the superior facilities of the National Archives, Grover wrote, "I leave it to your good judgment." Evans, confronted with the evidence and the archivist's ardent interest, gave in. Therefore, early in 1952, the two officials agreed upon a transfer of the papers after clearing the matter with the president and the necessary members of Congress. By May Congress's Joint Committee on the Library ordered the transfer of the precious documents to the National Archives. It was, as Luther Evans explained to his staff, "an emotional wrench to surrender the custody of the principal documents of American liberty. Logic and law require it, however." To Grover, Evans wrote of himself as being "darned broadminded and just a wee bit righteous." Grover added his own footnote to this "ahem, historic transaction," observing that "Jefferson wanted on his tombstone that he wrote the Declaration. I want on mine that I saw it safely enshrined in the Archives of the United States."[15]

The archivist had some extra funds available for the protection of documents, so he was able to speed what Evans called the "completion of the bridal chamber." The additional protective arrangement was that the Declaration of Independence, the Constitution, and the Bill of Rights could be, in case of emergency, mechanically lowered into a vault that was described as "the last word in fireproof, theft-proof, bomb-proof protection." In June the main body of the records of the Continental Congress and the Constitutional Convention, amounting to 190 cubic feet, was moved to the archives.

Grover made a grand event of the later transfer of the Declaration of Independence and the Constitution. That took place on 13 December 1952, when they were escorted down from Capitol Hill, along a route lined with servicemen and women and musical and other detachments from the Air Force, Army, Coast Guard, Marine Corps, and Navy. The documents traveled in an armored personnel carrier, which was preceded and followed by tanks. Two days later the dedication of the enshrinement of the documents took place in the archives building's exhibition hall in equally splendid ceremonies presided over by Chief Justice Vinson. After speeches by President Truman and Senator Theodore Green of Rhode Island, Archivist Grover and Librarian Evans unveiled the shrine in which lay the Declaration of Independence, the Constitution, and the Bill of Rights. Grover thought of this as the most stirring moment of his career.[16]

Although this may have been the most glorious occasion in the National Archives' history, it was not that institution's only "heart's desire" to be satisfied during the early 1950s. In March 1935 the question had been raised of incorporating the State Department's territorial papers project into the National Archives. Congress had funded the project in 1929 to make available in published form the most significant papers relating to the history of the territories of the United States; and it had been ably guided by Clarence E. Carter, its editor since 1931. Both Carter and Connor believed that the territorial papers project should become part of the National Archives, because of the advantage of the project being close to the documentation and because they assumed the archives would become the center for federal historical publications. The State Department raised no serious objection to the move. Yet the project's transfer was not consummated, apparently because Solon Buck, then the National Archives' publications chief, found almost everything but publications interesting to pursue.[17]

The question arose again in 1949 in connection with the Hoover Commission's work in reorganizing the executive branch. Clarence Carter, however, had changed his mind and was reluctant to see his unit moved out of the State Department, whether to the archives, the Library of Congress, or the Interior Department, as had been variously suggested. His reason was that none of them was conducting a program of extended historical research, while the State Department was, both in his project's work and in the Foreign Relations of the United States series. Nevertheless, the National Archives was eager to acquire the territorial papers project. Grover won Carter over in January 1950 by promising to continue his status, to transfer his coworkers with him, and to make special efforts to win additional financial support for the project. The State Department and the Budget Bureau agreed to the move. Certainly, it was in line with the already approved transfer of the preserving and publishing of constitutional amendments, materials regarding presidential electors and their votes, and the statutes at large. It was a small matter, all being agreed, to incorporate the transfer of those functions and of the territorial papers project to NARS into Reorganization Plan No. 20, which President Truman submitted to Congress on 13 March 1950.[18]

The plan went into effect on 24 May, and Carter and his small staff were immediately moved over to the National Archives Division. Moreover, in July Larson acted successfully to increase the project's annual funding from $30,000 to $50,000. Carter, in November, concluded that the transfer had been advantageous because of his "better and speedier" access to the pertinent records, the concentration of his staff in one place, and the integration of the project's research and publication operations. During the six years following the move, five large volumes in the distinguished Territorial Papers series were published under the auspices of the National Archives. NARS and GSA also sponsored the publication in 1952 of Carter's widely used fifty-page work, *Historical Editing*.[19]

During the first half of the 1950s, the National Archives Division had other goals that were less easily attained. One was fitting the division into GSA. As has already been noted, many archivists were pleased neither with the new organizational arrangement nor with the fact that they would have to change some of their procedures. Grover often urged the staff to make the transition cheerfully, but it was Schellenberg who carried most of the burden of cutting down on unnecessary paperwork, improving staff supervision, and reducing unfair caviling at GSA whenever anything went wrong. Each branch of the archives had to realize that it was not, as Grover put it, "a major organizational unit." They had to learn to work together and with GSA, and it was Schellenberg who taught his subordinates this lesson by demonstrating that only by cooperating and cocking an eye toward efficiency could they cope with the tasks ahead.[20]

There were problems of legislation, too. One long-term objective had been to get the House of Representatives to loosen restrictions on the use of its records in the National Archives. Finally, in June 1953 the House provided that researchers could examine not only its transferred archives of more than fifty years in age, but indeed any of them, regardless of age, if they had already been made public. In 1953, moreover, GSA accepted sponsorship of the National Archives' long-standing legislative request to permit the archivist (now through the administrator of general services) to effect the removal of any enduringly valuable federal records more than fifty years old unless the agency head certified that the records had to be retained in connection with current business. There was a four-year delay in the enactment of this legislation, for several agencies considered it too radical a step. Congress, however, passed the measure in June 1957, probably because agency heads had become convinced that no one would question their certification that records they did not want to release for other reasons (for example, embarrassment) were currently used for operational purposes.[21] Although representing no great advance, the legislation did strengthen the archives somewhat in its quest to acquire the older historically valuable records of the government.

Then there was the continuing problem of what to do about retiring officials who destroyed or took federal records with them. Despite the uproar about the Morgenthau diary in 1947, neither Congress nor the president had dealt with the situation. The issue again became lively after the 1952 elections when Republican Con gressman John Taber of New York questioned whether the out-going Democratic administrators might destroy records that they thought might embarrass them. Seeing this as partisan fluff, Theo-dore Schellenberg and Herbert Angel tried to calm genuine appre-hensions by stating that federal records were safe—all 24,800,000 cubic feet of them. Federal archivists and records managers, never-theless, privately considered the possible unauthorized removal of documents an agonizing problem. Lacking adequate authority to do much about it, they rendered yeomanly service in using persua-sion and what little law was available to keep appointed officials and civil servants from taking their files with them upon leaving office. It is impossible to determine how successful the archivists and records managers were, but surely the situation would have been worse had they been complacent about it.[22]

Staff was the most pressing problem of the National Archives during the first half of the 1950s. Although the division's regular staff allocation was 259.1 in fiscal year 1953, this was less than in 1940, 1941, or 1942, and indeed less by 22 positions than Gro-ver had estimated necessary for 1953. The situation deteriorated steadily during the next three years, with appropriated positions for other than special programs falling to 235.3 by fiscal year 1956. Clearly, the National Archives Division was not GSA's favorite and was being expected to do more with fewer employees. This could be only partly explained by the fluctuations in reference service and the transfer of some functions to GSA and the central adminis-tration of NARS. Many archivists believed that their staff level was being kept low to permit the development of other NARS programs, as the number of people engaged in trendier, more businesslike mi-crofilm and records-management projects grew rapidly. Whether or not this was true, Grover was not able to procure additional staff authorizations for the National Archives. An even greater problem by the middle 1950s was that the division found it difficult to recruit and retain qualified personnel. One part of the problem was that professional employees could be drawn only from the general entrance registers for federal positions, and another was that there were better paying jobs for qualified people elsewhere, both within and outside the government. Moreover, it was difficult for new professional employees to see how they could advance very far in archival service since the old-timers monopolized the top jobs and few of them were close to retirement. The staff situation along with the economy drive of the early years of Dwight Eisenhower's presidency affected the National Archives' work considerably. For example, the division was forced to slow down the preparation of preliminary inventories and to abandon revising the *Guide to the Records in the National Archives*. There was also a cessation of abstracting information for researchers from pension and bounty-land files, census schedules, and early passenger lists.[23]

Staff problems strengthened Theodore Schellenberg's determination to upgrade his personnel's effectiveness by instituting an in-service training program. Training, of course, had been an important objective of the National Archives during the late 1930s and early 1940s. Despite wartime exigencies, the archives courses operated by the American University had partially achieved the agency's training goals. After World War II, however, that program had less effect, apparently because the staff of the National Archives was less motivated to take advantage of it. It was clear by 1951 that more effective training was needed. By spring 1952 the National Archives Division had laid the basis for such training by drafting standards for the classification of professional positions and the compilation of uniform job descriptions.[24]

The training program began in 1953, when all GS-5 positions, the lowest on the professional scale, were declared training jobs. During their first year, persons occupying such positions received training in archival theory and practice and took tests which, if passed, led them to be considered full-fledged archivists and promoted to the grade of GS-7. Those who failed were discharged unless they had already acquired civil-service status, in which case they were ranked as subprofessionals in the GS-5 grade with the right to take the tests one more time. The division also encouraged employees to take advanced training and even graduate degrees so that as many persons as possible could be promoted from within the organization.[25]

This was just the beginning of what Schellenberg had in mind. Indeed, he threw himself into the development of the training program so much that it later contributed to an estrangement between himself and Grover. Schellenberg personally carried the major burden of the program, participating not only in training GS-5s, but also delivering most of the lectures in an advanced two-semester course for GS-7s. Part of his contribution was the collating and preparation of extensive reading materials, and the writing of his volume *Modern Archives: Principles and Techniques*, which was published in 1956, was partly motivated by his interest in the National Archives Division's training programs. By 1955 he had developed monthly seminars for supervisory employees, and he also encouraged and helped his branch chiefs to provide specialized on-the-job training. As Schellenberg saw it, all this was worth his time and that of his subordinates, for better-trained archivists were more efficient and contented archivists. He hoped that training would cut down the division's turnover rate by making professional jobs more attractive and by giving archivists a clearer idea of how they could gain advancement within the National Archives. It is impossible to measure the results except subjectively. Yet it is plain that although Schellenberg rubbed some of his employees raw with training, he achieved their considerable improvement not only as archivists, but often as supervisors and even occasionally as specialists.[26] His was a virtuoso educational performance.

In viewing happenings within the National Archives Division from its incorporation into GSA in 1949 to the middle 1950s, it is clear that the more it changed, the more it remained the same. It had, despite staff reductions and some unhappiness with GSA, become more thoroughly professional. Thanks to that and to its frequent success in meeting its problems, the division would be better prepared to cope with the challenges of the following decade.

15. And Everything Else

The National Archives and Records Service contained other though much smaller divisions than Records Management and the National Archives. These were the Federal Register Division, the Franklin D. Roosevelt Library, the National Historical Publications Commission, and, in effect, the archivist's office. None of these was without its moments of change and even excitement during the first half-dozen years under the General Services Administration.

The Federal Register Division assumed additional responsibilities in 1950 under the provisions of Reorganization Plan No. 20. The most significant was the publication of laws passed by Congress, first in slip form, within forty-eight hours after the president had signed them, and then in the volumes of the *Statutes at Large*. This added immensely to the division's work, partly because there was a backlog in the publication of the *Statutes at Large*. Thanks to its modernization of the format of the volumes and its use of advanced technological processes, the division not only caught up on the backlog by early 1952 but also improved on the expected time of publication of the laws at less cost. The Federal Register Division inherited from the State Department the tasks of advising Congress and the states on the certification of electors and of filing electors' votes, interstate compacts, and constitutional amendments. The division also made improvements in the production and format of its other publications, most importantly the *United States Government Organization Manual*; the *Federal Register*; and the new *Code of Federal Regulations*, the publication of which was completed in 1950. It rendered splendid service during the Korean War in response to the demands for more information from federal agencies, government contractors, and the public. The result was the preparation and distribution during the conflict of several editions of the *National Defense Appendix*, which concentrated appropriate administrative rules and regulations in one source; the *Handbook of Emergency Defense Activities*, which made available a list of who was doing what in connection with mobilization and defense operations; and *Abstracts of Defense Regulations*.[1] A hard-working, innovative group, the division's some forty employees had become essential to keeping the government moving.

The Franklin D. Roosevelt Library was the sparkling gem among the divisions of the National Archives and Records Service. This was partly because of the beauty of its building and grounds at Hyde Park, New York, and partly because of the importance of its holdings. Research began at the library in May 1946, although only a little material was then available. Thanks to the growing amount of research interest in the library's holdings, pressure never ceased to have all of them opened as soon as possible. Indeed, a few researchers such as William L. Langer and Herbert Feis sought privileged access, which Archivist Wayne C. Grover resisted, usually successfully. Another problem was the pressure from some people such as Laughlin Currie, to keep their materials among the Roosevelt papers closed in order to avoid embarrassment to themselves or to persons still active in government. Archival resistance in these cases was less successful, because too many powerful government officials believed that the arguments of national security and possible embarrassment justified keeping some of the library's files closed. Clearly, the question of what to open was difficult for the archivists, caught as they were between the spur of researchers and the bridle of "very important people." As less and less remained closed to research, the decisions would, as Herman Kahn, the library's director, wrote in 1950, get "difficulter and difficulter."[2]

By 1950 Grace Tully and Samuel I. Rosenman had finished screening Franklin D. Roosevelt's papers, a chore that had been assigned to them by the late president. About 85 percent of those documents were then opened for research. This was celebrated on 17 March in a ceremony highlighted by talks given by Mrs. Roosevelt, Waldo G. Leland, and Jess Larson. Administrator Larson also read a message from President Truman, who pictured the library as proof of the American principle of "full and free access to knowledge." Although Truman exaggerated, the occasion did mark the unprecedented opening of the bulk of a president's papers for research less than five years after the end of his administration. It was also officially contemplated that the rest would be opened by 1970, a goal that was largely achieved, partly because of continuing pressure from researchers.

What was available for research at the library in 1950 was substantial. By 30 June there were 5,900 cubic feet of manuscripts, chiefly those of Franklin D. Roosevelt; 51,700 books and other printed items; and significant quantities of motion and still pictures and sound recordings. There had been 660 visits for research purposes during fiscal year 1950, and 550 written responses had been made to other requests for research data. The museum had become a popular spot for tourist visits, attracting more than 250,000 persons that year. A beginning was made on preparing for publication some of Roosevelt's papers relating to conservation, and the staff worked steadily at arranging and describing holdings. Moreover, the library accessioned more of the late president's papers as well as materials pertaining to his family, people who had worked with him, and the Democratic National Committee. By the end of fiscal year 1955, the library contained 7,059 cubic feet of manuscripts and 66,410 books and other printed materials. There were 835 research visits that year and 636 written reference services. A number of significant articles and books had already been published based upon research at the library, including Frank Freidel's *Franklin D. Roosevelt: The Ordeal* and Herbert Feis's *The China Tangle*. There was no doubt by 1955 that the Franklin D. Roosevelt Library was a well established and useful research institution.[3]

The National Historical Publications Commission was the other division of NARS. Although theoretically independent, it was attached to the agency for administrative convenience and because the archivist was legally the commission's chairman. The NHPC had been written into the National Archives Act in 1934 in order to initiate a high-quality general federal program of publishing historical documents. It failed to blossom, however, partly because of a paucity of funds and partly because of the low level of interest in it by archivists Robert Connor and Solon Buck. Indeed, although its full membership was maintained, the NHPC did not even meet between 1940 and 1950.[4]

Grover saw the commission as an important channel of communication between NARS and scholarly organizations. Thus he fought to keep NHPC's statutory authorization in 1949–50, and he also sought a broader basis of support for the commission so that it would no longer be a cipher in the world of history. Before Congress considered appropriate legislation during the summer of 1950, another force, the president, came into play in NHPC's reactivation. Harry S. Truman prided himself on his knowledge of and interest in his country's history. It was, therefore, not difficult for the archivists and historians who wanted a functioning NHPC to arrange a ceremony in May to present him with a copy of the newly published first volume of *The Papers of Thomas Jefferson*, which Julian P. Boyd had edited under the auspices of Princeton University. The occasion sparked what its sponsors desired. Truman declared, "We need to collect and publish the writings of the men and women who have made major contributions to the development of our democracy." He specifically asked the NHPC to canvass scholars and to make recommendations for such a program.

Under the leadership of its chairman, Wayne Grover, and its secretary, Philip M. Hamer, the commission moved quickly in response to the president's request. It met on 15 June and adopted a resolution urging Congress to expand the membership of NHPC and to broaden its functions. Congress, with the support of GSA, acted favorably in the Federal Records Act of 1950. Not only did the legislators continue the enlarged commission's authority to make "plans, estimates, and recommendations" for historical publications; but they also charged it to "cooperate with and encourage appropriate Federal, State, and local agencies and nongovernmental institutions, societies, and individuals in collecting and preserving and, when it deems such action to be desirable, in editing and publishing the papers of outstanding citizens of the United States and such other documents as may be important for an understanding and appreciation of the history of the United States."[5]

Meanwhile, the archivist designated Philip Hamer to spend all of his time on the work of NHPC and especially to survey scholars, some 150 of them, for their advice on which documentary projects deserved first attention. Hamer was the logical choice on the NARS staff, having made his mark as a historian, a teacher, an archivist, and the editor of the *Guide to Records in the National Archives* and the *Federal Records of World War II*. While Hamer was gathering data and recommendations, the commission was being reconstituted. It included by December 1950 two representatives of the president; two from the AHA; and one each from the Senate, the House of Representatives, the Library of Congress, the State Department, the Defense Department, and the Supreme Court; with the archivist of the United States continuing ex officio as chairman.

The new National Historical Publications Commission first met in February 1951 and took action that led to the establishment of a small staff. It approved a program to encourage people to give personal papers to appropriate repositories and it endorsed the preparation of a comprehensive register of manuscripts collections in the United States. More central to its obligations, the commission considered recommendations to the president. This report was presented to Truman in May, and it urged that the highest priority be given to the publication of the papers of John Adams, John Quincy Adams, Benjamin Franklin, Alexander Hamilton, and James Madison. The report also mentioned the names of sixty other Americans who had achieved fame in various walks of life and whose papers should be seriously considered for publication in printed form or in microfilm. In addressing the president, the commission defined its main tasks as being to promote such publishing projects, to aid in finding funds for them, to assist in their planning, and to give technical advice. The idea was that the "work should be done objectively, impartially, and in the spirit of truthseeking that is the ideal of the scholarly world." President Truman approved those propositions, in effect charging the commission later to present a more detailed program.[6]

During 1952 and 1953, while a detailed report to the president was being prepared, NHPC undertook a number of activities. The commission sought advisory support from the Mississippi Valley Historical Association, which was the largest organization of historians specializing in the history of the United States, and the Pacific Coast Branch of the AHA. The MVHA responded in part by sponsoring a session on the commission's work at its 1952 convention. With Wayne Grover's cooperation, the Library of Congress transferred the project that produced the annual bibliographical volumes on *Writings on American History* to NHPC. Philip Hamer undertook the preparation of a volume that would indicate the location of manuscripts available for research in the United States. The commission promoted the publication of documents relating to the ratification of the Constitution and its first ten amendments and to the first Congress under the Constitution. Moreover, NHPC encouraged institutions interested in publishing the papers of John C. Calhoun, Archbishop John Carroll, Henry Clay, and James Madison.[7]

The commission presented its refined report to President Dwight D. Eisenhower in 1954. Entitled *A National Program for the Publication of Historical Documents*, it elaborated upon what had been contained in the 1951 report, indicated what activities had been begun since then, and identified the papers of 301 additional Americans that should be considered for publication. The president commented favorably, which NHPC took as encouragement to move ahead. And move ahead it did, under the guidance of Philip Hamer and his successor in 1961, Oliver W. Holmes. Hamer's *A Guide to Archives and Manuscripts in the United States* was published in 1961; even earlier, by 1955, with the commission's urging, the Library of Congress began a catalog of manuscripts in the United States, the first volume of which appeared in 1962 in the *National Union Catalog of Manuscript Collections*. With NHPC's technical advice and its assistance in securing funding, dozens of high-quality documentary publications projects sprang up all over the country. Their output included, among others, letterpress volumes of the correspondence of the Adams family, Calhoun, Clay, Franklin, Hamilton, Madison, and Woodrow Wilson, and microfilm editions of the records of the Continental Congress in the National Archives and the papers of the presidents in the Library of Congress. In short, it was a magnificent flowering of published primary documentation of the nation's history, even if it took chiefly a biographical approach. NHPC and the archivist's office unquestionably played the key role in this development. Fortunately for the interested parties, it came during decades when the government, academic institutions, philanthropic foundations, and private donors could contribute generously to support such publications.[8]

In viewing other concerns of the archivist's office, it comes as no surprise that Wayne Grover continued the policy of his predecessors of fostering his agency's good relationships with related organizations. A variety of federal offices (for example, the National Park Service) relied considerably on the staff of the National Archives in finding information necessary to their historical programs. Indeed, well before the 1950s informal groups of federal archivists, manuscript curators, and historians cooperated in a broad range of activities that forwarded one another's programs. NARS also continued to give assistance to, set examples for, and interact with archivists elsewhere, especially through the Society of American Archivists, of which it continued to be the largest supporter. This included aiding in the birth of new archival operations such as the Ford Motor Company Archives in 1953 and the establishment of a collection of plans for archival buildings in the National Archives as well as the advisory work of Victor Gondos, Jr., on architectural matters.[9]

Deterioration, however, had become evident in NARS's relations with scholars. The wish of many senior archivists, especially Solon J. Buck, to have close working contacts with social scientists had borne little fruit. Indeed, archival relationships with them and even with historians had weakened since the end of World War II. One can roughly locate the chief reasons for this. Few social scientists understood how they could use archival holdings in their work, and this number rapidly declined as the historical approach was increasingly eschewed in the social sciences. As for historians, those who had been most active in establishing and nurturing the National Archives during its first decade were seldom the ones who conducted research there. Moreover, many historians during the 1940s began to take the agency's existence for granted just as many archivists became too busy with other matters to cultivate effectively the support of historians.

Wayne Grover seemed to be at a disadvantage in dealing with this situation, since, unlike Connor and Buck, he was neither a historian by training nor prominent in scholarly circles when he became archivist. Yet he was keenly concerned with rebuilding a strong community of interest between his organization and the historical profession. He encouraged his staff's participation in the affairs of the leading historical associations during the 1950s, and he was pleased with the archival concerns of the AHA's Committee on Historians and the Federal Government. Grover and his staff successfully encouraged the interest of historians in both NHPC and the territorial papers project. Moreover, archivists and historians joined in placing greater emphasis on the holding of joint sessions of the SAA with the AHA and the MVHA. The AHA and NARS were particularly pleased with their mutual venture in making available microfilms of captured World War II German records, which extended the services of the National Archives to American scholars involved in studying recent European history.[10]

NARS had many reasons for promoting better relations between itself and historians; chief among them was the furthering of the use of archival materials and the joint support of programs. There is no doubt that during the 1950s archivists and historians were increasingly successful in rebuilding and traveling the bridges between their professions. And this was attributable not only to the efforts of Grover and his colleagues but also to the work of the leaders of the leading historical associations, particularly Executive Secretary Boyd C. Shafer of the AHA. All this was advanced by the increasing number of graduate students in history and of practicing historians, and especially by their greater interest in conducting original research, which was partly spurred by the mounting availability of archival and manuscript materials.

There was, however, probably another important reason why NARS increasingly cultivated historians. Wayne Grover must have hoped that he and his staff would not again find themselves isolated as they had been in 1949 during the reorganizational crisis that led to their agency being placed within the General Services Administration. Fortunately for all concerned, and largely because of Grover's astuteness and Larson's ability to make the new organization work, the fears that abounded among federal archivists in 1949 rarely materialized. In late 1952 and in 1953, however, a new crisis arose that tested how well NARS had bettered relations with historians and other archivists.

Soon after Dwight Eisenhower's election as president, rumors began circulating that a political appointee would replace Grover as archivist of the United States. The AHA council quickly acted to combat that possibility, calling in December 1952 for adherence to the precedents set by Franklin Roosevelt and Harry Truman in continuing a professionally qualified person as archivist. The council's resolution was premature, for no significant figure in the incoming administration had indicated that the position was considered a political one. It soon became obvious, however, that Senator Everett Dirksen, the Illinois Republican, was seeking Grover's replacement. The archivist saw the situation as one in which some of his staff were resorting to partisan politics in order to influence the operation of NARS. "Such is life in the jungles of Washington," he observed. Opposition to Dirksen's maneuver grew steadily. In fact, even before Eisenhower was inaugurated, educational leaders such as Waldo G. Leland joined the AHA council in seeking to thwart a political turnover in the leadership of NARS.[11]

There is little evidence that Grover's job was in jeopardy. The only real candidate to replace him was the controversial revisionist historian Charles Callan Tansill, who was considered to be Senator Dirksen's choice. Tansill, however, mustered little political and professional support, and he apparently encountered opposition from the new president's influential brother, Milton Eisenhower. There is no evidence, in any event, that anyone in the administration seriously considered Tansill for the archivist's position. It should also be noted that former Adjutant General Edward F. Witsell in late January wrote a strong letter in support of Grover, who had been one of his aides in the army. The friend to whom Witsell wrote was General Wilton B. Persons, who was one of President

Eisenhower's closest confidants in the administration and who quickly vouched for the reliability of Witsell's assessment.[12]

This information was known to few people outside the White House; consequently, a scare ran through the scholarly community. The word went out to fight to perpetuate professionalism in the archivist's job. The AHA formally transmitted its council's recommendation to the president on 2 February. Eisenhower's chief political aide, Sherman Adams, immediately replied that "the President will see to it that this office is maintained on the highest professional level." Other scholarly organizations rallied to Grover's support as the White House also received addresses from such organizations as the MVHA, the SAA, the American Association of State and Local History, and the American Musicological Society.[13]

The coming of a new administrator of general services in May 1953 was the occasion for another scare. Edmund F. Mansure, a fifty-two-year-old Chicago drapery manufacturer, was the appointee. Although Mansure apparently thought it necessary to become involved in patronage, he did not consider NARS a target for such activity. Senator Dirksen, however, who was one of his leading backers, placed pressure on him regarding the archivist's job. That led Mansure to indicate to Grover's friends that he would welcome letters from the academic community urging that partisan politics be kept out of NARS. Thus, another antipatronage campaign was launched by Waldo G. Leland, Clarence E. Carter and Theodore R. Schellenberg of the National Archives, and Julian P. Boyd of Princeton. The result of their efforts was an outpouring of letters not only from scholars and archivists, but also from President Robert G. Sproul of the University of California and Republican Senator H. Alexander Smith of New Jersey. It is questionable whether Mansure would have replaced Grover in view of the White House's disinclination to do so. The support, however, that Grover received in May and June did give the administrator sufficient ammunition to deal with Dirksen in a time-honored political way.[14] Whether or not the archivist had been in serious political jeopardy, the response of the scholarly community had been impressive. Grover's contribution to rebuilding bridges between NARS and academicians had thus been rewarded in a very personal way. More important was the setting of a precedent that a change of presidents or parties in control of the government should not disturb the tenure of a professionally qualified archivist of the United States.

Mansure and Grover got along well. Although the general services administrator felt bound to economize in his agency's operations, which did hamper the work of NARS, he found that attrition of staff was effective to the point where none of the bureau's personnel had to be discharged. Mansure, indeed, assured his subordinates that there was "going to be no revolution in GSA. There will be evolution." He adhered to this policy, which fitted in perfectly with the archivist's view of administration. The administrator also willingly accepted Grover's arguments regarding the importance of records management. Therefore, it was not long before Mansure was telling Eisenhower's cabinet, in a familiar parable, of the need for professional and economical administration of federal documents, because "the government now has enough records to fill the Pentagon Building seven times." For that, for eschewing patronage mongering in NARS, and for a generally satisfactory relationship with Mansure, it was not much of a sacrifice for Grover and his staff to accept the abolition of coffee breaks (which had a way of reemerging anyway), sharply restricted travel funds, and loyalty-security inquiries, which were mild in GSA during the age of McCarthyism.[15]

Whatever pinches were felt during Edmund Mansure's tenure in GSA, they did not stop Wayne Grover and his aides from dreaming. There was an abundance of ideas for the development of the Records Management Division and the establishment of a system of presidential libraries. Even more wide ranging was the archivist's interest in founding an American archives institute, which would "stimulate interest and pride in America's documentary heritage." His idea was to find support from numerous institutions, professional associations, and foundations in order to subsidize traveling exhibits of documents; a national register of manuscripts; new documentary training programs for archivists, editors, records managers, and high-school and college teachers; the preparation of archival and manuscript subject-matter guides; and the operations of SAA. The institute never came into being, but in one way or another most of what Grover had in mind during the middle 1950s was accomplished before his death in 1970.[16]

By 1955 the agency that had begun as the National Archives was far different than it had been at the time of its entry six years before in GSA. NARS had effectively demonstrated that it was more than an ornate storehouse for precious documents or even a research and cultural center. It had made itself indispensable to the government for the purposes of expert documentation and records management and to citizens seeking to support their claims against the government or each other. Many archivists and scholars, however, still had doubts about the wisdom of removing the archivist from direct responsibility to the president and incorporating the archives into the ranks of GSA, despite the material benefits involved. Then there were those who were disturbed by the prominence of records management in the operations of NARS. Also, some people were worried by what Ernst Posner called "the curse of bigness." The result of this in the world's largest archival establishment was that everything had to be minutely regulated, which seemed to deprive American federal archivists of the spiritual and scholarly rewards enjoyed by their European counterparts. It also made it difficult for them to relate to the problems of their colleagues in America's other archival and manuscripts agencies, which were much smaller than NARS. Only time would tell to what extent these were serious problems, and what might be done to remedy them.[17]

16. Paperwork Management

As we have seen, the Records Management Division of the National Archives and Records Service came into existence as a consequence of the work of the Hoover Commission of 1947–49. The division's work was considered successful. In fiscal year 1953 the General Services Administration estimated that its records-management operations had saved the government $34,170,000, which was $2,170,000 more than the annual amount that Emmett J. Leahy's Hoover Commission task force had contended was minimally possible. Moreover, during the following year the trend toward an ever larger accumulation of federal records was broken, with the volume of paper on hand dropping from 25,300,000 to 24,700,000 cubic feet.

The results, however, stemming from the recommendations of the first Hoover Commission were in no area of government as great as was possible, partly because of the exigencies of the Korean War. Thus at the end of the war, in 1953, Congress authorized the establishment of another Commission on Organization of the Executive Branch of the Government to pick up the sword of economy and efficiency where its predecessor had laid it down. Herbert Hoover was again chosen as chairman, and the group came to be known as the Second Hoover Commission. This commission also used the task-force approach, and again Emmett Leahy was named, in June 1954, to head the group that would look into problems connected with the administration of government records. Director of Records Management Herbert E. Angel represented NARS, and the remaining members included another person from government service and two people from private industry. The group took for itself the name Task Force on Paperwork Management, which symbolized its determination to deal with more than just the storage and disposal of federal records.[1]

Attempting to get at the root of records problems, the Paperwork Management Task Force sought ways to confine the creation of federal records to those that were absolutely necessary to the efficient functioning of government. The task force got down to business immediately and was able to submit its report to the Second Hoover Commission by 19 November 1954. The report recommended numerous ways to cut down on the quantity and types of records and on their handling, with the goals of increasing governmental efficiency and reducing the expenditures for personnel and equipment in the administration of federal records. The task force suggested that the records reforms could be facilitated by devising a comprehensive paperwork management program for all federal agencies and establishing a paperwork management service in GSA separate from NARS.

The Second Hoover Commission agreed with almost all of its Paperwork Management Task Force's findings and recommendations. In its report to Congress of 19 January 1955, the commission urged the reduction of the variety and amount of records that federal offices produced. The president would establish a government-wide paperwork management program, and GSA would be responsible for general supervision of that program. (Unlike the task force, the commission did not specify the creation of a separate paperwork management service.) What the commission's recommendations aimed at—and what largely defined paperwork management—were better-styled letters, fewer and simpler forms, fewer and better drawn-up reports, simplification and narrower distribution of directives and instructions, fewer duplicate records, improved filing systems, pools of office machines, random examination of outgoing materials for quality control, the employment of qualified people to conduct paperwork management, and the use of technical manuals to instruct employees on the economical and efficient use and administration of records. Moreover, the target for the amount of federal records to be deposited in storage space, as contrasted to the more expensive office space, was increased from the 20 percent set by the first Leahy task force to 50 percent as an additional way to reduce expenditures and to unclog the operating channels of government agencies. The commission believed that the implementation of its recommendations could result in slicing $255,000,000 from the annual cost of the government's paperwork, which was estimated at $4,000,000,000.[2]

There was no significant opposition to the concept of paperwork management. The only question was who would supervise the program, given the vagueness of the Second Hoover Commission's recommendation on its administration and the reluctance of Congress to rear another government bureau. The Records Management Division was clearly in the running to assume responsibility for the new program. Certainly, no other federal office was as competent at records administration, and a new government service could not begin paperwork management operations as quickly as could the division. NARS also commanded the inside track because of its close working relationship with the administrator of general services. Indeed, its records managers had already urged their staff to prepare "to advance paperwork management" and they had published before the end of fiscal year 1955 three handbooks pertinent to that subject: *Form Letters*, *Plain Letters*, and *Federal Records Centers*.[3]

In May 1955 GSA submitted to the Bureau of the Budget a program defining its responsibilities and those of other executive agencies in carrying out paperwork management. That program was approved, and on 12 August President Dwight D. Eisenhower asked the heads of all government agencies to work with GSA in the establishment and operation of federal paperwork management. He directed GSA to serve in an "assisting," advisory, and supervisory capacity in implementing the Second Hoover Commission's recommendations regarding paperwork management. GSA designated NARS as the organization responsible for such functions; this authority soon devolved upon the Records Management Division, which was in 1956 renamed the Office of Records Management.[4]

The Office of Records Management quickly followed up its beginnings in paperwork management. It laid plans not only to issue more instructional manuals, but also to hold training conferences in various parts of the country. The office critically analyzed records retirement schedules in order to reduce the inflated percentage of records that federal agencies considered to be of permanent value. New efforts were made to close out uneconomical agency records centers and to expand the amount of space available in GSA's federal records centers. To eliminate oversized paper and filing cabinets, NARS urged agencies to use fewer legal-sized documents. Ways were sought to achieve more efficient use of equipment for the creation and handling of records so that fewer replacements would need to be bought. Although the Budget Bureau took responsibility for reducing and simplifying the number of forms, reports, and questionnaires that businesses, citizens, and state and local governments had to fill out, GSA helped by compiling a list of federal requirements in this area.[5]

In short, NARS's records managers had not only to improve their original operations, but they had to take on a vast new program and at the same time justify that they were the ones best qualified to do it. This meant that in 1955 and 1956 they had to beat off the attempts of the Budget Bureau to assume responsibility for much of paperwork management and to argue against the recommendation of a private consulting firm engaged by the Budget Bureau that paperwork management should be handled elsewhere than in NARS. The Office of Records Management emerged the victor in those cases because of its effectiveness in the paperwork jobs it had already taken on and because of the patent interrelatedness of records and paperwork management. It made little sense, as Herbert Angel said, to establish a "new and untried organization when the existing one was already working so well."[6]

That raises the question of how well the records service of NARS did over the years in the related functions of records and paperwork management. The percentage of federal records in various kinds of storage space rose from about 14 in 1948 to 20 in 1952, but to 42 in 1956. From then on, the task resembled that of Sisyphus, for not until fiscal year 1971 was the Second Hoover Commission's goal of 50 percent met. Of course, most federal records were initially placed in agency storage space. As agency records centers were reduced (for example, from seventy-eight in

1954 to twenty in 1955), however, the holdings of NARS's federal centers grew, from 2,439,000 cubic feet in 1954 to 5,301,000 in 1960. The figure stood at 9,526,000 in 1968. Because of improved appraisal operations, the federal records centers were able to destroy 60 percent of the records received in 1968 as compared with 39 percent in 1956. Moreover, because of NARS's training and disposal scheduling activities, the originating agencies were able to destroy an increasing proportion of useless records over the years as well as to restrict the number of records created in the first place. Those and other programs of the Office of Records Management succeeded in reducing the volume of federal records during the middle 1950s to, for example, 23,800,000 cubic feet by the end of fiscal year 1955. The number soon rose again, and by 1968 it had reached about 29,000,000 cubic feet, 35 percent of which were in NARS's records centers. One shudders to think, however, what the situation would have been in terms of cost, government efficiency, and the saving of archival materials without records and paperwork management programs.

There are other things to be considered. The amount of space freed for reuse or other uses in federal agencies because of the removal of records was 619,000 square feet in 1956 and even 573,-400 in 1968. In the latter year the freeing for reuse of 72,800 filing cabinets, 8,900 transfer cases, and 570,500 linear feet of shelving compared quite favorably with 45,000 cabinets and 70,800 transfer cases freed twelve years earlier. Then too, the records service answered a vastly increased number of reference inquiries, rising from 1,868,000 to 6,165,103 between fiscal years 1956 and 1968. The savings here were great, for the federal records centers could efficiently and cheaply perform those reference services because of their specialized personnel and the superb concentration and organization of the records in their custody. Records centers were constructed less expensively on cheaper land with fewer maintenance costs than were other federal buildings. Moreover, NARS found ways to cram in more records per square foot of building space than other federal agencies did by using high ceilings filled with paper almost to the top on a double-shelving basis.[7]

Although the number of federal records centers dropped from

seventeen in 1958 to fourteen in 1969, their capacity greatly expanded during those years. That resulted partly because some of the regional centers moved into new and larger quarters and partly because of the addition to the NARS system of the Military Personnel Records Center at St. Louis in 1960 and the mammoth Washington National Records Center at Suitland, Maryland, in 1968. The number of federal records center employees also rose from 387 in 1952 to 1,173 in 1967. Clearly, the centers had become big business.[8]

Neither growth nor accomplishment was achieved without push and perspiration. Everett D. Alldredge, as chief of the Records Center Branch, was constantly pressing the deputy regional directors and center managers to do better. In his circular letter of February 1955 he complimented most of the regional directors on "doing a really perceptive reporting job," but he added, "some of you are ducking problems." In particular, he referred to records disposal where "we are falling increasingly behind schedule." Alldredge suggested that the regional directors ask his office for help, such as the loan of a "high-powered archivist"; and he urged that better employee-training programs should be initiated. In April he expressed his disappointment that only half of the regions were prepared to become involved in paperwork management. "If this is because the Center staff can not do the job, a higher calibre Center staff is needed." In July he offhandedly complimented the centers for accessioning some 50 percent more records than had been programmed. Alldredge added that the centers' disposal record was better than had been anticipated, although he criticized them for having drawn up too few agency records disposal schedules. On he went, month after month, neither sparing the rod nor spoiling the staff, whether the subject be disposal, accessioning, paperwork management, training, employee suggestions (the listing of which he "sincerely hoped . . . doesn't become a joke book"), or clinics for other civil servants.[9]

Yet Alldredge's bark was worse than his bite, and his subordinates knew that he had Archivist Grover and Records Management Director Angel behind him demanding results. All knew that if they failed the bite would almost always show up in their budget and

The Federal Records Center, Suitland, Maryland, soon after completion

their prestige within NARS instead of in purges or transfers. They also knew that if they cried for help, Grover, Angel, and Alldredge would do whatever they could to support them. It was a benevolently despotic system, but it worked. The records centers, where the bulk of the records-management staff and even the majority of NARS personnel were, took the essence if not the rhetoric of Alldredge's circulars seriously. Clearly, his message was the need for accomplishment.[10]

Along with the enlargement of the program came changes in titles and even in organization. After records management assumed the status of an office instead of a division in November 1956, Angel received the title of assistant archivist for records management, and Alldredge, as his chief aide, became director of the Program Development Division. (Theodore R. Schellenberg, as Angel's counterpart for the National Archives, also became an assistant archivist; the former assistant archivist, Robert H. Bahmer, took the new title of deputy archivist.) When Angel became GSA's director of administration in November 1959, Alldredge succeeded him as assistant archivist for records management, in which capacity he served, with few interruptions, until his retirement in 1971. Angel returned by 1964 as assistant archivist for the operation of records centers and, beginning in 1968, served for several years as deputy archivist.[11]

It serves no purpose to detail individual responsibilities from 1955 on in the limited space available, given the long interruption in Angel's service and the ultimate division of records work into two offices, one for management and the other for records centers. Suffice it to say that Angel was the chief draftsman for the paperwork management program and the strategist for developing that program and records management onto a government-wide basis. Alldredge, until he succeeded Angel, was commander and tactician of the forces in the field. Grover and Bahmer helped out in terms of strategy and tactics, but they were most concerned with getting approval from GSA, the Budget Bureau, and Congress for the staff and buildings necessary to carry out records and paperwork management. Even after the establishment of separate offices of records management and records centers and after Angel's return to NARS, these four men continued to work as a team until their retirement during the latter half of the 1960s.

Their work demonstrated that NARS was concerned with every aspect of the management of records from their creation, size, and design through their use and traffic patterns to their storage and their destruction or preservation. Of course, this included keen interest in the equipment, supplies, and personnel needed at the different stages in the lives of various types of records. NARS had to be flexible in the implementation of paperwork management; there were too many ways in which the baronies that make up the federal government could circumvent direct orders. As Wayne Grover advised Angel in 1956, it was difficult "to get top executives . . . to take action. . . . There is no point in wasting any more time arguing about regulations." NARS's records managers, therefore *encouraged* other federal agencies to adopt paperwork management programs. In cooperation with the general services administrator, they used a variety of techniques to spur the growth of such programs including appeals for "a one-time 'housecleaning'" of records, and the use of records surveys, pamphlets, and training workshops as well as more direct forms of salesmanship. And the emphasis was on paperwork management as a way to economize, not as something that would suggest "new people, new organizations, and the necessity to spend more money." NARS also gave special attention to promoting paperwork management in congressional offices, which not only helped congressmen, but placed the records managers in a more favorable position at the mouth of the great American public cornucopia.[12]

NARS sought to keep its organization flexible too. When Administrator Edmund Mansure questioned the bureau's lack of a "direct line of clear-cut authority," Grover replied that GSA fostered the situation, especially by making its regional directors responsible to both the administrator and the heads of the organizations under him on matters pertaining to their functions. Yet the archivist declared that all were living quite nicely within that sometimes confusing system because of its flexibility. More levels of administration and delegations of authority, he contended, would not likely facilitate action. "What GSA needs is not something to make everybody sore at each other."[13] Grover, however, did not win his point, for additional levels and delegations of authority were on their way throughout the government. At least as far as GSA was concerned, one result was that people on the lower part of the federal pyramid more often got "sore at" those who resided above the bureau level and seemed to be increasingly remote from the realities of line operations.

The amount of work the records managers assumed not only expanded greatly but also became more complex. NARS drew up plans in 1955 for handbooks, agency records surveys, training programs for agency personnel, and technical assistance efforts. The goal, of course, was to reduce the proliferation of the bulk and types of records as well as to make those that remained more useful, simpler, and less expensive. NARS cooperated with the American University, New York University, and Seattle University in offering records-management courses, for more personnel had to be recruited and trained for records and paperwork management. In fiscal year 1956 came the issuance of two manuals, *Guide Letters* and *Applying Records Schedules*, and the sponsorship of two-day management clinics for some 2,000 key federal employees in nineteen cities. The Interagency Records Administration Conference, which was governed by a committee composed of representatives from the Budget Bureau and NARS, stepped up its efforts to improve the exchange of information and ideas among federal records officers. By 1959 there were IRAC meetings in fifteen major American cities. Moreover, transcripts of the monthly conferences in Washington, as well as the IRAC bulletin, *Time Saver Ideas*, were available on request. Work was also begun in 1956 and completed four years later to establish an underground repository that would give special protection to the records vital to government operations in an emergency. NARS proceeded with management surveys, technical assistance programs, and special records and paperwork management training courses in a number of federal agencies.[14]

NARS had primarily held its clinics for the purpose of demonstrating to agency officials what could be accomplished through paperwork and records management. The clinics soon gave way to the development of one of the Office of Records Management's chief devices for training agency personnel, the specialized workshop. By the end of fiscal year 1960, 139,700 civil servants had attended workshops on records disposition, forms, mail management, and, by far the most popular, correspondence administration. Handbooks on those and related subjects had also been prepared for use as instructional guides either in connection with the workshops or for use in their own right. The Office of Records Management continued to offer technical assistance to other agencies, and it conducted paperwork and records-management surveys (eighty-three in 1960) to show what needed to be done and how simply it could be done. By the end of the decade it was clear that paperwork management, as integrated with records administration, was an established function and an effective weapon in the struggle against waste and inefficiency in government.[15]

It is impossible to say how much money paperwork management saved, for one does not know how far government agencies would have gone in creating additional records, either in terms of kind or amount, or how much additional personnel and equipment would have been required to handle them. Nor does one know what federal agencies would have done on their own or in response to outside pressures in dealing with the proliferation of records.

The important thing is that NARS, even though it never received full cooperation from many government agencies, successfully persisted with its innovative paperwork management efforts. In 1963, for example, GSA announced that between 1960 and 1962 the total quantity of government records had risen by only 0.3 percent, which was far less than the increase during those years in federal expenditures. The records managers continued to produce handbooks (they dealt with seven topics by 1957 and with nineteen by 1971) and went on with paperwork management surveys, technical assistance to other agencies, and workshops. In fiscal year 1963 NARS began auditing records programs in various agencies to see how closely they were adhering to the Federal Records Act and the standards promulgated under it. There was also a campaign to teach civil servants how to deal economically and efficiently with source data automation, which saved an estimated minimum of $1,000,000 in 1963 and was just a token of the costs that could be eliminated. In 1968 GSA announced that federal agencies reported savings totaling more than $10,000,000, as well as improvements in quality and faster service resulting from NARS's sixty-eight paperwork management surveys and some 150 technical assistance efforts. There was, of course, no way to put a total price tag on the paperwork and records-management programs, especially as they worked to achieve greater efficiency. That they had beneficial impact no one in government doubted; that more could have been done, with better funding and authority, was also seldom questioned. Whether paperwork management saved at least the $255,-000,000 per year estimated by the Second Hoover Commission was impossible to tell. Yet it was remarkable what had been done by the some thousand NARS employees who worked in the records centers and the less than a hundred who were involved in paperwork management programs.[16]

It always seemed touch and go, however, as to whether enough was being done to keep the government from being smothered in its own paper. As Theodore Schellenberg pointed out in late 1959, government typewriters were pounding out 4,000,000 documents each working day. Indeed, 485,000 federal employees were making records, but only 5,500 people in NARS and other agencies were working to keep those materials under control. There were clearly too few people engaged in limiting the unnecessary growth of federal records on hand. NARS tried desperately to contain the situation by enlarging the capacity of its records centers as well as by controlling the creation of documents. Despite the efforts of the records managers, there was the omnipresent threat that matters would get out of hand.[17]

NARS was sometimes criticized for not doing enough. A report of the General Accounting Office, issued in 1962, scored the Office of Records Management for having insufficient control over agency records programs. Although not critical of NARS, in 1964 Congressman Arnold Olsen of Montana called the attention of the House of Representatives to the vital need to cope with federal records problems. It was plain, he said, that the "natives are becoming restless" in the "Paperwork Jungle." This view coincided with Grover's conviction that Congress was not appropriating enough money for his agency to do an adequate job in any area of its work. Although NARS, like any federal bureau, seldom thought that it had enough cash and staff, things improved somewhat for the next several years. Especially important was the funding of GSA's plans for expanding records-management programs, including the construction of the huge new records and archives center at Suitland, Maryland. Indeed, NARS could bask in the Budget Bureau's rating of its records-management efforts as "quite good" and the compliments of a senior member of Congress, Edward P. Boland of Massachusetts, regarding its contributions to government economy as well as to "cultural and educational enrichment."[18]

The impact of the records and paperwork management programs was felt outside federal agencies. Private organizations and businesses as well as state and local officials often used NARS's publications and participated in meetings that it organized. In 1957 and 1958 Pan American World Airways, American Telephone and Telegraph, Northrup Aircraft, Ford Motor Company, Radio Corporation of America, Cooper Tile and Rubber, Richfield Oil, and Remington Rand were among the businesses that sought from or exchanged with NARS information on records management. At that time the federal records managers also supplied assistance to state officials in fifteen states and the territories of Alaska and Hawaii. This effort reached out beyond the nation's boundaries, as it had earlier with archival administration. For example, in 1958 Herbert Angel addressed the Canadian government's Senior Records Management Conference. The title of his talk was "Economy of a Good Records Program." NARS gave records-management training to 129 foreign officials in fiscal year 1960. More so even than its archivists, America's records managers were setting the pace for the world.[19]

While the records managers were teaching others, they were seeking training themselves. The American University had begun offering courses in records administration at the beginning of the 1940s, and during the 1950s and 1960s other universities entered this area of instruction. That, however, was inadequate to the needs of records-management officials. As early as fiscal year 1954 Angel and Alldredge attempted to provide in-service training opportunities for personnel working in the records centers. That was not enough, either. Alldredge lamented in 1955 that he could not procure funds for a "national get-together of Center Chiefs" to facilitate better training of their employees. Undoubtedly, he was stimulated by Theodore Schellenberg's success with the instructional program of the National Archives. Prodded by Alldredge, the records centers experimented with training programs in 1955 and 1956, but their content and effectiveness varied greatly and funds were unavailable to coordinate or standardize these efforts. Alldredge complained in March 1957 that the training programs were "still lagging" and urged the center chiefs to devote more attention to the problem.[20]

By 1958 Angel and Alldredge found a way to help fill the gap in training their field employees. They enlisted Schellenberg's services in this work, and although his intensive courses were primarily archival in nature, they added an extra dimension to training professional-level employees in the records centers. In 1958 and 1959 Schellenberg became a circuit rider, visiting center after center to give three-day courses. And these short courses were not confined to center employees, for archivists and historians were invited to participate. This was only a stop gap. In the future reliance had to be placed on the development of in-service training, workshops, the use of reading materials, and enrollments in courses offered by universities.[21]

It is not surprising that Angel and Alldredge accepted formal training for their staffs in archival administration. That was partly because the records centers were also archival repositories and partly because of the intimate connection between the archival and records-management professions in the United States. When federal records centers began being established in 1950, it was assumed that archival materials would be centralized in Washington. By 1955, however, the National Archives was no longer eager to fill its scarce space with field records. Moreover, some archivists believed that field archives should be kept in the regions, either in presidential libraries or records centers. In fact, Congress had enacted legislation authorizing such disposition by 1955, and the National Archives had stopped accessioning most permanently valuable field records. Plainly, a policy had to be developed. Everett Alldredge vigorously and successfully contested the views that there were large amounts of permanently valuable records in the centers and that such material should ultimately be deposited in presidential libraries. He championed taking steps to formulate and apply more rigorous standards in appraising the value of records; and he indicated that archivists in the records centers were best prepared to determine and administer the small amounts of archives of regional research interest that were located in the field.[22]

Some of the center chiefs were also interested in developing field archives. In 1956 Philip C. Brooks, who was then chief of the records center in San Francisco, planned to propose that a Western regional federal archives be established in his center. He also published that year an article in the *Mississippi Valley Historical Review* urging historians to conduct research in the archival holdings of federal records centers. In February 1957 Acting Archivist Robert Bahmer enunciated NARS's policy along similar lines in response to a question from Senator Prescott Bush of Connecticut as to why field records should not be deposited in local archives and libraries. Bahmer pointed out that they were federal records and that the government had a responsibility to see they were properly administered. Some of the field records, moreover, had national as well as local significance and consequently belonged in the National Archives. As for those of regional importance, he wrote that "records centers are a more desirable alternative" than using a great variety of libraries and historical societies to care for and to make federal field records available for research. Whatever the policy, by 1957 it was true that several records centers had made arrangements for research by historians and other private citizens. The dual archival and records-management functions of the centers would grow over the years. By 1966 more than two hundred scholars and students conducted research in the centers and the first guide to archival holdings in a federal records center was published. Indeed, by 1968 scholarly advisory groups had been formed, and NARS was making plans formally to establish archival units in the centers.[23]

Many records managers felt compromised by such developments, for they considered their profession to be quite distinct from that of the archivists. Indeed, professional organizations of records officers developed rather early. Some of the records people considered IRAC to be such, and others, particularly those working outside the federal government, formed local records-management groups. By 1956 the first of their national societies, the American Records Management Association, was founded; it was followed the next year by the establishment of the Association of Records Executives and Administrators. NARS took no part in the formation of these two groups, which appealed chiefly to business and state and local records managers. NARS, however, could not ignore ARMA and AREA or their respective publications, *Records Management Quarterly* and *Records Management Journal*. Thus, the bureau soon encouraged its records-administration employees to be active in the affairs of the two associations.

Wayne Grover believed that archivists and records managers had much in common, indeed that they were probably interchangeable as would be seen in the careers, for example, of Philip Brooks, Edward G. Campbell, Lewis Darter, Jr., and Elizabeth Drewry. In his presidential address to the Society of American Archivists in 1954, Grover warned archivists that they had to keep the doors open to all who might be affected by their work. This point of view was also pressed on federal records managers. For example, in 1957, NARS let each of its regional directors understand that he "should know the key state, local and institutional historians and archivists in his region. They should be kept informed as to our developments in the records program." Although this policy was designed partly for promotional and even recruitment purposes, it was largely aimed at maintaining a confederation of those who had an interest in records at any stage in their life span.[24]

It was not only Grover and Bahmer who were proud to function as archivists and records managers. Alldredge and Angel kept active in SAA and even served as presidents of the organization in 1963–64 and 1966–67, respectively. Alldredge also launched a continuing series of meetings of archivists, historians, librarians, and records managers sponsored by NARS, SAA, and state organizations. The first of these symposia was held in Atlanta in April 1964. They were a success, for by the end of 1966 two dozen of them had been held in seventeen different cities, with attendance ranging from 30 to 150. Out of the symposia came not only valuable exchanges of information, but also stimuli for the establishment of regional advisory groups and regional archives in connection with the work of the federal records centers.[25] Although the resulting dialogue occasionally became testy, the variety of people involved was proof that NARS had a constituency that was not only among the elite of the American Historical Association.

Certainly, the seizing of responsibility for paperwork management by NARS was not accidental. Angel and Alldredge expected that this approach would have to be taken and were eager to do so, and Grover and Bahmer, as experienced records managers, were equally interested in this development and confident of their organization's ability to carry out the job. Yet for all their concern for records and paperwork management, none of them forgot that such work was an integral part of the records process, which included archives and research. They were all experienced and trained archivists. Moreover, Bahmer, Angel, and Alldredge were trained historians; and Grover had a superb grasp of and an intense interest in historical activities. It was fortunate for NARS and the country that they could see the overall picture, the intricate relationships be-tween public administration, records management, archives, schol-arship, and service to citizens. There were, of course, missteps and occasionally unwelcome orders from superiors. Nevertheless, NARS was reasonably successful in balancing its legitimate interests so that they could be mutually reinforcing.

17. The Presidential Library System

In odd moments while the Franklin D. Roosevelt Library was being established, Robert D. W. Connor envisioned it as being the first of many such institutions. If, however, Solon J. Buck, Connor's successor as archivist, had such a dream, it was well hidden. Indeed, in 1947 Buck's deputy, Dan Lacy, recommended to the Budget Bureau about possible legislation that "the papers accumulated by a President while in office . . . may not be disposed of by the President or his heirs except by deposit in the Library of Congress."[1] That was a far cry from what Connor had wanted and from what would eventuate during Wayne C. Grover's tenure as archivist of the United States.

Harry S. Truman and his aides were not prepared to see presidential papers declared public property, but they were concerned lest White House files be lost to posterity. President Truman was shocked to learn that a great amount of his predecessors's correspondence had been destroyed by their heirs or through natural causes. He resolved that "such destruction should never again be permitted"; since the "truth behind a president's actions can be found only in his official papers, and every presidential paper is official." As early as 1949, Truman began depositing films, scripts, and recordings of his speeches in the National Archives. In 1950 he asked Archivist Grover to incorporate in the proposed Federal Records Act a section that would allow the National Archives to receive papers of the presidents and other high government officials. Grover did this, and the provision became part of the new law.[2]

President Truman soon decided not to deposit his papers in the National Archives but to establish a presidential library under the jurisdiction of the archivist, as Franklin D. Roosevelt had done. Truman, his staff, his friends, Grover, and General Services Administrator Jess Larson began planning for this in 1950. Indeed, on 8 July 1950, the Harry S. Truman Library, Incorporated, was formed to raise funds for the construction of an appropriate building. Although some money was received, the corporation was largely inactive until late 1952, when it was reorganized. By 1957 some 17,000 persons and groups had contributed $1,800,000 for the establishment of the Harry S. Truman Library. Truman, following Roosevelt's precedent, emphasized that the library would not be a personal memorial, but a government-owned center for research. The Missourian, too, formed an advisory committee of scholars to assist in planning the library, which he originally intended to locate in Grandview, Missouri, the site of his family's farm.[3]

Of course, Truman had motives other than the promotion of research in seeking to establish his own presidential library. The huge amount of records that he had accumulated as president had to be housed and administered, and Truman did not have the wealth to pay for that. Since he believed that his presidential papers were his personal property, as tradition dictated, and since he thought that the material should be made available for his as well as the public's use, Truman accepted the idea of founding a privately built but federally owned and administered library near his home. Such an institution would serve his needs and those of legitimate researchers under restrictions that would give no advantages to his and his associates' political enemies and would not reveal secret information so early that it could jeopardize the national interest. Moreover, the library would be used as a museum to display, for public instruction, appropriate papers as well as gifts that Truman had received during his presidency. Professional administration of the library would ensure that his papers and museum objects would be opened to the public as soon as possible and would be given maximum protection against scattering, damage, and destruction. All in all, this research and museum facility

would constitute a valuable new addition to the educational resources of the Middle West and the nation.[4]

The preparations and the rationales for building the Truman
Library did not settle the question of what to do with the president's
papers between the time he left office and the time the library was
ready for occupancy. There was some consideration of leaving
security-classified materials in the White House as long as they
would be useful to Truman's successor, Dwight D. Eisenhower;
transferring others to a federal records center; and shipping the
rest to Kansas City for Truman's use. In the end, President Truman
decided to take everything back to Missouri with him. The idea
was that it would be under his personal supervision until the library was built, at which time he would deed the material over to
the government. On 19 January 1953, Larson assured Truman
that two archivists could be detailed to assist him.[5]

The decision, however, was not Larson's to implement; indeed, it caused a good deal of discussion among White House aides
during the early days of the Eisenhower administration. One of
the new president's assistants, Val Peterson, contended that presidential papers were public, not private, property. As such, they
should be turned in to the government "for deposit at a common
point, preferably in the Capital City." That argument did not carry
the day, although Eisenhower's aides could not come to a quick
decision regarding the assignment of some archivists to help Truman with his papers. In May the White House staff asked Wayne
Grover for his advice. He replied that funds were available to
provide professional assistance to Truman. (Obviously concerned
with what Eisenhower and Truman might do in the future, the
archivist added that the establishment of presidential libraries outside of Washington would be of positive benefit in broadening
research opportunities over the country.) The White House took
Grover's advice in order to encourage that presidential papers
become public property and agreed that two archivists be detailed
to help organize Truman's papers.[6]

While Harry Truman awaited the construction of the presidential library that would bear his name, two other important
developments took place. One concerned the interest of his aides

in following another of Franklin Roosevelt's precedents with respect to presidential papers. That was the publication of the essential documentation of Truman's presidency, as Samuel I. Rosenman
had done for Roosevelt in the thirteen volumes entitled *Public
Papers and Addresses of Franklin D. Roosevelt.* Although nothing
came of this when George M. Elsey and Wayne Grover first discussed it in 1949, the idea was not forgotten. Elsey raised the question again at a luncheon in the fall of 1954 with Grover and two
other former Truman aides, David D. Lloyd and Kenneth Hechler.
All four of them agreed that it was difficult for researchers to find
recent key presidential documents and that the government should
consider the publication of a series of volumes for the presidents
comparable to the *Congressional Record* and the Supreme Court's
United States Reports.[7]

Grover had a staff study prepared for the White House, the
National Historical Publications Commission, and Elsey, Lloyd,
and Hechler. The Eisenhower administration's response to the proposal to publish the public papers of the presidents was favorable.
Events, however, moved slowly. It was not until September 1955
that the archivist felt he was on sure enough ground to raise the
question of the project's legality. In December GSA's acting general
counsel indicated that apparently NARS's Federal Register Division,
upon securing the approval of the NHPC, would have the statutory
authority to publish recent presidential documents.[8]

The project was not pressed further in 1956, for fear it would
become involved in the politics of that presidential election year.
The National Historical Publications Commission and the Federal
Register Division, however, were ready to go forward in 1957.
The commission recommended the project on 2 March, and the
series was given the name The Public Papers of the Presidents.
Under the law, the Federal Register Division could handle the
series because of its authority to publish special editions of the
Federal Register. The division also had the employees and the experience to initiate and carry on such a monumental project. NHPC,
of course, contributed in an advisory capacity because of its staff's
skill at historical editing. The two organizations agreed that each
volume in the new series would encompass a year of presidential

pronouncements, including "Formal messages to the Congress," "Messages to the People," "Executive documents," "Significant messages to sovereigns, heads of state, representatives of foreign governments," released press conference transcripts, and selected letters.

The first volume of The Public Papers of the Presidents was published in 1958 and contained selected papers of Eisenhower for 1957. By 1959 the Federal Register Division's administrative committee, which was composed of the archivist, the public printer, and a representative of the attorney general, had approved the publication of volumes for the early years of the Eisenhower administration and the entire Truman presidency. The first volume for the Truman period appeared in 1961. Thus was an important documentary series established, which has been continued to the present time. The Public Papers of the Presidents could not answer all the questions that researchers asked. It has been, however, of immense reference value to those who are interested in recent presidential history as well as an improved continuation of Rosenman's work on Roosevelt and of James D. Richardson's volumes relating to earlier presidents, which were entitled *A Compilation of the Messages and Papers of the Presidents.*[9]

The other development that occurred before the Harry S. Truman Library was completed was more important than either the new documentary project or the new presidential library. That was the provision of continuing arrangements to preserve presidential papers for public use. The establishment of the Roosevelt Library, of course, had represented a haphazard approach to the problem. Since Val Peterson's suggestion that presidential papers belonged to the public and thus should be passed to the government at the end of each administration had sparked no favorable response, there was still need for some method of regularization. The concept of the presidential library offered a possibility of that. NARS by early 1954 was, as Assistant Archivist Robert Bahmer wrote, "considering the possibility of trying to influence . . . the development of [presidential libraries] in some way that will make the end result more acceptable than the prospect of an increasing number of Libraries set up in home towns." The big problem was how to guide a retiring president on the disposition of his papers. Truman had originally agreed to place his papers in the National Archives, but after reconsideration he decided to have his own library. Probably other presidents would want to do the same thing, Bahmer believed. In any event, he had come to question "whether it is advisable to centralize all such materials." Perhaps the solution was "to tie in the Presidential Libraries with Universities some way that would permit us to administer the collections professionally while the University or College carried the cost of physical maintenance."[10]

By 1955 NARS had devised a plan to deal with these issues, especially the regularization of the federal government's acquisition of presidential papers and administration of presidential libraries. Indeed, support for the plan was impressive and bipartisan, as was indicated in the sponsorship of the necessary resolution by House Majority Leader John W. McCormack and Minority Leader Joseph W. Martin, Jr. The House of Representatives held hearings on 13 June on the legislation, which would authorize GSA to accept not only the papers and other historical materials of or relating to any president and other high officials of the government, but also land, buildings, and equipment donated to the United States in order to create a presidential library. The general services administrator would be empowered to "maintain, operate, and protect them as a presidential archival depository." Moreover, his agency could enter into agreements to operate as presidential libraries property made available by a state or local government, college, university, foundation, or institute, without receiving the title thereto, for that purpose. What was crucially important to regularizing the process was that the administrator would not need positive congressional action to do these things. He would only be required to report in writing to Congress about such arrangements, including descriptions of the historical materials and property involved; the estimated cost of extra equipment needed; and the cost of the operation, maintenance, and protection of the new "presidential archival depository." If sixty days of continuous session of Congress passed after the filing of this report without legislative action preventing the consummation of such an agreement, then the administrator could implement it.[11]

The House and the Senate passed the bill without controversy by August 1955, and President Eisenhower signed it into law on the twelfth. The legislation had been well designed. It satisfied the needs of NARS for regularizing the acceptance and administration of presidential papers and libraries; of Eisenhower's and Truman's aides for a smooth way to establish their presidential libraries as federally maintained institutions; of scholars for additional, valuable research material; of local boosters for prestigious tourist enterprises; and of various parties for the dispersal of such facilities to the advantage of citizens in outlying areas and, in case of war, to the nation. It was plain that the libraries could fulfill significant educational functions, especially in their museum activities. Moreover, the possibility of having a former president and some of his former aides available on occasion was an attraction, for it might allow the public and researchers to have access to living history. When all was said, however, the overarching reason for supporting the legislation was, as Administrator Mansure pointed out, that it provided "a foundation for the systematic preservation and use of the papers of the American Presidency." He added that the legislation was "historic in every sense of the word." This certainly was true for NARS, for it thus added another major function to its operations, the supervision of the presidential library system.[12]

Not everyone was happy with the Presidential Libraries Act. In April 1956 the council of the American Association for State and Local History protested it as a menace to the manuscript-collecting activities of historical societies. What they objected to was the "sweeping inclusiveness of authorizing the National Archives to accept for deposit 'other papers relating to and contemporary with any President or former President of the United States.'" There were several answers to this criticism, which Herman Kahn of the Franklin D. Roosevelt Library gave. First, the authorization theoretically did not apply to all former presidents, only in effect to currently living former presidents, the incumbent, and future presidents. Second, granted that presidential libraries would solicit as well as receive historical materials, their collecting activities would emphasize the papers of those persons and groups that played a *"nationally significant* role in the period of the public life of the President . . . for whom a library has been established." Third, Kahn questioned whether there was really a problem. Probably not, for there were far more papers available than collecting institutions could currently administer properly.[13] Of course, AASLH's fears were understandable, for there was little to keep the presidential libraries from skimming off the cream of American historical papers. Be that as it may, presidential libraries have largely confined themselves to what is directly related to a given president; and state, local, and private repositories have found that they have a great deal in common with presidential libraries in the work of preserving historical materials. There certainly has been no shortage of things worth collecting for research.

Although the Presidential Libraries Act had been passed and a controversy over it weathered, a presidential library system had yet to be established. All that existed in 1955 and 1956 was the Franklin D. Roosevelt Library, the beginnings of a Harry S. Truman Library, and plans for a Dwight D. Eisenhower Library. For NARS, that meant only one such institution in hand, with two in the bush. The Truman Library had received about half of its intended private funds by 1954 as well as several offers of land for the building. That summer the corporation accepted an offer of 13.2 acres from the city of Independence, Missouri. The property was located in a park, only five blocks from the Truman residence in Independence. The corporation soon directed architects to draw up plans for the library, and in May 1955 ground for the structure was broken on the crest of a gentle hill. Work on the capacious one-story limestone building, the architecture of which could be called semicircular federalese, progressed well. In February 1957 the building, site, and most of Truman's historical materials were offered to the government under the terms of the Presidential Libraries Act. The administrator of general services made the prescribed report to Congress and the necessary sixty days passed. Thus by spring GSA's agreement to accept responsibility for operating the Harry S. Truman Library became binding. The federal government received custody of the new institution in July during dedication ceremonies that were presided over by Chief Justice Earl Warren with Truman, Herbert Hoover, and Eleanor Roosevelt in attendance.[14]

The veteran archivist, Philip C. Brooks, became director of the Truman Library, a post he would hold for almost fifteen years. Truman and he intended that the institution's program would be more than a carbon copy of that of the Roosevelt Library. Of course, the Truman Library would receive and solicit pertinent historical materials, both for research use and museum display. It would also show films and hold meetings in connection with its purposes and even those of the community. Moreover, a private organization was formed in May 1957 to foster the maximum scholarly use of the library's resources and facilities. That was the Harry S. Truman Library Institute for National and International Affairs, whose directors included Truman, various other national figures, scholars, local worthies, and representatives of universities in the region. The idea was that the institute would establish a book collection in the Truman Library, finance conferences of scholars and public figures, and give grants-in-aid for research. That the institute did, and more, over the years. Its additional accomplishments included publishing the proceedings of several scholarly conferences and a newsletter that reported the library's activities and holdings, subsidizing oral history projects, funding special research projects, and awarding the David D. Lloyd Prize for the best book published every two years dealing with the period of Truman's presidency.

In May 1959 the Truman Library opened its research room to researchers, more than 700 of whom had used its resources by 1970; even earlier its museum was opened to the public and almost 2,000,000 people had visited it by 1970. The library's research holdings were substantial, numbering by 1963 over 50,000 printed items and some 3,244 cubic feet of the papers of President Truman and of groups and persons who had been associated with him. There were available in addition large collections of microfilm, motion-picture film, still photographs, and sound recordings. Not only had the library quickly established itself as an important research institution, it had also pioneered for other presidential libraries and similar organizations in fostering research and bringing together scholars and public figures. Indeed, many of the people who attended conferences and conducted research at the Truman Library considered themselves the equivalent of alumni. They proved, as such, to be both the library's closest friends and sharpest critics.[15]

The basis for the Eisenhower Library was laid well before Dwight Eisenhower became president of the United States. Before the end of the Second World War, a group of citizens from Kansas, the state in which Eisenhower had been raised, proposed the building of a war memorial, including museum and library, as a tribute to the general and veterans. This proposal led to the incorporation of the Eisenhower Foundation in July 1945. The foundation acquired the Eisenhower home in Abilene, Kansas, in December 1946 and bought additional land for the memorial. In April 1952 construction was begun on the museum, which was opened to the public two years later. The library was a separate rectangular building of two stories, construction on which was started in October 1959 and completed in May 1962, when it was turned over to the government along with Eisenhower's papers. The Eisenhower home and museum and a newly built chapel, the Place of Meditation, were not deeded over to the public until 1966, the same year that the library was opened for research. Like Roosevelt and Hoover before him and Truman later, Eisenhower's final resting place was on the grounds of his library, for he was entombed in the Place of Meditation in 1969.

As with the other presidential libraries, the Eisenhower Library became more than a repository for documents and a tourist attraction. It launched a substantial oral history project in 1963 and cooperated in the editing and publication of General Eisenhower's papers by Johns Hopkins University. The library also became a meeting place for conferences on Western history and sponsored other significant events, including a symposium of scholars on the invasion of Normandy and exhibitions of Western art. From 1968 through 1973, 2,275,000 visitors came to the Eisenhower Center, as the whole complex of buildings is called. By the end of 1973, 369 researchers had used the library and had examined more than

116,000 research items. The holdings by the end of fiscal year 1973 consisted of almost 17,000,000 pages of manuscripts and oral histories of Eisenhower and the people and groups associated with him; 42,000 printed items; and considerable quantities of photographed, filmed, microfilmed, and sound-recorded materials.[16]

The advantageous stipulations of the Presidential Libraries Act led former President Hoover to decide to move his papers from the Hoover Institution at Stanford to a federal repository. Therefore, upon his initiative and that of a group of Iowans, the Herbert Hoover Presidential Library was constructed with private funds in 1962 and transferred to the government in 1964. This institution was situated in Hoover's birthplace, West Branch, Iowa, and opened for research in 1968. Because of Hoover's one term in office and the relative smallness of government operations during his presidency, this library is the smallest of all. Its manuscript and oral history holdings ran about 2,000 linear feet in 1971. Yet its collections have excited considerable interest, so that in 1973 it ranked third out of the six presidential-records depositories in the number of visits by researchers. The Hoover Presidential Library also contains a fine collection of books and museum pieces; and it sponsored, through its private fund-raising group, four scholarly seminars on Hoover's life during the centenary of his birth in 1974. The institution is part of a complex of buildings encompassing not only the handsomely designed limestone library and museum structure, but also several frame buildings administered by the National Park Service that give a taste of the atmosphere of small-town Iowa in the nineteenth century. One of these is the house in which Hoover was born.[17]

The Roosevelt, Truman, Eisenhower, and Hoover libraries were the only operating units in the presidential library system by 1968. Steps, however, were already well advanced by then for the establishment of presidential archival depositories named after John F. Kennedy and Lyndon B. Johnson. Kennedy's prepresidential papers had been transferred to the custody of NARS five days after he was inaugurated president in 1961. A few days after Kennedy's assassination in 1963, Archivist Grover and General Services Administrator Bernard Boutin met in the White House

Lyndon Baines Johnson Library, Austin, Texas

with several of Kennedy's aides and friends to discuss the building of the Kennedy Library and the initiation of an oral history project. Despite the fiascos involved in the private fund-raising corporation's attempts to find a site in the Boston area for the library, which were not resolved until 1975, President Kennedy's papers and related materials were soon placed in various NARS facilities. In 1969 these were concentrated in the Federal Records Center at Waltham, Massachusetts, where since 1970 increasingly large amounts of them have been available for research.[18]

The White House and NARS began planning to establish the Lyndon B. Johnson Library soon after the new president took office in November 1963. This became a matter of high priority after 1965, when the University of Texas offered land and an appropriately equipped building in Austin for the Johnson Library. By 1967 the site was being cleared. The library was built to be larger than life, like Texas. Towering eight stories high and made of pale beige travertine, the building is fronted by reflecting pools and a fountain that can spout a jet of water forty feet in the air. Lyndon B. Johnson's Texas Taj Mahal was dedicated in May 1971, and the first group of papers was opened to researchers the following January. Although the University of Texas holds title to the building, NARS has a permanent occupancy permit to administer the voluminous research materials in its custody there.[19]

Plainly, by the end of the 1960s the Presidential Libraries Act of 1955 had proved its worthiness. The presidents were impressed with the advantages that the legislation offered, and they and their families and associates moved quickly to plan presidential archival depositories and to prepare historical materials for deposit and use therein. If many of the papers were not opened as soon as scholars often justifiably wanted, it cannot be gainsaid that much more was made available for research and many other services offered than could have been expected had there been no presidential libraries. Individual presidential archives, of course, might have developed without the existence of the Presidential Libraries Act, but, clearly, having to be separately considered, such institutions would have come along slowly and perhaps with less professional regulation.[20]

It was the responsibility of NARS to find ways of supervising the presidential library system. Beginning in 1957, Archivist Grover and Deputy Archivist Bahmer directly administered the Roosevelt Library and the Truman Library, basically under the same regulations. Thus, the pattern was set early for operating the libraries under similar rules for soliciting and organizing historical materials and making them available for research use. Wayne Grover took his new responsibility seriously. As Director Philip C. Brooks of the Truman Library noted, "The presidential libraries are very close to his heart." So they were, but their operation posed weighty problems, such as dealing with the egos of large numbers of donors, sponsors, and researchers who were or thought they were very important people. It was plain that Grover and Bahmer, who were burdened with many other duties, did not have enough time to do the complete job of supervision. Therefore, in 1957 they used Karl L. Trever to help them, with the title of special assistant to the archivist for presidential libraries. After Trever's retirement by 1964, Herman Kahn, the former director of the Roosevelt Library, took over the rapidly growing job as the first assistant archivist for presidential libraries. That put the administration of the presidential library system on a par with the other major offices in NARS.[21]

NARS, of course, deemed the development of the new office necessary not only because four presidential libraries would be fully open for use by 1968, but also because of the enormous amount of work that was required in planning the projected Johnson and Kennedy depositories. Moreover, after the election of a new president in 1968, another project began. Richard M. Nixon late in 1968 began to turn over many of his prepresidential papers to NARS and early in 1969 indicated plans to establish his own presidential library. The plans for a Nixon library were disrupted by the controversies related to his resignation in 1974 and the action of Congress in impounding his presidential records. Nevertheless, in February 1975 he stated his intention to deed another 1,300 cubic feet of his prepresidential papers to GSA in an agreement that bound the agency to cooperate in the ultimate creation of a Nixon library. Public access to his presidential records awaits the long, tedious sorting out of them, which NARS began after federal courts awarded custody of the papers to the government in 1977.

Since the foundation of the Roosevelt Library, the question had occasionally been raised as to who really owned the records of the presidents and other federal officials. The issue became heated in 1974 as the Watergate investigations reached their peak, with most researchers, much of the press, and many politicians demanding that the government be declared the owner of such material. In response to this, Congress, when it impounded the Nixon papers in December 1974, established a commission on public documents to make recommendations as to the control, disposition, and preservation of the records of federal officials. Whatever action Congress takes on the commission's 1977 conclusions that such materials should be considered public property,[22] there seems little doubt that presidential libraries will still be constructed as the repositories for the records of the presidents. Two important issues are whether a clear distinction can be made between the private and the public papers of federal officials and whether future incumbents will preserve their records as well as their twentieth-century predecessors had when such material had been considered personal property. Another crucial question is, Would the government be as willing as soon to open such papers to public scrutiny as the donors of materials to existing presidential libraries have been? It is no evasion to say, assuming the records of officials are declared public property, that only time will tell.

Regardless of what the debates on those issues lead to, the salient fact is that the presidential library system was firmly established by the end of Lyndon B. Johnson's administration. The Roosevelt, Truman, Eisenhower, and Hoover Libraries, and later the Johnson and Kennedy depositories, however, did not all operate in the same way. There were advantages and disadvantages to their dissimilarities. The chief advantage was that each institution could develop its own particular programs, apart from the common ones of serving research, display, and tourist purposes. Thus, the Roosevelt Library worked with local and naval history, the Truman Library became a center for the study of the institution of the presidency, the Eisenhower Library reflected the general's military career and his interest in art and in the West, and the Hoover

Library emphasized Chinese art as well as America's overseas relief efforts. Some libraries were more interested in sponsoring conferences on scholarly and public issues than were the others, which in turn might be more concerned with awarding grants-in-aid to facilitate research. The variety of the interests of any single presidential library was considerable and the range of concerns of all of them together was impressive. It was obvious, that each was stimulating the others to consider and launch new programs. Certainly, NARS's Office of Presidential Libraries encouraged this cross-fertilization, and seldom were the results unsuccessful.

There was one index of success on which the libraries were highly rated by 1973: they were all substantial research and, except for the Kennedy depository, tourist centers. The pages of their manuscript, microfilm, and oral-history holdings ran from 4,865,-967 in the Hoover Library to 38,392,667 in the Johnson Library. All six of the repositories had significant collections of museum and printed materials as well as of sound recordings and motion and still pictures. And by no means was the Hoover Library the smallest or the Johnson Library the largest institution in all categories. The number of visits during fiscal year 1973 by researchers ranged from 342 at the Eisenhower Library to 1,345 at the Roosevelt Library, and the number of museum visitors, keeping in mind that there was no Kennedy museum yet, ranged from 82,870 at the Hoover Library to 694,180 at the Johnson Library. Although none of the presidential libraries was as inexpensive for the federal government to operate as the $150,000 yearly figure estimated by Archivist Grover in 1955, none could be considered, in view of inflation and approved new services, to be dear. This was shown in their expenditures for 1973, which ranged from $265,980 for the Hoover Library to $650,260 for the Johnson Library.[23]

Yet there were some disadvantages to the dissimilarities among the libraries. There had been traces of patronage at a couple of the depositories because of the influence of their political founders. A related problem was that in all the libraries some members of the affiliated private fund-raising groups had swayed policy decisions. Moreover, the prominent role that scholars had played in the establishment of the Roosevelt, Truman, and Kennedy repositories was not emulated in the other three institutions. Scholars, indeed, were not always prominent in the work of the private support groups, although the professional staff was usually more willing to listen to academicians than were many of the "very important people" who were interested in the various presidential libraries. That mirrored the fact that the staffs of the libraries were professionally competent and were supervised by a highly qualified group of people in NARS's Office of Presidential Libraries. Yet archivists too often exercised excessive caution in making decisions, particularly in determining what materials should be opened for research, and they were sometimes timid in considering changes suggested by researchers. It was not only the influence of the "very important people" at work here or the natural caution of many archivists. Part of the situation developed because the personnel at the libraries often believed that they had to follow suggestions slavishly from other government agencies on the use of materials that had originally been in their offices. Unfortunately for relations between NARS and the scholarly world, these problems have not always been satisfactorily resolved; the results were, are, and will probably continue to be the airings of grievances by researchers.

There is no doubt that the presidential libraries were, as Herman Kahn called them, "a new institution." This was partly because of their focus upon the career and interests of a chief executive; partly because of their integration of research, museum, and even conference functions; and partly because they provide a continuing and systematic way of collecting historical materials of the highest interest. The presidential depositories have also been controversial, whether the issue be decentralization, competition with other collecting organizations, the availability of materials to researchers, or the occasional involvement of political figures in their operations. Yet the common goals of the presidential libraries, which Franklin D. Roosevelt originally stated, have been considerably fulfilled. The first was to preserve the papers of the presidents, which had not been well done before Roosevelt's time. The second was to deed them over to the federal government, since only until recently had it been almost universally accepted that such documents were private property. The third was to open the papers, on equal terms, to researchers within a reasonably short span of time. If this objective has not been as well achieved as many wish, it must be agreed that much success has been attained in this area. A fourth goal—one more easily achieved—was to display the other historical materials that recent presidents collected or acquired. There have been, of course, dividends beyond those four activities, and not just in terms of conferences and other educational services and the provision of financial aid for research. The specialized nature of the presidential libraries has led to the development of staffs that can render expert service to researchers. This "new institution" has also stimulated historical publication, as the hundreds of books and articles based on the holdings of the libraries demonstrate. The establishment of the libraries has also encouraged dozens of other institutions, especially universities, to preserve manuscript collections. Equally important, a goal for presidential libraries that Roosevelt voiced only later has been pursued with great success. That is the collection of the papers and oral histories of the people and groups associated with the presidents. Despite the pains the presidential libraries suffered at birth and through their growing up, they have provided notable and increasing service to researchers and the public. There is no doubt that archivists and especially researchers will not silently suffer any diminution of the quality of that performance.[24]

18. Progress, Programs, and Problems, 1957–1967

The National Archives and Records Service operated reasonably well, given the funds available, during the second half of Wayne C. Grover's tenure as archivist of the United States. As I have shown, the integration of paperwork management with records administration and the establishment of the presidential library system proceeded with no serious hitches; as I shall demonstrate, the Federal Register Division continued the high quality of its work and the National Historical Publications Commission grew in impact. The Office of the National Archives, the heart of the system, was where the serious problems arose. Yet even it was usually able to take them in its stride.

The holdings of the National Archives expanded from a post-World War II low of 749,500 cubic feet in 1955 to 895,807 in 1967, including some 3,620,000 photographs, 1,551,000 maps and charts, 64,900 reels of motion pictures, and 34,300 sound recordings. The number of documents furnished to researchers and the number of inquiries answered rose from a combined total of 416,500 in 1955 to 566,700 in 1967. Neither in holdings nor service, however, was this growth steady.[1]

The National Archives by 1960 was bulging at the seams, with almost 912,000 cubic feet in its possession, some 13 percent of which was stored in a warehouse in Alexandria, Virginia. Despite strenuous efforts to cope with this problem through better appraisal and reappraisal, the situation grew worse during the early 1960s. Not only did many of the government's archives remain in inadequate housing, but considerable amounts of valuable material were not accessioned. Only the building of the Washington National Records Center in 1967 and the establishment of regional archives in federal records centers allowed the National Archives to bring its holdings under better control. As for the reference services provided, they were even less under the ability of NARS to control since no one could predict well how many researchers would use the National Archives or how much staff time working with them would consume. This was a problem insofar as it was difficult to make budget personnel in the General Services Administration, who increasingly thought in terms of "targets" and "missions," understand that the amounts of service that researchers required were unequal and that the work needed to serve them and indeed their very numbers could not be forecasted accurately from year to year. Thus the National Archives usually either "failed" to reach or overshot the "unit-cost" goals that GSA set for its reference service. Consequently, the archives was often inadequately budgeted; indeed, that part of NARS had fewer employees in 1967 than the old National Archives had in 1941![2]

Yet the National Archives did make some progress. One example of this was in the preservation of fragile documents. This was largely a result of the decision made in 1956 to microfilm most of the endangered archives instead of flattening or laminating them. The number of sheets preserved rose from 617,000 out of the more than 13,000,000 requiring attention in fiscal year 1955 to 3,140,000 in 1962, more than two-thirds of which were microfilmed. Thus considerable progress was made in catching up on the backlog of documents needing preservation. Terror, however, struck the hearts of archivists in 1963 as some agencies reported discovering blemishes on microfilm. Although these spots were microscopic and none had been detected on microfilm that the National Archives had processed or stored, the General Services Administration in January 1964 notified all federal agencies that until the problem was resolved it would not approve the disposition of any permanently valuable records that had been microfilmed. The National Bureau of Standards inaugurated research on this problem. Although the government hoped that the mystery of the blemishes would be quickly solved, work on the question continued into fiscal year 1968. By then it was plain that the appearance of the blemishes came from the failure of some offices to follow prescribed standards in processing and storing microfilm. The crisis of microfilm blemishes had proved that the standards of NARS were satisfactory.[3]

The massive effort of microfilming fragile documents for preservation also enlarged the amount of material included in the file microcopy or, as it became called during the 1950s, microfilm publications program. The National Archives had begun microfilming in 1936 in order to augment its finding aids, but by 1940 it planned to microfilm documents to reduce the handling of often-consulted records and to facilitate the use of archives by researchers who found it difficult to spend time in Washington. By 1965 some 67,000 rolls were available for sale and researchers had bought 48,715 rolls that year. And that was not all, for many of the microfilm publications, for example, at least 29,319 rolls in fiscal year 1961, were used in the archives building's search rooms. The success of the National Archives with microfilm publications prompted other institutions, most notably the Library of Congress, the Massachusetts Historical Society, and the State Historical Society of Wisconsin to launch similar programs by the early 1960s. By 1964 the National Historical Publications Commission procured funds from Congress to stimulate other institutions to begin such programs. By 1970 many of the other archival and manuscript repositories in the United States had made microcopy programs an integral part of their operations, much to the benefit of scholarship.[4]

The strides forward taken in preserving archives were accompanied by an impressive production of guides to the research materials. The 1957 list of publications of the National Archives included ninety-eight preliminary inventories and thirteen special lists; but that increased by 1973 to 170 inventories, thirty-two special lists, and sixty-nine guides to microfilms of the captured German and Italian records that the archival service formerly possessed. To complement this program, the National Archives prepared a large number of unpublished inventories and lists for staff use. Forty-nine of these were produced in fiscal year 1964 and ninety-five the following year. Using these approaches, the National Archives soon brought most of its holdings under bibliographical control, which saved staff members and researchers a great deal of time.

Both the published and unpublished inventories and lists provided a good basis for the compilation during the 1960s of lengthy published guides on special topics. Most notable among these were the *Guide to Federal Archives Relating to the Civil War*, by Kenneth W. Munden and Henry P. Beers; the *Guide to the Archives of the Government of the Confederate States of America*, by Beers; the *Guide to Materials on Latin America in the National Archives*, by John P. Harrison and George S. Ulibarri; and the *Guide to Genealogical Records in the National Archives*, by Meredith B. Colket, Jr., and Frank E. Bridgers. Unfortunately, the National Archives did not bring its splendid comprehensive guide of 1948 up to date for more than a quarter of a century. Researchers and archivists often requested a new edition of it, but no formal action was taken until 1966 when a blue-ribbon staff committee urged the need for a revised guide. Even at that, work on it was delayed until 1968, and the new *Guide to the National Archives of the United States* was not published until 1974. At its appearance many prayers were offered that archivists and researchers would not have to wait until the following century for the next edition. The provision for automated updating of the guide's contents should help answer those prayers.[5]

It is appropriate to mention here that the long-time editor of the Territorial Papers of the United States, Clarence E. Carter, died in 1961. During his editorship, twenty-six volumes in this distinguished series of documents on the territories found in federal archives had been published. The new editor, John Porter Bloom, continued to apply the high standards that Carter set for the series in both printed volumes and microfilm publications.[6]

Over the years, the facsimile program of the National Archives expanded, in terms of both the number of reproductions of famous documents available and their sales, which reached about 90,000 in 1963. The exhibition hall of the National Archives also constantly grew in popularity as a tourist stop in Washington. During fiscal year 1960 the number of visitors reached 625,000 and by 1965 more than 1,320,000. The various centennial exhibits on Civil War themes were of particular interest during those years.[7]

The National Archives increasingly rendered technical service to individuals, businesses, and government agencies. Perhaps most exciting in this respect was the organization's encouragement and help, beginning in 1952, in establishing archives in the territories. This led first to the enactment of appropriate legislation by Puerto Rico in 1955 and the detailing of Oliver W. Holmes the following year to advise the commonwealth on its planned new institution. During fiscal year 1958 Charles E. Dewing of the National Archives served as the acting director of the Archivo General de Puerto Rico in its initial year of operation. That same year Archivist Grover detailed another of his staff members to assist in the further development of Hawaii's Archives Division. The National Archives extended similar assistance to Alaska before it reached statehood. Another noteworthy venture was Karl L. Trever's work during the early 1960s in setting up the Sam Rayburn Library in Texas, along the lines of a presidential library, in honor of the long-time Speaker of the House of Representatives.[8]

Grover and NARS had not lost the taste for new programs after the founding of the records service and the presidential library system. The archivist was eager to have his staff meet more often with potential users of federal records. One result of this, as we have seen, was the symposia that NARS and the Society of American Archivists administered for archivists, historians, librarians, and records managers. Additionally, the bureau's personnel often spoke to campus groups. One dramatic illustration of this occurred in 1962 when Grover and the directors of the Roosevelt and Truman libraries lectured to audiences on five campuses over a telephone network organized by the University of Omaha. NARS also procured funds from the Ford Foundation to survey the problems that dissertation writers encountered during their training and research. Operating between 1965 and 1967, the National Historical Publications Commission administered this Survey on the Use of Original Sources in Graduate History Training. Walter Rundell, Jr., the survey's director, visited 112 universities and research repositories;

interviewed 557 archivists, graduate students, librarians, and professors; and sent out questionnaires to almost 200 others. He concluded that there were three general problems hampering research on the history of the United States: the limitations on access to source materials, mediocre communication between researchers and custodians, and less than excellent training in historical research methods. In a spate of lectures and articles and in a book, Rundell elaborated on these problems and possible solutions to them. Thus the survey contributed to bettering American historical research by forcefully calling attention to the need and the ways to improve training, communication, and access.[9]

NARS also became increasingly alert to the rising importance of machine-readable and taped records. By December 1964 it and the Budget Bureau completed a survey of automated records in the government. The study concluded that the disposition practices of federal agencies for such material had to be brought in line with those for paper records. NARS, therefore, laid plans to issue a general disposition schedule for automated data during fiscal year 1966 with the chief objective of saving valuable information that would otherwise be destroyed. The survey also indicated that the government should consider establishing a central archives for automated records. The Committee on the Preservation and Use of Economic Data of the Social Science Research Council originally proposed this and the location of such a center in NARS, and many officials in NARS were in agreement. The committee, however, reversed itself in March 1965, contending that an electronic data center might better be an independent operation that would have concerns beyond those of NARS.

More than a decade later a federal data center had not been established, largely because of a continuing national controversy as to whether the government would use it, as it had used other of its instrumentalities, to pry into the privacy of American citizens. That controversy also took place within GSA, with the administrator's office often pressing for an electronic data center under its control and with many leading archivists arguing against it on the grounds that NARS was bringing automated records under control through its management operations without being deemed a threat to American liberties. It should be emphasized that machine-readable records became neither the mere "intermediate worksheets" that NARS originally considered most of them nor until the middle 1970s a major new program that some archivists had sought. It was, however, no small accomplishment for NARS to begin integrating such a sophisticated form of record into its operations of appraisal, accessioning, disposal, training, and reference work. Whether the organization could keep abreast of the rapid developments in automated materials and their use is a question that has deeply concerned NARS to the present time. Of one thing archivists and records managers were sure: such materials would become increasingly significant in research and government administration.[10]

During the latter half of Wayne Grover's tenure, the National Archives added a clever innovation to its campaign to preserve the estimated 2 percent of federal records that were enduringly valuable. It seemed logical that if there were disposal schedules for records, there should also be schedules to identify better those materials that should be retained. Thus NARS in 1962 began preparing records retention plans, which became an asset in developing comprehensive records programs and disposal schedules as well as in clarifying what records needed the best of care in the agencies and facilitating their transfer to the National Archives. By the end of fiscal year 1964 the service had prepared retention plans for all or part of sixty-nine federal agencies.[11]

The National Archives used its increasing interest in automated data techniques to try to gain improved knowledge of what it and other repositories had on hand. In fiscal year 1967 NARS procured $40,000 from the Council on Library Resources, Inc., to establish a project for computer indexing of finding aids from a variety of American archival and manuscript institutions. Frank G. Burke left the Library of Congress to head this program and thus to follow up the breakthrough he had made there in selective permutation indexing. The eventual goal of his project, called SPINDEX II, was to provide centralized bibliographical control of and computerized information retrieval service for archival and manuscript repositories across the country.[12] Although SPINDEX II facilitated information retrieval in a number of institutions, it was too large and expensive a task to succeed. Thus one of NARS's prime objectives during the 1970s was to find less costly ways to bring its own archival holdings under better bibliographical and retrieval control and to cooperate with other advanced repositories in exchanging the fruits of such efforts.

The Federal Register Office continued to work smoothly during the rest of Wayne Grover's years as archivist of the United States. After acquiring the additional job of publishing the Public Papers of the Presidents, most of the office's work was concerned with handling its always increasing load and making improvements in its operating methods and services. In August 1965 it began preparing for publication in a *Weekly Compilation of Presidential Documents* the news-conference transcripts, statements, messages, speeches, and other materials issued by the president. This new publication proved to be of distinct service to government agencies, journalists, scholars, and others.[13]

When Philip M. Hamer retired from the executive directorship of the National Historical Publications Commission in 1960, its work had been well begun. Hamer's successor at the commission's helm was Oliver W. Holmes, another veteran of service in the National Archives, the recipient of a Ph.D. from Columbia University, and a former president of SAA. Holmes continued NHPC's work in encouraging, coordinating, and advising on the publication of the papers of illustrious Americans in what Hamer had so well labeled "well-edited and beautifully printed volumes." The funding for the documentary publications came from a wide variety of sources, including universities; philanthropic foundations; state and local governments; and private enterprises such as Time, Inc., and the New York Times Company. The ongoing result of NHPC's efforts under Hamer and Holmes was not only the wider accessibility of documentary materials for research, but a renaissance in historical editorship in the United States.[14]

New initiatives, however, were in the offing. By December 1962 NHPC had taken a fresh look at its program and had prepared recommendations for President Kennedy on what it thought should be done in the future. The commission reported in this published document on the more than two dozen major editorial projects with which it had been involved. There was also reference to NHPC's role in supporting the publication of the Public Papers of the Presidents, *The National Union Catalog of Manuscript Collections*, and Hamer's *Guide to Archives and Manuscripts in the United States*, as well as its responsibility for the annual bibliographical compendium, *Writings on American History*. For the next decade, the commission requested support for a campaign to raise $5,000,-000 from private donors to establish capital funds for the completion of major projects such as the Adams and Jefferson papers and the allocation of $1,000,000 annually to NHPC, half from Congress and half from private sources, to finance a grants-in-aid program for other projects including microfilm publications.[15]

As chairman of the commission, Wayne Grover sent a copy of the report to Presidential Assistant Arthur M. Schlesinger, Jr., for President Kennedy to see in December 1962. General Services Administrator Bernard L. Boutin officially transmitted the report on 10 January 1963 to Kennedy, who soon endorsed its recommendations. In May Congressman Jack Brooks of Texas introduced legislation in Congress to authorize the acceleration of NHPC's work. The White House gave considerable support to the bill, which Congress soon enacted and the president, on 28 July, approved. All was not gained, however, for Congress had yet to appropriate monies. There was a hullabaloo in the House as to what *editing* meant. Many representatives defined the term in its journalistic instead of its historical sense and expressed their fear that the projects would lead to a rewriting of the words of great Americans. Fortunately for NHPC, a majority in Congress was convinced that historical editing referred to making the published documents as faithful as possible to original meanings and texts. Yet the misunderstanding about terminology as well as some congressional reservations about such a "frill" as historical documentary publication resulted in the appropriation not of the authorized $500,000, but of only $350,000 for fiscal year 1965.[16]

GSA was partly responsible for NHPC's continued underfunding, for after Congress had appropriated $350,000 during each of the fiscal years 1965 and 1966, the administrator's office requested only that much for 1967. Yet the commission was heartened in

1968 when Congress extended both the legislation of 1963 and the authorization for expenditures of $500,000 annually. Eventually, with the approach of the nation's bicentennial, NHPC gained additional appropriations to support its editorial programs. Private, state, and local donors also helped out, again not to the commission's full satisfaction, but substantially. For example, in October 1964 the Ford Foundation granted $2,000,000 to be spent over ten years in financing editorial projects, the training of editors, and Walter Rundell's Survey on the Use of Original Sources. This grant particularly enabled NHPC to support microfilmed documentary projects. By 1967 twenty-three repositories in seventeen states had been involved in the microfilm editing program and had already produced sixty-one microfilm publications that totaled over one thousand rolls of film.[17]

By the 1970s NHPC would come under well-publicized attack for dealing with the papers, as one critic said, of only "Great White Men." Yet there was earlier criticism. Leo Marx suggested in 1961 that "possession of the documents" is far from being "possession of the past," and five years later Page Smith asked if the historical editors were not providing scholars with more than they need to know. In 1965 an archivist, Charles Lee, declared his perplexity at "the sudden popularity of these documentary projects, particularly of the 'great man' variety." Some scholars asked, if *sotto voce*, why so much was invested in editing while they found it difficult to get very modest grants to prepare secondary works on a great variety of historical topics that might be more widely read. Others were critical of the fact that most of the editing projects dealt with colonial and early national history. Yet a careful student of NHPC could not help but notice that the commission tried to listen to the critics. Its support of microfilm programs and the broadening of people and groups included in its projects indicated that. If NHPC moved slowly in heeding its critics, at least it moved. If considerable money was poured into the editing projects, few claimed that it would otherwise have been invested elsewhere in Clio's work. Certainly, the projects carried out the commission's goal of making more documentary material more widely available, and with editing of high quality. This monumental undertaking also attracted continuing national attention and thus generated additional public interest in the work of historians and archivists. Those were substantial achievements, which were superbly supported by NHPC's work in tracking down documents and in serving as a clearinghouse for a broad range of historical and archival activities. And, as Burl Noggle wrote in 1967, "The age of the historical editor has merely begun." No one knows how long it will last. The balance sheet, however, shows more in the editors' column of assets than in their column of debits.[18]

The work of NHPC was just one example of how, under Wayne Grover's leadership, the leading American temple of archives had been plucked from jeopardy during the late 1940s and set on the road to bigger things. That had been done at a price, however. There were always tensions within NARS, especially between archivists, who often believed that their interests were being sacrificed to boost those of others, and records managers, who often believed that they were given insufficient credit for their contributions. Thus one of the main tasks of Grover and Deputy Archivist Robert Bahmer was to keep things as well in balance as possible, given GSA's frequent underfunding of the National Archives. That this was a problem was particularly seen by 1956 in the relations between the archivist and his deputy on the one hand and Theodore R. Schellenberg, the assistant archivist for the National Archives, on the other hand.[19]

The root cause of the unpleasantness was the difference of opinion between the men as to how the National Archives should be operated. Because of this Grover often tried to serve as the director of the National Archives as well as the head of NARS, and Schellenberg felt free, especially as his reputation as an archival theorist increased, to give unsolicited advice on the administration of NARS. The archivist constantly prodded Schellenberg to improve his division's administration, and Schellenberg complained that Grover had not delegated enough authority to him to do that. Grover viewed Schellenberg's many nonadministrative activities, especially his writing and teaching, as hampering his executive effectiveness; but Schellenberg believed that he gave them so much attention because the archivist insisted on really running the National Archives. In January 1956 Grover moved to effect "a more harmonious working relationship in the front offices." This resulted in weekly conferences among him and Bahmer, Schellenberg and his assistant, G. Philip Bauer, and the records management heads, Herbert E. Angel and Everett O. Alldredge. What these conferences led to was a series of confrontations, with Schellenberg often charging that a double standard was being disadvantageously applied to the National Archives, and with Angel and Alldredge replying that the personnel of the National Archives were not cooperating in the development of records-management programs.[20]

The conferences of February 1957 illustrate how bitterly divided Schellenberg and Grover were. Then, there was pressure on executive agencies to reduce their requests for appropriations for fiscal years 1958 and 1959. It was agreed, therefore, at the 27 February conference, that NARS would ask for no budget increases except for the operation of the federal records centers, which demonstrably saved the government funds. Despite this decision, Schellenberg declared in his diary that the centers neither saved money nor promoted efficiency, but indeed possibly allowed federal agencies to postpone solving their records problems. It was also on 27 February that the archivist privately told Schellenberg and Bauer the "National Archives was being administered too loosely, and that the accomplishment of the staff was inadequate." Schellenberg conceded that this was true regarding the production of finding aids, but he argued justifiably that the National Archives had had to operate on a tight budget in terms of staff for the past seven years. He held that his emphasis on defining his office's objectives and developing the *Handbook of Procedures*, the employee-training program, and informational materials was proper. On 28 February Grover called Schellenberg and Bauer in again to say that he had no criticism of the training project, but that the photographic, repair and rehabilitation, and reference-service operations needed upgrading. The archivist reiterated that he wanted Schellenberg to become more involved in the administration of the National Archives, which he had not been because of his official and unofficial writing and teaching endeavors. The two men then proceeded to argue whether the spelling out of staff responsibilities in the *Handbook of Procedures* would "straight-jacket" the National Archives and allow Schellenberg to "domineer" its operations. Schellenberg denied wanting to do anything more than "to hold people accountable for their time and production," and he passed the responsibility for the *Handbook* on to Bauer, who had finished its preparation. Schellenberg, however, agreed to give high priority to studying his office's reference-service operations.[21]

The warfare went on and on. In April 1957 Schellenberg exulted in a private survey's criticism of federal records centers for tending to delay the making of disposal decisions by government agencies. (Grover, incidentally, had written "nonsense" in the margin next to this comment in the report.) That finding was undoubtedly tied in with Schellenberg's complaint to the archivist several months later that circumstances were forcing the National Archives to revert to Sir Hilary Jenkinson's theoretical position of archival repositories "receiving what is passed on . . . without actively trying to determine what shall be passed on." He urged that there be more appraisal of the records in the originating agencies and closer relations between those agencies and his staff. Schellenberg took the opportunity to point to the results of his training program, reporting that 60 percent of the professional staff of the National Archives had taken the course. He had also gone further afield by assuming the direction of the American University's summer archival administration course from Ernst Posner, who had become the graduate dean there. By July 1958 Schellenberg reported with pride that of the 140 professionals on his staff, 18 held a Ph.D. degree, 59 had taken a second degree or had completed academic work beyond it, and 56 possessed a bachelor's degree or had taken additional credits.[22]

The biggest battle between Schellenberg and the archivist began in March 1958. Then, Grover and Bahmer proposed that the National Archives be reorganized on a functional basis. In that way records would be administered more by related groups (that is, all military records would be grouped together), and the staff would operate as specialists at, say, appraisal, arrangement, or description. Schellenberg thought this would make sense regarding records, but that functional staff specialization "would be a big step backward. It would create temporary anarchy, and would render the institution sterile from a scholarly point of view." He believed his staff members should become, although they currently were not, subject-matter specialists who could perform a wide range of archival work among the records in their custody. Since functionalism was largely the basis for the operation of records centers, Schellenberg saw all this as further evidence of bamboozlement and aggrandizement by records managers.[23]

After extended and often bitter debate, a compromise seemed to be reached in November 1960 when Schellenberg and Bauer proposed consolidating the National Archives into two major functional divisions, one for civilian records and the other for military records. The impending retirement of Chief Archivist Thaddeus Page of the General Records Division and the probability that the head of the Natural Resources Records Division, Oliver Holmes, would become executive director of NHPC meant this could be done without any serious staff tension. Grover and Bahmer agreed that this consolidation was a good plan and could be carried out when Holmes received his new post the next year. The hitch came in December 1960 when Schellenberg and Grover disagreed on who should head the proposed military records division. Schellenberg championed the brilliant but controversial military archivist Dallas Irvine, and Grover wanted Sherrod East, a military records manager and a seasoned archivist. As he often did, Schellenberg personalized the battle, charging in his diary that Grover was excessively concerned with personal loyalty and was taking credit for what Schellenberg did. Grover and Bahmer blamed the trouble on Schellenberg's crankiness.[24]

Another crisis developed in August 1961 when the archivist established an Accessioning Policies Review Board to formulate uniform standards for appraisal. This was Grover's answer not only to Schellenberg's complaints that the National Archives had too little say in appraising the records it received but also to the demands of the General Accounting Office on NARS to relieve agency pressure for more space to store archives. Schellenberg, however, considered the new board "unnecessary and highly inappropriate," arguing that for a year he had been conferring with his chief aides to carry out a careful reappraisal of the materials in their custody. He was, in effect, reversing his position by holding that appraisal was the responsibility of the Office of Records Management since "valuable records get stuck [in the records centers] and never get out." Moreover, he was irritated that Herman Kahn (whom he identified with the presidential libraries, not the National Archives) had been named to head the new board.[25]

In effect, Schellenberg had plotted his own future. Grover and Bahmer took due note of his severe complaint about the Accessioning Policies Review Board. However brilliant a theoretician their assistant archivist for the National Archives was and whatever he had achieved as an administrator, he was too personal and divisive in his tactics within NARS, and, they believed, he spent insufficient time on administration. Schellenberg had to go, though not in a way that would deprive NARS of his talents and prestige. The archivist and his deputy, therefore, devised a plan of organization that would accomplish that and serve the goals of appraisal and functionalism that they had in mind. On 15 December 1961, Grover and Bahmer called Schellenberg into conference to inform him of a reorganization of NARS. The Office of the National Archives was to be divided into three offices headed by assistant archivists, each of which would rank with the Office of Records Management. These three would be the Office of Military Archives, headed by G. Philip Bauer; the Office of Civil Archives, headed by Herman Kahn; and a new, small Office of Records Appraisal, which was offered to Schellenberg.

When Schellenberg remarked that "the organization involved quite a 'come-down'" for him, the archivist replied that that was the objective, for he had found him increasingly nettlesome. Schellenberg asked about retiring, but Grover said that he was not looking for that. Bahmer commented that the job of operating the new Office of Records Appraisal was a difficult and important one and that Schellenberg clearly had the qualifications to set and implement improved standards for records appraisal. Grover also ordered Schellenberg to stop his participation in the summer archival institute at the American University and the National Archives training program, although he could teach an archival course the next year at the University of Washington. Schellenberg's reaction to the conference was one of "utter consternation and despair." He fulminated about how toadyism, jealousies, and institutional politics had brought this to pass. He saw the reorganization as shelving his closest allies, Dallas Irvine and Herman R. Friis, while elevating those whom he had come to see as his enemies, Kahn, East, and even Bauer. Indeed, Schellenberg acted so badly that Grover almost retracted his offer of the position of assistant archivist for records appraisal.[26]

Of course, Grover was after more than Schellenberg's reassignment in the new organization of NARS. The shake-up also came in response to the GAO's 1961 recommendations for better agency disposal programs as well as to provide for more flexibility in NARS. Schellenberg agreed that something had to be done to tighten up disposition schedules so that records disposal and the accessioning activities of the National Archives would be better carried out. What he regretted was that his new office was charged with developing better plans for this and finding a way to audit their implementation, a task that he believed should largely be the responsibility of the Office of Records Management. Yet he had come to agree that the functional organization of the National Archives and its staff, which was built into Grover's plan, was considerably justified as a way to achieve further flexibility in the service's operation, even though he still thought that it would damage professionalism among the staff. Schellenberg had arrived at some intellectual accommodation with Grover and Bahmer despite their fights during the past six years. He could even say, when Grover won the Career Service Award of the National Civil Service League in 1962, "It is probably a deserved honor," although he added that the archivist's "chief contributions to the management of public records lie outside the National Archives."[27]

Schellenberg carried on for two years with considerable success in developing disposal and retention schedules and firming up appraisal and accessioning operations. After he retired in December 1963, the archivist abolished the Office of Records Appraisal and soon transferred its functions to the new Office of Federal Records Centers, an action that partly bore out Schellenberg's observation that his office had been established to carry out functions that the records managers had done inadequately. Yet he mainly saw this and the reorganization of NARS which took place soon after his retirement as further exalting those whom he considered his foes. Herbert E. Angel was named to head the Office of Federal Records Centers, and Everett Alldredge remained in charge of the Office of Records Management. NARS established another new office with the designation of Herman Kahn as assistant archivist for presidential libraries. Bauer moved over to fill Kahn's spot as head of the Office of Civil Archives, and, in turn, Sherrod East was promoted to take his place as assistant archivist for military archives.

Although Schellenberg was no longer on the staff of NARS, he was far from retired as an archivist. He worked with great effect as a teacher and writer on archival subjects during the half-dozen years before his death. In addition to a new book, *The Management of Archives*, which appeared in 1965, he wrote seven other published papers. He continued to be controversial, championing the training of archivists in library schools and greater freedom for archivists to rearrange records if that would make the materials more comprehensible and serviceable. If Schellenberg was often cool with researchers and his staff and arrogant with his equals and superiors, he had won many admirers for his challenging intellect and intense convictions. One did not have to like him to recognize that he had more impact as an archival theoretician than any other person of his time, although, ironically, this was probably more so abroad than in his own country.[28]

That the reorganization of 1961 reduced the complexity of the National Archives is debatable, since it only replaced that office with two slightly less complicated organizations. Another goal of the reorganization, of course, was to multiply the staff's senior specialists by eliminating a dozen lesser administration positions, thus releasing those who filled them to work as archivists instead of as administrators. Although this action simplified the hierarchy a bit, many observers believe that it also resulted in a number of senior personnel being frustrated administrators who sought to infuse their archival jobs with informal administrative tasks. The functional assignment of archivists was more successful, for specialization allowed some staff members to develop technical skills that were valuable at a time when the need for such skills was expanding. Moreover, rotation of personnel over various projects was encouraged so that those skills could be practiced broadly and archivists could become acquainted with a variety of record groups and projects. By 1966, however, it was recognized that functional specialization was not working out as well as had been anticipated. This was because archivists too often had to perform several skilled functions. For example, it was difficult to prepare a finding aid without being skilled at arranging records or at providing reference service. Thus a price was paid in terms of some confusion and morale problems among the staff in order for archivists to gain increased flexibility and a greater breadth of knowledge of archival operations.[29]

A new reorganization in 1966 took cognizance of much of this. The archivist then designated Sherrod East as acting assistant archivist in charge of both civil and military archives. Moreover, a new Office of Administrative and Technical Services, headed by Walter Robertson, Jr., was created to carry out the most crucial specialized services. This meant the abandonment of the technical specialization of archivists as well as provision for better coordination of the activities of the civil and military archives divisions, although rotation of junior staff was still to be practiced. Even this reorganization had its problems, for East headed the National Archives for only a few months to be succeeded briefly in an acting capacity by Lewis Darter, Jr. Not until Edward G. Campbell became its assistant archivist in 1967 did the Office of the National Archives settle down. There were minor reorganizations in NARS later, but the overall lines of the 1966 reorganization held up rather well. Despite the coming and going of personnel, the major offices continued to be the NHPC, Federal Register, Presidential Libraries, Records Centers, Records Management, and National Archives, with its two divisions of civil and military archives.[30]

NARS, particularly through the National Archives and the presidential libraries, continued striving to maintain good relations with people in related professional associations. Not only did the National Archives and the American Historical Association participate in some joint projects such as the microfilming of captured German records, but numerous archivists attended the AHA's annual convention. Relations between the archivist and AHA Executive Secretary Boyd C. Shafer were cordial. Indeed, Shafer, in 1961, took the trouble to write General Services Administrator John Moore of the AHA's keen interest in the National Archives and to praise Grover for his "outstanding work for history and historians." NARS in its turn got GSA to support legislation of interest to historians. For example, in 1958 and 1959 then Administrator Franklin Floete urged Chairman William L. Dawson of the House Committee on Government Operations to endorse a bill authorizing the appropriation of some $500,000 for the microfilming work of the Civil War Centennial Commission. Relations between NARS and the Mississippi Valley Historical Association and its successor, the Organization of American Historians, became closer during the 1960s. Indeed, between 1964 and 1967, William D. Aeschbacher, the director of the Eisenhower Library, also served as secretary-treasurer of the OAH. One must observe, however, that relations with researchers were sometimes strained because GSA's underfunding of the archives resulted in a diminution of service.

Grover was interested, too, in expanding contacts with librarians and others such as historians of science. NARS continued to be of vital importance to the operations of the Society of American Archivists, particularly in underwriting the editing of *The American Archivist*. In no small part because of NARS's continuing commitment to its success, SAA had become a mature and vigorous organization by 1969, with a variety of programs and with 2,250 members. The group had also found a way to honor its most eminent members, a large proportion of whom were current or former personnel of NARS, by naming them fellows of the society. The only problem was that by 1975 so many fellows (109) had been elected that they might as well have been called Guys and Dolls.[31]

There is no doubt that NARS's relations with the professional associations, if not with individual researchers, were closer by the time Grover retired in 1965 than when he had become archivist in 1948. There was, however, a point during those years when his bureau's relations with some groups were very poor. This was a result of the controversy over certain papers of the explorers Meriwether Lewis and William Clark. In 1952 some field notes and observations written by Captain Clark with some contributions by Lewis during their famous expedition of 1803–1806 were found in an old desk once owned by General John Henry Hammond. These papers were stored in the Minnesota Historical Society and it seemed possible that the society would receive permanent custody of them. The problem arose when Hammond's heirs in 1953 sought title to the Clark papers, apparently with the intention of breaking them up for private sale. It was at this point that the United States government, on the advice of NARS, decided to seek title to the Clark materials. The government contended that Clark wrote the papers in his official employment, which made them federal records. The National Archives would not have entered the case had the papers been given to the Minnesota Historical Society, for that organization undoubtedly would have given them excellent care and would have opened them to public use. As Deputy Archivist Bahmer put it, "We do not believe that historical scholarship would be served by permitting the Clark papers to remain in private hands. These documents belong to the nation. They should not be regarded as merchandise nor should they be handled in any way that will expose them again to the several dangers of loss, withdrawal, and dispersal."[32]

Had the Clark case been just a struggle between Hammond's heirs and the government, little attention would probably have been paid to it. The crisis arose when manuscript dealers, private collectors, libraries, and historical societies concluded that Leviathan was trying to close one of their best hunting preserves. This view was especially emphasized by individual collectors and the merchandisers of manuscripts, whose concern for scholarship was usually marginal. As for libraries and historical societies, they were creating a specter, for the National Archives had no intention of taking back federal papers that were being professionally administered and made available for research. The only basis for their fears was that the government might change its policy in the future. Regardless of the merit of such views, a crisis had developed by the time the case came before the court in 1955. By then many collectors, dealers, librarians, and historical societies had organized a campaign to support the proposition that the Clark materials had been written and maintained as private, not government documents. Wayne Grover's attempts to have the AHA appoint a committee representing various scholarly interests to sort out the matter failed, although as time went by a number of scholars did support NARS's view of the issue.[33]

The federal district court in Minnesota ruled against the United States in the Clark case, holding that the papers were rough working notes and therefore not government records. This decision was affirmed upon appeal. NARS, thus, had lost its case. It had also incurred the ill will of manuscript collectors. Yet as Julian P. Boyd, the distinguished librarian and editor at Princeton, pointed out, the case had not decided the right of the government to recover its records. Boyd endorsed the guidelines that the archivist should never try to recover records that were being properly administered, and he reprimanded librarians and historical societies for assuming without justification "the hostile motives of archivists." As he declared, "A government that has at times throughout history yielded up too readily the public rights to lands, forests, mineral deposits, water power, and other natural resources should not be attacked for standing steadfast in its duty of protecting the public records. For these are not only among our most precious monuments: they are *our* property."[34]

Perhaps Boyd's words were taken to heart, for not much time passed before NARS, the historical societies, and the great libraries were again cooperating in the pursuit of their many common interests. A similar case during the 1960s in which Kenneth D. Sender sought title to official Spanish and Mexican documents, which he had purchased, dealing with New Mexico failed to stir up much sentiment except among private collectors and dealers. Again the government lost, although on grounds that did not deny its right to recover records. The irony in both the Clark and Sender cases is that in the course of the legal struggles, NARS obtained copies of a great number of the documents involved when court exhibits became official records and were soon transferred to federal records centers.[35]

One of the greatest fears of the administrators of the National Archives from the time its doors were opened to researchers was the theft of documents. The institution was relatively vulnerable because of the huge ratio between the number of staff members and the bulk of records in their custody. Thanks to the honorable intentions of almost all researchers and employees, the vigilance of the archivists and guards, and the methods established to protect many of the most valuable documents, no serious theft took place during the 1930s, 1940s, and 1950s, and when loss did occur the documents were easily recovered. The fear of theft remained strong, however, and it was justified by an incident that occurred in 1962.

The first evidence of the crime was noted in September 1963. Then an autograph dealer disclosed that he had received three letters, including one signed by Ulysses S. Grant and another by Andrew Jackson, that undoubtedly belonged to the National Archives. The letters were returned to NARS, and agents of the Federal Bureau of Investigation began hunting for the thieves. As the search continued, it became clear that the culprits had used the aliases of Dr. and Mrs. Bradford Murphy to establish their good faith at the National Archives, although they used at least eight additional aliases in their other operations. The couple was eventually identified as Robert and Elizabeth Murphy. In January 1964 FBI agents found them in an apartment in Detroit along with fifty stolen documents, most of which bore presidential signatures and some of which had been taken from institutions other than the National Archives. The Murphys were convicted of theft in June, and each was sentenced to ten years in prison.[36]

To say that the National Archives was shaken by this crime is an understatement, especially since the institution had not become aware of the theft until a private citizen brought forth evidence of it. Archivists immediately began considering ways in which records could be better protected from thieves. From 1963 on, at least in theory, the security of documents was to have priority over what Deputy Archivist Bahmer called "customer convenience." Consequently, the archives developed a system of requiring identification of researchers and of checking them in and out at a single business entrance and the search rooms, which had already been drastically reduced in number. Moreover, the exhibition hall was sealed off from the building's office and research areas so that casual visitors could not roam the halls at will. Efforts were made to increase surveillance of researchers and to improve reports on what records they used. The National Archives also began stamping loose documents in order to identify them as its property, although there was a limit to this, both in terms of the hundreds of millions of papers involved and the fragility of some of them. Of course, the devising of security procedures became an ongoing program at the archives and other NARS facilities. It has been rather successful, thus far, and carried out with a minimum of inconvenience to researchers and staff members. Still, there is the fear that someone else might try to outwit the system and, worse yet, might succeed.[37]

As I have noted earlier, one of NARS's constant problems has been averting the threat of having insufficient facilities to take care of the records it accessions. The 1950s reappraisal and rearrangement programs of the National Archives as well as the work of the federal records centers temporarily took care of this. The threat, however, reappeared by 1958, due largely to the success of accessioning programs. This was seen particularly with respect to military records. Many of the army's records of enduring value were not receiving appropriate archival care, nor, as long as they were in the army's custody, was it certain that they would be available for research reasonably soon. Archivist Grover had been seeking possession of those records for years. He also felt obliged by the Hoover Commission's recommendations to crusade against the maintenance of agency records centers, which were more expensive to operate than GSA's records centers.

In 1957 the army, now convinced that NARS would provide excellent service and significant budgetary savings, agreed to phase out its records centers. Consequently, during the next few years, NARS acquired a string of army and, through similar agreements, other service records centers. The pearl of the group was the military records center in Alexandria, Virginia, which contained highly important records not only of the army, but also of the office of the secretary of defense and the air force. The transfer "with certain exceptions" of the Army Departmental Records Branch in

Alexandria took place in January 1958 and included its property, personnel, and funds. Before the year's end, GSA designated the former army facility as an annex of the National Archives. The National Archives accessioned most of its holdings from 1939 to 1951, along with related navy and air force records, and combined them into a World War II Records Division. This meant that almost instantly NARS had acquired some 100,000 cubic feet of archives for which it had insufficient space in the archives building and inadequate facilities in Alexandria.[38]

The pressures caused by this transfer led Grover immediately to seek a second suitable building for the National Archives. By 1959 he had persuaded General Services Administrator Franklin Floete to endorse the construction of "a War Archives Annex" to be sited across Constitution Avenue from the archives building. That proposed underground structure would house military archives and be topped by a "Heroes Memorial" which was to contain research and exhibition areas. Grover and Floete obviously hoped that this appeal to patriotism would lead the government to provide proper facilities for the military records of World War II. This proposal failed to win approval, but some support developed for a less expensive alternative. That was to use as a defense archives the handsome, structurally sound, seventy-six-year-old former pension office building at Fifth and F Streets, Northwest, and thus preserve an existing war memorial. In December 1959 the National Capital Planning Commission approved the plan. Despite a considerable publicity campaign by NARS, this proposal also fell by the wayside.

Grover, therefore, was forced to make do with what space he had in the federal records centers and the deteriorating archives annex in Alexandria. As previously observed, NARS kept the immediate problems posed by the increasing accession of records from getting out of hand by improved space utilization and the implementation of better appraisal and reappraisal techniques. A major containing action came only with the opening of a gigantic new combined records center and archival annex in Suitland, Maryland, in February 1967. Even that would not meet all future problems. Indeed, in July 1969 NARS requested the construction of another building across Pennsylvania Avenue from the archives. This proposal had already gone through several phases by the middle 1970s, and no one was sure of the final outcome.[39] There was no doubt, however, that pressures would continue to mount for the provision of additional housing for the archives of the federal government.

The problems of the National Archives during the 1960s led some researchers to complain about service. Certainly, after most researchers were located in the Central Search Room by 1962, many older hands were irritated by being far removed from the archivists of a particular record group and having to work more often through less expert intermediaries.[40] That situation was aggravated by the occasional shortage of the carts needed to move archives, which sometimes prolonged a researcher's wait for records. It was also inconvenient to wait for records to be transferred from outside the building or, later, to journey to Suitland to examine pertinent materials. And, as with any operation, there were sometimes personality clashes between staff and clients. Nevertheless, a reasonably high level of satisfaction was reached in reference service, because most researchers quickly learned to make good use of the National Archives and archivists usually accommodated themselves well to the varying requirements and levels of sophistication of their clients.

Yet there was one problem that grew larger, particularly by the 1960s. This was the imposition of restrictions on the use of archives. As earlier mentioned, during the 1940s archivists as well as other federal officials became more conscious of security. The National Archives seldom fought to keep down the level of restrictions, which was a growing problem as more and more government agencies placed limitations on the use of their records. Even though NARS was increasingly successful in accessioning the archives among those records, restrictions continued to keep some of them out of the hands of researchers. Given the high tide of public confidence in whatever the government did in the interest of security during World War II and the Cold War, scholars, journalists, and even government researchers rarely challenged the restrictions until the middle 1960s. It is not surprising that the archivists did little more.[41]

Until 1940 restrictions were based on only the customary right of a federal agency to limit access to its records. The National Archives Council had had the legal power to deal with that by requisitioning records and fixing rules for their use, but it soon discovered that agencies could obstruct the application of that authority by noncooperation, destruction of records, and exertion of political influence. Thus most things had to be negotiated, which often included the accessibility of archives to researchers. It is plain in retrospect that the situation took a turn for the worse after 22 March 1940, when President Roosevelt issued Executive Order 8381 establishing, pursuant to an Act of Congress of 12 January 1938, security classifications for documents of the departments of War and the Navy. President Truman extended this in Executive Order 10104 of 1 February 1950, although his Executive Order 10290 of 24 September 1951 established procedures for reviewing, declassifying, and downgrading the security classifications of certain records. President Eisenhower, in Executive Order 10501 of 5 November 1953, moved a bit further in this latter direction, as did his Executive Order 10816 of 7 May 1959, which allowed private researchers to be considered for access to restricted materials. It must be pointed out, however, that E.O.s 10290, 10501, and 10816 in theory and especially in practice did little to breach the walls of excessive security classification. This was largely because too many people—tens of thousands of them—in too many agencies by then exercised the power, without very exact guidelines, to restrict the use of federal documents. Abetting the problem was that very few people challenged the situation or even sought the limited relief offered under E.O.s 10290, 10501, and 10816.[42] Patriotism, therefore, became not only the safest haven of scoundrels but also of meek bureaucrats who, in case of doubt, security-classified everything in sight and shrank from declassifying anything, even for their brethren in other federal offices.

Other factors made the situation worse. These included the practices of many agencies of restricting the use of their records without clear legal authority and not identifying security-classified records. Moreover, there were no systematic declassification schemes for many materials. Even where private or government researchers could gain access to classified records, the procedure for doing so was discouraging, for a researcher had to have a security clearance and access clearance, which, if granted, took months to secure. If allowed to see the records, one often found that one's notes had to be reviewed by the authorities and sometimes withheld, and even that one's manuscript had to be cleared for publication by the agency that originated the documents.

NARS tried to ease the effects of the system by securing in 1956 an amendment to the Federal Records Act more strictly limiting agency and security restrictions to fifty years. This, of course, did not apply to such things as census records, the use of which was specifically restricted by Congress. Moreover, in practice there were numerous exceptions to the fifty-year rule. During the Kennedy presidency, therefore, NARS sought absolute power to remove restrictions on all security-classified documents more than fifty years old. The most that was achieved was Executive Order 10964 of 20 September 1961, which only slightly liberalized the review, downgrading, and declassification of security-classified records.[43]

Under the Federal Property and Administrative Services Act of 1949, NARS had to implement the use restrictions set by law or by the agencies originating the records. One could not criticize archivists fairly for carrying out this mandate. The trouble came in part because agencies sometimes formulated the restrictions vaguely, which occasionally led archivists to show documents that should not have been seen and more often, in order to be beyond the censure of officialdom, to withhold records that probably should have been served up. A related problem was that some agencies contended their restrictions applied to communications from them found in the records of other offices and even in private manuscript collections. This was an arguable claim legally, but one that archivists were disinclined to contest given the power of the agencies involved. It was in these gray areas that most of the confusion and controversy was to develop between researchers and archivists.

In dealing with these problems, NARS contented itself during Grover's tenure with passing on to the originating agencies requests for access from researchers and sometimes endorsing them as a way of encouraging "liberal policies of access." The archivist probably believed he was being daring even by occasionally mentioning that concept. Certainly, it was not a policy with which everyone on his staff agreed. There were, after all, those in NARS who had to be discouraged from imposing additional use restrictions, for example, on materials that contained any comment deemed derogatory to government agencies and officials, which Grover warned would "in effect censor . . . individual researchers."[44] Of course, few people outside of NARS knew of the continuing debate in the organization between those who sought fewer restrictions on the use of archives and those who, motivated by heightened consciousness of security or a greater concern for citizen privacy, wanted additional restrictions. This is a debate that remains unsettled, although it has been taken up in Congress. And the question of whether the right of citizens to know what their government is doing is paramount to their right to have records pertaining to them as individuals kept private or even the government's need to keep its most sensitive business confidential will not likely be decided on objective grounds.

The presidential libraries had special problems. Of course, they abided by congressional and security-classification restrictions as well as by those placed upon their collections by the private donors. The presidential libraries, however, occasionally went beyond this to suggest restrictions to donors when the donors themselves had not thought of them. Indeed, on their own initiative the library staffs sometimes screened out "derogatory" materials and interpreted questionable agency classifications as applying to their holdings, even when the donors had not called for such restrictions. There was even some question as to whether the presidential libraries had interpreted agency and donor restrictions too strictly. Yet the libraries were in a delicate position, under pressure from originating agencies to respect their restrictions and in fear that they might, through some hypothetically embarrassing disclosure, discourage prospective donors from transferring materials. As long as researchers seldom objected, it was understandable that archivists often yielded to pressures from those federal officials who were most sensitive to possible embarrassment. An example of what this could lead to is the voluminous Henry Morgenthau Diary in the Roosevelt Library. It was long subject to many of its parts, including unclassified materials, being kept from access, even when a researcher had a security clearance and Morgenthau's approval for use. In all fairness, however, it must be stated that the presidential libraries also frequently reviewed their holdings ever with a view toward increasing the proportion of materials open for research. If they sometimes did not go as far as researchers wanted, it is clear that they were trying to respond to the needs of researchers.[45]

That the problem of restrictions was not small was demonstrated early. For example, in 1956 the National Archives had custody of 24,000 cubic feet of security-classified records and there were hundreds of additional cubic feet of such documents in the Roosevelt Library. This was soon substantially increased with the addition of materials in the new Truman Library and the former army records center in Alexandria. Indeed, with the absorption of those materials, archivists became more alert to the need to declassify as many of their holdings as possible. Although this movement was chiefly aimed at benefitting government researchers, it was also of some help to private scholars. In October 1958, therefore, the National Archives gained the responsibility for reviewing, subject to final military approval, the classifications on army records in its custody that had been created before 1946. The Department of Defense, in June 1960, extended the reviewing authority of the archivists to all military records in NARS's possession. Issued partly in response to pressure from NARS, President Kennedy's Executive Order 10964 of 1961 systematized automatic downgrading and declassification procedures and slightly accelerated them. Security clearances, of course, were still hard to get, and the military's permission for access to the records even more so. The National Archives also gained some concessions in liberalizing access to military records less than fifty years old.[46] Potentially, this also eased access problems in the presidential libraries.

This newly found authority, however, led to no great change. By January 1964 there were only 25,972 regradings of documents incident to the archival arrangement of military records, and 11,-820 regradings, including 5,722 declassifications, in response to reference service requests. Considering that there were some 140,-

ooo cubic feet of security-classified records in the custody of the National Archives by August 1963, this activity had barely made a dent in the problems of access. Archivist Grover then sought substantial independent authority for NARS to decide upon the downgrading of all security-classified material and the allowing of access to it, since Executive Order 10964 had accomplished so little. Moreover, if matters moved slowly in the military area, they were worse with agencies outside the Defense Department, none of which had established declassification programs. The overall situation deprived citizens and often officials of access to valuable but no longer genuinely sensitive documents. It also placed an onerous burden on NARS, which had to inform researchers of the varying, complicated, and usually discouraging ways established by the originating offices for applying for access. The solution, according to Grover, was the systematic downgrading of *all* security-classified records and the setting of procedures that would allow researchers to secure a single clearance and a single permission for access that would apply to the examination of any classified document.[47]

The Interdepartmental Committee on Internal Security, which was wrestling with coordination of the government's security program, took Wayne Grover's complaints to heart. A subcommittee of it readily agreed with the archivist's statement of the problem and voted to recommend that first a single security clearance and permission system be established, to be operated through GSA, and then that action be taken to encourage all agencies to adopt systematic programs to downgrade and to declassify their records.[48]

A vote to recommend, though, was not tantamount to accomplishment. Nevertheless, by 1967 GSA was operating a single security clearance system. Not all agencies accepted its clearance, and none surrendered the right to reserve the granting of access to its records that were in the custody of NARS. This, however, was a step in the right direction, especially when no other federal agency joined the military services in establishing systematic declassification programs. There was also the problem of unauthorized classifications, such as "For Official Use Only," "Eyes Only," and even "Cosmic Top Secret," which the National Archives, under the provisions of the Federal Records Act, had felt obligated to observe.

Yet by 1965 NARS challenged these indicia, asking the Justice Department to interpret Executive Order 10501 of 1953, which had abolished the "Restricted" category as a security classification, as rendering invalid such of those markings that did not apply to genuinely security-sensitive material. No clear interpretation could be given, but many archivists felt freer to disregard certain markings such as "Confidential" when not used in an authorized classification scheme, and "Eyes Only" when the material involved plainly did not pertain to national security.[49]

Also in 1965 the chairman of the Interdepartmental Committee on Internal Security, John F. Doherty, urged federal agencies to begin a continuous review of their classified records and each to nominate one of its staff members to work with the archivist on this. Another, more important advance was the passage of the Freedom of Information Act in 1966. Unfortunately, that legislation was not drafted tightly enough to open up records, whether in the custody of the originating agencies or of NARS to the extent desired for research. Agencies such as the Justice Department that were excessively sensitive still found ways to evade obeying the spirit of the law. Yet many federal offices did reduce the obstacles to access. There was also the additional prize, as a result of the act, that archivists and researchers could henceforth be more precisely informed as to what use restrictions were.[50]

The problems concerning restrictions on access to federal records became of public interest partly because by the middle 1960s an increasing number of researchers were studying topics documented by restricted documents. That was attributable not only to the booming production of Ph.D.s, but also to the rising interest in recent history. Many of those researchers became increasingly irritated at being stymied in their work by archivists brandishing notices of use restrictions. Moreover, the Freedom of Information Act encouraged their unrest. Pulitzer Prize-winning historian Herbert Feis in January 1967 expressed the frustration of many scholars with the government's system of documentary restrictions. In an article in *Foreign Affairs*, he lashed out at the shackles that secrecy placed upon scholarship. Restrictions on the use of records, he declared, would not prevent the writing of histories of recent times;

they would only contribute to the survival of "unjust and uninformed evaluation of policies, decisions, and persons."[51]

This was just the beginning of the controversy, as more and more researchers pressed the government and archivists to permit greater public access to federal records. The mounting dissatisfaction with the Vietnamese War and the differences perceived between what government officials said and what they did certainly were contributing factors. Historians, journalists, and other researchers wanted to know more than ever what the documents contained, and they were no longer greatly impressed by the forbidding incantation of "national security" in their quest for data. Their pressure, along with that from the public and sympathetic—or harrassed—archivists, was unrelenting, and it would have favorable results. By the late 1960s NARS was increasing its efforts to make more material accessible, whether it was agency-restricted or security-classified, and to inform researchers of what was available and what was restricted. Of great assistance to all involved was President Nixon's Executive Order 11652 of 8 March 1972, drafted upon NARS's initiative, that allowed federal archivists to increase monumentally the number of classified records open for study. Moreover, amendments to the Freedom of Information Act in 1974 improved the ability of the public to get at federal documents.[52] Despite these and other advances toward sweeping away unreasonable obstacles in the way of public access to government records, archivists and researchers were still keenly aware that a mutually satisfactory solution to the restricted use of documents had yet to be found.

Of course, all of this illustrates the fact that NARS and the National Archives as part of it had increased their usefulness to the nation and had made progress in dealing with long-standing concerns. They had also been confronted with serious problems during the late 1950s and the 1960s: microfilm blemishes, reorganization, use restrictions, space, theft, and GSA's often inadequate funding of archival operations. As one veteran archivist observed, "It was just one damned thing after another." The institution, nevertheless, had survived. Indeed, it emerged stronger than ever, even if it could be compared to a phoenix that had arisen too large from the ashes. If there were those at earlier times who had thought that the National Archives would go on quietly through the years with a small staff puttering with old documents and genteelly working with researchers, they learned by the middle 1960s that the organization, now including all of NARS, could not be static, for the society in which it operated was marked by rapid change. Archivists and records managers, too, had to change with society. By definition, that meant that in order to survive and to progress they had to cope with problems. It meant that "one damned thing after another" was likely to be their lot indefinitely.

19. *The Independence Movement*

One change that chafed many archivists over the years was the location of the National Archives and Records Service in the General Services Administration. Although Archivist Wayne C. Grover's official position always had to be that NARS's subordination to GSA was salutary, there were obvious problems because of the arrangement. Most important was that there was a limited relationship between the functions of NARS and GSA's other services. Therefore, there had always been reservations about, as Congressman Charles McC. Mathias, Jr., of Maryland put it, "the concept that GSA should become the guardian of history as well as the custodian of wash-rooms, store-rooms, and work-rooms."[1] The underlying fear was that the administrator of general services and his chief aides would have inadequate comprehension of or interest in NARS's work, which could result in the organization being poorly supported and having inappropriate and even political goals applied to it.

It is true that NARS's relations with the general services administrators had varied. From NARS's point of view, the first three administrators were satisfactory. Not only had Jess Larson delegated his statutory archival and records authority to the archivist of the United States, he had fairly well let Grover run NARS as he saw fit. Other administrators, until the 1970s, had followed Larson's precedent in delegating their archival and records authority. Yet there was always the fear among archivists that a new administrator might not do so. Larson's immediate successor, Edmund F.

Mansure, has often been pictured as something of a villain. He was identified with tight budgets and the movement in 1953 to remove Grover from office, and he resigned office in 1956 in connection with a congressional investigation of GSA contract procedures and awards. His reasons for leaving, however, had nothing to do with NARS and, far from pushing for Grover's dismissal, Mansure and the archivist had gotten along rather well. Moreover, the tight-budget policy was that of the Eisenhower administration, and it was not applied discriminatorily against NARS. Franklin G. Floete, the new administrator, indeed inherited that policy. Like his predecessors, Floete was a businessman. He had taken a law degree from Harvard and had been a veteran of World War I, and before becoming administrator of general services he had been an assistant secretary of defense. Despite the financial stringency in effect when Floete arrived, he soon favored NARS and during his almost five years in GSA he got along famously with Grover.[2]

The archivist's irritations with GSA, like those of many people in NARS, grew during the John F. Kennedy and Lyndon B. Johnson administrations. President Kennedy's first appointment to the General Services administratorship was John L. Moore, the vice-president for financial affairs at the University of Pennsylvania. Moore, however, resigned his post in November 1961, declaring that government service was "just too much." The practical result was almost a year wasted in dealing with GSA's and NARS's affairs. Moore's successor was Bernard L. Boutin, who was thirty-eight and had been a businessman and the Democratic national committeeman for New Hampshire. Restiveness quickly mounted in NARS as Boutin and his successor in 1965, career civil servant Lawson B. Knott, Jr., applied jargon-laden programs of management to GSA. Whether called "missions," "targets," or "program charters," they all meant the same thing: supposedly measurable goals being set for and penalties being applied to any operation that overestimated or underestimated its ability to reach those objectives in terms of business efficiency.

The setting of short- and long-range goals was far from reprehensible in itself. After all, it did encourage civil servants to think more about what they were doing and to justify it. The problem was that many of the new management concepts that worked well in most of GSA were not easily adaptable within NARS. Many of its cultural activities were not quantifiable and much that was (for example, the amount of reference work) could not be accurately forecasted. Moreover, business objectives of gain and loss and of productivity could not always be applied to what archivists and even records managers did in working with people instead of buildings and with material of intangible value instead of easily priced hardware. NARS's budget suffered during most of the Kennedy-Johnson years as a result of GSA's hyperopia in applying the newer administrative concepts to the square peg among the round ones. Although the average annual number of positions in NARS had shot up from 335 to 893 while Larson was Administrator (1949–53), to 932 when Mansure resigned (1956), and to 1,832 at the end of Floete's years (1961); it dipped to 1,716 by 1966. The demoralizing thing was that this decline took place (with the attendant problem of slow promotions) while GSA's expectations of NARS rose substantially and were fulfilled, although this performance was achieved only by deferring much work that the archivists believed to be vital to the preservation and administration of records.[3]

In public Wayne Grover continued to seem pleased with the relationship between NARS and GSA. Privately, however, by 1965 the archivist had reconsidered his earlier faith in the value of the connection. He was appalled by the growing hunger of the administrator's office for detailed reports and for restrictions on decision making in the bureaus. GSA seemed to be more interested in accountability than service, in reports than fresh ideas. Not only did that impinge on staff time, but it did so while the work load rose without a growth of staff. Moreover, because the administrator and his aides monopolized their agency's relations with the White House and Congress, there was no one to whom Grover could turn to break what he considered to be GSA's stranglehold on NARS's operations. Indeed, the situation was aggravated by the fact that the administrator, who was often sympathetic to NARS's problems, was frequently unavailable for consultation; thus the organization would find itself in the hands of his assistants who were usually less oriented toward dealing with archival matters. Then too, GSA reported to committees in Congress and the Bureau of the Budget that were concerned with management issues instead of with cultural and educational affairs, which put NARS at a further disadvantage.

Plainly, the situation in which NARS found itself raised serious fears. Could not NARS's cultural functions be throttled by GSA's business-management attitude, by the principle that everything had to be viewed in terms of economy, efficiency, and measurable productivity? Could not politics enter the picture and be equally destructive to archival and scholarly principles by leading to the use of documents or the presidential libraries for partisan purposes? Indeed, could not the top administrators in NARS eventually become so oriented toward business-management concepts that they would be more concerned with getting rid of archives than with preserving them?[4]

Grover had spent thirty-two years in federal service, seventeen of them as archivist of the United States. During a year of taking stock in 1965, he decided to retire. Indeed, he elected to use the occasion of his retirement as a way, without seeming self-serving, to make a final important contribution to NARS. That contribution was to beseech the president to reconstitute the organization as an independent federal agency. Since he had been appointed by a president, Archivist Grover believed he had the right to inform a president of his retirement and his convictions about the future of NARS. He called this maneuver "Operation Exit." In planning it, he consulted with his deputy, Robert H. Bahmer; Executive Director Oliver W. Holmes of the National Historical Publications Commission; the editor of the Jefferson Papers and the immediate past president of the American Historical Association, Julian P. Boyd; and another distinguished historical editor, Lyman H. Butterfield, who edited the Adams Papers.

Grover sent his letter to Lyndon B. Johnson on 2 November 1965. After advising the president of his impending retirement, he recommended the recreation of the National Archives Establishment as an independent government agency, containing the archives, the Federal Register, the presidential libraries, and the records centers, managed by the archivist of the United States under a board of governors. In addition to supervising the work of the archivist, the board of governors would also assume the functions of the Administrative Committee of the Federal Register, the Federal Records Council, the National Archives Trust Fund, and the NHPC, all of which committees could then be abolished. The proposed board would consist of the living former presidents of the United States, "about eight" appointees of the incumbent president, the public printer, two nominees of the AHA, and one representative each from the House of Representatives, the Senate, and the Supreme Court. NARS's work with the creation of federal records, which was primarily concerned with applying automation to office paper-work, could remain with GSA.

In justifying his proposal, Grover emphasized his fear that "political pressure from Congress or . . . the carelessness or irresponsibility of a newly appointed Administrator of General Services" could in some future administration lead to misuse of the "precious" and "sensitive" documents in the presidential libraries. Since NARS had achieved the purposes of federal records management envisioned by the Hoover Commission, it could now be divorced from GSA, which was basically concerned with business operations, not the supervision of cultural and educational activities. Such action would not only shore up NARS's responsibilities in those areas and militate against misuse of the presidential libraries but would give former presidents an officially recognized role in the administration of the libraries. The retiring archivist indicated that he had already discussed the outlines of his proposal with former presidents Dwight D. Eisenhower and Harry S. Truman, who had authorized him to advise President Johnson of their approval of it. Grover also took the opportunity to endorse Bahmer's appointment as the new archivist in view of his key role in the development of NARS. He closed by offering his assistance in helping Johnson develop his own presidential library.[5]

It was a skillfully written letter, well calculated to appeal to a president's personal interests, but it was only one facet of Operation Exit. Grover apparently had not discussed his proposal with Administrator Knott. Indeed, he sent his letter to the president while Knott was out of town. From 2 November on, Grover acted with Boyd and Butterfield, while Holmes served as secretary of the little group, in directing the independence movement. He wrote to a number of prominent friends and acquaintances, including Eisenhower and Truman, Chief Justice Earl Warren, and Civil Service Commission Chairman John W. Macy, Jr., soliciting written support for his proposal. Boyd was in touch with Eric F. Goldman, his colleague at Princeton University, who was then serving as a consultant to the president. On 3 November Boyd also drafted a letter to send to Mrs. Lady Bird Johnson asking her for an interview with Butterfield and Grover. Butterfield thought it should be dispatched immediately; Grover, however, insisted that they wait until the president replied to his letter of 2 November. Neither Johnson nor Knott responded to Grover's proposal for freeing NARS from GSA, although the president sent a telegram praising Grover's service and the administrator attended the archivist's retirement party on 5 November.[6]

The matter rested there for a while. Bahmer served as the acting head of NARS until 16 January 1966, when his appointment by Knott as archivist of the United States was announced. Thus, at least that part of Grover's wish was achieved. He had pressed Bahmer's appointment as a matter of continuity and competence. Grover knew that Bahmer wanted to remain in government service for only another two or three years. Both of them believed that it was time for a new generation of leadership to come forth, and they wanted to give the younger group a chance to prepare for the tasks ahead of them. Their candidate for Bahmer's successor was thirty-seven-year-old James B. Rhoads, who had joined the staff of NARS in 1952 after receiving bachelor's and master's degrees from the University of California at Berkeley. He later took the Ph.D. in history at the American University. After serving ably in a variety of jobs in the National Archives, Rhoads succeeded G. Philip Bauer as assistant archivist for civil archives in April 1965. A year later Bahmer appointed him his deputy with the understanding that he would recommend Rhoads's succession to the position of archivist when Bahmer retired. Both Grover and Bahmer agreed that, whether or not NARS achieved independence, this was the best way to begin transferring responsibility to a younger generation of archivists.[7]

Lyndon B. Johnson had not ignored Wayne Grover's plea to liberate NARS. The president had placed the matter in the hands of one of his aides, Douglass Cater, who had previously been an editor of the news magazine *The Reporter*. Cater in turn asked for analyses of Grover's proposal from the Bureau of the Budget and from Richard E. Neustadt, a former assistant to President Truman and an expert on political affairs at Harvard University. Neustadt responded first, on 3 January 1966, supporting the idea of an independent NARS especially as a way to protect the integrity of the presidential libraries. He differed with Grover only in that he believed the archivist should report directly to the president and the proposed board of governors should be only advisory. A few days later the reply of the Budget Bureau came. Director Charles L. Schultze argued against a separate archival agency on the grounds that, first, the bulk of NARS's functions were administrative, not cultural and educational in nature, and, second, the authority of the proposed board of governors would remove control of the government's "operating records" from the president and Congress. He did agree that there was a touchy problem with respect to the presidential libraries and recommended that his organization should study further the question of whether they should remain within GSA's jurisdiction.[8]

Obviously, the issue was not to be easily settled, thanks to the differing reports from Neustadt and Schultze, although the door was now open for some significant change with respect to NARS. Also in January two other quarters were heard from. Administrator Knott had not been oblivious to Grover's opening of what GSA might consider Pandora's box. Knott told Secretary S. Dillon Ripley of the Smithsonian Institution about the former archivist's proposal and reportedly indicated that there was something to be said for transferring the scholarly functions of NARS to the Smithsonian. Indeed, this idea resembled what Bahmer had already suggested could be a satisfactory disposition of the case. Ripley apparently was interested, though he did little more than wait on the fence to see if part of NARS might be joined to his empire of scattered cultural enterprises.[9]

Meanwhile, Grover's group sallied forth again, alarmed by the lack of White House action and the surfeit of rumors and information they had about what other interested parties were thinking. They arranged, by early March, an audience with Lady Bird Johnson because of her interest in cultural matters. Boyd and Butterfield went to the White House and discussed Grover's proposal with the president's wife, but this led to no immediate results. In April a Budget Bureau aide, David F. Reynolds, prepared a paper that smacked of being his agency's last word on the issue. His report concluded that NARS was too reticent in pressing for budget increases and that Administrator Knott was "somewhat too critical" in evaluating its requests, especially with respect to records appraisal and management, Federal Register activities, and the establishment of regional archives. Yet Reynolds had little sympathy for the archivists, writing that they tended to be "poor managers and not aggressive enough." He preferred that records managers have more influence in NARS. In any event, he saw no reason to separate the bureau from GSA.[10]

Lyman Butterfield tried to shake up the situation on 9 May, when he addressed the Extraordinary Congress of the International Council on Archives in Washington. Although he did deal with what he knew best, documentary publication, Butterfield was chiefly concerned with calling attention to how he believed the National Archives of the United States had been hobbled by its relationship with GSA. "The restoration of the National Archives," he declared, "to its pre-1969 name, dignity, and independent status as an 'establishment' in the Executive Branch, responsible directly to the President, is a measure imperative to the well-being of both our archivial patrimony and the scholarship dependent upon it." Butterfield could not have believed that the Extraordinary Congress would rise to help strike GSA's fetters from the body of captive NARS. His aim was publicity, and he got a good deal of that in professional circles. As the Budget Bureau later noted, his speech set off enough of a stir among America's archivists and historians to convince the bureau's personnel that NARS's constituency was restive and wanted improvements made.[11]

Butterfield's speech and the Budget Bureau's recognition of it, however, led to neither action nor response from the federal government. In late September Grover was not cheerful about the whole business, writing that it "is now likely to be a long drawn out tussle." He was disappointed that former presidents Truman and Eisenhower had not lent him effective support; he was also disappointed in himself, believing that he had "either waited too long or not long enough" to press for an independent NARS. "Unless enough powerful people can be convinced simply that the status and environment of the National Archives Establishment should be improved, I am afraid that we have little hope but to wait for GSA to make a mistake." The former archivist clearly still pinned his hopes upon "powerful people," particularly the Johnsons. He was, furthermore, still in touch with Mrs. Johnson, thanks to his recently assumed role as consultant in planning the Lyndon B. Johnson Library. Although she agreed that it was strange to have to check out matters pertaining to the projected library with the administrator of general services, Lady Bird Johnson averred that the president then had no time to consider archival problems. Consequently, in November 1966, Boyd and Butterfield suggested that their little group seek to force the issue with a resolution from the AHA Council. Grover and Holmes, however, had reservations about such a step, for President Johnson did not like "to be pressured in that manner."[12]

Whether Lyndon B. Johnson liked "to be pressured" or not, that is what happened. Boyd soon prepared for action, going so far as to inform Mrs. Johnson on 20 December that although he had the year before dissuaded the AHA from making a statement regarding NARS's status, it was clear that the council, of which he as a past president of the AHA was a member, would act now. He had, moreover, won Grover's blessing, despite the latter's fear for what probably would be a long battle, one that would make life "uncomfortable as hell for the present Archivist." On 27 December Boyd introduced and the AHA Council adopted a statement pointing out the dangers involved in the subjection of NARS "to an agency bound by no professional standards and obligations and concerned not with our cultural patrimony but with efficiency in the housekeeping operations of government." The council then resolved to invite the Organization of American Historians and the Society of American Archivists to join the AHA in establishing an ad hoc committee to explore the question of whether the National Archives should be an independent federal agency, and, if so, how organized. On 29 December the AHA's membership, assembled in their annual business meeting, approved the council's resolution. The OAH and SAA responded affirmatively to the AHA's invitation. The Joint Committee on the Status of the National Archives was soon formed, with Boyd and former Army Chief Historian Kent Roberts Greenfield representing the AHA, Fletcher M. Green of the University of North Carolina and David A. Shannon of the University of Maryland being the OAH's nominees, and William T. Alderson of the American Association for State and Local History and State Archivist H. G. Jones of North Carolina being the SAA's designees.[13]

While the joint committee was organizing, developments were occurring elsewhere. In January 1967 Mrs. Johnson had Douglass Cater urge the Budget Bureau to restudy the question of, in Cater's words, "getting the National Archives out from under the GSA" since it was "obviously something about which the historians care a great deal." The AHA's resolution and Grover's contact with the president's wife were having results. In effect, Lady Bird Johnson had become part of the independence movement, for, as Grover said, she "had been needling everyone about doing something about the Archives situation." The consequence was that in February the Budget Bureau decided to make a full-scale study of the question. At Mrs. Johnson's request, Butterfield, Grover, and Holmes compiled a list of archivists, historians, and records managers whom the bureau could interview in connection with its investigation.[14]

The Bureau of the Budget moved quickly. On 16 February Hirst Sutton, the chief of its General Government Division, got in touch with Ernst Posner of the American University, who was considered the dean of the nation's archivists. By the end of the first week of March, the bureau's officials had met with a number of archivists and historians, including Posner again, Boyd, Butterfield, and the AHA's executive secretary, Paul Ward. The Budget Bureau also elicited the views of General Services Administrator Knott, who indicated that archival and presidential library functions might be pared from GSA though not be established as a separate agency. Then too, there were the opinions of Archivist Bahmer to be considered. He was not about to preside over the breakup of NARS. Although he favored shifting his organization to the Smithsonian Institution, he had serious reservations about independent status for fear that NARS would be budgetarily vulnerable on its own as had been the old National Archives. He also had to cope with the desires of his overlord, the administrator of general services, who was unlikely to let the records centers and perhaps the Office of the Federal Register go without a fight. Indeed, he believed that Knott would not cheerfully relinquish any part of NARS. Bahmer's goal, therefore, was somehow to keep all of NARS together, except for the small records-creation unit, and even to exploit the situation to improve his bureau's operations. Bahmer had given fair warning of his intentions at the time of his appointment as archivist in January 1966. Then he pointed out that he would emphasize the obligations of archivists to the scholarly world, both in assisting researchers and in working as scholars. Plainly, service was as important as status to Bahmer.

The administrator and the archivist could form a community of interest. Knott acted first, on 27 February 1967, when he asked Congress to authorize giving NHPC $500,000 annually for grants-in-aid of publication for fifteen years. Knott intended to demonstrate that he was taking good care of NARS not only by raising the ante from the $350,000 that GSA had been supporting and by trying to extend considerably the period of authorized funding, but also by stressing the commission's support of microfilm publications that affected a wide range of archivists and historians. In March Bahmer proposed and Knott approved a study to convert the occasionally published *National Archives Accessions* into a scholarly journal that would rouse more interest in NARS and its holdings as well as encourage federal archivists to contribute further to their profession's literature. These would be only the first of several program improvements initiated internally while the battle over NARS's status took place.[15]

On 15 April 1967, the Joint Committee on the Status of the National Archives met for the first time. The representatives of the

AHA, OAH, and SAA concluded that a detailed study of NARS and its historical development had to be made, and with some dispatch. With a grant of $2,500 from the Council on Library Resources, Inc., the committee was able to engage the services of one of its own members, H. G. Jones, to conduct such a study. He began his work in May and would complete it in October. Then the joint committee would review what Jones had done and write its report. The joint committee also voted to keep in touch with the Budget Bureau, obviously to learn what it could from the bureau's inquiries and to serve as a lobby.[16]

Even before the joint committee met, the Budget Bureau had gotten far enough with its investigation to conclude that its negative reaction to Wayne Grover's proposal had to be revised. This was partly because Bahmer's retirement as archivist in a year or two would mean a complete change of the guard in NARS, partly because archivists and historians were upset about the organization's position in GSA, and partly because NARS should be enabled to provide better leadership in and service to scholarship.[17] The Budget Bureau personnel must have been pleased to hear of the results of the joint committee's first meeting, for it was then clear that they should be able to report well before the committee could.

Ernst Posner had been serving as something of a liaison officer between the Budget Bureau and the joint committee. On 5 May he reported to Julian Boyd on the progress of the bureau's study, and what he wrote could not have caused joy among the participants in the independence movement. The bureau's working team did not believe that NARS had made the most of the cultural mission assigned to it. Although they seemed to think that the National Archives should be divorced from GSA, they believed that the records centers as well as records management should be separated from archival functions and perhaps should even remain in GSA.[18]

Posner was rather well on target. The Budget Bureau's Office of Management and Organization, on 15 May, sent its report to the director of the Budget. The office indicated its preference for transferring the National Archives, NHPC, presidential libraries, and related technical services to the Smithsonian Institution, with the appointment of the archivist by the president. That would avoid establishing a vulnerable "splinter agency" by merging the archival services with a strong cultural and educational organization. The president's appointment of the archivist would provide the direct line of communication that both officials apparently wanted. To cope with the growing archival holdings of federal records centers, the National Archives would be permitted to station regional archivists in the centers in order to assist scholarly researchers. The offices of Federal Records Centers, the Federal Register, and Records Management would remain part of GSA.[19]

Although the Budget Bureau's Office of Management and Organization had made its report, it did not become official policy because other elements in the bureau had different ideas about NARS's destiny. The Education, Manpower, and Science Division preferred that NARS's cultural functions be transferred to the Library of Congress instead of the Smithsonian Institution because of the superior budgetary consideration Congress was likely to give the library. The General Government Division took even stronger exception to OMO's report. Not only did that division favor the establishment of an independent archival agency, but it recommended that the agency should include the Office of the Federal Register because of its documentary functions. The division argued that independent status would permit the executive branch better control of the National Archives with respect to restricted documents, records appraisal, and presidential libraries, which operations mainly concerned executive agencies. Such control would not be available in the Library of Congress and would be far from effective in the Smithsonian Institution given its direction by an independent board of governors. After OMO and the two divisions had been heard from, Deputy Director of the Budget Phillip S. Hughes came up with a fourth position, which was to leave NARS "in GSA with new dough, leadership, [civil-service] grades, an advisory board, and some insulation." The immediate result of this remarkable divergence of opinion was that the contending factions in the Budget Bureau consulted with each other to see if they could reach some agreement.[20]

No significant progress was made in that direction. Indeed, representatives of the bureau sounded out GSA to see if it might indicate something that would help the director of the Budget to decide his agency's position on NARS. With the passage of time, however, and encouraged by the stalemate within the Budget Bureau, Lawson Knott and his staff had become intractable on the question of separation. When approached in July 1967 with the Budget Bureau's findings, GSA's reaction was that they did not know there was a problem regarding the administration of NARS or that the proposed alternatives would be superior to the current organizational arrangement. Administrator Knott, from that point on, was intent upon keeping NARS within GSA. Since the Budget Bureau's staff could not agree upon how to slice up NARS and where to put the pieces, and since GSA did not volunteer to surrender any of NARS, the Budget director did not issue any recommendations for reorganization.[21]

GSA, however, did pay attention to various suggestions for improving archival programs. In particular, Knott approved the replacement of the *National Archives Accessions* with a scholarly journal published by NARS to develop the relationship of archivists with historians. This eventuated in the establishment of *Prologue: The Journal of the National Archives*, the first issue of which appeared in 1969. In the same spirit, Knott also showed interest in providing an advisory council for NARS composed of representatives of interested scholarly organizations.[22]

H. G. Jones had meanwhile completed his study for the Joint Committee on the Status of the National Archives. After reviewing his work, the committee prepared its report and forwarded it to the AHA, OAH, and SAA on 14 December. It contended that the intimate relationship between archivists and records managers required they not be separated into what would be two conflicting authorities, and that NARS's educational and cultural programs must be better funded to allow the organization to accomplish its missions. Most striking was the committee's demand that the "national archival and records management system should be restored to independent status as the National Archives and Records Authority, administered by an Archivist of the United States appointed by the President and responsible to a Board of Regents." This board would consist of the living former presidents, the attorney general, the administrator of general services, the public printer, three public members appointed by the president, and one member each from the House, the Senate, the judiciary, the AHA, the OAH, the SAA, and the American Records Management Association.[23]

The release of the report on 27 December 1967 caused a considerable stir. Although Archivist Bahmer had furnished information for and knew of the general contents of the report, the joint committee had not consulted him in its drafting. Encouraged by Administrator Knott, Bahmer, in turn without consulting the scholarly associations, publicly called the report "all wet" and "absolutely wrong." Deputy Archivist Rhoads also reacted strongly, charging that it was replete with "allegations that do great disservice to us" because of their "preconceived notion" that NARS should be independent. The *Washington Post* and the *New York Times*, however, were moved to call for the independence of the National Archives from GSA. The Council of the SAA endorsed the joint committee's recommendations at its December meeting, although Boyd stayed the AHA Council from taking similar action because of the probable need to discuss the report. Members of Congress soon entered the picture. In January 1968 Senator Hugh Scott of Pennsylvania and Congressman Charles McC. Mathias of Maryland, both Republicans, announced that they were drafting legislation based on the joint committee's recommendations. Division was clearly the reaction to the report among interested parties.[24]

Bahmer and Knott followed up in a way designed to continue the split and to make the joint committee's report a dead issue. Both of them were probably aware that the Budget Bureau and even the White House would be happy to settle for improvements in NARS's operations. Moreover, Bahmer was dead set against the independence movement because he feared, although it was not the movement's intention, that it would lead to the separation of the records centers from the rest of the archival service. He was also probably fearful that the administrator might not appoint his intended successor, James B. Rhoads, as archivist.

The Budget Bureau, on 9 January, asked GSA for its reaction to the joint committee's report. The answer came back on 13 February in a double-barreled charge, a long letter from Knott and a twenty-eight-page commentary (along with several appendices) from Bahmer. Contending that the archival program had improved, not suffered since NARS was incorporated in GSA, Administrator Knott stressed his disappointment "that men educated to the objective consideration of carefully collected evidence would prepare a one-sided pronouncement rather than a fact-finding inquiry." He also suggested that H. G. Jones's study was replete with errors; and he wondered how many members of the AHA, OAH, and SAA were aware of what the joint committee was doing "in the names of their organizations." Bahmer's commentary was directed at reiterating these comments and providing supporting documentation.[25]

Elements in the Budget Bureau were alarmed at the argumentative tone of Knott's letter, especially since the White House wanted the level of controversy toned down. One can assume that this reinforced the bureau's interest in settling the matter through the improvement of NARS's programs in GSA instead of issuing a report on its organizational status that probably would have been scathingly attacked on all sides. Julian Boyd was outraged with Bahmer's stand, especially his indication that a small group of men, and particularly, without naming him, Boyd, were presuming to speak for all historians and archivists. Just as the archivist believed that Boyd had become overbearing, so Boyd thought that what the joint committee reported was the considered judgment of the majority of archivists and historians. In addition, ugly rumors were soon being circulated about the motives of the people involved, for example, that Jones was ambitious to become the next archivist of the United States.[26]

Meanwhile, NARS had been sending copies of Bahmer's commentary to people who inquired about the allegations made in the joint committee's report. Deputy Budget Director Hughes apparently soon requested Administrator Knott to stop this, on the grounds that it was only supplying more fuel for the controversy. Since the joint committee decided to stop distributing its report after reading the archivist's comments, NARS likewise halted distribution of the commentary. H. G. Jones asked Bahmer for detailed comments on his study for the joint committee, which the committee had decided to have published as a book. The archivist agreed to provide such comments to Jones as well as to the Budget Bureau. Discussion of the joint committee's report and Bahmer's commentary would continue, particularly after the committee prepared a rebuttal to Bahmer's statement by April. Nevertheless, the basis had been planted for obscuring the controversy.[27]

Far more important was that the Budget Bureau was willing to let the question of the organizational status of NARS ride if progress were made in better supporting its operations. GSA came to the same conclusion, partly because of the Budget Bureau's suggestions and partly out of the conviction that that was the only way it could prevent its loss of NARS. From the beginning of the controversy, the Budget Bureau had indicated its interest in NARS reaching its "optimum potential" as a cultural, archival, and records-management organization. NARS plainly needed better salaries, encouragement of leadership, and an advisory board to improve relations with the academic community. General Services Administrator Knott had, in 1967, shown interest in this. By February 1968 he had become a champion of additional funding for a broad range of programs in NARS, including among others machine-readable records and employee training. There is no doubt that the administrator's enthusiasm was very much related to the pressure he felt from the Budget Bureau and the joint committee to make substantial changes. Moreover, the archivist's office was fully prepared to take advantage of this.[28]

The results of the government's willingness to give more support to archival services were highly encouraging. Most important was the rise in NARS's budget from $18,300,000 to $20,800,000 between fiscal years 1968 and 1969 and of its number of employees from 1,808 to 2,316. The organization also allowed its professional staff up to 10 percent of their working hours, if they could find the time, for research activity. Plans were accelerated to establish regional archives units in the federal records centers and even to develop regional advisory councils, which had been encouraged informally in some regions as early as 1966. The administrator approved intensive study of plans to place copies of NARS's microfilm publications in the records centers for use by local researchers. In July 1968 Knott established the national Archives Advisory

Council to advise on "policies, procedures, programs, objectives, and other matters relating to the effectiveness of the federal archival program in providing a maximum contribution to society." He designated the archivist as chairman; and a large majority of the other members were representatives of scholarly organizations, including the AHA, OAH, and SAA. Moreover, the government set up a program to recruit new archivists and to give them a lengthy period of training and apprenticeship. Bahmer made progress in advancing his favorite program, audiovisual services. In 1966 he had appointed a specialist in this area with the intention, largely being fulfilled by 1968, of making NARS an information and distribution center for the older audiovisual materials of federal agencies. The archivist secured financing from the Council on Library Resources, Inc., to hold a planning conference on automated indexing for archives, which was consonant with his interest in the SPINDEX II project. The National Archives also held in 1967 the first of its many well publicized conferences in Washington for scholars on specialized subjects.[29]

This burst of activity did not satisfy all historians and archivists, particularly those connected with the independence movement. It did, however, represent a considerable advance in NARS's development both in service to and liaison with scholars. Moreover, it contributed greatly to scattering the independence movement. Robert H. Bahmer's commentary on the joint committee's report prompted the AHA Council to request the committee to clarify its position. Chairman Boyd reconvened the joint committee on 11 April 1968. The committee reaffirmed its views, but it also decided to modify the text of its report somewhat. Five of the six committee members approved the revision in May; Julian Boyd dissented because he believed that the report did not then sufficiently emphasize the need "at all costs" to keep archival administration and records management together in one organization, whether independent or not.

The revised report came too late to stop the fragmentation of the forces connected with the independence movement, and Boyd's dissent seemed only to have encouraged confusion and dissension in its ranks. On 18 April the SAA Council, although it still favored reestablishment of an independent federal archival agency, withdrew its approval of the joint committee's report because the archivist of the United States had not approved its contents. The OAH Executive Board the previous day endorsed, with three abstentions, the joint committee's original recommendations. Later the AHA Council approved the modified report, although the group was clearly interested in working through the new Archives Advisory Council to improve the status of NARS. By the end of 1968 nothing had happened that could significantly alter Boyd's complaint in April that the scholarly associations were not effectively supporting the work of their joint committee. He could only pin his dwindling hopes on congressional action with support from individual scholars and based upon whatever sentiment would be stirred up by the publication of H. G. Jones's book-length study of the status of the National Archives.[30]

Archivist Bahmer concluded early in 1968 that the independence movement was moribund. He retired from federal service on 8 March, convinced that he had achieved all that any reasonable person could want to at that point in improving NARS. As far as he was concerned, the substance of what he, and even Grover, had wanted had already been implemented or soon would be. It was time for a younger person, James B. Rhoads, to take over and to carry the changes further. Spring was a good time for the switchover, for it was likely that Rhoads would be appointed the new archivist and thus would be ensconced in office before the probable change in presidential administration the following year. Soon after Bahmer's retirement support for Rhoads came from several sources, most notably the Council of the Society of American Archivists. Of course, Bahmer, Rhoads, and Knott had developed a community of interest during the time of the independence movement, however different the archivists' motivations might have been from the administrator's. Thus, Knott could respond to the support for Rhoads with some enthusiasm. He consequently appointed Rhoads the fifth archivist of the United States on 2 May.[31]

Bahmer's retirement and Rhoads's succession marked the end of the domination of NARS by the generation that had joined the staff of the National Archives during the 1930s. This change had

Robert H. Bahmer, fourth archivist of the United States, 1965–1968

been underway since the early 1960s, for most of the prominent figures from the depression generation had already retired, including Philip Hamer, Dallas Irvine, G. Philip Bauer, Theodore Schellenberg, and, of course, Grover. Rhoads quickly reached out for people of his own generation for support. Although the new archivist named Herbert Angel as his deputy, Daniel J. Reed of the Manuscript Division of the Library of Congress replaced Herman Kahn, the retiring assistant archivist for presidential libraries, later in 1968. James E. O'Neill of Loyola University of Chicago succeeded Elizabeth Drewry as director of the Roosevelt Library; a couple of years later he took Angel's place as deputy archivist when Angel retired.[32] As a number of younger outsiders came to leadership in NARS, there were some complaints that those who had long been with the organization, and particularly those who had come during the 1940s, were being passed over. Whether that was accidental or intentional, it was clear that Rhoads was following the wish of his two predecessors that younger and more variously experienced persons be brought into the highest levels of NARS.

As for the joint committee's report, the AHA, OAH, and SAA never did synchronize their reactions to it, partly because of Bahmer's and NARS's opposition, partly because many archivists and historians considered the report to have been too hastily put together, and partly because of Boyd's dissent from the modified version. In September 1968 the SAA reviewed the report. The organization, however, limited its approval to the concepts that the integrity of the whole federal archival program must be preserved and that NARS's cultural and educational functions must be strengthened. In short, "NARS should be given sufficient autonomy, either under GSA or as an independent governmental agency, to maintain its position as one of the leading archives of the world." The AHA and OAH stood by their endorsements, though they did little to act upon them as the organizations became embroiled in other issues. Indeed, their low level of action and the SAA's position could be taken as approval of what had occurred within NARS in 1967 and 1968. The result obviously was the sidetracking of the independence movement. When H. G. Jones's book appeared in 1969, under the title *The Records of a Nation*, it seemed more of an envoi from a lost cause than the prologue to change. As Wayne Grover wrote to Jones, the book "looks good, reads well and may in the long run accomplish its purpose. . . . The very least it can do is serve as a good text book for new Administrators of General Service. You may consider this small comfort, but I could have used even that."[33] Even those in Congress who had been interested in legislation to create an independent archival agency found other matters more absorbing. No doubt there was a connection between that and Senator Scott's successful championing of one of his former aides, Robert L. Kunzig, to be the new administrator of general services in 1969.

In retrospect, it is plain that left to themselves the White House, the Budget Bureau, and Administrator Knott would have done little to advance the work of NARS. It is also unlikely that Bahmer and Rhoads, for all their interest and ability, could have moved their masters very far off dead center. Grover's dramatic gesture in his letter of retirement, the supporting activities of Boyd, Butterfield, and Holmes, and the work of the Joint Committee on the Status of the National Archives were what made the difference. If the independence movement, because of tactical errors or whatever, failed to achieve its primary goal, it certainly deserves much of the credit for the substantial changes in NARS's operations that were initiated during the three years after Grover's departure.

20. *Old and New Challenges*

It is obvious that when Robert D. W. Connor and the early staff members of the National Archives took up their work, they did not quite know what it was all about. Their relative amateurishness, as it turned out, held more advantages than disadvantages for them as they went about building the new archival institution. Confronted with an unusually large volume of records that were highly diverse in origins, types, and organization, the federal archivists were therefore conceptually unfettered in devising ways to bring that material under control. They were also fortunate in having at their disposal an enormous building that, thanks to the foresight of its planners, was already equipped to deal with problems of temperature and humidity as well as fire and chemical dangers. Whatever the planners had not foreseen, the early staff worked with great success to remedy.

That staff, and those who joined and succeeded them during the next two decades, were pioneers of the archival profession. A list of their innovations would resemble a mail-order house catalog. Generally it would have to include cleaning, repair, rehabilitation, records reproduction, storage equipment and methods, appraisal, disposal, arrangement, client service, management of current and semicurrent records, paper-work management, guides, documentary publications, and administrative organization. A detailed list would contain, for example, such specific innovations as the airbrush, microfilm publications, general disposal schedules, the record group, and the life-cycle concept of managing records.

From its earliest days, the archives aimed at being a coordinated organization dealing with federal records in diverse ways and providing an unusual range of services for government, researchers, and ordinary citizens. This was seen in the establishment of the *Federal Register*, the audiovisual and museum work of the National Archives, and in the authorization for the National Historical Publications Commission. As time passed, presidential libraries, various records-management activities, and a functioning NHPC were added to the agency's operations. These mounted the works of the National Archives and its successor, NARS, far beyond the traditional aspects of archival administration.

NARS has continued to develop outstanding new programs in all the areas within its jurisdiction. For example, its work with films and recordings was expanded in 1969 with the establishment of the National Audiovisual Center as a lending operation and in 1975 with the program to receive television-news videotapes for preservation and research use. Also in 1975, thanks to the push of Charles Lee of South Carolina and other archivists, the NHPC was reorganized as the National Historical Publications and Records Commission in order to give assistance to other archival repositories, historical societies, and manuscript collections in carrying out a variety of germane projects. The federal records centers have been producing guides to their more permanent holdings, and since 1969 NARS has established service to area researchers on older federal records of regional interest. In recent years the Washington National Records Center has stored the papers of members of Congress on a courtesy basis, which is not only a gesture of goodwill, but also a way of encouraging senators and congressmen to consider the eventual preservation of their records in the repositories of their choice.

Since 1968 there have also been dramatic developments of slightly earlier interests. The SPINDEX II program has been used successfully to produce NARS's microfilm catalog, guides to captured German records, and an index to the papers of the Continental Congress. Developed as well have been the NARS-5 and NARS A-1 systems, which provide computer control, respectively, of materials in the federal records centers and in the National Archives. By 1977 these systems put NARS well beyond any other archival institution in the control of records by computer operations. NARS led all others, too, except possibly the Canadians, in coping with the handling of machine-readable records. Moreover, the agency made strenuous efforts to follow up on its initiatives to better relations with researchers, particularly through the work of its national Archives Advisory Council, the success of *Prologue*, and the holding of research conferences and the publication of their proceedings.

Returning to NARS's older accomplishments, it won the battle with the proponents of a hall of records by its successful establishment and operation of a centrally controlled chain of records centers. This has not been without its problems, for there continue to be strains between federal archivists and records managers, who have sometimes tended to see their particular group as Jack Sprat and the other as his well-fed wife. Be that as it may, both groups largely agree that they must stand together, and not just to protect each other's flanks from the marauders who stalk the bureaucratic jungle. More important, they have come to realize that each has skills that the other needs if they are best to carry out their complementary functions in dealing with federal records during their life span. This means it has become solidly established in professional thought that there is and should be only one organization—not two, several, or even one in each agency—dealing with federal records when the immediate needs of government agencies for them have ceased. Of course, one cannot expect that the work of the archivists and records managers will always be fully coordinated, given the preservationist bent of the one and the economical outlook of the other. NARS nevertheless has seen to it that federal records are rather uniformly administered with a high level of preservation, efficiency, and economy as well as comparatively liberal access for researchers.

In reviewing NARS's history from 1934, it is clear that the institution came along at a propitious time. The founding of the National Archives during the Great Depression enabled the new agency to recruit an exceptionally able professional staff and to retain their services long enough so that a remarkably high percentage of them decided to remain with the organization throughout most of their careers. A less lean and hungry staff probably would not have given such devoted service. Moreover, the establishment of the National Archives coincided with the great expansion of the federal government and was soon followed by the rise of the United States to preeminence as a world power. The young archival agency benefited from both occurrences because it received more initial financial support than it would otherwise have enjoyed much earlier or later and because it shared in the rising prestige of the federal government at home and of the United States abroad.

All this allowed the National Archives to have great impact on the development everywhere of archival administration, records management, and the availability of research materials. Adding to this was the fact that many of the agency's early leaders were historians and teachers who were highly concerned with opening to research use the material in their custody and sharing the archival techniques that the archives developed. One consequence of that is the great influence they and their successors have had on the archival and records-management professions. This came through their publications and addresses, symposia, workshops, and training programs as well as the Society of American Archivists, the Interagency Records Administration Conference, and the International Council on Archives, all three of which the personnel of the National Archives had so much to do with founding and sustaining. Another result is the easier access researchers have to the older records of the government of the United States and even to archives and personal papers elsewhere in the country and the world. And this came about not just by the wider opening of the doors of archival institutions, but also through the production of documentary publications and the application of microfilm and other ways to reproduce records for researchers. Undoubtedly, some of these changes would have occurred had the National Archives not been established, but only some of them and to a lesser degree. No one disputes that between 1934 and 1968—or today—the establishment of the National Archives was magnificently justified.

Since 1968 everything in connection with NARS has increased substantially, including budget, programs, research users, visitors, publications, and employees, even in the archives itself. I shall leave it to future historians to detail these and other facets of the organization's record since then. It is pertinent to this study, however, to mention some of these in connection with a brief analysis of the major challenges that confront NARS.

One of these challenges concerns the size, diversity, and geographical dispersal of NARS. In 1954 Ernst Posner alluded to this "curse of bigness." He suggested that it would deprive America's federal archivists of much initiative because everything would have to be minutely regulated. NARS today is roughly three times as large as it was then, with over 3,000 employees in 1976 located at more than twenty facilities from coast to coast, and there are indications that Posner's fears have some substance. The top leadership encourages initiative, but there are too many layers of NARS and GSA administration for it to be often remarkably successful. One seldom dares to do important things on one's own. The alternative is to seek permission through channels, across divisions, and often over many miles, a process that frequently discourages the innovative spirit. The problems of size, diversity, and dispersal are also likely to be seen in other ways. One is that the top level of NARS administration, try as hard as it does to avoid it, is far away from most operating personnel. Caught up in pressing day-to-day tasks of administration, and especially relations with GSA, the leadership has found it more difficult both to ponder ideas suggested from down the line and to devise changes. The result is that significant innovation has sometimes become blocked on both ends. Indeed, one can suggest that despite able leadership and despite many recent accomplishments the pace of conceiving new theory and practice has slackened since the middle 1950s. However, the "curse of bigness" is not the only and perhaps not the most important reason for this, for the increased number of problems burdening NARS since 1968 has drained away some of the time that the archivist and his deputies could have used for salutary innovations. It is fair to say, too, that NARS has at least held its own in contributing to recent archival advances, regardless of the problems confronting it.

Another group of challenges is professional in nature. There always seem to be too many records being created, and Congress and the White House have been insufficiently tough in containing, contracting, or refusing to authorize many federal programs that contribute to this and other wasteful results. Moreover, NARS has not always been given the tools to help reduce the records glut, and it always finds it difficult to get enough space for the increased amount of records that it must handle. This is particularly a problem with archives, for as the records centers deal with more records, the volume of material of an archival nature mounts. The problem is that the archival service has had greater trouble in obtaining suitable space than have the records managers. Even if the federal government acts to pare the production of records that NARS must handle, there is little likelihood that new material of archival value will be reduced in the near future, for most of it is already wending its way by way of schedules into the hands of the National Archives. Hopefully, the Federal Records Management Amendments of 1976 and the work of the Federal Paperwork Commission, which Congress established in 1974, will give agency records officers and NARS additional weapons to control the creation of government records. Congress will also have to consider seriously providing additional space for archives, the size of which will increase regardless of whether the government handles its records more effectively.

There are other professional challenges of long standing. In one area, control of fire, NARS had made heartening progress, though not before, despite its cries for improvement, fire destroyed much valuable material in the National Personnel Records Center in St. Louis in July 1974. There are areas, however, in which NARS has made little recent progress. One is that records managers have not found the formulas or possibly the funds to be more precise now than they were twenty-five years ago in calculating the accumulation of federal records as well as the funds saved and costs avoided as a result of their work. Improvement here is important if only to prod Congress and the White House better to provide for dealing with records. Another problem is disposal. In 1970 Congress provided that disposal lists and schedules did not have to be submitted to it for approval. Congress is to be consulted only on records of special interest to it. This would be a step forward if the archivist and his staff, with their professional knowledge, were the only ones involved in disposal matters outside the creating agencies. At least theoretically, however, the administrator of general services is the one empowered to make such decisions, a legal provision that could lead to a crisis in the disposal of federal records.

A related and highly controversial issue concerns restrictions on the use of records. This came to the forefront during the middle of the 1960s and has remained there since. Although NARS does not determine security classifications and agency restrictions on records, it must by law administer them with respect to the records in its custody. Therefore, NARS has been a target, rather unfairly so, of those fighting against security classifications and agency restrictions as well as, sometimes justifiably so, for how it has carried out those restrictions and donor restrictions on the private papers among its holdings. The excessive restrictiveness of the regulations governing the use of many federal records has been cut down, beginning with the passage of the Freedom of Information Act in 1966 and with later amendments to it and the implementation of President Nixon's 1972 Executive Order 11652 on declassification. Moreover, NARS has become increasingly sensitive to administering classified and restricted material more in the favor of researchers, so one can say that the situation has very much improved since 1966.[1] Indeed, the agency, under the leadership of Archivist James B. Rhoads, has become unique among national archival institutions by virtue of its playing an important role in declassifying documents.

One thing that may offset this progress was the passage of the Privacy Act in 1974, the same year in which Congress added liberalizing amendments to the Freedom of Information Act. The Privacy Act may lead to the imposition of restrictions on records that could become just as important to research as the material that has recently been thrown open to scholars, journalists, and other citizens. The balancing of the needs of researchers against the legitimate requirements of individuals for privacy of the information about themselves in the records may become the great issue before archivists and their clients during the next decade. Elected officials will not find it an easy one to resolve.

It should also be said that the independence movement has been revived in recent years. This vindicates Wayne C. Grover's

*James B. Rhoads, fifth archivist of the United
States, 1968–*

statement in 1966 about the attempt to regain separate status for
NARS: "I believe we are on the right course in what is now likely to
be a long drawn out tussle. . . . Sooner or later the leadership of
GSA will make a mistake that the historical profession will not be
able to stomach."[2] The agency's mistakes did accumulate under
general services administrators Robert L. Kunzig (1969–72) and
Arthur F. Sampson (1972–75), both of whom were Pennsylvania
Republican political figures. It was not just a matter of too much
centralization, the imposition of management goals that were often
not applicable to NARS, and the frequently inept performance of

services by GSA. These had long been bones of contention between GSA and NARS. Rather, intimidation, partisanship, and capriciousness seemed on the rise in GSA after 1968.

It was not until 1974, however, after the resignation of Richard Nixon, that the worst came and the spirit of the independence movement stirred again. This was in connection with the question after the Watergate scandal of what would happen to Nixon's official papers. NARS was affected because GSA did not seek its advice on the controversial agreement relating to the custody of the former president's tapes and other materials, and because Administrator Sampson placed a special representative instead of qualified archivists in charge of Nixon's presidential materials. One result of the furor over Nixon's resignation and his papers was that late in 1974 Congress impounded the documents, which NARS later came to administer. It also established the National Study Commission on Records and Documents of Federal Officials to make recommendations on the status, disposition, and administration of the papers of high government officials.[3]

Equally important for the purposes of this study is the question of what should be the status of NARS within the federal government. The events of 1974 and 1975 added up to the "mistake" of which Grover wrote that would drive scholars to demand that NARS be returned to status as a separate agency of the United States government. Although the American Historical Association pressed strongly for impounding the Nixon papers, historians were slow in mobilizing to raise the issue of an independent archival agency again. The first blow was struck by the American Assembly conference, called "The Records of Public Officials," in April 1975. With a number of archivists and historians participating, that Forty-eighth American Assembly called for public ownership of presidential records, improved methods of determining the preservation of and access to federal records, and "the establishment of a new, independent, [sic] archival and records management system." The AHA council endorsed this in December and adopted it as the association's policy in May 1976. That same year the executive board of the Organization of American Historians and the SAA council voted their support of divorcing NARS from GSA, and in 1977 the

National Study Commission on Records and Documents of Federal Officials recommended that "NARS should be independent of the General Services Administration . . . and insulated from partisan political influences."[4] What all this will lead to is hard to say. It would appear, however, that what might be called the second independence movement is more unified as to what it wants and has enlisted more widespread support among archivists, historians, and the public than did Grover's movement a decade before. Therefore, one must conclude that there is a chance NARS will be given a different status as a federal agency.

Well-considered legislation can make NARS into a better and stronger institution than it has been. That does not mean, however, that all its problems will be solved. The theoretically ideal National Archives Act of 1934 did not make the agency invulnerable to regrettable pressures from politicians and other federal agencies. Although the lodgment of the National Archives within the folds of GSA reduced external pressures on the archivists, it succeeded in substituting for them often unwise moves from GSA itself. Whether or not NARS achieves independent status again or more autonomy within GSA, its future will be as unpredictable as its past has been. That is inherent in the life of any institution.

It is essential from the standpoints of archival thought, public administration theory, and historical analysis that NARS be protected from the arbitrary interference of either well-meaning or predatory bureaucrats and politicians on professional archival matters. With appropriate statutory protection, NARS is now a large enough and sufficiently visible entity with enough of a clientele to be able to stand on its own as an agency of government. Only thus can it best carry out its mission of professionally ministering to the creation, management, preservation or disposal, and research use of federal records. Only thus can it build on its continuing record of highly innovative and influential accomplishments. And only thus can it serve the nation and its people for all seasons and not just when an overseer decides.

NOTES

1. U.S., *Statutes at Large*, 48:1112–24.

2. The standard work on ancient archives is Ernst M. Posner, *Archives in the Ancient World*.

3. For additional information, see Wayne C. Grover, "Government Records for Research"; Boyd C. Shafer, ed., *Historical Study in the West*; Direction des Archives De France, *Manuel D'Archivistique*; Friedrich Kahlenberg, *Deutsche Archive in West und Ost*.

4. On the influence of "scientific" history in the United States, see Jurgen Herbst, *The German Historical School in American Scholarship*; and John Higham with Leonard Krieger and Felix Gilbert, *History*.

5. Victor Gondos, Jr., "The Movement for a National Archives of the United States, 1906–1926," pp. 4–9.

6. Ibid., passim.

7. Ibid.; Fred Shelley, "The Interest of J. Franklin Jameson in the National Archives," pp. 99–130; David D. Van Tassel, "John Franklin Jameson," pp. 81–96.

8. Gondos, "The Movement for a National Archives," p. 406.

9. Percy Scott Flippin, comp., "The Archives of the United States Government," 22:7–8, 63.

10. Record Group 51, "Records of the Bureau of the Budget" (hereafter cited as RG 51), Series 21. 1, National Archives General #1, H. L. Ickes to Roosevelt, 12 May 1934, J. L. Keddy to F. J. Bailey, n.d. (between 12 and 24 May 1934), Bailey memorandum, 22 May 1934; Official File 221, Lincoln Colcord to Roosevelt, 29 Jan. 1934, L. M. Howe to Ickes, 18 May 1934, Roosevelt Papers.

11. J. G. Bradley to R. D. W. Connor, 15 Feb. 1936, 6 Oct. 1938, Connor Papers; J. F. Jameson to Bradley, 7 Feb. 1934, 6, 7, and 12 Mar. 1934, 6 June 1934, Bradley to Jameson, 26 Apr. 1934, 5 June 1934, Jameson Papers; Gondos, "The Movement for a National Archives," pp. 418–19.

12. Gondos, "The Movement for a National Archives," p. 419; U.S., *Statutes at Large*, 48:1112–24, 1026.

13. U.S., *Statutes at Large*, 48:1112–24.

14. Ibid.

15. Ibid.

16. Ibid.

CHAPTER 2

1. Regarding the state of archival affairs at the time of the establishment of the National Archives, see Christopher Crittenden, "The Archivist as a Public Servant," p. 4, and Mary Givens Bryan, "Changing Times," pp. 3–4.

2. Shelley, "The Interest of J. Franklin Jameson in the National Archives," p. 129; J. F. Jameson to Albert Shaw, 28 Mar. 1933, Jameson to R. P. Chiles, 1 Apr. 1933, Jameson Papers; OF 221, W. E. Dodd to Secretary of State Hull, 16 May 1933, Roosevelt Papers.

3. R. P. Chiles to J. F. Jameson, 27 Mar. 1933, Jameson to Chiles, 1 Apr. 1933, Jameson Papers; R. D. W. Connor Journal, vol. 1, p. 7; Jameson to Conyers Read, 18 May 1934, Jameson file.

4. For information on the development of the historical profession in the United States, see John Higham with Leonard Krieger and Felix Gilbert, *History.* See also Marcus W. Jernegan, "Productivity of Doctors of Philosophy in History," pp. 1–22, and William B. Hesseltine and Louis Kaplan, "Doctors of Philosophy in History," pp. 765–800.

5. Secretary file (Ex.), S. J. Buck to Conyers Read, 10, 16 May 1934, American Historical Association Papers (hereafter cited as AHA Papers).

6. Secretary file (Ex.), Conyers Read to J. F. Jameson, May 11 1934, AHA Papers; *American Historical Review* 40 (Apr. 1935):579.

7. Secretary file (Ex.), Minutes of the Meeting of the Executive Committee, 20 May 1934, AHA Papers; Conyers Read to J. F. Jameson 24 May 1934, Jameson file.

8. J. F. Jameson to Conyers Read, 28 May 1934, Jameson file; Jameson to R. D. W. Connor, 28 May 1934, Connor to Jameson, 31 May 1934, Connor Papers.

9. Robert R. Simpson, "Leland to Connor," pp. 513–22; Waldo G. Leland, "Robert D. W. Connor, First Archivist of the United States," pp. 45–54; Hugh T. Lefler, "Robert Digges Wimberly Connor," pp. 109–23; *Dictionary of American Biography*, s.v. "Connor, Robert Digges Wimberly."

10. J. F. Jameson to Conyers Read, 28 May 1934, Jameson file.

11. Conyers Read to J. F. Jameson, 1 June 1934, Jameson file; OF 221A Misc., Executive Committee AHA to Roosevelt, 5 June 1934, Roosevelt Papers; Read to R. D. W. Connor, 5 June 1934, Connor Papers.

12. R. D. W. Connor to Conyers Read, 7 June 1934, Connor to F. P. Graham, 18 June 1934, Connor Papers.

13. J. F. Jameson to S. F. Bemis, 19 June 1934, Jameson to Conyers Read, 18 June 1934, Jameson Papers; Read to Jameson, 21 June 1934, Jameson file; Read to R. D. W. Connor, 21 June 1934, Connor Papers.

14. OF 221A Misc., Rudolph Forster to Marvin McIntyre, 22 June 1934, Roosevelt Papers; J. G. Bradley to K. E. Keller, 22, 29 June 1934, Connor Papers; J. F. Jameson to R. D. W. Connor, 22 June 1934, Jameson file.

15. F. P. Graham to R. D. W. Connor, 22 June 1934, Connor to J. F. Jameson, 22 June 1934, Connor to Conyers Read, 22 June 1934, Connor to Graham, 23 June 1934, Read to Connor, 23 June 1934, Connor Papers.

16. R. D. W. Connor to Conyers Read, 25 June 1934, J. F. Jameson to F. P. Graham, 25 June 1934, Connor Papers; James to Read, 27 June 1934, Jameson

file; OF 221, W. E. Dodd to Secretary of State, 25 June 1934, Cordell Hull to Roosevelt, 25 June 1934, Roosevelt Papers.

17. Lefler, "Connor," pp. 109–14; Leland, "Connor," pp. 45–51; W. W. Pierson to R. D. W. Connor, 7 July 1934, D. R. Fox to Connor, 5 July 1934, F. P. Graham to Connor, 30 June, 8 July 1934, J. F. Jameson to Connor, 9 July 1934, Connor to W. G. Leland, 9 July 1934, Connor Papers; Jameson to W. E. Lingelbach, 7 July 1934, Jameson file. Jameson was either premature or immediate in arranging for Cordell Hull to propose Connor to Roosevelt, for Under Secretary of State William Phillips informed Jameson on 9 July that Secretary Hull had sent Connor's name to the president for consideration. This made no difference by 9 July, for Connor was then the AHA's nominee for archivist. See William Phillips to Jameson, 9 July 1934, Connor Papers.

18. Connor Journal, 1:34–36, 76, 84, 47.

19. Ibid., vol. 1, passim; Jameson file, passim; OF 221A, Connor and Rowland folders, Roosevelt Papers.

20. Connor Journal, 1:35, 65, 104–5, 107–8, 112, 115, 117–18, passim.

21. Jameson file, passim; Connor Journal, 1:89, 127–29; OF 221A, W. E. Dodd to Secretary of State, 9 Aug. 1934, enclosed in Cordell Hull to Roosevelt, 10 Aug. 1934, J. F. Jameson to Marvin McIntyre, 20 Sept. 1934, Jameson to Roosevelt, 20 Sept. 1934, and Connor folder, Roosevelt Papers.

22. OF 221A, Connor folder, J. F. Jameson to Marvin McIntyre, 20 Sept. 1934, Roosevelt Papers; McIntyre to Connor, 27 Sept. 1934, Connor Papers.

23. Connor Journal, 1:134–37; Connor to Sadie Connor, 3 Oct. 1934, Connor Papers; Robert D. W. Connor, "FDR Visits the National Archives," pp. 323–25.

24. Connor Journal, 1:134–37; Connor to Sadie Connor, 3 Oct. 1934, Connor Papers; Connor, "FDR Visits the National Archives," pp. 323–35; Lefler, "Connor," pp. 116–17.

25. Cordell Hull to Connor, 15 Oct. 1934, Connor Papers; OF 221, Memo for the Press, 10 Oct. 1934, Roosevelt to Pat Harrison, 12 Oct. 1934, Roosevelt Papers; Connor Journal, 1:146 and "Confirmation."

26. Conyers Read to Connor, 22 Oct. 1934, W. E. Dodd to Connor, 31 Oct. 1934, Connor Papers.

27. Connor Journal, 1:3.

Chapter 3

1. Connor to Sadie Connor, 3 Oct. 1934, Connor Papers; Connor Journal, 1:138.

2. Connor Journal, 1:139–40.

3. Robert H. Bahmer, "The National Archives after 20 Years," pp. 198–99; OF 221, Roosevelt to Secretary of the Interior, 10 Sept. 1934, H. L. Ickes to Roosevelt, 12 Sept. 1934, Roosevelt Papers.

4. Robert D. W. Connor, "Adventures of an Amateur Archivist," p. 8; Bahmer, "The National Archives after 20 Years," p. 199; Connor Journal, 4:13–19, especially copies of letters from H. L. Ickes to Connor, Connor to Ickes, Ickes to Roosevelt, all dated 23 Nov. 1935.

5. Bahmer, "The National Archives after 20 Years," pp. 195–205.

6. Connor Journal, 1:140–41, 146–52; Connor to Harriet Root, 27 Oct. 1934, Connor Papers.

7. OF 221, J. R. Pope to F. A. Delano, 3 June 1933, Roosevelt Papers; Record Group 66, "Records of the Commission of Fine Arts" (hereafter cited as RG 66), J. R. Pope, "Archives Building, Washington D.C.," 21 Sept. 1934; The National Archives, *First Annual Report of the Archivist of the United States*, pp. 5–6 (hereafter cited as RAUS with the appropriate report number).

8. Flippin, "The Archives of the United States Government," 22:53–54; RAUS, 1:6,9.

9. RAUS, 1:5–8; RG 66, "The National Archives Building," apparently by J. R. Pope, ca. 1934, Charles Moore to L. A. Simon, 4 Dec. 1934.

10. RAUS, 1:6,8; RAUS, 3:3 and plates between pp. 2 and 3; *New York Times*, 15 Nov. 1936.

11. OF 221, F. A. Delano to Roosevelt, 5 June 1933, and enclosures of J. R. Pope to Delano and Pope to L. W. Robert, both dated 3 June 1933, Roosevelt Papers; RG 66, Pope, "Archives Building, Washington, D.C.," 21 Sept. 1934; RAUS, 1:6.

12. RG 66, Charles Moore to L. A. Simon, 25 Feb. 1935, Moore to J. R. Pope, 26 Feb. 1935; OF 221, Roosevelt to Secretary of the Treasury and C. J. Peoples, 6 Mar. 1935, Roosevelt Papers.

13. RG 66, L. A. Simon to J. R. Pope, 7 June 1935, Pope to Simon, 11 June 1935, Simon to Charles Moore, 12 June 1935, Moore to Simon, 13 June 1935, I. D. Matthew to H. P. Caemmerer, 4 Nov. 1937.

14. RAUS, 1:20, 25–26, 33–34.

15. For a justification of the metal boxes, see Record Group 64, "Records of the National Archives and Records Service" (hereafter cited as RG 64), Archival Service—Director, D. W. Hyde, Jr., to Connor, 11 Mar. 1935.

16. RAUS, 4:1–2; RAUS, 1:34; RAUS, 2:1–2, 23–25, 44, 60–61; RAUS, 3:2–3, 41, 59–60; RG 64, Archivist 71.1, R. D. W. Connor to L. A. Simon, 22 June 1938, Simon to W. E. Reynolds, 2 Feb. 1940, and Central Files 82.3, "Background Material," FY 1949, p. 23.

17. OF 221 and 221A, 1933–35, Roosevelt Papers; Roosevelt to R. D. W. Connor, 11 Oct. 1934, enclosing Sol Bloom to Roosevelt, 6 Oct. 1934, Connor Papers; Connor, "Adventures of an Amateur Archivist," p. 4; Connor Journal, vol. 6, "Patronage."

18. Connor to Emil Hurja, 6 Sept. 1935, Connor Papers; Connor, "Adventures of an Amateur Archivist," p. 5.

19. Secretary file (Ex.), Conyers Read to R. D. W. Connor, 4 Mar. 1935, Connor to Read, 2 Jan. 1936, AHA Papers; Jameson to Connor, 12, 14, and 31 Oct. 1934, Connor to Jameson, 16 Oct. 1934, 13 Jan. 1937, Connor Papers; Connor, "Adventures of an Amateur Archivist," p. 6.

20. Connor Journal, vol. 1, "The Triumphant Historians," vol. 6, "Patronage"; *New York Times*, 9 May 1935; Pat Harrison to Connor, 30 Jan. 1935, Connor to Dunbar Rowland, 22 Nov. 1935, Connor to W. W. Old, Jr., 9 Jan. 1935, Connor to Roosevelt, 10 June 1935, Connor to Harrison, 26 Sept. 1935, Connor Papers; OF 221, Roosevelt to Connor, 12 July 1935, Connor to Roosevelt, 15 July 1935, Roosevelt Papers.

21. Connor, "Adventures of an Amateur Archivist," p. 6; Jameson to W. E.

Dodd, 31 Oct. 1934, Connor Papers; Connor Journal, vol. 6, "Patronage"; RAUS, 1:35–36.

22. RG 64, Archivist's File, Office of the Administrative Secretary, "Journal —The National Archives"; OF 221, R. D. W. Connor to Roosevelt, 21 May 1935, Roosevelt to Acting Director of the Bureau of the Budget, 21 May 1935, D. W. Bell to Roosevelt, 7 June 1935, Rudolph Forster to J. A. Farley, 10 June 1935, Roosevelt Papers; *Washington Times-Herald*, 15 Dec. 1936; RAUS, 2:10.

23. D. W. Hyde, Jr. to Connor, 1 and 4 Dec. 1934, 3 Jan. 1935, Hyde Papers; RG 64, Statistical Issuances and Organization Charts, "The National Archives, General Organization Chart, Nov. 27, 1935"; RAUS, 2:19–36.

24. RG 64, Collas G. Harris oral history transcript, passim; T. R. Schellenberg to parents et al., 5 Jan., 20 Aug. 1935, Schellenberg to Alma Schellenberg, 26 Mar. 1935, V. D. Tate to Schellenberg, 17 Jan., 8 Mar. 1935, P. C. Brooks to Schellenberg, 7 Feb. 1935, Schellenberg Papers.

25. RAUS, 1:20; RAUS, 2:10–11; RAUS, 3:57–58; RAUS, 4:3–4. The early staff of the National Archives had an impressive background. A survey taken in November 1936 showed that the agency's then 98 professional and subprofessional and 124 administrative and clerical employees included 78 who read and 25 who spoke twenty-one foreign languages or dialects, 106 who had received degrees, and 24 who had finished some college work. Incidentally, among the 106 degree holders were twenty-six Ph.D.s, fifty-two masters, and nine bachelors of law (Buck Papers, C. G. Harris to Buck, 27 Nov. 1936).

CHAPTER 4

1. Robert D. W. Connor, "Adventures of an Amateur Archivist," pp. 2–17; Robert D. W. Connor, "The National Archives," p. 558.

2. RG 64, Archivist—Reading file, Connor, Memorandum, No. 20, 15 Oct. 1935, Memorandum No. 26, 12 Nov. 1935, "Journal—The National Archives" (25 May 1926–30 June 1936), and Official Memoranda file, No. A–82, 8 July 1938, No. A–129, 5 July 1940; National Archives file, Minutes, Advisory Council, 1 Feb. 1936.

3. Buck to Connor, 28 June 1937, Buck Papers; OF 221, Roosevelt to Acting Director of the Budget, 2 Aug. 1937, Roosevelt Papers; Connor to N. V. Russell, 1 Dec. 1938, Connor Papers; *Washington Times-Herald*, 27 Sept. 1939; RAUS 4:4, 41; RAUS 5:44–45; RAUS, 6:38–39.

4. Jameson to Connor, 14 Nov. 1934, Connor Papers; Connor Journal, vol. 2, 4 July 1938; *Time*, 22 Oct. 1934; Thaddeus Page, "R. D. W. Connor, 1878–1950," pp. 99–101.

5. W. E. Dodd to Connor, 2 Sept. 1938, Connor Papers.

6. Connor Journal, vol. 2, 13 Mar. 1935; *Congressional Record*, 13 Mar. 1935, 3568–74.

7. C. A. Woodrum to Connor, 22 Nov. 1935, Connor to Woodrum, 26 Nov. 1935, Connor Papers; RG 64, Archivist—Reading file, Connor to Carter Glass, 4 Feb. 1936, and Central Files, Alphabetical Subject file, Visitors—Capitol, 1935–1937.

8. RG 64, Administrative Secretary Correspondence, J. J. Cochran to Cordell Hull, 20 Jan. 1936; Cochran to Hull, 25 Jan. 1936, Connor Papers.

9. J. J. Cochran to Connor, 27 Jan. 1936, Connor Papers; Connor to Buck, 10 Sept. 1941, Buck Papers.

10. Connor Journal, vol. 2, "Transfer of War Department Records to the National Archives"; Connor, "Adventures of an Amateur Archivist," pp. 8–9; RAUS, 2:17; RAUS, 3:21; RAUS, 4:36–37; RAUS, 5:49–50.

11. Connor, "FDR Visits the National Archives," pp. 331–32; Connor to J. W. Bailey, 28 Feb. 1938, Connor to Morris Sheppard, 28 Feb. 1938, Connor Papers.

12. R. R. Hill to Connor, 18 Feb. 1935, Connor to Herbert Putnam, 19 June 1935, Connor Papers; Connor Journal, vol. 2, 20 Aug. 1935, 10 June 1937, vol. 6, pp. 8 and 72–93; *Washington News*, 25 Mar. 1937; Connor, "The National Archives," pp. 590, 594; Connor, "Adventures of an Amateur Archivist," pp. 10–12.

13. RAUS, 2:8–9.

14. U.S., *Statutes at Large*, 49:5005–03. Congress had already provided for delivery to the National Archives of copies of printed legislative documents and Supreme Court opinions as well as publications of other federal agencies in Public Law 151 of the Seventy-fourth Congress.

15. OF 221, Connor to Roosevelt, 26 Aug. 1935, H. M. McIntyre to Connor, 26 Aug. 1935, and OF 221–B, 1935–36, Roosevelt Papers; RAUS, 2:9–10, 61–62; RG 64, Archivist—Reading file, e.g., Connor to Postmaster General, 25 Sept. 1935.

16. RAUS, 2:61–63.

17. Ibid., 62; RAUS, 3:54–56; RAUS, 5:40–41; RAUS, 7:38–39.

18. RAUS, 1:11–12.

19. RAUS, 2:7, 33–35, 85–87; RAUS, 3:68–69; RAUS, 4:34; RAUS, 5:93–94; RAUS, 6:87–90; RAUS, 7:88; RAUS, 8:81; RAUS, 9:64; RAUS, 10:74; RAUS, 11:56.

20. RAUS, 1:17, 21–22, 30–31; RAUS, 2:58–61, 66, 82.

21. OF 221, Connor to Roosevelt, 23 Oct. 1935, 16 Feb. 1938, Roosevelt to Connor, 30 Oct. 1935, 3 Jan. 1939, Roosevelt Papers.

22. RG 64, Archivist 28.5, J. G. Bradley to Connor, 19 Dec. 1935; OF 221, Connor to Roosevelt, 23 Apr. 1937, Roosevelt to Connor, 14 May 1937, Roosevelt to Connor, 14 May 1937, Roosevelt Papers; RAUS, 1:30; RAUS 2:58; RAUS, 3:40; RAUS, 4:19–22; RAUS, 5:15–17.

23. RG 64, Archivist—Reading file, form letter, 12 Apr. 1935, Connor to Federal Reserve Board, 6 Sept. 1935.

24. RAUS, 1:21, 26–28. It should be noted that there was not then and still is not a precise legal distinction between records and archives.

25. RAUS, 2:11–12, 36–38; RAUS, 3:7–8, 26–30; RAUS, 4:7–8; RAUS, 5:3–4; RAUS, 6:10–11.

26. RAUS, 2:6, 14–17, 20, 40; RAUS, 3:9–10, 23, 25, 66; RAUS, 4:2–3.

27. RAUS, 4:9–10.

28. RAUS, 3:66; RAUS, 5:4–8; RAUS, 6:12–14; U.S., *Statutes at Large*, 53:1219–21, 54:958.

29. RAUS, 2:12, 88–103; RAUS, 3:8–9, 50, 93–110.

30. David L. Smiley, "The W.P.A. Historical Records Survey," pp. 3–28; RAUS, 3:93–110; RAUS, 4:62–64; RAUS, 5:89–91; RAUS, 6:91–93; RAUS,

7:89–90; RAUS, 8:82; RG 64, Archivist file 17.2, Dan Lacy to Buck, 27 May 1947.

31. RG 64, Archival Service—Director, A–Z file, D. W. Hyde to Chief, Division of Accessions, 16 Sept., 3 Oct. 1935.

32. OF 221, Roosevelt to Mac, 26 Dec. 1935, Roosevelt Papers; RAUS, 2:4–6.

33. RAUS, 5:92; RAUS, 8:80; RAUS, 9:59–60.

CHAPTER 5

1. RAUS, 2:13–14, 20; RAUS, 3:10–11, 14–18; RAUS, 4:12–13; RAUS 5:11–12; RAUS, 6:16–18; RAUS 7:20–26; Wayne C. Grover, "Research Facilities and Materials at the National Archives," pp. 976–83.

2. Robert D. W. Connor, "Adventures of an Amateur Archivist," pp. 9, 12–13; e.g., *Washington Star*, 12 Dec. 1936; *New York Times*, 18 Apr. 1937, IV; *Washington Post*, 24 Mar. 1935; RAUS, 2:79–84; RAUS 3:85–92; RAUS, 4:53–61; RG 64, Archivist 18.

3. RAUS, 3:49, 82.

4. RAUS, 3:126–30, 142, 156–57, 161–63; RG 64, Archivist 44, Connor to Attorney General, 23 Jan. 1939; OF 25 Misc., Connor to Roosevelt, 16 Dec. 1938, Roosevelt Papers.

5. RG 64, Administrative Secretary Correspondence, Connor to J. J. Cochran, 17 Mar. 1937; Connor Journal, vol. 6, "Transfer of State Department Archives"; RAUS, 4:12, 19, 42.

6. RAUS, 3:11; RAUS, 4:12, 19, 23; Connor, "Adventures of an Amateur Archivist," pp. 14–15; OF 221, Roosevelt to H. L. Ickes, 22 Aug. 1935, Roosevelt Papers; Connor Journal, vol. 2, "Transfer of War Department Records to the National Archives."

7. OF 25, Roosevelt to Harry Woodring, 17 June 1937, Woodring to Roosevelt, 6 July 1937, Roosevelt Papers.

8. Ibid., F. D. Roosevelt to Connor, 7 July 1937, Connor to Roosevelt, 20 July 1937.

9. Ibid., Roosevelt to Harry Woodring, 22 July, 3 Aug. 1937, Woodring to Roosevelt, 29 July, 7 Aug. 1937, Connor to Roosevelt, 2 Aug. 1937, Woodring to Connor, 6 Aug. 1937; Connor, "Adventures of an Amateur Archivist," pp. 15–16; RAUS, 4:12; RAUS, 5:11–12.

10. OF 25 Misc., Connor to Roosevelt, 16 Dec. 1938, Roosevelt to Harry Woodring, 19 Dec. 1938, Woodring to Roosevelt, 21 Dec. 1938, Roosevelt Papers; Connor Journal, vol. 2, "Transfer of War Department Records to the National Archives."

11. RAUS, 2:40–44; RAUS, 3:30–31; RG 64, Archivist—Memos from Chiefs, A. E. Kimberly to Archivist, 4 May 1936; Kimberly, *Repair and Preservation in the National Archives.* It is worth noting that the National Archives initiated a Works Progress Administration project, employing several hundred workers between 1938 and 1941, that flattened more than 100,000,000 documents (RAUS, 5:20; RAUS, 6:24; RAUS, 7:27).

12. RAUS, 2:v; RAUS, 3:v; RAUS, 4:v, 16.

13. RG 64, Archival Service—Director/A–Z, D. W. Hyde to Connor, 5 Feb.

1936, Archivist—Memos from Chiefs, A. H. Leavitt to Connor, 27 Apr. 1936, F. W. Shipman to Connor, 4 May 1936; RAUS, 3:13; RAUS, 5:23. Two observations are in order here. One is, as Hyde's letter and Connor's statement suggested, American archivists tended to view the two principles as one. Indeed, many archivists lumped the two ideas together under the term *provenance*. Another is that Arthur H. Leavitt, a chief of one of the two original archives divisions, made an essential contribution to better American understanding of *provenance* in his translation of the 1920 edition of the classic Dutch archival work by S. Muller, J. A. Feith, and R. Fruin, *Manual for the Arrangement and Description of Archives*.

14. National Archives file, N. M. Blake to R. R. Hill, 17 Mar. 1939, A. H. Leavitt to Hill, 13 Mar. 1939, and also Archival Terminology file, Buck Papers; Roscoe R. Hill, "Archival Terminology," pp. 206–11. For later, solid work on terminology, see Frank B. Evans, Donald F. Harrison, Edwin A. Thompson, and William L. Rofes, "A Basic Glossary for Archivists, Manuscript Curators, and Records Managers," pp. 415–33.

15. Frank B. Evans, "Modern Methods of Arrangement of Archives in the United States," pp. 243–56; RAUS, 1:15, 21; RAUS, 2:45–48; RG 64, Archivist —Memos from Chiefs, Roscoe R. Hill to Connor, 27 Apr. 1936; Roscoe R. Hill, "Classification in the National Archives," pp. 60–77; RAUS, 5:24–25; RAUS, 7:39–40.

16. RAUS, 1:15–16; RAUS, 2:49–50; RG 64, Archivist—Memos from Chiefs, J. R. Russell to Connor, 24 Apr. 1936; RAUS, 3:44–47; RAUS, 4:25–26; RAUS, 5:25–26; RAUS, 6:28, 38; RAUS, 7:39–40; Evangeline Thurber, "Suggestions for a Code for Cataloging Archival Material," pp. 42–53.

17. RAUS, 1:14–18; RAUS, 2:36–40; RAUS, 5:9, 42.

18. RG 64, Archivist—Memos from Chiefs, N. V. Russell to Connor, 24 Oct. 1938; RAUS, 1:16; RAUS, 4:2–3.

19. RAUS, 1:16; RAUS, 2:54–55; RAUS, 3:50, 67; RAUS, 4:2, 4.

20. Cf. RG 64, Statistical Issuances and National Archives Organization Charts file, The National Archives, General Organization Chart, 27 Nov. 1935, with RAUS, 4:2–3, and RAUS, 5:41–43.

21. Donald R. McCoy, "The Beginnings of the Franklin D. Roosevelt Library," pp. 137–50.

22. W. G. Leland to Connor, 19 Nov. 1934, Connor Papers; RAUS, 3:6–7; "The 50th Anniversary Meeting," 424, 432–433; AHA file, Buck to Connor, 13 Sept. 1935, Connor to A. R. Newsome, 17 Sept. 1935, Buck Papers.

23. RAUS, 2:79–84; RAUS, 3:85–92; RAUS, 4:53–61; RAUS, 5:83–88; RAUS, 6:76–85; RAUS, 7:79–86; Philip M. Hamer, "The Records of Southern History," pp. 3–17; National Archives file, Buck to Connor, 18 Mar. 1937, 1 June 1938, Buck Papers.

24. RAUS, 2:79–84; RAUS, 3:65, 85–92; RAUS, 4:53–61; RAUS, 6:41–42; *New York Times*, 12 Sept. 1937, IV, 9 Jan. 1939; *Washington News*, 9 July 1938.

25. RAUS, 2:30; RAUS, 3:65; RG 64, Archivist—Reading file, R. R. Hill to L. S. Rowe, 13 Dec. 1935, and Central Files—Alphabetical Subject file, Visitors, 1935–38.

26. Robert D. W. Connor, "The National Archives of the United States," p. 35. For different figures, see RAUS, 4:26–29.

27. RG 64, Statistical Issuances file, passim; RAUS, 4:27–30; RAUS, 5:29–35; RAUS, 6:30–35; RAUS, 7:21, 31–35. It must be noted that the service figures of the National Archives are not completely reliable. Not only were changes made in the agency's statistical bases without a complete record of why they were made, but the divisions within the National Archives often interpreted the reporting criteria differently.

28. Robert C. Binkley, *Manual on Methods of Reproducing Research Materials*; RG 64, Archivist—Memos from Chiefs, V. D. Tate to Connor, 6 May 1936; V. D. Tate, "Microphotography in Archives," pp. 103–108; Preston W. Edsall, "The File Microcopy Program of the National Archives," pp. 9–14; V. D. Tate, "File Microcopy Projects—The National Archives," pp. 227–35; RAUS, 1:20, 37; RAUS, 2:63–38; RAUS, 7:33, 35–36.

29. Philip M. Hamer, "Finding Mediums in the National Archives," p. 83; Robert D. W. Connor, "The National Archives: Objectives and Practices," pp. 588–90.

CHAPTER 6

1. Robert D. W. Connor, "The National Archives: Objectives and Practices," pp. 587–90.

2. Connor to A. R. Newsome, 22 Mar. 1935, Connor to J. F. Rippy, 7 and 8 Oct. 1935, Connor Papers; RAUS, 2:33; William F. Birdsall, "The Two Sides of the Desk," pp. 159–72; Conference of Archivists file, Buck to T. C. Blegen, 15 Oct. 1935, Buck to L. J. Cappon, 23 Oct. 1935, Buck to Newsome, 4 Mar. 1936, Buck to W. G. Leland, 28 Mar. 1936, Buck Papers; *American Historical Review* 41 (Apr. 1936):456. See also William F. Birdsall, "The American Archivists' Search for Professional Identity, 1909–1936."

3. Society of American Archivists, *Proceedings, Providence, R.I., December 29–30, 1936, and Washington, D.C., June 18–19, 1937*; Lester J. Cappon, "The Archival Profession and the Society of American Archivists," pp. 199–201.

4. SAA, *Proceedings, Providence . . . and Washington*, pp. 65–74; Cappon, "The Archival Profession and the Society of American Archivists," p. 199; N. V. Russell to Buck, 18 Dec. 1935, Buck Papers.

5. Robert D. W. Connor, "Adventures of an Amateur Archivist," p. 7.

6. SAA, *Proceedings, Providence . . . and Washington*, p. 14.

7. See Cappon, "The Archival Profession and the Society of American Archivists," pp. 195–204, for a discussion of many of the points touched on above.

8. SAA, *Proceedings, Providence . . . and Washington*, p. 24; *American Historical Review* 41 (Apr. 1936):456; *American Archivist* 1 (July 1938):111–16; 2 (Apr. 1939):106–14, 126–27; 2 (Jan. 1939):55–57.

9. *American Archivist* 2 (Jan. 1939):55–57, 2 (July 1939):197–98. See also Theodore R. Schellenberg, *European Archival Practices in Arranging Records*, Solon J. Buck, *Selected References on Phases of Archival Economy*, and Ryszard Przelaskowski, *Schedule of Internal Work in Modern Archives*. With considerable help from Olga Paul, the archives had other pertinent articles from European journals translated into English and placed on file in its library.

10. RG 64, Archivist file 77.3; RAUS, 4:6; RAUS, 5:45–46; RAUS, 6:39–40; RAUS, 7:41; RAUS, 8:41.

11. Columbia University file, R. C. Binkley to Connor, 6 Dec. 1934, Connor to A. P. Evans, 3 Dec. 1935, Connor to Buck, 7 Feb. 1936, Buck Papers; RG 64, Archivist file, Buck to Evans, 14 Feb. 1936.

12. American University file, E. S. Griffith to Buck, 27 Jan. 1937, Buck to Griffith, 30 Jan. 1937, 27 Apr. 1938, ALA file, Buck to A. F. Kuhlman, 10 June 1937, Buck Papers; Connor to S. F. Bemis, 2 Aug. 1937, Connor Papers; Samuel Flagg Bemis, "The Training of Archivists in the United States," pp. 154–61. See also Frank B. Evans, "Educational Needs for Work in Archives and Manuscripts Depositories," pp. 13–19.

13. RG 64, Archivist 77, O. W. Holmes memorandum, 11 Apr. 1947; Buck to Connor, 27 Aug. 1938, Connor Papers.

14. H. G. Jones, "Archival Training in American Universities, 1938–1968," p. 139; American University file, Buck to J. M. Gray, 22 Dec. 1938, E. N. Anderson to Buck, 20 May 1939, Buck Papers; Solon J. Buck, "Essentials in Training for Work with Public Archives and Historical Manuscript Collections," p. 119.

15. Paul Lewinson, "Introduction: The Two Careers of Ernst Posner," pp. 8–11; American University file, course list and outline, Oct. 1939–Feb. 1940, for History and Administration of Archives, Buck Papers; Buck, "Essentials in Training," p. 120; RAUS, 6:40; RAUS, 7:41; RAUS, 8:41.

16. RG 64, Archivist 77, Buck to Connor, 28 Jan. 1939, and Archivist 77.3; Buck, "Essentials in Training," p. 120; RAUS, 7:41; RAUS, 8:41; RAUS, 9:46; RAUS, 10:57.

17. Jones, "Archival Training in American Universities," p. 141; RG 64, Archivist 77, O. W. Holmes memorandum, 11 Apr. 1947; Buck, "Essentials in Training," pp. 114–15.

18. Buck, "Essentials in Training," p. 121; RAUS, 11:33; *American Archivist* 12 (Apr. 1949):204; Jones, "Archival Training in American Universities," pp. 148, 142–43.

19. Karl L. Trever, "The Organization and Status of Archival Training in the United States," pp. 155, 158–59; *American Archivist* 24 (July 1961):371; 30 (Jan. 1967):214; Jones, "Archival Training in American Universities," pp. 144–45; Archival Training file, Brooks Papers; Thornton W. Mitchell, "The State of Records Management," p. 263.

20. William D. Overman, "The Pendulum Swings," pp. 3–4, 6; Christopher C. Crittenden, "The Archivist as a Public Servant," p. 4; Mary Givens Bryan, "Changing Times," pp. 3–5.

21. For a perceptive commentary, see John Melville Jennings, "Archival Activity in American Universities and Colleges."

CHAPTER 7

1. See, for example, Karl L. Trever, "Administrative History in Federal Archives," pp. 159–69, and Henry P. Beers, "The Bureau of Navigation, 1862–1942," pp. 212–52.

2. Frank B. Evans, "Modern Methods of Arrangement of Archives in the United States," pp. 241–56; RG 64, Memorandum No. A–122, 1 Mar. 1940.

The debate over applying concepts of library science to archives was by no means over, even though the National Archives and almost all other repositories rejected most of those ideas. See William Van Schreeven's review of Margaret C. Norton's "Archives and Libraries, a Comparison Drawn," in *American Archivist* 6 (July 1941):291–92; Randolph W. Church, "The Relationship between Archival Agencies and Libraries," pp. 145–50, and Herman Kahn, "Libraries and Archivists—Some Aspects of Their Partnership," pp. 243–51.

3. RG 64, Finding Mediums Problem file, passim, Memoranda No. A–142, 28 Feb. 1941, A–144, 3 Mar. 1941, A–146, 15 Mar. 1941; RAUS, 7:65–68; Mario D. Fenyo, "The Record Group Concept," pp. 229–32.

4. RG 64, Advisory Committee on Finding Mediums, especially minutes of 25 Mar. 1941; Fenyo, "The Record Group Concept," pp. 229–39; RAUS, 9:29–33.

5. RAUS, 8:25–27 and unpaged "Printed and Processed Material Issued by the National Archives"; RAUS, 9:29–31; RAUS, 10:35–37; RAUS, 11:22–24.

6. Meyer H. Fishbein, "A Viewpoint on Appraisal of National Records," pp. 176–77; Emmett J. Leahy, "Reduction of Public Records," p. 13.

7. Leahy, "Reduction of Public Records," pp. 13–28.

8. Philip C. Brooks, "The Selection of Records for Preservation," pp. 221–34. See also Helen L. Chatfield, "The Problem of Records from the Standpoint of Management," pp. 93–101.

9. Fishbein, "A Viewpoint on Appraisal of National Records," pp. 176–77; RG 64, Archivist 14.54, G. Philip Bauer, "An Essay on the Appraisal of Current and Recent Records," stamped "Received 22 Sept. 1944."

10. RAUS, 7:44, U.S., *Statutes at Large*, 55:581.

11. RG 64, Archivist 14, Connor to Accessions Advisory Committee, 22 Sept. 1939.

12. RG 64, Archivist—W. C. Grover file, M. W. Price to Connor, 20 Sept. 1940 and enclosures; Connor Journal, Vol. 5, 1 Oct. 1940; Philip C. Brooks, "Archives in the United States During World War II, 1939–1945," p. 276.

13. Waldo G. Leland, "The Archivist in Times of Emergency," pp. 1–12; Brooks, "Archives in the United States during World War II," pp. 264–65; *American Archivist* 4 (July 1941):210.

14. *American Archivist* 4 (July 1941):210, 212; 5 (Apr. 1942):124–25; Brooks, "Archives in the United States during World War II," p. 264.

15. Brooks, "Archives in the United States during World War II," p. 264; RAUS, 5.11–12, RAUS, 6.1–6, 16–18; RAUS, 7:8–12, 20–21.

16. Connor Journal, Vol. 5, 11 and 17 July 1941; OF 221, Connor to Roosevelt, 18 and 22 July 1941, Roosevelt to James Rowe, Jr., 21 July 1941, Roosevelt Papers.

17. OF 221, Roosevelt to James Rowe, Jr., 21 July 1941, Rowe to Roosevelt, 23 July 1941, Roosevelt to Rudolf Forster, 28 July 1941, Roosevelt Papers.

18. OF 221A, Bernard Kennedy, Thomas M. Owen, Jr., Ruth Bryan Rohde, and Joseph Broadman files, Roosevelt Papers; Secretary file (Ex.), Connor to G. S. Ford, 7 Aug. 1941, AHA Papers.

19. Secretary file (Ex.), Archivist of the U.S. folder 1941, AHA Papers; OF 221A, Solon J. Buck file, Roosevelt Papers.

20. For discussions of Connor and Buck, see RG 64, oral history transcripts of Herbert E. Angel, Robert H. Bahmer, Lester J. Cappon, Collas G. Harris, Thaddeus S. Page, Ernst Posner, Vernon D. Tate, and Karl L. Trever.

Chapter 8

1. RG 64, Archivist 71.1, C. G. Harris to W. E. Reynolds, 29 Sept. 1941, Archivist 71.3, S. J. Buck's note on Chief, Division of Building Management and Service to Executive Officer, 14 Nov. 1941, Harris to E. B. Morris, 3 June 1942, Harris to E. F. Addiss, 16 Sept. 1942, M. W. Price to Chiefs of Records Divisions, 28 Nov. 1942.

2. RG 64, Archivist 14, Buck to H. B. Mitchell, 17 Oct. 1941.

3. RG 64, Archivist 14 Special, C. G. Harris to H. D. Smith, 7 Oct. 1941; RG 51, Ser. 39.32, F7–21/41.1, Memorandum re conference with S. J. Buck, 29 Oct. 1941; RAUS, 8:v, 36–39.

4. RAUS, 9:42–45; RAUS, 10:ii, 52–57.

5. RAUS, 8:36–38; RAUS, 9:42–43; RAUS, 10:52; C. G. Harris file, Harris to S. J. Buck, 4 Nov. 1944, Buck to Harris, 22 Nov. 1944, Buck Papers.

6. RG 64, Statistical Issuances file. The composition of the statistics relating to service was changed in 1941, so there is no adequate basis for precise comparison with preceding years. It is also doubtful that all of the National Archives' divisions totaled things the same way on the new basis of reporting services rendered by telephone calls, letters, reports, personal conferences, loans to agencies, search room visits, and reproductions made.

7. RG 64, Thaddeus S. Page oral history transcript, pp. 8, 24, Vernon D. Tate oral history transcript, p. 18.

8. RG 64, Guy Lee oral history transcript, pp. 13–14, Archivist 13 Special, Minutes of Administrative Conference, 30 July 1942; RAUS, 7:40; RAUS, 8:40–41, RAUS, 9:43–46; RAUS, 10:54–56; RAUS, 11:37–38.

9. RG 64, Archivist 14, M. W. Price to Chiefs of Custodial Divisions and Chief, Reference Division, 29 Dec. 1941, Chief, Reference Division to Committee on Protection Against the Hazards of War, 16 Dec. 1941, Minutes of a Meeting of the Heads of Operating Units, 16 Feb. 1942.

10. RG 64, Archivist 14 Special, C. G. Harris to Buck, 3 Dec. 1941, Archivist 14, Harris to Buck, 13 Feb. 1942.

11. RG 64, Archivist 14, Minutes of a Meeting of the Heads of Operating Units, 16 Feb. 1942, Memorandum No. A–179, 16 Feb. 1942.

12. RG 64, Archivist 14, R. D. Hubbard to Buck, 21 Feb. 1942, C. G. Harris to Buck, 24 Feb. 1942, Archivist 14 Special, Survey folders, 18–21 Feb. 1942, Archivist 13 Special, Minutes of the Advisory Council, 2 Mar. 1942.

13. RG 64, Archivist 14, J. G. Bradley to Buck, 8 Dec. 1941, with Buck's note of 11 Mar. 1942, Archivist 71.1, Buck to Executive Officer, 21 Apr. 1942; RAUS, 8:2–9.

14. RG 64, Archivist 75, Buck to L. W. Crammer, 15 Apr., 4 Sept. 1942.

15. RG 200, Grover Papers, Budget Digest, Sept. 1948; RG 64, Archivist 10, Buck to H. D. Smith, 21 Sept. 1942, Wayne Coy to Buck, 16 Oct. 1942.

16. RAUS, 7:15–37; RAUS, 8:12–34; RAUS, 9:15–38; RAUS, 10:19–43; RAUS, 11:10–28.

17. RAUS, 8: unpaged section, "Printed and Processed Material Issued by the National Archives"; RAUS, 9:29, 48; RAUS, 10:58–59; RAUS, 11:29–30.

18. RG 64, Archivist 78, Roosevelt to Connor, 13 Feb. 1942, Archivist 82.2, Press Release 6, 10 Apr. 1942, Press Release 11, 23 June 1942; RAUS 7:5, 17.

19. RAUS, 8:8, 11, 33–34; RAUS, 9:39–40; RAUS, 10:44–45; RAUS, 11: 19, 24–25, 28, 41.

20. Edward G. Campbell, "Old Records in a New War," pp. 156–68; Philip C. Brooks, "Archives in the United States during World War II," p. 269.

21. Public Information Office, NARS, Press Releases, 1935–58.

22. RAUS, 8:24; RAUS, 9:52; RAUS, 11:21, 39; OF 221, Buck to Roosevelt, Oct. 12, 1942, Roosevelt Papers. During the war, the staff moved highly valuable documents to the lower levels in the center of the archives building.

23. RG 64, Archivist 71, C. G. Harris to Connor, 23 July 1940, Vernon D. Tate oral history transcript, p. 20, Archivist 75.3, Routing Slip, 28 May 1943, Archivist 71.1, Assistant to the Archivist to Buck, 10 May 1943; RAUS, 9:51.

24. RG 64, Archivist 41, especially P. M. Hamer to Archivist, 19 Mar. 1942, Memorandum A–183, 28 Mar. 1942, Minutes of Conference of Chiefs of Records Divisions, 5 July 1943, Official Circular No. 44–71, 10 May 1944, H. E. Edmunds to E. G. Campbell, 2 Oct. 1944.

25. RG 64, Archivist 71.1, C. J. Streeter to C. G. Harris, 5 Sept. 1942, M. W. Price to Buck, 30 Sept. 1942, Buck to Commissioner of Public Buildings, 24 Oct. 1942; RAUS, 9:50–52; RAUS, 10:60–61; RAUS, 11:40.

26. OF 221–B, Buck to Roosevelt, 27 July 1942, H. D. Smith to Roosevelt, 5 Dec. 1942, Roosevelt to Buck, 5 Dec. 1942, Roosevelt Papers; U.S., *Statutes at Large*, 56:1045.

27. E.g., RG 64, Archivist 44, Buck to G. F. Milton, 10 Feb. 1942.

28. RG 64, Archivist 29, S. J. Buck to Secretary of State, 22 June 1942, 18 Mar. 1943, 24 Apr. 1944, Buck to G. H. Shaw, 2 Sept. 1944; RAUS, 9:67; RAUS, 10:81.

29. RG 64, Archivist 44, P. M. Hamer to Buck, 19 Nov. 1942, Dan Lacy to Roosevelt, 8 Jan. 1944, Lacy to Henry Morgenthau, 7 Aug. 1944, Buck to H. D. Smith, 28 Feb. 1945, Archivist 14, Buck to Smith, 19 Oct. 1944; Brooks, "Archives in the United States during World War II," p. 272.

30. RG 64, Archivist 14, P. M. Hamer to Buck, 31 Dec. 1941, 22 Jan. 1942, Non-Government Organizations file, Buck to Director and Assistant Director, Records Accessioning and Preservation, 29 Jan. 1942; "Plans for the Historiography of the United States in World War II," pp. 243–45.

31. "Plans for the Historiography of the United States," pp. 245–52.

32. RG 64, Archivist 14, Buck to R. F. Nichols, 8 and 21 July 1942, Archivist 14.52, "Conference on a National War History Commission," 29 Dec. 1942, D. D. Irvine to Buck, 14 Nov. 1942, Dan Lacy to F. W. Shipman, 26 June 1943; Guy Stanton Ford, "Your Business," pp. 481–94; "Plans for the Historiography of the United States," pp. 249–51; Roosevelt to Ford, 17 Feb. 1944, reprinted in *American Historical Review* 49 (Apr. 1944):601.

33. *American Historical Review* 51 (Apr. 1946):578–79, 607–8; Walter Rundell, Jr., "Uncle Sam the Historian," pp. 3–20; National Archives file, R. F. Nichols to Connor, 28 Oct. 1940, P. M. Hamer to Buck, 22 Jan. 1942, Buck

Papers; RG 64, Archivist 14, Hamer to Buck, 31 Dec. 1941, P. W. Edsall to Director of Research and Records Description, 24 Mar. 1942.

34. RG 64, Archivist 19, Buck to Cordell Hull, 29 June 1942, Sumner Welles to Buck, 21 Sept. 1942; Emeterio S. Santovenia, "El Archivo Nacional de Cuba," pp. 59–60; RAUS, 10:45–46; RAUS, 11:32–33.

35. Oliver W. Holmes, "The National Archives and the Protection of Records in War Areas," pp. 110–111; Ernst Posner, "Public Records under Military Occupation," pp. 213–27. See also Gerald K. Haines, "Who Gives a Damn about Medieval Walls," pp. 97–106.

36. Holmes, "The Protection of Records in War Areas," pp. 111–16.

37. Ibid., pp. 111, 117–18; OF 221, F. W. Shipman to Roosevelt, 6 Jan. 1944, Roosevelt Papers; H. E. Bell, "Archivist Itinerant," pp. 172–73; see also Bell, "The Protection of Archives."

38. Holmes, "The Protection of Records in War Areas," pp. 119–22.

39. Ibid., pp. 122–27; RG 64, Archivist 19; Journal of Oliver W. Holmes, (in Dr. Holmes's possession), 5–9 Mar. 1945; American Archivist 10 (Oct. 1947): 399–400; 12 (July 1949):308–9; 17 (Apr. 1954):172.

40. Holmes, "The Protection of Records in War Areas," p. 126; American Archivist 8 (Apr. 1945):286.

41. National Archives file, "Statements of Dr. Solon J. Buck, Archivist of the United States; John L. Wells, Budget Officer; and Thad Page, Administrative Secretary," 17 and 21 Feb. 1944, pp. 348–80, 449–520, Buck Papers.

42. P file, S. J. Buck, "Some Notes on the Posner Affair," 1 March 1944, Buck Papers.

43. Mac file, Kenneth McKellar to Buck, 1 June 1944, Buck to McKellar, 5 June 1944, Buck Papers; RG 64, Administrative Secretary Correspondence, McKellar to Thad Page, 17 and 26 Jan. 1945, Page to McKellar, 24 Jan. 1945; Independent Offices Appropriation Bill for 1946, pp. 233–57.

44. Holmes Journal, 5–9 Mar. 1945; RG 64, Administrative Secretary Correspondence, W. B. Dinsmoor to O. W. Holmes, 16 Mar. 1945, Buck to Dinsmoor, 29 Mar. 1945; Lewinson, "The Two Careers of Ernst Posner," pp. 7–19; Wolfgang A. Mommsen, "Ernst Posner, Mittler Zwischen deutschem und amerikanischem Archivwesen," pp. 218–30; Philip C. Brooks, "The Archival Contributions of Ernst Posner," pp. 1–8.

45. RAUS, 8:47; RAUS, 11:43.

CHAPTER 9

1. Wayne C. Grover, "The National Archives at Age 20," pp. 99–100.

2. Solon J. Buck, "Let's Look at the Record," pp. 110–11; see also Edward G. Campbell, "The National Archives Faces the Future," pp. 441–43.

3. Wayne C. Grover, "A Note on the Development of Records Centers in the United States," pp. 160–63; RG 64, Archivist 21.5; Philip C. Brooks, "Archives in the United States during World War II," p. 267; American Archivist 4 (Apr. 1941):135.

4. Frank B. Evans, "Archivists and Records Managers," pp. 45–58; RAUS, 7:1–8; RAUS, 8:3–9.

5. RG 64, Archivist 23, Dorsey W. Hyde, Jr., "The Field Service Problem of the National Archives," 1 Apr. 1942, M. W. Price to F. R. Holdcamper, 25 Apr. 1942, Buck to Holdcamper, 16 Oct. 1942, G. L. Litton to Price, 21 May 1943, Buck to C. C. Crittenden, 23 June, 3 July 1943; *American Archivist* 5 (Apr. 1942):196, 6 (Oct. 1943):259; Oliver W. Holmes, "The Problem of Federal Field Office Records," pp. 84–90, 102–4.

6. RG 64, Archivist 21, Emmett J. Leahy, "Proposal Establishing Records Officers in Each of the Principal Departments and Agencies of the Federal Government and a Council of Records Administration in the Bureau of the Budget," 13 Apr. 1942, enclosed in Buck to H. D. Smith, 22 May 1942.

7. RG 64, Archivist 21, especially "Summary of Conference at the Bureau of the Budget, June 4, 1942, Concerning Proposed Designation of Records Officers and Establishment of a Records Council."

8. RG 64, Archivist 24, Buck to H. D. Smith, 5 Aug. 1942, and enclosed "Draft of An Act to Provide for the Disposal of Certain Records of the United States Government," F. J. Bailey to Buck, 22 Sept. 1942, Archivist 14, C. G. Harris to Buck, 26 Aug. 1942; Harris file, Harris to Buck, 21 Sept. 1942, Buck Papers; RG 51, National Archives General file, Ser. 39.1 N6.

9. RG 64, Archivist 24, Buck to F. J. Bailey, 22 Oct. 1942.

10. RG 64, Archivist 21, P. C. Brooks to Buck, 28 Nov. 1942, 3 June 1943, Paul Lewinson to Brooks, 25 Nov. 1942.

11. National Archives file, Buck to H. D. Smith, 14 Sept. 1942, Harris file, Buck to C. G. Harris, 4 Nov. 1942, Buck Papers.

12. OF 221, H. D. Smith to Roosevelt, 5 Nov. 1942, Roosevelt Papers.

13. OF 221, Wayne Coy to Rudolph Forster, 10 Nov. 1942, Roosevelt Papers; RG 64, Archivist 14, Roosevelt to Buck, 10 Nov. 1942.

14. RG 64, Archivist 40, especially P. M. Hamer to Buck, 18 Nov. 1942, R. D. Hubbard to Buck, 23 Nov. 1942, Herman Kahn to Buck, 23 Nov. 1942.

15. RG 64, Archivist 40, M. W. Price to Chiefs of Records Divisions, 18 Nov. 1942, Buck to Roosevelt, 23 Nov. 1942.

16. RAUS, 9:53–54; RAUS, 10:62–63.

17. OF 221, H. D. Smith to Roosevelt, 5 Nov. 1942, Roosevelt Papers; RG 64, Archivist 44, P. M. Hamer to Buck, 19 Nov. 1942, Archivist 40, Buck to Director of Records Accessioning and Preservation, 9 Dec. 1942.

18. RG 51, National Archives General file, Ser. 39.1 N6; U.S., *Statutes at Large*, 57:380–83; RAUS, 9:13–15; RG 64, Archivist 24, Buck to A. J. Elliott, 12 Feb. 1943.

19. U.S., *Statutes at Large*, 57:380–83.

20. RAUS, 10:70–71.

21. U.S., *Statutes at Large*, 59:434; RG 64, Archivist 24, Buck to H. D. Smith, 10 Nov. 1944, F. J. Bailey to Buck, 23 Nov. 1944; RAUS, 10:2; RAUS, 11:4, 11–13.

22. RAUS, 8:80; RAUS, 9:13, 59–60; RAUS, 10:69; RAUS, 11:51.

23. Philip C. Brooks, *The Functions of Records Officers in the Federal Government*, pp. 1–3; RG 64, Archivist 21, Brooks to E. F. Poeppel, 20 Feb. 1943.

24. RG 64, Archivist 21, P. C. Brooks to Buck, 3 June 1943, Buck to Brooks,

24 July 1943, Brooks to Buck 24 July 1943, Archivist 13, especially Official Circular No. 44–21, 18 Sept. 1943, Central Files 13.85, Minutes of Meeting of Open Conference on Administration, 3 July 1944.

25. Harris file, Buck to C. G. Harris, 1 Aug. 1944, Buck Papers; RG 64, Central Files 17.2, H. D. Smith to Buck, 23 Sept. 1944, Buck to Smith, 14 Oct. 1944.

26. RG 64, Archivist 14, Buck to H. D. Smith, 13 Dec. 1944.

27. RAUS, 11:passim; RG 64, Archivist 24.5, H. O. Brayer to Buck, 22 Dec. 1944, Dan Lacy to Brayer, 30 Dec. 1944, Archivist 22, Paul Lewinson to L. J. Cochrane, 22 Dec. 1944, 16 Feb. 1945, Central Files 22, Buck to Luther Gulick, 1 May 1945.

28. RAUS, 6:40, Brooks, *The Functions of Records Officers in the Federal Government*, pp. 2–3.

29. Emmett J. Leahy, "Records Administration and the War," pp. 97–108; Herbert E. Angel, "Highlights of the Field Records Program of the Navy Department," pp. 174–80; Ollon D. McCool, "The Metes and Bounds of Records Management," p. 87; Sherrod East, "Archival Experience in a Prototype Intermediate Repository," p. 43.

30. Wayne C. Grover, "A Note on the Development of Records Centers," pp. 160–63; Richard B. Morris, "The Federal Archives of New York City," p. 272; Jesse Dunsmore Clarkson, "Escape to the Present," p. 525; Connor Journal, vol. 5, 18 Sept. 1941; H. G. Jones, *The Records of a Nation*, p. 36.

31. Wayne C. Grover, "A Note on the Development of Records Centers in the United States," pp. 160–63; Robert H. Bahmer, "The National Archives after Twenty Years," pp. 200–01; RG 64, Robert H. Bahmer oral history transcript, p. 20; Herbert E. Angel, "Archival Janus," pp. 5–12. Angel points out that by 1943 England's Public Record Office established the first of several records repositories around London, although neither during nor after the war were they operated on as far-reaching a scale as those in the United States. It should also be mentioned that North Carolina pioneered in records management and center concepts on the state level during World War II, but its work did not affect developments in the federal government nor did it develop very substantially or successfully until after the war. See Fannie Memory Blackwelder, "The North Carolina Records Management Program," pp. 340–57; and Christopher Crittenden, "The North Carolina Records Center," pp. 53–57.

32. RG 64, Archivist—Memoranda to the Archivist, C. G. Harris to Buck, 5 Aug. 1942; Richard B. Morris, "The Need for Regional Repositories for Federal Records," pp. 115–22; Oliver W. Holmes, "The Problem of Federal Field Office Records," pp. 84–90, 95–97, 102–4; Thomas C. Mendenhall, "Carrying on," pp. 569–70.

33. RG 64, Archivist 23, Buck to R. B. Russell, 2 Oct. 1944.

34. *American Archivist* 8 (Jan. 1945):87; RAUS, 10:3–4; RAUS, 11:4.

35. Edward G. Campbell, "The National Archives Faces the Future," p. 441.

CHAPTER 10

1. *American Archivist* 4 (July 1941):215; RG 64, Archivist 14.54, C. G. Harris to Buck, 5 Aug. 1943, Minutes of Conference of Staff Officers, 5 May

1943, Archivist 14, D. W. Hyde, Jr., "The Place of the National Archives in Relation to State and Local Governments, Libraries, Museums and Research Institutions," 20 Mar. 1943, Buck to Hyde, 1 Apr. 1943, Hyde to Buck, 2 Apr. 1943; Archives file, 1944–47, Buck Papers; Isadore Perlman, "General Schedules and Federal Records," pp. 27–38; Oliver W. Holmes, "Areas of Cooperation Between the National Archives and State Archives," and William D. McCain, "Some Suggestions for National Archives Cooperation with the State Archives," pp. 213–28.

2. RG 64, Central Files 19.5; Henry E. Edmunds, "The Ford Motor Company Archives," p. 99.

3. RG 64, Archivist 14, D. W. Hyde, Jr., "Undeveloped Research Possibilities in the National Archives," 9 Apr. 1943, Archivist 14.5, Dan Lacy to Buck, 9 July 1943, with comments by S. J. Buck, 10 July 1943.

4. See Herman Kahn, "Records in the National Archives Relating to the Range Cattle Industry, 1865–1895," pp. 187–90; Carl J. Kulsrud, "The Archival Records of the Agricultural Adjustment Program," *Agricultural History* 22 (July 1948):197–204; Harold T. Pinkett, "Records in the National Archives Relating to the Social Purposes and Results of the Operation of the Civilian Conservation Corps," pp. 46–53; Thomas W. Owen, Jr., "How the National Archives Can Aid Genealogists," pp. 37–41.

5. W. Turrentine Jackson, "Materials for Western History in the Department of the Interior Archives," pp. 61–76.

6. RAUS, 12:25–34; RAUS, 13:19–26; RAUS, 14:21–33; RAUS, 15:19–31; RG 64, Statistical Issuances file, Archivist 15.4, T. R. Schellenberg et al. to Grover, 13 June 1957.

7. Archives file, 1944–47, Buck Papers; *American Archivist* 8 (Apr. 1945): 162; 9 (Oct. 1946):394; 11 (Apr. 1948):157–58; RAUS, 12:34–38; RAUS, 13:28–30; Solon J. Buck, "The Archivist's One World," p. 13.

8. RG 64, Archivist 19, *Proposal for the Establishment of a UN Archives.* For a fuller account of the National Archives' participation in the development of the UN Archives and the International Council on Archives, see Oliver W. Holmes, "Toward an International Archives Program and Council, 1945–1950," pp. 287–99.

9. Buck, "Archivist's One World," pp. 13–16; Robert Claus, "The United Nations Archives," pp. 129–32; Claus, "The Archives Program of the United Nations," pp. 195–202; Claus, "The Proposal for a United Nations Archival Agency," pp. 26–27; Purnendu Basu, "The United Nations Archives," pp. 105–18; Archives file, 1945–46, Buck Papers.

10. RAUS, 13:27–30; RG 64, Archivist 14.54, L. K. Born to Buck, 26 Aug. 1946, Buck to William Benton, 9 Sept. 1946, Archivist 19, H. P. Leverich to Buck, 30 Sept. 1946; Buck, "Archivist's One World," pp. 10–13, 17.

11. Buck, "Archivist's One World," pp. 17–18; Hilary Jenkinson, "An International Council on Archives," pp. 5–6; RAUS, 13:27.

12. Buck, "Archivist's One World," pp. 18–20; RAUS, 13:27–28; *American Archivist* 10 (Apr. 1947):210–11.

13. RAUS, 13:28; International Council on Archives file, Buck to E. J. Carter, 16 Jan. 1947, Buck to W. G. Leland, 10 June 1947, Buck Papers; *American Archivist* 10 (July 1947):227–31; Jenkinson, "International Council on Ar-

chives," pp. 6–8; Herbert O. Brayer, "Report on the Meeting of Professional Archivists Called by the United Nations Educational, Scientific, and Cultural Organization, June 9 to 11, 1948, Paris, France," pp. 325–28; RAUS, 14:33–34.

14. RAUS, 15:31–32; Margaret C. Norton, "The First International Congress of Archivists, Paris, France. August 21–26, 1950," pp. 13–32; "The First International Congress of Archivists," *Indian Archives* 5 (1951):54–59.

15. William J. Van Schreeven, "The International Congress on Archives, 1953," p. 37; Robert H. Bahmer, "The Third International Congress of Archivists," p. 159; Ernst Posner, "Round Table on Archives—Warsaw, 1961," p. 21.

16. Fritz Epstein, "Archives Administration in the Soviet Union," p. 144; Bahmer, "Third International Congress of Archivists," p. 155; Posner, "Round Table on Archives," pp. 15–23; RG 200, Grover Papers, Day file, Bogdan Popovich to Grover, 18 Nov. 1953, Grover to F. W. Shipman, 24 Dec. 1953, Grover to Popovich, 24 Dec. 1953.

17. *American Archivist* 5 (July 1952):276–77; Bahmer, "Third International Congress of Archivists," pp. 156, 160–61; Posner, "Round Table on Archives," pp. 16, 23.

18. RAUS, 13:27–28; RAUS, 14:34; Lester K. Born, "The Archives and Libraries of Postwar Germany," p. 50.

19. RG 64, Central Files 19.5; RAUS, 14:35; RAUS, 15:32; *American Archivist* 14 (Oct. 1951):366–69; 15 (Jan. 1952):71, 92; Society of American Archivists, *Directory of Individual and Institutional Members, 1970*, passim; e.g., Etienne Sabbe, "The Safekeeping of Business Records in Europe," Allen Horton, "Archival Backgrounds in New South Wales," G. Belov, "History that Lives again—Archives in the U.S.S.R.," Bogomir Chokel, "The Archives of Bulgaria," and Rodolfo Ramos Choto, "Los Archivos en El Salvador, C.A." G. Philip Bauer, Kenneth W. Munden, Harold T. Pinkett, Edward Weldon, and C. F. W. Coker were the staff members of the National Archives who succeeded Karl L. Trever as editors of the *American Archivist* to 1978.

20. See, for example, *Indian Archives* 3 (1949).

21. Bernard Wellbrenner, "The Public Archives of Canada, 1871–1958," pp. 101–13; W. Kaye Lamb, "The Fine Art of Destruction," pp. 54–55; Lamb, *Report of the Public Archives for the Year 1951*, passim; Lewis H. Thomas, "Provincial Archives in Canada," pp. 343–44; Wilfred I. Smith, "The Public Archives of Canada," p. 24.

22. *American Archivist* 14 (July 1951):271–2.

23. C. E. W. Bean, *First Annual Report of the Commonwealth Archives Commission*, passim; *American Archivist* 18 (Jan. 1955):86; H. L. White, "Foreword," and Theodore R. Schellenberg, "Preface," in Schellenberg, *Modern Archives*, pp. vii–xi.

24. *American Archivist* 18 (Jan. 1955):80–81; 19 (Jan. 1956):72; 21 (Oct. 1958):434–45; David S. MacMillan, "Archival Reform in Australia," pp. 210–13; MacMillan, "Business Archives," p. 123; MacMillan, "Archives in New South Wales," p. 52; Ian MacLean, "Australian Experience in Record and Archives Management," pp. 387–88.

25. T. R. Schellenberg to A. C. Schwarting and family, 7 July 1954, Schellenberg Papers. Sir Hilary had recently retired as the operating head of England's Public Record Office. His manual had originally been published in 1922, and

Percy Lund, Humphries & Co. of London had issued a revised edition of it in 1937.

26. Schellenberg, *Modern Archives*, passim. See also J. H. Collingridge's review in *Archives* 3 (Lady Day 1957):53, 56.

27. Philip C. Brooks, "Archival Heritage Meets Modern Records in Panama," pp. 151–59; T. R. Schellenberg to H. E. Angel, 8 Nov. 1954, Angel to Schellenberg, 12 Nov. 1954, Schellenberg Papers.

28. Theodore R. Schellenberg, "Applying American Archival Experience Abroad," pp. 33–38.

29. Diary, 3 Sept. 1962, Schellenberg Papers; RG 64, Planning and Control Case (hereafter referred to as P & C) No. 066–79, Register of Foreign Visitors, and Office of Records Management, RM (Gen.) Foreign Governments file; RG 200, Grover Papers, Day file, W. C. Grover to Staatsarchivrat Herzog, 9 July 1957; *American Archivist* 23 (Oct. 1960):477–78; Lloyd C. Gwam, "The First Permanent Building of the Nigerian National Archives," p. 67; Rhodesia and Nyasaland, the National Archives, *The National Archives and Your Records*.

30. See, for example, *American Archivist* 15 (Apr. 1952):172–73; 20 (Jan. 1957):84.

31. *American Archivist* 23 (Oct. 1960):465.

32. RG 64, P & C 062–131; George S. Ulibarri, "The Inter-American Technical Council on Archives," pp. 73–80.

33. Bahmer, "The Third International Congress of Archivists," p. 159; *American Archivist* 18 (Jan. 1955):74; E. E. Burke, "Some Archival Legislation of the British Commonwealth," pp. 280–82; John H. Collingridge, "Implementing the Grigg Report," pp. 179–84; Felix Hull, "'Modern Records' Then and Now," pp. 395–99.

34. Herbert E. Angel, "Archival Janus," p. 7; RG 200, Posner Papers, Wolfgang Mommsen to Ernst Posner, 20 Mar. 1967; Wilfred I. Smith, "Archives in Developing Countries," p. 155; Morris Rieger, "The Regional Training Center Movement," pp. 163–71; Ben Oliver, "R M is Becoming International," pp. 16–21; *Records Management Journal* 11 (Winter 1973):6. For further information on the development of French and German archival institutions, see Direction des Archives de France, *Manuel d' Archivistique*, and Kahlenberg, *Deutsche Archive in West und Ost*.

35. Robert W. S. Turner, "To Repair or Despair," pp. 327–28, 322, 325, with commentary by James L. Gear, pp. 329–34; Peter J. Scott, "The Record Group Concept," pp. 493–504, and discussion of this article in *American Archivist* 30 (Jan. 1967):239–40; 30 (July 1967):541–42.

36. Morris Rieger, "Archives for Scholarship," pp. 81–82; *American Archivist* 28 (July 1965):469–70; 29 (Jan. 1966):142.

37. Rieger, "Archives for Scholarship," pp. 83–84; *Archivum* 16 (1966):21–32, 35–40, 210–11, 79–99, 127–50; see also *National Archives Accessions*, no. 60 (Dec. 1967):67.

38. *Archivum* 16 (1966):passim, especially 232–27; H. G. Jones, *The Records of a Nation*, p. 240.

39. *American Archivist* 30 (July 1967):533–34; *Archivum* 18 (1968):17–20, 25–93.

40. *Archivum* 18 (1968):212–19.

41. Rieger, "Archives for Scholarship," p. 89.

42. Charles Kecskeméti, "The Spirit of Washington," pp. 133–38; Robert Claus, "The Proposal for a United Nations Archival Agency," p. 25.

CHAPTER 11

1. RG 64, Central Files 13.85, Minutes of Open Conference on Administration, 12 Mar. 1945.

2. New York Times, 7 June 1945; RAUS, 12:33–34; RAUS, 13:25–26; RAUS, 14:20–21, 25, 32–33; RAUS, 15:30–31.

3. RAUS, 12:39–41; RAUS, 13:32–33; RAUS, 14:37–39.

4. RG 64, Archivist 42, especially E. G. Campbell to Archivist, 17 Feb. 1947, National Archives Trust Fund Cases, R. H. Bahmer to R. P. Bieber, 7 June 1949; RAUS, 12:28, RAUS, 13:20–21; RAUS, 14:24–25; RAUS, 15:22–23; Albert H. Leisinger, "Microreproduction of Archives for Reference and Publication Purposes," pp. 135–39.

5. RAUS, 12:16–23; RAUS, 13:12–17; RAUS, 14:12–18, 27.

6. RAUS, 12:23–28; RAUS, 13:17–20; RAUS, 14:19–24.

7. RAUS, 12:1–16.

8. RG 64, Central Files 12.1, Official Circular No. 46–25, 22 Aug. 1945.

9. RAUS, 12:3–4; G. Philip Bauer, The Appraisal of Current and Recent Records, passim; RAUS, 14:1.

10. RAUS, 12:15, 25; RAUS, 13:18; RAUS, 15:18–19; RG 64, P & C 145–101, Endorsement Sheet, 29 Nov. 1945.

11. RG 64, Central Files 22, L. B. Hershey to Buck, 15 Nov. 1946, Buck to Hershey, 29 Nov. 1946, Dan Lacy to J. E. Webb, 26 Dec. 1946, P & C 047–151, P & C 047–166, Archivist 71.1, Lacy to W. E. Reynolds, 26 Dec. 1946, Buck to Reynolds, 26 Feb. 1947; RAUS, 14:11.

12. RG 64, Conferences-Councils-Meetings, Minutes of the Archivist's Conference, 7 and 14 Feb. 1947, Official Circular 48–15, 10 July 1947; RAUS, 13:40–41; RAUS, 14:19, 43–44; RAUS, 15:40.

13. RAUS, 13:11; RAUS, 14:10–11; RAUS, 15:10.

14. Irving P. Schiller, "The Archival Profession in Eclipse," pp. 227–33; OF 221, Buck to Truman, 18 Feb. 1946, Truman Papers.

15. RAUS, 12:12, 58–59; RG 64, Archivist 21 (1946); see also RG 64, Archivist 14, Lincoln Gordon to Buck, 19 Feb. 1946, Buck to Gordon, 28 Feb. 1946, Buck to H. D. Smith, 28 Feb. 1946.

16. RG 64, P & C 047–142, Archivist 21 and 82.1 (1946–49); RAUS, 12:11–12, 44–45; RAUS, 13:2–3, 6–13; RAUS, 14:7–10; RAUS, 15:7. Brooks, as chairman of the SAA's Committee on Records Administration, also wrote another influential booklet entitled Public Records Management.

17. RAUS, 13:1–2; RAUS, 14:6–9, 11–12. See also RG 64, Archivist 22.

18. RAUS, 12:2–3; OF 221, J. A. Kennedy to James Forrestal, 19 Mar. 1946, Forrestal to M. J. Connelly, 19 Mar. 1946, Connelly to E. A. Locke, Jr., 3 Apr. 1946, Truman to Buck, 4 June 1946, Buck to Truman, 29 July 1946, Truman to Buck, 10 Aug. 1946, Truman to J. E. Webb, 10 Aug. 1946, Truman Papers; RG 64, Archivist 14, Buck to P. H. French, 31 May 1946; RAUS, 13:3, 42.

19. RAUS, 13:3–4, 21; RAUS, 14:2, 5, 23–24.

20. Howard K. Beale, "The Professional Historian," pp. 238–39; Arthur M. Schlesinger, Jr., *The Imperial Presidency*, passim; E. O. 11652, 8 Mar. 1972.

21. That service to the federal government had the highest priority is documented in RG 64, Central Files 13.85, Minutes of Open Conference on Administration, 12 Mar. 1945, and in P & C 046–140 (7), Official Circular 46–91, 24 June 1946. Those seeking to establish or to maintain legal rights ranked second; scholars third; and others, such as journalists and novelists, fourth.

22. RG 64, Archivist 44, Dan Lacy to Buck, 5 Oct. 1945, E. G. Campbell to H. F. Angel, 27 Mar. 1947, W. C. Grover to K. C. Royall, 9 Mar., 8 Apr. 1948, Official Circular 46–83, 16 May 1946, P & C 047–141, Ken Hechler to Agency Historians, 6 Sept. 1946, P. C. Brooks to Dr. Noble, 3 Nov. 1947, P & C 047–167, especially Lacy to Buck, 19 Apr. 1947, Campbell to Ira Nunn, 8 July 1947, Buck to Alexander Wiley, 31 July 1947, and P & C 047–123.

23. RAUS, 14:31; *American Archivist* 16 (Oct. 1953):352–53. For a discussion of restrictions, see *Guide to the National Archives of the United States* (1974), pp. 11–17.

24. RG 64, Archivist's Controlled Project/Security, D. D. Eisenhower to Directors of Army General Staff Divisions and Chiefs of Army Special Staff Divisions, 20 Nov. 1947; Charles A. Beard, "Who's to Write the History of the War?", passim. See also Harry Elmer Barnes, *The Struggle Against the Historical Blackout*.

25. RAUS, 14:31, *Statutes at Large*, 62:58; Beale, "The Professional Historian," pp. 239–40.

26. Herman Kahn, "World War II and Its Background," pp. 149–62; Schlesinger, *The Imperial Presidency*, pp. 337–67.

27. RG 64, Archivist 14, Buck to R. A. Taft, 4 July 1945; American Historical Association, *Annual Report of the American Historical Association for the Year 1945*, 1:8.

28. *Washington Post*, 26 Jan. 1947; *New York Times*, 28, 29, 30 Jan. 1947, *Christian Science Monitor*, 29 Jan. 1947; *Washington Star*, 29 Jan. 1947.

29. RG 64, P & C 047–141, Dan Lacy to Buck, 27 Jan. 1947, Lacy to Kenneth Hechler, 3 Feb. 1947.

30. *New York Times*, 4, 12, 14 Feb. 1947; *Congressional Record*, 11 Feb. 1947, 93:1017–22.

31. *Chicago Tribune*, 21 Mar. 1947; *Washington Post*, 2, 8, 9, 26 May 1947; *New York Herald Tribune*, 9 May 1947; *Washington Star*, 26 May 1947.

32. *New York Times*, 22 July 1947; *Eighth Annual Report of the Franklin D. Roosevelt Library*, p. 1; RG 64, P & C 048–91, Buck to Owen Brewster, 25 July 1947.

33. RG 64, P & C 047–141, Dan Lacy to G. M. Elsey, 24 Mar. 1947; Elsey to C. M. Clifford, 15 Oct. 1947, Elsey Papers.

34. RAUS, 13:51.

35. *Washington Post*, 21 Dec. 1945; RG 64, Archivist 17.2, "Organizational Changes in the National Archives Since September 18, 1941," 29 May 1947, P & C 046–130, memoranda of 21, 26, 28, 29 Dec. 1945, Buck to H. D. Smith, 21 Jan. 1946.

36. RG 51, Ser. 39.32, F7–21/41.1, Buck to John Keddy, 17 June 1946; RG

64, Archivist—Lacy files, Dan Lacy to Buck, 15 Aug. 1946, P & C 046–130, Buck to J. E. Webb, 7 Oct. 1946; National Archives file, Lacy to Buck, 20 Aug. 1946, Buck Papers.

37. RAUS, 13:iv, 33–36; RAUS, 12:iv; RG 64, Central Files 12.1, Official Circular 47–27, 31 Dec. 1946, Archivist 17.2, "Organizational Changes in the National Archives Since September 18, 1941," 29 May 1947, Conferences-Councils-Meetings, Minutes of the Archivist's Conference, 24 Jan., 23 May, 27 June 1947.

38. National Archives file, "Why the National Archives Needs More Money," 20 Jan. 1947, Buck to John Phillips, 27 May 1947, Buck Papers; RG 64, Archivist 17.2, Buck to E. M. Dirksen, 3 Feb. 1947.

39. RG 64, Director of Operations and Assistant Archivist, Dan Lacy to Buck, 4 June 1947; National Archives file, a former employee to Buck, 24 May 1947, Buck to John Phillips, 27 May 1947, Buck Papers.

40. RG 64, Central Files 82.3, Background Material Notebook (1948), Archivist 17.2 and 17.4, Dan Lacy to Buck, 13 June 1947. The budget was so tight that the archivist asked his executive staff if the National Archives should continue to provide free reference service to private citizens. No decision was made to charge for such service. RG 64, Conferences-Councils-Meetings, Minutes of the Archivist's Conference, 27 June 1947.

41. National Archives file, Buck to R. B. Wigglesworth, 18 June 1947, Dan Lacy to F. P. Graham, 18 June 1947, Buck to G. S. Ford, 19 June 1947, "Statement of Dr. Solon J. Buck. . . . Before the Independent Offices Subcommittee of the Senate Appropriations Committee," 23 June 1947, Buck Papers; *New York Times*, 25 June 1947.

42. RG 64, Director of Operations and Assistant Archivist, Dan Lacy to Buck, 10 July 1947, Central Files 82.3, Background Material Notebook (1948); National Archives file, Buck to Wigglesworth (draft), 14 July 1947, Buck to J. P. Boyd, 8 Aug. 1947, Buck Papers.

43. *New York Times*, 1 Aug. 1947; OF 221, Buck to D. S. Dawson, 23 Apr. 1948, Truman Papers.

44. RAUS, 14:2, 21–22, 41; RG 64, P & C 048–105 and 046–130; National Archives file, W. C. Grover to Buck, 2, 17 Oct. 1947, Buck Papers.

45. RG 64, George M. Elsey oral history transcript, p. 2; OF 221–A, Buck to D. S. Dawson, 24 Mar. 1948, Truman Papers.

46. Library of Congress file, L. H. Evans to Buck, 28 Apr. 1948, Buck Papers; OF 221, Buck to D. S. Dawson, 18 Apr. 1948, Dawson to Truman, 12 May 1948, Buck to Truman, 12, 27 May 1948, Truman to Buck, 13, 28 May 1948, Truman Papers.

Chapter 12

1. OF 221, Buck to D. S. Dawson, 18, 23 Apr. 1948, Dawson to Truman, 12 May 1948, OF 221–A, E. D. Thomas to Truman, 10 May 1948, A. V. Watkins to Truman, 11 May 1948, Truman Papers; *Washington Post*, 14 Aug. 1948; *New York Times*, 14 May, 4 June 1948.

2. *American Archivist* 11 (July 1948):274; *New York Times*, 23 Jan. 1966.

3. RAUS, 14:44; RAUS, 15:13–17, 31, 37, 40–41.

4. RAUS, 15:5–11.

5. Ibid., 11, 39–40.

6. Ibid., 6, 17–23, 30; RG 64, Archivist 46–A.

7. RAUS, 15:30–31, 34–36, 6, 23–29; RG 64, Statistical Issuances.

8. RAUS, 15:3, 5, 10–11, 40; RG 64, Conferences-Councils-Meetings, Minutes of the Archivist's Conference, 23 Nov., 21 Dec. 1948, 8 Mar. 1949; Wayne C. Grover, "Recent Developments in Federal Archival Activities," p. 5.

9. RG 64, Conferences-Councils-Meetings, Minutes of the Archivist's Conference, 23 Nov. 1948, 29 Mar., 10 May 1949, Central Files 12.1, Official Circular 49–36, 15 Dec. 1948.

10. Oliver W. Holmes, "The National Archives at a Turn in the Road," p. 340; Robert W. Krauskopf, "The Hoover Commissions and Federal Recordkeeping," pp. 374–75.

11. Grover, "Recent Developments in Federal Archival Activities," p. 9; Holmes, "The National Archives at a Turn in the Road," pp. 347–48; Krauskopf, "The Hoover Commissions and Federal Recordkeeping," pp. 375–76; RG 64, Archivist 21, W. C. Grover to F. P. Brassor, 3 Mar. 1948, E. J. Leahy to H. E. Miller, 23 Mar. 1948; RG 264, "Records of the Commission on the Organization of the Executive Branch of the Government" (hereafter cited as RG 264), Research and Library Section, Records Management folder, Pearson Winslow to S. A. Mitchell, 10 Mar. 1948; Commission on Organization of the Executive Branch of the Government, *Records Management in the United States Government*, p. 2.

12. Commission on Organization of the Executive Branch, *Records Management in the United States Government*, pp. 1–2, 4, 8–12, 39–40; Krauskopf, "The Hoover Commissions and Federal Recordkeeping," pp. 377–78.

13. RG 200, Grover Papers, Hoover Commission file, Herbert Hoover to W. C. Grover, 22 Oct. 1948, Grover to Hoover, 2 Nov. 1948; RG 64, Conferences-Councils-Meetings, Minutes of the Archivist's Conferences, 21 Dec. 1948, P & C 050–77, Thaddeus Page to Grover, 5 Jan. 1949, Page memorandum, 6 Jan. 1949; interview with Robert H. Bahmer, Washington, D.C., 19 June 1974; Grover, "Recent Developments in Federal Archival Activities," pp. 6–12.

14. RG 51, Ser. 39.32, F2–81/49.1, R. C. Atkinson to Arnold Miles, 15 Apr. 1948, "Reorganization of the Executive Branch," 16 Apr. 1948, Atkinson, "Draft—A Plan for the Reorganization of the Executive Branch of the Government," 12 May 1948.

15. Interview with R. H. Bahmer, 19 June 1974; Holmes, "The National Archives at a Turn in the Road," p. 348; RG 64, P & C 049–106; RG 264, Executive Director, Records Management folder, Grover to Herbert Hoover, 28 Jan. 1949. For a trenchant criticism of the Leahy report, see Krauskopf, "The Hoover Commissions and Federal Recordkeeping," pp. 379–82.

16. RG 264, Project File 22, Records Management folder, J. D. Millett to S. A. Mitchell, 26 Oct. 1948; Krauskopf, "The Hoover Commissions and Federal Recordkeeping," p. 378; Commission on Organization of the Executive Branch of Government, *Office of General Services—Supply Activities*, pp. 3, 8, 12–13; H. R. 2641 and S. 991, Eighty-first Congress, First Session.

17. RG 64, Conferences-Councils-Meetings, Discussion at the Archivist's Conference, 15 Feb. 1949, and P & C 049–106.

18. RG 64, Conferences-Councils-Meetings, Minutes of the Archivist's Conference, 8, 9, 17 Mar. 1949, and P & C 049–106.

19. RG 200, Grover Papers, Hoover Commission file, Grover to Truman, 21 Mar. 1949, Grover to Buck, 24 Mar. 1949; RG 64, P & C 049–106, Grover, Statement Relating to the Hoover Commission Report on Records Management, 21 Mar. 1949, P. C. Brooks to Grover, 23 Nov. 1949; interview with Oliver W. Holmes, Washington, D.C., 29 Dec. 1974.

20. RG 51, Ser. 39.32, F1–20/46.1, R. C. Atkinson to C. B. Stauffacher, 25 Mar. 1949; RG 200, Grover Papers, Hoover Commission file, Grover to Buck, 24 Mar. 1949.

21. RG 51, Ser. 39.32, F1–20/46.1, Frank Pace, Jr., to Truman, 28 Mar. 1949; Commission on Organization of the Executive Branch of Government, *Office of General Services–Supply Activities*, pp. 3, 12–13.

22. Holmes, "The National Archives at a Turn in the Road," p. 349; RG 64, Archivist 00, R. H. Bahmer to J. L. McClellan, 28 June 1949, P & C 049–106, W. C. Grover to Bahmer, 20 May 1949, Conferences-Councils-Meetings, Minutes of the Archivist's Conference, 3 and 10 May 1949.

23. Holmes, "The National Archives at a Turn in the Road," pp. 349–50; RG 64, George M. Elsey oral history transcript, p. 5, P & C 049–106, P. C. Brooks to Grover, 23 Nov. 1949; RG 51, Ser. 39.32, F 1–20/46.1; U.S., *Statutes at Large*, 63:377.

24. Holmes, "The National Archives at a Turn in the Road," pp. 350–54; *American Archivist* 12 (Apr. 1949):205.

Chapter 13

1. General Services Administration, *Report of the Administrator of General Services to the Congress, July Through December 1949*, p. 2 (hereafter cited as RAGS with the appropriate date); Oliver W. Holmes, "The National Archives at a Turn in the Road," p. 350; Bill file, H. R. 4754, Truman to Larson, 30 June 1949, Truman Papers; RG 64, Central Files 12.1, Official Circular 50–5, 7 July 1949.

2. RG 200, Grover Papers, Personal files, Grover to Preston, 2 Aug. 1949; RG 269, "Records of the General Services Administration" (hereafter cited as RG 269), Administrator, Correspondence file (Historical), Administrative Order 27, 1 Dec. 1949; RG 64, Archivist 15.4, Grover to Assistant Archivist and Administrative Officer, 30 Oct. 1950, Central Files 12.1, Official Circular 50–5, 7 July 1949.

3. RG 64, Conferences-Councils-Meetings, Minutes of the Archivist's Conference, 2 Dec. 1949.

4. RAUS, 15:41–42; Wayne C. Grover, "Recent Developments in Federal Archival Activities," pp. 9–10; RG 64, Conferences-Councils-Meetings, Minutes of the Archivist's Conference, 16 Aug. 1949, 2 Nov. 1951.

5. RAGS, July–December 1949, p. 36; Grover, "Recent Developments in Federal Archival Activities," pp. 8–11.

6. RG 64, P & C 050–77, Thaddeus Page memoranda, 6 Jan. 1949, 14 June 1949, R. H. Bahmer to Chet Holifield, 14 June 1949, Archivist 00, Bahmer to

Holifield, 22 June 1949, Bahmer to J. L. McClellan, 28 June 1949; RAGS, July–December 1949, p. 36; RG 51, Ser. 39.32, F 1–20/46.1.

7. RG 64, P & C 050–77, Thaddeus Page memorandum, 8 July 1949; RG 200, Grover Papers, GSA file, Grover to Larson, 14, 25, 26 July 1949, Transcript of telephone conversation between Grover and Larson, 10 Aug. 1949.

8. RG 64, P & C 050–77, Thaddeus Page to Grover, 31 Aug., 14 Sept. 1949, 9 Jan. 1950; RG 200, Grover Papers, GSA file, Grover to Larson, 7 Oct. 1949.

9. RG 64, P & C 050–77; Grover, "Recent Developments in Federal Archival Activities," pp. 11–12; Bill file, S. 3959, Russell Forbes to F. J. Lawton, 1 Sept. 1950, Lindsay Warren to Lawton, 5 Sept. 1950, Truman Papers; U.S., *Statutes at Large*, 64:583.

10. U.S., *Statutes at Large*, 64:583.

11. Robert W. Krauskopf, "The Hoover Commissions and Federal Record-keeping," pp. 384–85; RAGS 1951, p. 5; U.S., *Statutes at Large*, 64:583.

12. RG 64, P & C 049–106, Grover to R. H. Bahmer, 20 May 1949.

13. RAUS, 15:50–51; Herbert E. Angel, "Federal Records Management since the Hoover Commission Report," pp. 15–17; Isadore Perlman, "General Schedules and Federal Records," p. 28; *American Archivist* 15 (Apr. 1952):182; RAGS 1952, pp. 59–61.

14. Caskie Stinnett, "Lacking Wastebaskets, Bureaucrats Have to 'Downgrade' Their Debris," p. 12; William Knapp, "Death of a Document," p. 38; Helen L. Chatfield, "Records and the Administrator," pp. 119–22.

15. National Archives, *The Federal Records Problem*, passim; *Washington Star*, 21 Oct. 1949; RAGS, July–December 1949, pp. 37–39.

16. RG 64, Conferences-Councils-Meetings, Minutes of the Archivist's Conference, 27 Jan. 1950; *American Archivist* 36 (Oct. 1973):636–38.

17. RG 64, Conferences-Councils-Meetings, Minutes of the Archivist's Conference, 3 Mar. 1950.

18. RAGS 1950, pp. 52–59; RG 64, Conferences-Councils-Meetings, Minutes of the Archivist's Conference, 7 June 1950.

19. RAGS 1951, pp. 6, 12–13; RG 64, Archivist 17.2, Recommended Forecast of Programs Fiscal Year 1954, 21 Apr. 1952; RG 200, Grover Papers, GSA file, R. H. Bahmer to Administrator, 27 Feb. 1950, W. C. Grover to Deputy Administrator, 18 July 1950; *American Archivist* 17 (July 1954):282; Angel, "Federal Records Management Since the Hoover Commission Report," pp. 18–19; Interview with R. H. Bahmer, Washington, D.C., 19 June 1974.

20. Angel, "Federal Records Management since the Hoover Commission Report," p. 18; RAGS 1953, pp. 30–34; Everett O. Alldredge, "The Federal Records Center, St. Louis," p. 113; *American Archivist* 17 (Jan. 1954):73, RG 64, Records Management Office, Alldredge to Deputy Regional Directors, 13 May 1955.

21. RG 64, Archivist 17.2, Recommended Forecast of Programs Fiscal Year 1954, 21 Apr. 1952; RG 200, Grover Papers, Day file, Grover to Director, Records Management Division, 23 June 1953, Alphabetical Correspondence file, Grover to R. B. Bradford, 9 Mar. 1951; Jim Lum to Brooks, 11 Jan. 1955, Brooks Papers; Interview with W. D. White, Kansas City, Mo., 21 Nov. 1973; Angel, "Federal Records Management since the Hoover Commission," pp. 18–19; Interview with R. H. Bahmer, 19 June 1974.

22. RG 64, P & C 051–78, R. G. Bahmer to Larson, 8 Sept. 1950, Grover to Larson, 18 Sept. 1950, Minutes of Federal Records Council, 19 June 1951, 14 May 1953.

23. Angel, "Federal Records Management since the Hoover Commission Report," pp. 16–17, 22–26; Krauskopf, "The Hoover Commissions and Federal Recordkeeping," p. 385; RAGS 1952, pp. 60–61.

24. RAGS 1953, pp. 26–34; RAGS 1954, pp. 11–19.

25. Wayne C. Grover, "The National Archives at Age Twenty," pp. 100–101.

26. RG 64, P & C 055–59, W. C. Grover to Assistant to the Administrator, 14 Oct. 1953.

CHAPTER 14

1. RG 200, Grover Papers, Day file, Grover to M. L. Radoff, 1 Feb. 1954; Wayne C. Grover, "Recent Developments in Federal Archival Activities," pp. 5–7, 10–11; Grover, "The National Archives at Age Twenty," pp. 102, 105.

2. RG 64, Central Files 12.1, Official Circular 50–33, 31 Mar. 1950.

3. RG 200, Grover Papers, GSA file, Grover to Larson, 14 July, 7 Oct. 1949, Grover and Larson telephone transcript, 10 Aug. 1949, Day file, Grover to J. A. Klein, 21 Oct. 1954, 1 July 1957; RG 64, Marcus W. Price oral history transcript; RAGS 1952, p. 76; RAGS 1953, p. 41; RAGS 1954, p. 29; RAGS 1955, pp. 52–53; RAGS 1956, p. 33; RAGS 1957, p. 9.

4. RG 64, Conferences-Councils-Meetings, Minutes of the Archivist's Conference, 27 July 1949, 28 June 1950, 2 Nov. 1951; RAGS 1950, pp. 63, 65; RAGS 1951, pp. 14, 17; RAGS 1952, pp. 72, 75.

5. RG 200, Grover Papers, GSA file, Grover to Larson, 7 Oct. 1949.

6. Staff Member, NA, Personal Observations file, Statement made in 1950 in defense of my plans of administering the National Archives, Schellenberg Papers.

7. Frank B. Evans, "Modern Methods of Arrangement of Archives in the United States," pp. 257–58.

8. RAGS 1950, pp. 59–61; RAGS 1951, pp. 18–21; RAGS 1952, pp. 70–72; RAGS 1953, pp. 34–35; RAGS 1954, pp. 20–21; RAGS 1955, pp. 50–52.

9. RAGS 1952, p. 76; RAGS 1953, p. 41; RAGS 1954, p. 28–29; RAGS 1956, p. 33.

10. RAGS 1950, p. 61; RAGS 1951, p. 21; RAGS 1952, p. 76; RAGS 1953, pp. 40–41; RAGS 1954, p. 29; RAGS 1955, p. 53; RAGS 1956, p. 34; RAGS 1957, p. 9.

11. RAGS 1950, pp. 63–65; RAGS 1951, pp. 16–18; RAGS 1952, pp. 74–75; RAGS 1953, pp. 38–40; RAGS 1954, pp. 26–28; RAGS 1955, pp. 53–54.

12. RAGS 1950, pp. 65–66; RAGS 1951, pp. 14–15; RAGS 1952, p. 72; RAGS 1953, pp. 36–37; RAGS 1954, pp. 22–24; RAGS 1955, pp. 55–56; RAGS 1956, pp. 37–38; RG 64 Archivist 15.4, Grover to Director of Archival Management, 2 Oct. 1951. T. R. Schellenberg to Grover, 13 June 1957; Etienne Sabbe, "Les Archives de l'État," p. 37.

13. Boyd C. Shafer, "Lost and Found," pp. 220, 222–223; Lester J. Cappon, "Tardy Scholars among the Archives," pp. 6, 15–16; David C. Duniway, "On the Use of Archives by Historians," pp. 285–86.

14. RG 200, Grover Papers, Day file, Grover to Director of Archival Management, 26 June 1952; RAUS, 15:31; RAGS 1950, pp. 65–66; RAGS 1951, pp. 16, 18; RAGS 1954, p. 28; RAGS 1956, pp. 38–39; RAGS 1957, p. 12.

15. Grover, "The National Archives at Age 20," p. 103; Milton O. Gustafson, "The Empty Shrine," pp. 273–85; RG 64, P & C 052–114, Grover, Memo for Record, 29 Aug. 1952, Grover to Evans, 24 Jan. 1952, Evans to Grover, 5 May 1952, Grover to Evans, 15 May 1952; *Information Bulletin, Library of Congress* 11 (5 May 1952).

16. RG 64, P & C 052–114, L. H. Evans to Grover, 5 May 1952, Grover, Memo for Record, 29 Aug. 1952, Release GSA–188, 7 Dec. 1952; OF 2310–I, Truman Papers; RG 200, Grover Papers, Day file, Grover to Assistant to the Administrator, 14 Oct. 1953; *American Archivist* 16 (Apr. 1953):180; Gustafson, "The Empty Shrine," pp. 271–72.

17. C. E. Carter to A. R. Newsome, 2 Mar. 1935, Carter Papers; Connor to Newsome, 22 Mar. 1935, Connor Papers; Clarence E. Carter, "The Territorial Papers of the United States," pp. 510, 512.

18. C. E. Carter to G. B. Noble, 10 Feb. 1949, Carter Papers; RG 64, P & C 050–103, Grover to Assistant Archivist, 19 Jan. 1950, Grover to Larson, 25 Jan. 1950; *Washington Star*, 13 Mar. 1950.

19. RG 64, P & C 050–103, Release GSA–65, 30 June 1950; Bill file, S. 2348, 7 July 1950, Truman Papers; C. E. Carter Memorandum, 16 Nov. 1950, Carter Papers; RAGS 1950, p. 64; RAGS 1951, p. 17; RAGS 1954, p. 28; RAGS 1956, p. 37.

20. RG 64, Conferences-Councils-Meetings, Minutes of the Archivist's Conference, 9 Sept. 1949, Archivist 15.4, Grover to Assistant Archivist, 30 Oct. 1950, Grover to Director of Archival Management, 28 May 1951.

21. RG 64, Conferences-Councils-Meetings, Minutes of the Archivist's Conference, 6 Apr. 1951, P & C 056–77, I. H. Nunn to R. R. Hughes, 1 Nov. 1955, R. H. Bahmer to Floete, 27 June 1956; *American Archivist* 17 (Jan. 1954):73; RAGS, 1953, pp. 91–92; RAGS 1956, pp. 96–97; RAGS 1957, pp. 82–83.

22. *Washington Post*, 1 Dec. 1952; RG 64, P & C 054–109.

23. RG 64, Archivist 17.2, Recommended Forecast of Programs FY 1954, 21 Apr. 1952, Statistical Issuances, National Archives Personnel; Staff Member, NA, Analytical Reports, T. R. Schellenberg et al. to Grover, 5 Sept. 1956, Schellenberg Papers; RG 200, Grover Papers, GSA file, Grover to Mansure, 27 Aug. 1953; *American Archivist* 17 (Jan. 1954):72; RG 269, Administrator, General Subject Files, Organization and Management 7, NARS, Annual Report on Management Improvement Program, enclosed in Grover to Director, Office of Management, 30 July 1954.

24. RG 64, Conferences-Councils-Meetings, Minutes of the Archivist's Conference, 2 Nov. 1951, Quarterly and Annual Reports, Report on Archival Developments by the Director of Archival Management for Fiscal Year 1952.

25. RG 200, Grover Papers, GSA file, Grover to Director, Office of Management, 3 July 1953, G. Philip Bauer, "Recruitment, Training, and Promotion in the National Archives," pp. 298–303.

26. Bauer, "Recruitment, Training, and Promotion in the National Archives," pp. 304–5; Staff Member, NA, Analytical Reports, T. R. Schellenberg et al. to Grover, 5 Sept. 1956, Schellenberg Papers; *American Archivist* 19 (Oct. 1956): 374.

CHAPTER 15

1. RAGS 1950, pp. 66–69; RAGS 1951, pp. 23–26; RAGS 1952, pp. 77–80; RAGS 1953, pp. 42–44; RAGS 1954, pp. 30–32; RAGS 1955, pp. 57–59; RAGS 1956, pp. 39–41.

2. OF 158–D, W. L. Langer and S. E. Gleason to Truman, 6 Dec. 1948, G. M. Elsey to Grover, 20 Dec. 1948, Grover to Elsey, 22 Dec. 1948, Truman Papers; RG 64, Archivist—Roosevelt Library file, Herman Kahn to Grover, 2 Sept. 1952, Laughlin Currie to Kahn, 4 Jan. 1950, S. I. Rosenman to Kahn, 18 Jan. 1950, Kahn to Grover, 20 Jan. 1950.

3. *New York Herald Tribune*, 18 Mar. 1950; RAGS 1950, pp. 69–72; RAGS 1952, p. 81; RAGS 1954, p. 34; RAGS 1955, pp. 59–61; RG 64, Archivist—Roosevelt Library file, E. B. Nixon to Herman Kahn, 25 Oct. 1951, R. H. Bahmer to Kahn, 4 Jan. 1952.

4. See the reports of the secretary of the National Historical Publications Commission in the second through the fifteenth *Annual Report of the Archivist of the United States*, and Robert L. Brubaker, "The Publication of Historical Sources," pp. 195–96.

5. RG 200, Grover Papers, GSA file, Grover to Larson, 26 July 1949; RAGS 1951, p. 29; RAGS 1950, p. 72; Brubaker, "The Publication of Historical Sources," pp. 194–96; *Public Papers of the Presidents of the United States, Harry S. Truman, 1950*, pp. 416–18; RG 64, Central Files 06, Chairman, National Historical Publications Commission, to Chet Holifield, 27 June 1950.

6. RAGS 1951, pp. 28–31; *American Archivist* 14 (Oct. 1951):370–72.

7. RAGS 1952, p. 85; *Mississippi Valley Historical Review* 39 (Sept. 1952): 284; *American Historical Review* 58 (Apr. 1953):767.

8. L. Q. Mumford to the Librarian, 7 Mar. 1955 (in the author's possession); RAGS 1955, pp. 61–62; Brubaker, "The Publication of Historical Sources," pp. 194, 200, 210–15.

9. Charles W. Porter, III, "Documentary Research Methods Applied to Historic Sites and Buildings," pp. 205–6; Oliver W. Holmes, "Areas of Cooperation Between the National Archives and State Archives," pp. 213–22; William D. McCain, "Some Suggestions for National Archives Cooperation with the State Archives," pp. 223–28; Katherine E. Brand, "Developments in the Handling of Recent Manuscripts in the Library of Congress," pp. 101–3; Lester J. Cappon, "The Archival Profession and the Society of American Archives," pp. 197–203; Henry E. Edmunds, "The Ford Motor Company Archives," p. 99; *American Archivist* 17 (Jan. 1954):90–91.

10. RG 64, P & C 051–83; *Mississippi Valley Historical Review* 38 (Sept. 1951):370–71; 41 (Sept. 1954):308; 42 (Sept. 1955):294; Wayne C. Grover, "The National Archives at Age 20," pp. 99–107; *American Historical Review* 57 (Apr. 1952):839–40; 64 (Oct. 1958):248–49; 65 (Jan. 1960):477–78; RG 200, Grover Papers, AHA file.

11. *American Historical Review* 58 (Apr. 1953):779; Professional Correspondence file, D. C. Duniway to Douglas McKay, 16 Feb., 2 Mar. 1953, Schellenberg Papers; Grover to W. G. Leland, 7 Jan. 1953, Leland to G. S. Ford, 9 Jan. 1953, Leland Papers.

12. GF 48–F–1, Eisenhower Papers.

13. Ibid.; *Mississippi Valley Historical Review* 40 (Sept. 1953):396–97.

14. OF 23, especially [GSA] Staff Meeting, Washington, D.C., 4 May 1953, enclosed in E. F. Mansure to W. B. Persons, 7 May 1953, and GF 48–F–1, Eisenhower Papers; RG 200, Posner Papers, Grover file, C. E. Carter to Ernst Posner, 20 May 1953, M. L. Radoff to Posner, 2 June 1953, Posner to Mansure, 22 May 1953; W. G. Leland to G. S. Ford, 31 May, 4 June, 19 June 1953, Leland Papers; RG 64, Director of Archival Management, Correspondence: Domestic, T. R. Schellenberg to G. L. Anderson, 20 May 1953, Schellenberg to W. E. Lingelbach, 20 May 1953. The later rumor that Schellenberg worked to remove Grover in 1953 is unsupported by the documentation in his personal papers, the Eisenhower papers, and the records of the National Archives.

15. OF 23, Staff Meeting, Washington, D.C., 4 May 1953, enclosed in E. F. Mansure to W. B. Persons, 7 May 1953, Mansure to Cabinet, 26 June 1953, Eisenhower Papers; RG 64, P & C 055–59, Mansure to Grover et al., 8 May, 21 Aug. 1953; RG 200, Grover Papers, GSA file, B. I. Shacklette to W. C. Grover, 6 Nov. 1953, Day file, Grover to Director, Office of Management, 2 Sept. 1955.

16. RG 200, Grover Papers, Day file, Grover to M. L. Radoff, 1 Feb. 1954, Trust Fund Plans file, memorandum of 7 Apr. 1953, Grover to H. E. Edmunds, 7 Jan., 1 Feb. 1954, Grover to Ernst Posner, 13 June, 14 Sept. 1956, L. J. Cappon to Grover, 1 June 1957.

17. Ernst Posner, "The National Archives and the Archival Theorist," 207–16.

CHAPTER 16

1. Robert W. Krauskopf, "The Hoover Commissions and Federal Record-keeping," pp. 385–89.

2. Ibid., pp. 390–92; Commission on Organization of the Executive Branch of the Government, *Paperwork Management, Part I, in the United States Government, A Report to the Congress*, pp. 3, 5–21; Everett O. Alldredge, "Records Centers," pp. 2–3.

3. RG 64, Office of Records Management, E. O. Alldredge to Deputy Regional Directors, 22 Apr. 1955; General Services Administration, *Annual Report on the Management Improvement Program, Fiscal Year 1955*, p. 27.

4. Krauskopf, "The Hoover Commissions and Federal Recordkeeping," pp. 393–94; RG 64, Quarterly Reports, Records Management Division, Report to the Archivist for the Quarter Ending 30 Sept. 1955.

5. Krauskopf, "The Hoover Commissions and Federal Recordkeeping," pp. 394–98; RG 64, P & C 056–77, Scope of GSA Authority and Responsibility in RM, Fiscal Year 1956.

6. RG 64, Office of Records Management, RM (General), H. E. Angel to Christopher Crittenden, 24 Oct. 1957; *Washington Star*, 12 Sept. 1956. In 1956 NARS also had to contend with Emmett Leahy's recommendation that separate holding areas be established to handle and assess records in order to reduce the number of federal records centers. Grover countered Leahy's suggestion by showing that the existence of holding areas would require unnecessary movement of records and use of personnel. RG 200, Grover Papers, Day file, Grover to Director, Records Management Division, 12 Sept. 1956.

7. Everett O. Alldredge, "Records Centers—A Historical Footnote," pp. 2–3; RAGS 1954, pp. 17–18; RAGS 1956, pp. 30–33; RAGS 1960, p. 12; RAGS 1965, p. 30; RAGS 1968, p. 7; RAGS 1969, p. 28; *American Archivist* 19 (Jan. 1956):84; GSA, *Annual Report on the Management Improvement Program, 1955*, p. 28; RG 269, GSA, Office of Administration, Program Plans, NARS Schedule of Program Plans Fiscal Years 1965–1969, 15 Mar. 1963.

8. RG 64, Archivist 17.2, Recommended Forecast of Programs Fiscal Year 1954, 21 Apr. 1952, Office of Records Management, Meetings, NARS Regional Directors, 28 Sept.–3 Oct. 1958; RG 51, Budget Bureau, F6–1, vol. 1, 1967; *Washington Post*, 18 June 1967.

9. RG 64, Office of Records Management, E. O. Alldredge to Deputy Regional Directors, 14 Feb., 22 Apr., 29 July 1955, 13 Apr., 15 May, 18 June 1956.

10. Interview with W. D. White, Kansas City, Mo., 21 Nov. 1973.

11. *American Archivist* 36 (Oct. 1973):637–38; 20 (Apr. 1957):179; 27 (July 1964):446; *National Archives Accessions*, no. 55 (May 1960), p. 32.

12. RG 200, Grover Papers, GSA file, Grover to H. E. Angel, 22 May 1956; RG 269, GSA, Office of Administrator, General Subject Files, Organization & Management 7, Grover to Assistant Administrator, PP&C, 8 Aug. 1956.

13. RG 64, Records Management, Organization & Management, Grover to Administrator, 15 Sept. 1955.

14. RAGS 1955, pp. 44–48; RAGS 1956, pp. 27–30; *American Archivist* 23 (Jan. 1960):108; RG 64, P & C 057–080, Minutes of Federal Records Council, 17 June 1960.

15. RAGS 1960, pp. 10–13.

16. RAGS 1963, pp. 51–52; RAGS 1968, pp. 6–7; RG 64, Archivist 17.2, Recommended Forecast of Programs Fiscal Year 1954, 21 Apr. 1952; RG 51, Budget Bureau, F6–1, vol. 1.

17. *Washington News*, 11 Nov. 1959; RAGS 1958, p. 11; RAGS 1959, pp. 26–27; RG 64, P & C 063–77, W. C. Grover to Assistant Administrator of General Services, 22 Aug. 1962, P & C 065–80, Minutes of Federal Records Council, 29 July 1964.

18. Comptroller General's Report to the Congress, *Review of Certain Records Management Activities*; *American Archivist* 27 (July 1964):363– 70; 28 (Jan. 1965):157; RG 269, GSA, Administrator, Reading file, Grover to Administrator, 20 May 1964; RG 51, Budget Bureau, GSA–G6, 1965, Records Management, L. V. Lewis to Broadbent, 22 Apr. 1965; *Congressional Record*, 6 Mar. 1968, H–1742.

19. RG 64, Records Management Office, RM (General), 1957–58, P & C 060–131; RG 200 Grover Papers, Day file, Grover to W. E. Hendrickson, 5 June 1957; Herbert Angel, "Archival Janus," p. 7; Ken Munden, "Records Essential to Continuity of State and Local Government," pp. 25–27; Edward N. Johnson, "Trends in County Records Management," pp. 297–301.

20. RG 269, GSA, Administrator, General Subject Files, Organization & Management 7, Grover to Director, Office of Management, 30 July 1954; RG 64, Records Management Office, E. O. Alldredge to Deputy Regional Directors, 14 Feb. 1955, 15 Mar. 1957; Federal Records Center (San Francisco) file, P. C. Brooks to Federal Records Center Staff, 28 Sept. 1955, Brooks Papers.

21. Lecturer—Federal Records Centers, 1958—file, Schellenberg Papers;

RG 64, Records Management Office, Numbered Memoranda, NR 58–42, 25 Apr. 1958; Everett O. Alldredge, "Archival Training in a Record Center," pp. 401–7.

22. Robert H. Bahmer, "The National Archives after Twenty Years," p. 201; RG 64, Military Archives Office, Misc. Subject file, Grover to Director, Records Management Division, 2 Sept. 1955, E. O. Alldredge to Director, Records Management Division, 4 Oct. 1955.

23. *San Francisco Call-Bulletin*, 12 Dec. 1956; Philip C. Brooks, "The Historian's Stake in Federal Records," pp. 267–68; RG 200, Grover Papers, Day file, R. H. Bahmer to Prescott Bush, 20 Feb. 1957; Harry L. Weingart, *Guide to the Records in the Federal Records Center, Kansas City, Missouri* (Kansas City, Mo.: Federal Records Center, 1966); Gerald T. White, "Government Archives Afield," pp. 838–41; William R. Petrowski, "Research, Anyone?", pp. 581–92.

24. Wayne C. Grover, "Archives," pp. 3–10; RG 64, Records Management Office, Meetings file, Consolidated Report of Panel Discussions at Conference of Regional Directors, NARS, 14–18 Oct. 1957, Numbered Memoranda, NR 57–53, 11 June 1957.

25. Everett D. Alldredge, "Still to be Done," pp. 12, 3; see also *American Archivist* 27 (July 1964):442; 30 (Apr. 1967):349–50.

CHAPTER 17

1. RG 64, P & C 047–141, Dan Lacy to Kenneth Hechler, 3 Feb. 1947.

2. *American Archivist* 24 (July 1961):312; OF 221, R. A. Conway to J. A. Cummings, 10, 17 Feb. 1949, Conway to Grover, 7 Oct. 1949, Truman Papers; RG 51, Budget Bureau, Ser. 47.1, F4–6/50.1, G. M. Elsey to Roger Jones, 5 Jan. 1950; Robert H. Bahmer, "Legislative Background of Presidential Libraries," p. 2.

3. *New York Herald Tribune*, 12 Oct. 1951; Document Book, vol. 1, Harry S. Truman Library, hereafter referred to as HSTL; PPF 1–L, press release, 8 Jan. 1953, Truman Papers.

4. David Lloyd, "The Harry S. Truman Library," pp. 99–110.

5. W. C. Grover memoranda, 8 Dec. 1952, 16 Jan. 1953, Brooks Papers; Document Book, vol. 1, esp. Truman to Larson, 17 Jan. 1953, Larson to Truman, 19 Jan. 1953, HSTL.

6. OF 101–EE, Val Peterson to Sherman Adams, 23 Feb. 1953, Charles Willis, Jr. to Adams, 6 Mar. 1953, Arthur Minnich to B. M. Shanley, 17 Mar. 1953, Grover to Shanley, 15 May 1953, Minnich to Adams, 9 June 1953, Adams to E. F. Mansure, 9 June 1953, Eisenhower Papers. For a penetrating commentary by an Eisenhower administration official on the public character of presidential papers, see Frederick W. Ford, "Some Legal Problems in Preserving Records for Public Use," pp. 41–47.

7. RG 200, Grover Papers, Alphabetical file, Grover to G. M. Elsey, 4 Oct. 1949, Elsey to Grover, 10, 18 Oct. 1949; RG 64, P & C 055–114, Grover memorandum, 15 Sept. 1955.

8. RG 64, P & C 055–114, W. C. Grover memorandum, 15 Sept. 1955, D. C. Eberhart to Archivist, 7 Sept. 1955, Grover to General Counsel, GSA, 16 Sept. 1955, Acting General Counsel, GSA, to Grover, 6 Dec. 1955.

9. RG 64, P & C 055–114, D. C. Eberhart to Grover, 5 Apr. 1957; Warren R. Reid, "Public Papers of the Presidents," pp. 435–39.

10. OF 101–PP, Eisenhower Papers; RG 200, Grover Papers, Day file, R. H. Bahmer to Herman Kahn, 5 Feb. 1954.

11. *Hearing Before a Special Subcommittee of the Committee on Government Operations, House of Representatives, Eighty-Fourth Congress, First Session, on . . . Bills to Provide for the Acceptance and Maintenance of Presidential Libraries . . . June 13, 1955,* passim. The legislation also stipulated that "any former President of the United States" could have "reasonable office space in any Presidential archival depository" and that such institutions could accept "any federal records appropriate for preservation therein."

12. Ibid.; Public Law 373, Eighty-fourth Congress, 1st Session; U.S., *Statutes at Large,* 69:695; Elizabeth H. Buck, "General Legislation for Presidential Libraries," pp. 337–41.

13. "Remarks of Herman Kahn at SAA Meeting, Columbus, Ohio, Oct. 4, 1957," copy in possession of author.

14. Document Book, vol. 1, HSTL; Philip D. Lagerquist, "The Harry S. Truman Library as a Center for Research on the American Presidency," p. 34.

15. Document Book, vol. 1, HSTL; *American Historical Review* 63 (July 1958):1123–24, 64 (July 1959):1074; Philip C. Brooks, "The Harry S. Truman Library," pp. 25–37; *Harry S. Truman Library Research Newsletter, April 1963,* pp. 25–37; Lagerquist, "The Harry S. Truman Library as a Center for Research on the American Presidency," p. 35.

16. Administrative files, Eisenhower Library, passim; D. W. Wilson to D. R. McCoy, 10 Dec. 1973, D. J. Reed to McCoy, 29 Nov. 1973, in possession of author.

17. *Historical Materials in the Herbert Hoover Presidential Library,* passim; D. J. Reed to D. R. McCoy, 29 Nov. 1973, in possession of author.

18. RG 64, P & C 062–126, Grover to Assistant Administrator, GSA, 30 Aug. 1961, P & C 067–80, Federal Records Council minutes, 20 July 1967; RG 200, Grover Papers, Day file, Grover to K. L. Trever, 26 Nov. 1963, R. H. Bahmer to Deputy Administrator, GSA, 26 Feb. 1964; O'Neill, "Will Success Spoil the Presidential Libraries?" p. 341; *Kansas City Star,* 16 Feb. 1975, 12 June 1977.

19. James E. O'Neill, "Will Success Spoil the Presidential Libraries?" p. 341; Mrs. Lyndon B. Johnson, "Welcome to the LBJ Library," passim; *The Lyndon Baines Johnson Library—Five Year Report* (n.d.), enclosed in *Among Friends of LBJ,* no. 9 (Sept. 6, 1976).

20. For pertinent discussions, see Elizabeth B. Drewry, "The Role of Presidential Libraries," pp. 53–65; Richard S. Kirkendall, "Presidential Libraries," pp. 441–48; Kirkendall, "A Second Look at Presidential Libraries," pp. 371–86; William R. Petrowski, "Research, Anyone?" pp. 581–82; O'Neill, "Will Success Spoil the Presidential Libraries?" pp. 339–51.

21. Document Book, vol. 1, HSTL; P. C. Brooks to R. W. S. Turner, 21 July 1960, Brooks Papers; *National Archives Accessions,* No. 58 (Sept. 1964), p. 18; J. B. Rhoads to D. R. McCoy, 14 Sept. 1976, in possession of author.

22. J. B. Rhoads to D. R. McCoy, 14 Sept. 1976, in possession of author;

AHA Newsletter 13 (Jan. 1975):2–3; *New York Times*, 29 June 1977; *Lawrence Journal World*, 17 January 1978; National Study Commission on Records and Documents of Federal Officials, *Final Report*, pp. 10–11.

23. Comparative Statistical Summary of Presidential Libraries, Fiscal Year 1973, enclosed in D. J. Reed to D. R. McCoy, 29 Nov. 1973, in possession of author; Buck, "General Legislation for Presidential Libraries," p. 340.

24. Herman Kahn, "The Presidential Library, A New Institution," pp. 106–13; Drewry, "The Role of Presidential Libraries," pp. 53–65; O'Neill, "Will Success Spoil the Presidential Libraries?" pp. 339–51.

CHAPTER 18

1. The 1967 figures were not the highest till then in the history of the National Archives; its holdings ran to 914,102 cubic feet in 1962 and the number of services it provided was 599,738 in 1966. RAGS 1955, pp. 51, 55; RAGS 1962, p. 44; RAGS 1966, p. 23; RAGS 1967, p. 24.

2. RAGS 1960, p. 14; RAGS 1961, pp. 18–19; RAGS 1968, p. 3; RG 269, GSA, Office of Administration, Program Plans, W. P. Turpin to Administrator, 30 Aug. 1963, Turpin to Archivist, 30 Aug. 1963.

3. RAGS 1959, p. 28; RAGS 1962, p. 45; RAGS 1963, p. 54; RAGS 1964, pp. 55–56; RG 64, P & C 065–77, R. H. Bahmer to General Counsel, GSA, 25 Aug. 1964, P & C 067–80, Minutes of Federal Records Council, 15 July 1966, 20 July 1967.

4. Wayne C. Grover, "Toward Equal Opportunities for Scholarship," pp. 715–24; RAGS 1961, p. 20; RAGS 1965, p. 33; Walter Rundell, Jr., "Uncle Sam the Historian," p. 15.

5. Cf. *Publications of the National Archives* (1957), pp. 5–8, 11, with *Select List of Publications of the National Archives and Records Service* (1973), pp. 2–32; RAGS 1964, p. 55; RAGS 1965, 33; RG 64, Archivist's Controlled Project No. 1, Final Report, 27 Jan. 1966; interview with Robert H. Bahmer, Washington, D.C., 19 June 1974; J. B. Rhoads to D. R. McCoy, 14 Sept. 1976, in the author's possession.

6. Rundell, "Uncle Sam the Historian," p. 14; RAGS 1960, p. 16.

7. Oliver W. Holmes, "Territorial Government and the Records of Its Administration," pp. 105–6; RAGS 1963, p. 56; RAGS 1965, p. 33.

8. RG 64, P & C 053–77, Grover to Antonio Fernós-Isern, 27 Feb. 1953; *American Archivist* 20 (Jan. 1957):84; 20 (July 1957):269; Luis M. Rodriguez Morales, "Puerto Rico—The Documents Administration Program," *American Archivist* 26 (July 1963):379–82; Elizabeth H. Wray, "The Archives of the State of Hawaii," *American Archivist* 23 (July 1960):279–80; Diary, 26 Feb. 1962, Schellenberg Papers.

9. *American Archivist* 26 (Apr. 1963):277; Walter Rundell, Jr., *In Pursuit of American History*, passim; and, for example, Rundell, "Relations between Historical Researchers and Custodians of Source Materials," pp. 466–76, and "Clio's Ways and Means," pp. 20–40.

10. RG 64, P & C 064–101, Administrator's Controlled Project 64–1, Final Report, 31 Dec. 1964, M. H. Fishbein to L. J. Darter, Jr., 30 Apr. 1965; *Ameri-*

can Archivist 35 (Jan. 1972):134; James B. Rhoads, "The Future of Hard Copy," pp. 2–10; *Prologue* 1 (Fall 1969):38–40; Milton O. Gustafson, "Archival Implications of State Department Recordkeeping," pp. 36–38.

11. RAGS 1963, pp. 53–54; RAGS 1964, pp. 54–55.

12. RAGS 1967, p. 25; Frank G. Burke, "Automation in Bibliographical Control of Archives and Manuscript Collections," pp. 98–102; Burke, "SPINDEX II," pp. 19–23.

13. RAGS 1962, p. 47; RAGS 1963, p. 57; *American Archivist* 28 (Oct. 1965):594–95.

14. Philip M. Hamer, " . . . authentic Documents tending to elucidate our History," pp. 9–11; Julian P. Boyd, "In Memoriam: Philip May Hamer, 1891–1971," pp. 285–87; Robert L. Brubaker, "The Publication of Historical Sources," pp. 210–13; Oliver W. Holmes, "Recent Writings Relevant to Documentary Publication Programs," pp. 137–42.

15. National Historical Publications Commission, *A Report to the President Containing a Proposal by the National Historical Publications Commission*, pp. 1–2, 32–61.

16. RG 200, Grover Papers, Day file, W. C. Grover to A. M. Schlesinger, Jr., 13 Dec. 1962; National Historical Publications Commission, *A Report to the President*, iii–v; Brubaker, "The Publication of Historical Sources," pp. 223–24; Public Law 88–383, Eighty-eighth Congress, HR 6237.

17. Brubaker, "The Publication of Historical Sources," p. 224; RG 51, Budget Bureau, F6, Communication and Documentation, W. D. Carey to Hayes Redmon, 19 Sept. 1966; *American Archivist* 32 (Jan. 1969):75; 28 (Apr. 1965): 309; Fred Shelly, "The Choice of a Medium for Documentary Publication," pp. 363–68; National Historical Publications Commission, *Catalog of Microfilm Publications* (1967), pp. 1–21.

18. Jesse Lemisch, "The American Revolution Bicentennial and the Papers of Great White Men," pp. 7–21; *AHA Newsletter* 10 (May 1972):38; Esmond Wright, "The Papers of Great Men," pp. 197, 213; Leo Marx, "The American Scholar Today," pp. 48–52; *Journal of American History* 53 (Dec. 1966):590–91; Charles E. Lee, "Documentary Reproduction," p. 361; Burl Noggle, "A Note on Historical Editing," pp. 288–97.

19. Interview with Robert H. Bahmer, 19 June 1974.

20. Schellenberg diary, 3, 5, 6 Jan. 1956, 28 Feb. 1957.

21. Schellenberg diary, 27, 28 Feb. 1957; H. G. Jones, *The Records of a Nation, Their Management, Preservation, and Use*, pp. 70–71.

22. Schellenberg diary, 12 Apr. 1957; Staff Member, National Archives, Personal Observations, T. R. Schellenberg to Grover, 6 Nov. 1957, 24 July 1958, Schellenberg Papers.

23. Schellenberg diary, 10 Mar. 1958, 19 Jan. 1962.

24. Schellenberg diary, 28 Nov., 18 Dec. 1960; interview with Robert H. Bahmer, 19 June 1974.

25. Schellenberg diary, 14 Aug. 1961, and accompanying memorandum from W. C. Grover of same date.

26. *American Archivist* 25 (Apr. 1962):277–78; interview with Robert H. Bahmer, 19 June 1974; Schellenberg diary, 15, 19 Dec. 1961.

27. Schellenberg diary, 20 Dec. 1961, 19 Jan., 26 Feb. 1962.

28. *American Archivist* 27 (July 1964):446; *Archives* 3 (Lady Day 1957):53–56; 8 (Apr. 1967):55–56; "In Memoriam: Theodore R. Schellenberg," essays by Lester J. Cappon, James B. Rhoads, Ernst Posner, Ian MacLean, Aurelio Tanodi, Clinton V. Black, and George S. Ulibarri, pp. 190–202.

29. Schellenberg diary, 20 Dec. 1961, with GSA Order ADM 5450.3 CHGE 36 and NAR 5450.1A, both dated 22 Dec. 1961, and NAR 1848.2, 26 Dec. 1961; Robert H. Bahmer, "The Management of Archival Institutions," pp. 3–10; interview with Robert H. Bahmer, 19 June 1974.

30. *American Archivist* 30 (Jan. 1967):231; interview with Robert H. Bahmer, 19 June 1974.

31. *Washington Post*, 29 Dec. 1958; RG 200, Grover Papers, Personal files, B. C. Shafer to John Moore, 7 Mar. 1961, Day file, K. L. Trever to R. M. Brown, 31 Jan. 1958; RG 64, P & C 059–77; Franklin Floete to W. L. Dawson, 12 June 1959; *Mississippi Valley Historical Review* 52 (Sept. 1965):325; *Journal of American History* 54 (Sept. 1967):478; Wayne C. Grover, "Federal Government Archives," pp. 390–96, and "The Role of the Archivist in the Preservation of Scientific Records," passim; *American Archivist* 33 (Jan. 1970):121; 38 (Jan. 1975):4.

32. RG 200, Grover Papers, Day file, J. L. Rankin to W. C. Grover, 1 Oct. 1953; Robert H. Bahmer, "The Case of the Clark Papers," pp. 19–22; *Washington Post*, 29 Dec. 1958.

33. Richard Maass, "Arguments Heard in the Clark Case," pp. 113–16; Grover Papers, Day file, Grover to Turner Catledge, 13 Dec. 1955, Alphabetical Correspondence file, Grover to J. P. Boyd, 4 Oct. 1955; Robert F. Metzdorf, "Lewis and Clark I," pp. 226–30.

34. Julian P. Boyd, "These Precious Monuments of . . . Our History," pp. 178–80.

35. Burt Griffin, "Lewis and Clark II," pp. 64–67, 72–73; *American Archivist* 20 (Jan. 1957):83; Paul V. Lutz, "Government Loses Suit for Documents," pp. 9–11; *Antiquarian Bookman* 42 (16 Sept. 1968):835; interview with R. Reed Whitaker, Kansas City, Mo., 21 Feb. 1975.

36. *New York Times*, 26 Sept., 14 Oct. 1963, 7 Jan., 18 Sept. 1964; Schellenberg diary, 11 Nov. 1963; *Washington Star*, 10 Nov. 1963; RG 200, Grover Papers, Day file, R. H. Bahmer to Homer Hower, 16 Apr. 1964; Philip P. Mason, "Archival Security," pp. 480–87.

37. RG 200, Grover Papers, Day file, R. H. Bahmer to Archivist, 20 Feb. 1964; RG 64, Office of Military Archives, P & C Case files, NAR 1848.5, 16 Sept. 1964, and Archivist's Controlled Project No. 1, Final Report, 27 Jan. 1966; interview with Robert H. Bahmer, 19 June 1974.

38. RG 64, P & C 058–114, W. M. Bruckner to F. G. Floete, 24 Oct. 1957, Floete to Secretary of the Army, 6 Nov. 1957, R. H. Bahmer to Administrator, 17 Jan. 1958, memorandum for Percival Brundage, 18 Jan. 1958, and Office of Records Management, Meetings, Minutes of Administrator's Staff Meeting, 27 May, 25 Feb., 14 Jan. 1958; Walter Stender and Evans Walker, "The National Personnel Records Center Fire," pp. 521–22; *Washington Post*, 29 Dec. 1958; *American Archivist* 21 (Oct. 1958):445.

39. RG 51, Budget Bureau, F6–13/3, National Archives, F. G. Floete to Wilton Persons, 18 Mar. 1959, Floete to R. E. Merriam, 2 Apr. 1959, E. B. Staats

to Merriam, 24 Apr. 1959; *American Archivist* 23 (Apr. 1960):220; RG 64, P & C 057–080, Minutes of Federal Records Council, 17 June 1960, including *Proposal, Defense Archives Annex for the National Archives*, and Reports, Assistant Archivist for the National Archives to Archivist, Aug. 1967; *Washington Post*, 25 July 1969; *Washington Star-News*, 25 Mar. 1974.

40. Interview with Robert H. Bahmer, 19 June 1974. See also, Bahmer, "The Management of Archival Institutions," pp. 3–10.

41. Arthur M. Schlesinger, Jr., *The Imperial Presidency*, chap. 10, esp. pp. 367–70. It should be mentioned that there are three significant types of restrictions on the use of records: those imposed (1) by Congress, for example, on atomic data, (2) by agencies under security-classification regulations, especially on military and diplomatic materials, and (3) by agencies in general, for example, by the Federal Bureau of Investigation on its investigative files. The archivist of the United States also occasionally imposes restrictions at the behest of an agency, as with health and psychiatric files, and some records are temporarily withdrawn from use for repair, reproduction, and rearrangement.

42. RG 64, Office of Military Archives, P & C I–NM–14 (12), Dallas Irvine to Assistant Archivist, Military Archives, 31 Jan. 1962; Walter Rundell, Jr., "Restricted Records," pp. 41–43.

43. RG 64, P & C 061–106, W. C. Grover to L. T. DeLisio, 28 Aug. 1963, P & C 052–77, Grover to General Counsel, GSA, 14 Nov. 1951, P & C I–MN–14 (12), Dallas Irvine to Assistant Archivist, Military Archives, 31 Jan. 1962; RG 200, Grover Papers, Day file, Grover to Director, Office of Management, GSA, 2 Sept. 1955.

44. RG 200, Grover Papers, Day file, Grover to Louis Wright, 21 Dec. 1964; RG 64, Archivist 44, Grover to Assistant Archivist, National Archives, 28 May 1956.

45. RG 64, Archivist—Roosevelt Library, especially Grover to Director, Roosevelt Library, 22 Aug. 1952, P & C 062–132, and Office of Military Archives, P & C MN–166–S; RG 200, Grover Papers, Day file, Herman Kahn to Grover, 2 Nov. 1955, B. I. Shacklette to J. E. Hoover, 3 Apr. 1956, Grover to J. M. Blum, 11 June 1956, R. H. Bahmer to Rudolph Winnacker, 25 Apr. 1957, Grover to G. A. Eddy, 6 May 1957, Bahmer to Director, Roosevelt Library, 7 May 1957, Bahmer to E. F. Kelly, 30 Mar. 1960; Access to Papers file, P. C. Brooks to Research Archivist, Truman Library, 29 Mar. 1968, Truman Library file, Brooks to NKL (Stewart), 14 Feb. 1969, Brooks Papers; William J. Stewart, "Opening Closed Material in the Roosevelt Library," pp. 239–41.

46. RG 200, Grover Papers, Day file, R. H. Bahmer to R. A. Winnacker, 11 July 1956; RG 64, Security (Access-Release of), 1958–63, especially D. A. Quarles to F. G. Floete, 30 Jan. 1959, Adjutant General to Grover, 8 Dec. 1959, S. E. East to Chief, Records Administration Branch, Adjutant General's Office, 7 June 1963, Reports, East to Assistant Archivist for Military Affairs, 16 Jan. 1962, Office of Military Archives, P & C I–NM–1, Dallas Irvine to Assistant Archivist, Military Archives, 12 Jan. 1962, and P & C 061–106.

47. RG 64, Reports, S. E. East to Assistant Archivist for Military Archives, 16 Jan. 1962, Projects Branch to Assistant Archivist, Military Archives, 10 Jan. 1964, Reference Branch to World War II Records Division, 10 Jan. 1964, P & C 061–106, Grover to L. T. DeLisio, 28 Aug. 1963.

48. RG 64, P & C 061–106, R. H. Bahmer to L. T. DeLisio, 31 Oct. 1963.

49. RG 200, Grover Papers, Day file, R. H. Bahmer to J. W. Yeagley, 2 Aug. 1965.

50. RG 64, Office of Military Archives, P & C MN–165–5, e.g., J. F. Doherty to Secretary of Labor, 21 Jan. 1965, and Reports, J. F. Smith to E. G. Campbell, 12 July 1967.

51. Herbert Feis, "The Shackled Historian," pp. 332–43; see also Rundell, "Restricted Records," p. 40, and Henry Steele Commager, "Should Historians Write Contemporary History?" pp. 18–20, 47.

52. R. A. Jacobs to D. R. McCoy, 18 Aug. 1976, Jacobs's memoranda for the record, 11, 16, 25 Feb., 10 Mar. 1972, enclosed in Jacobs to McCoy, 19 Aug. 1976, in the author's possession; *Prologue* 7 (Spring 1975):59; David R. Young, "Secrecy and Disclosure," 41–42; James E. O'Neill, "Secrecy and Disclosure," pp. 43–45; Edwin A. Thompson, "Records Declassification in the National Archives," pp. 235–38.

CHAPTER 19

1. RG 200, Grover Papers, Personal—Operation Exit, C. M. Mathias, Jr., to A. O. Aldridge, 17 Oct. 1963.

2. David A. Frier, *Conflict of Interest in the Eisenhower Administration*, pp. 92–101, 115–29; RG 64, Karl L. Trever oral history transcript, p. 60; interview with Robert H. Bahmer, Washington, D.C., 19 June 1974.

3. *New York Times*, 23 Nov. 1961; e.g., RG 269, GSA, Office of Administration, Program Plans, W. P. Turpin to Administrator, 30 Aug. 1963, Turpin to Acting Administrator, 11 Jan. 1965, E. J. Rouhana to Administrator, 4 Feb. 1966; *Program Charters: Blueprint for the Future*, passim; RG 51, Budget Bureau, F6–1, vol. 1, National Archives Study (1967); RG 64, Robert H. Bahmer oral history transcript, pp. 47–49. It should be noted that Lawson B. Knott, Jr., had thirty years of service as a civil servant, including four as deputy administrator of general services. Age fifty-three at the time of his appointment as administrator, he was a graduate of Duke University and held a law degree from National University.

4. Interview with Robert H. Bahmer, 19 June 1974; RG 64, Robert H. Bahmer oral history transcript, pp. 32, 35–36; O. W. Holmes to D. R. McCoy, 4 Aug. 1976, in the author's possession; RG 51, Budget Bureau, F6, Communication and Documentation, Grover to Johnson, 2 Nov. 1965, enclosed in Charles L. Schultze to Johnson, 7 Jan. 1966; *AHA Newsletter* 13 (Sept. 1975):7–8.

5. *AHA Newsletter* 13 (Sept. 1975):7–8.

6. Ibid.; RG 200, Grover Papers, Personal—Operation Exit, Grover to Earl Warren, 2 Nov. 1965, Grover to Eisenhower, 4 Nov. 1965, Grover to Truman, 4 Nov. 1965, Grover to J. W. Macy, Jr., 4 Nov. 1965, J. P. Boyd to E. F. Goldman, 3 Nov. 1965, Grover to Boyd, 30 Mar. 1966, Warren to Grover, 5 Apr. 1966; Oliver W. Holmes, confidential notes (in Dr. Holmes's possession), 3, 5, 18, 20, Nov. 1965.

7. RG 200, Grover Papers, Personal—Operation Exit, Grover to J. W. Macy, Jr., 4 Nov. 1965, Grover to V. W. Clapp, 3 Nov. 1965; interview with Robert H.

Bahmer, 19 June 1974; *American Archivist* 28 (July 1965):472, 29 (Apr. 1966): 307, 310; 29 (July 1966):450; 31 (July 1968):330.

8. RG 200, Grover Papers, Personal—Operation Exit, R. E. Neustadt to Juanita Roberts, 3 Jan. 1966; RG 51, Budget Bureau, F6, Communication and Documentation, C. L. Schultze to Johnson, 7 Jan. 1966.

9. Interview with Robert H. Bahmer, 19 June 1974; O. W. Holmes, confidential notes, 21 Jan. 1966.

10. RG 200, Grover Papers, Personal—Operation Exit, L. H. Butterfield to Mrs. L. B. Johnson, 14 Mar. 1966; RG 51, Budget Bureau, G6, 1966 Misc. GSA-NARS, D. F. Reynolds for the Files, 8 Apr. 1966.

11. Lyman H. Butterfield, "The Scholar's One World," pp. 21–32; RG 51, Budget Bureau, G6, GSA, 1966 Misc.

12. RG 200, Grover Papers, Personal—Operation Exit, Grover to J. P. Boyd, L. H. Butterfield, and O. W. Holmes, 26 Sept. 1966, O. W. Holmes, confidential notes, 14 Nov. 1966.

13. *American Historical Review* 72 (Apr. 1967):1200–2, 1205–6; RG 200, Grover Papers, Personal—Operation Exit, J. P. Boyd to Mrs. L. B. Johnson, 20 Dec. 1966, Grover to Boyd, 22 Dec. 1966; H. G. Jones, *The Records of A Nation, Their Management, Preservation, and Use*, pp. ix, 273. The AHA appointed Louis Morton of Dartmouth College to the joint committee following the death of Greenfield in July 1967.

14. RG 200, Grover Papers, Personal—Operation Exit, Douglass Cater to Bill Carey, 14 Jan. 1967; O. W. Holmes, confidential notes, 13, 14, 15 Feb. 1967; RG 51, Budget Bureau, Office of Executive Management, Government Organization Staff, F6–1 NA Study, Harold Seidman to Hirst Sutton, 24 Jan. 1967, Prospectus for a Study of Federal Archival Functions, 16 Feb. 1967.

15. O. W. Holmes, confidential notes, 16, 17 Feb. 1967; RG 51, Budget Bureau, Office of Executive Management/Government Organization Staff, F6–1 NA Study, Harold Seidman to Messrs. Carey and Jones, 24 Feb. 1967, L. B. Knott, Jr., to Hubert Humphrey, 27 Feb. 1967, Olga [?] to Messrs. Holden, Greenstone, Schnoor, and Messner, 6 Mar. 1967, P. S. Hughes to John Roche, 25 Mar. 1967; *American Archivist* 29 (Apr. 1966):310–11; RG 269, GSA, Office of Administration, PPB 5–3, Controlled Projects, R. H. Bahmer to Director, Office of Program and Policy Planning, 3 Mar. 1967, with Knott's annotation of 17 Mar. 1967; RG 200, Posner Papers, Joint Committee file, draft of Ernst Posner to G. T. White, 28 Feb. 1967.

16. Jones, *Records of A Nation*, p. 274; *American Archivist* 30 (Oct. 1967): 622.

17. RG 51, Budget Bureau, Hirst Sutton to Harold Seidman, 23 Mar. 1967.

18. RG 200, Posner Papers, Joint Committee file, Ernst Posner to J. P. Boyd, 5 May 1967.

19. RG 51, Budget Bureau, F6, Communication and Documentation, Howard Schnoor to Director, 15 May 1967.

20. Ibid., Hirst Sutton to Director, 18 May 1967, and route slip from Howard Messner and Seymour Greenstone, 16 May 1967, with P. S. Hughes's annotation, 25 May 1967.

21. RG 51, Budget Bureau, F6–1, vol. 1, National Archives Study (1967–), S. D. Greenstone, meeting at GSA on the archives paper, 26 July 1967, L. B.

Knott, Jr., to W. D. Carey, 26 July 1967, F6, Communication and Documentation, Carey to Knott, 17 Aug. 1967.

22. RG 269, GSA, Office of Administration, PPB 5–3, Controlled Projects, R. H. Bahmer to Assistant Administrator for Administration, 28 Nov. 1967, with L. B. Knott's annotation, 8 Dec. 1967; *American Archivist* 31 (Apr. 1968): 213.

23. Jones, *Records of a Nation*, pp. 274–95.

24. Interview with Robert H. Bahmer, 19 June 1974; H. G. Jones to D. R. McCoy, 13 Aug. 1976, in the author's possession; *Washington Star*, 27 Dec. 1967; *Federal Times* (Washington, D.C.), 7 Feb. 1968; *Washington Post*, 28 Dec. 1967, 20 Jan. 1968; *New York Times*, 5 Jan. 1968; *American Archivist* 32 (Jan. 1969):93; 31 (Apr. 1968):213; *American Historical Review* 73 (Apr. 1968): 1346; *AHA Newsletter* 6 (Feb. 1968):59–60; *Congressional Record*, 19 Jan. 1968, p. 5170; RG 200, Grover Papers, Personal—Jones Report file, Grover to P. C. Brooks, 22 Jan. 1968.

25. RG 51, Budget Bureau, F6–1, vol. 2, NA Study, L. B. Knott, Jr., to P. S. Hughes, 13 Feb. 1968, enclosing R. H. Bahmer, comments on *A Report on the Status of the National Archives*.

26. RG 51, Budget Bureau, F6–1, Howard Schnoor to P. S. Hughes, 23 Feb. 1968; RG 200, Grover Papers, Personal—Jones Report file, J. P. Boyd to R. H. Bahmer, 27 Feb. 1968; H. G. Jones to D. R. McCoy, 13 Aug. 1976, in the author's possession.

27. RG 51, Budget Bureau, F6–1, vol. 2, NA Study, L. B. Knott, Jr., to P. S. Hughes, 28 Feb. 1968; H. G. Jones to D. R. McCoy, 13 Aug. 1976.

28. RG 51, Budget Bureau, F6–1, vol. 2, NA Study, L. B. Knott, Jr., to P. S. Hughes, 13 Feb. 1968, enclosing R. H. Bahmer's comments.

29. RG 269, GSA, Office of Administration, PPB 5–3, Controlled Projects, J. B. Rhoads to Administrator, 29 Mar. 1968, with L. B. Knott's annotation, 5 Apr. 1968, Director of Management Systems to Deputy Assistant Administrator for Administration, 10 Apr. 1968, Assistant Administrator for Administration to Administrator, 25 June 1968, with L. B. Knott's annotation, 29 June 1968, Office of Administration, Budget file, Knott to C. L. Schultze, 3 July 1967, enclosing GSA 1967 Expenditure Status; interview with Robert H. Bahmer, 19 June 1974; GSA Order ADM 5420.25, 29 July 1968; J. B. Rhoads to D. R. McCoy, 15 Oct. 1976, in the author's possession; *New York Times*, 23 Jan. 1966; *American Archivist* 31 (Apr. 1968):220–21; 31 (Oct. 1968):410–11, 414; 32 (Jan. 1969):75.

30 Jones, *Records of a Nation*, pp. 274–95; *American Archivist* 31 (July 1968):326–27; H. G. Jones to D. R. McCoy, 13 Aug. 1976; RG 200, Grover Papers, Personal—O. W. Holmes, J. P. Boyd to O. W. Holmes, 16 Apr. 1968; *Annual Report of the America Historical Association for the Year 1968*, 1:41, 44, 60; *Journal of American History* 55 (Sept. 1968):462.

31. Interview with Robert H. Bahmer, 19 June 1974; *American Archivist* 31 (July 1968):326–28, 330.

32. *American Archivist* 31 (Oct. 1968):412–13; *Prologue*, 4 (Spring 1972): 57.

33. *American Archivist* 32 (Jan. 1969):93, RG 200, Grover Papers, Personal—Jones Report file, Grover to H. G. Jones, 16 Mar. 1969.

CHAPTER 20

1. Richard W. Leopold, "Crisis of Confidence," pp. 139–55; *Final Report of the Joint AHA–OAH ad hoc Committee to Investigate the Charges against the Franklin D. Roosevelt Library and Related Matters*, passim; T. A. Wilson to D. R. McCoy, 22 Dec. 1969, and J. B. Rhoads to D. R. McCoy, 4 Mar. 1970, both in the author's possession; Gregory L. Waple, "Freedom of Information Act," pp. 894–959; Benedict K. Zobrist II, "Reform in the Classification and Declassification of National Security Information," pp. 110–43.

2. RG 200, Grover Papers, Personal—Operation Exit, Grover to J. P. Boyd, L. H. Butterfield, and O. W. Holmes, 26 Sept. 1966.

3. Walter Robertson, Jr., "NARS," pp. 485–92; National Study Commission on Records and Documents of Federal Officials, *Final Report*, pp. 9–11.

4. *The Records of Public Officials*, pp. 3–8; Mack Thompson to D. R. McCoy, 30 Aug. 1976, and E. L. Leffler to D. R. McCoy, 31 Aug. 1976, both in the author's possession; *SAA Newsletter* (Nov. 1976), p. 12; National Study Commission on Records and Documents of Federal Officials, *Final Report*, p. 43.

Bibliography

I have not intended this bibliography to be a record of everything that I examined during the course of my research. It is, instead, a list of the most important sources cited in the notes. Of course, two of the most significant sources are series of published government reports, and they deserve special notice. They are the first through the fifteenth volumes of the *Annual Report of the Archivist of the United States* (Washington: Government Printing Office, 1936–50); and, since 1949, the annual *Report of the Administrator of General Services to Congress* (Washington: Government Printing Office, 1950–). The discontinuance of the annual reports of the archivist was a great loss to archival administration and scholarship. The slender sections on the National Archives and Records Service in the reports of the Administrator of General Services, while useful for reference purposes, fall far short of compensating for that loss.

I should mention also that I dipped into obvious sources such as the United States *Statutes at Large*; the *Congressional Record*; *Time*; and, among other newspapers, the *New York Times*; the *Washington Post*; and the *Washington Star* for appropriate material. Moreover, I interviewed several dozen archivists and records managers. There were, however, only four of these interviews that were both formally conducted and open to attribution, those with Robert H. Bahmer, Washington, D.C., 19 June 1974; Oliver W. Holmes, Washington, D.C., 29 December 1974; W. D. White, Kansas City, Missouri, 21 November 1973; and R. Reed Whitaker, Kansas City, Missouri, 21 February 1975.

Archives and Manuscript Collections

Abilene, Kans.
  Dwight D. Eisenhower Library
    Administrative Files
    Dwight D. Eisenhower Papers
Chapel Hill, N.C.
  Southern Historical Collection, University of North Carolina Library
    Robert D. W. Connor Papers and Journal
Hyde Park, N.Y.
  Franklin D. Roosevelt Library
    Matthew M. Epstein Papers

Franklin D. Roosevelt Papers
Franklin D. Roosevelt Library, Inc., Papers
Independence, Mo.
Harry S. Truman Library
Philip C. Brooks Papers
Document Book
George M. Elsey Papers
Harry S. Truman Papers
Topeka, Kans.
Kansas State Historical Society
Theodore R. Schellenberg Papers
Washington, D.C.
Manuscript Division, Library of Congress
American Historical Association Papers
Solon J. Buck Papers
Clarence E. Carter Papers
Dorsey W. Hyde, Jr., Papers
J. Franklin Jameson Papers
Waldo G. Leland Papers
National Archives
J. Franklin Jameson File, Office of the Archivist
Percy Scott Flippin, comp. "The Archives of the United States Government—A
Documentary History." Typescript and scrapbook. 24 vols.
National Archives Oral History Project: Transcripts
Herbert E. Angel, Washington, D.C., 24 Jan., 13 Feb., 5 April 1973
Robert H. Bahmer, Washington, D.C., 10, 19 Sept. 1972, 3 Jan., 8 May
1973
G. Philip Bauer, Washington, D.C., 24 April 1973
Lester J. Cappon, Written Statement, June 1974
George M. Elsey, Washington, D.C., 3 Nov. 1972
Collas G. Harris, Great Falls and Alexandria, Va., 13 Jan., 28 July 1972
Oliver W. Holmes, Washington, D.C., 10 July 1973
Guy A. Lee, Alexandria, Va., 14 Mar. 1973
Thaddeus S. Page, Alexandria, Va., 2 Feb., 28 July 1972
Ernst M. Posner, Washington, D.C., 19 Oct., early Dec. 1973
Marcus Price, Washington, D.C., 25 Sept. 1972
Vernon D. Tate, Alexandria, Va., 8 June 1973
Karl L. Trever, Washington, D.C., 20 Feb., 19 Mar. 1973
Record Group 51, "Records of the Bureau of the Budget"
Record Group 64, "Records of the National Archives and Records Service"
Record Group 66, "Records of the Commission of Fine Arts"
Record Group 200
Wayne C. Grover Papers
Ernst M. Posner Papers
Record Group 264, "Records of the Commission on the Organization of the
Executive Branch of the Government"
Record Group 269, "Records of the General Services Administration"

GOVERNMENT DOCUMENTS

Australia
  Bean, C. E. W., *First Annual Report of the Commonwealth Archives Commission*. Canberra: The Commission, 1952.
Canada
  Lamb, W. Kaye. *Report of the Public Archives for the Year 1951*. Ottawa: Edmond Cloutier, 1952.
France
  Direction des Archives de France. *Manuel d'Archivistique: Théorie et Pratique des Archives Publiques en France*. Paris: Imprimerie national, 1970.
Rhodesia and Nyasaland
  The National Archives. *The National Archives and Your Records*. n.p.: The National Archives, 1963.
United States
  Bauer, G. Philip. *The Appraisal of Current and Recent Records*. Staff Information Circular no. 13. Washington: National Archives, 1946.
  Brooks, Philip C. *The Functions of Record Officers in the Federal Government*. Washington: National Archives, 1943.
  Buck, Solon J. *Selected References on Phases of Archival Economy*. Staff Information Circular no. 6. Washington: National Archives, 1939.
  Commission on Organization of the Executive Branch of the Government. *Office of General Services—Supply Activities*. Washington: Government Printing Office, 1949.
  ————. *Paperwork Management, Part I, in the United States Government, A Report to Congress*. Washington: Government Printing Office, 1955.
  ————. *Records Management in the United States Government, A Report with Recommendations. Task Force on Records Management. Prepared for the Commission on Organization of the Executive Branch of the Government*. Washington: Government Printing Office, 1948.
  Comptroller General. *Report to the Congress, Review of Certain Records Management Activities: National Archives and Records Service, General Services Administration, Dec. 1961*. Washington: Government Printing Office, 1962.
  Congress, House, *Hearing Before a Special Subcommittee of the Committee on Government Operations, House of Representatives, Eighty-fourth Congress, First Session, on . . . Bills to Provide for the Acceptance and Maintenance of Presidential Libraries . . . June 13, 1955*. Washington: Government Printing Office, 1955.
  Congress, Senate, *Independent Offices Appropriation Bill for 1946. Hearings Before the Subcommittee of the Committee on Appropriations. United States Senate. Seventy-ninth Congress, First Session*. Washington: Government Printing Office, 1945.
  General Services Administration. *Annual Report on the Management Improvement Program, Fiscal Year 1955*. Washington: General Services Administration, 1955.
  ————. *Program Charters: Blueprint for the Future*. Washington: General Services Administration, 1964.

Kimberly, Arthur E. *Repair and Preservation in the National Archives*. Staff Information Circular no. 4. Washington: National Archives, 1939.

National Archives. *The Federal Records Problem*. Washington: National Archives, 1949.

————. *Guide to Records in the National Archives*. Washington: Government Printing Office, 1948.

————. *Proposal for the Establishment of a United Nations Archives*. Washington: National Archives, 1945.

National Archives and Records Service. *Disposition of Federal Records*. Washington: Government Printing Office, 1949.

————. *Guide to the National Archives of the United States*. Washington: Government Printing Office, 1974.

The National Archives and Records Service Newsletter 1973–77).

National Archives and Records Service. *Public Papers of the Presidents of the United States, Harry S. Truman, 1950*. Washington: Government Printing Office, 1965.

————. *Publications of the National Archives*. Washington: General Services Administration, 1957.

————. *Select List of Publications of the National Archives and Records Service*. Washington: General Services Administration, 1973.

National Historical Publications Commission. *A National Program for the Publication of Historical Documents*. Washington: Government Printing Office, 1954.

————. *A Report to the President Containing a Proposal by the National Historical Publications Commission*. Washington: Government Printing Office, 1963.

National Study Commission on Records and Documents of Federal Officials. *Final Report*. Washington: National Study Commission, 1977.

Przelaskowski, Ryszard. *Schedule of Internal Work in Modern Archives*. Staff Information Circular no. 10. Washington: National Archives, 1940.

Schellenberg, Theodore R. *European Archival Practices in Arranging Records*. Staff Information Circular no. 5. Washington: National Archives, 1939.

BOOKS AND ARTICLES

Alldredge, Everett O. "Archival Training in a Record Center." *American Archivist* 21 (Oct. 1958).

————. "The Federal Records Center, St. Louis: Personnel Files and Fiscal Records." *American Archivist* 18 (Apr. 1955).

————. "Records Centers—A Historical Footnote." *Records Management Journal* 10 (Spring 1972).

————. "Still to be Done." *American Archivist* 28 (Jan. 1965).

American Assembly. *The Records of Public Officials*. New York: The American Assembly, 1975.

American Historical Association. *Annual Report of the American Historical Association for the Year 1945*. Washington: Government Printing Office, 1945.

American Historical Association. *Annual Report of the American Historical Association for the Year 1968*. Washington: Smithsonian Institution Press, 1969.

Angel, Herbert E. "Archival Janus: The Records Center." *American Archivist* 31 (Jan. 1968).

―――. "Federal Records Management since the Hoover Commission Report." *American Archivist* 16 (Jan. 1953).

―――. "Highlights of the Federal Field Records Program of the Navy Department." *American Archivist* 7 (July 1944).

Bahmer, Robert H. "The Case of the Clark Papers." *American Archivist* 19 (Jan. 1956).

―――. "Legislative Background of Presidential Libraries." In *Presidential Libraries; Their Growth and Development*. Washington: Interagency Records Administration Conference, 1958.

―――. "The Management of Archival Institutions." *American Archivist* 26 (Jan. 1963).

―――. "The National Archives after 20 Years." *American Archivist* 18 (July 1955).

―――. "The Third International Congress of Archivists." *American Archivist* 20 (Apr. 1957).

Barnes, Harry Elmer. *The Struggle Against the Historical Blackout*. n.p., n.d. (ca. 1950).

Bauer, G. Philip. "Recruitment, Training, and Promotion in the National Archives." *American Archivist* 18 (Oct. 1955).

Basu, Pernendu. "The United Nations Archives." *Indian Archives* 5 (1951).

Beale, Howard K. "The Professional Historian: His Theory and His Practice." *Pacific Historical Review* 22 (Aug. 1953).

Beard, Charles A. "Who's to Write the History of the War?" *Saturday Evening Post* 220 (4 Oct. 1947).

Beers, Henry P. "The Bureau of Navigation 1862–1942." *American Archivist* 6 (Oct. 1943).

Bell, H. E. "Archivist Itinerant: Jenkinson in Wartime Italy." In *Essays in Memory of Sir Hilary Jenkinson*. Edited by Albert E. J. Hollaender. Chichester, Eng.: Society of Archivists, 1962.

―――. "The Protection of Archives: Some Lessons from the War in Italy." *Indian Archives* 4 (1950).

Bemis, Samuel F. "The Training of Archivists in the United States." *American Archivist* 2 (July 1939).

Binkley, Robert C. *Manual on Methods of Reproducing Research Materials*. Ann Arbor, Mich.: Edwards Bros., 1936.

Birdsall, William F. "The American Archivists' Search for Professional Identity, 1909–1936." Ph.D. dissertation, University of Wisconsin, 1973.

―――. "The Two Sides of the Desk: The Archivist and the Historian, 1909–1935." *American Archivist* 38 (Apr. 1975).

Blackwelder, Fannie Memory. "The North Carolina Records Management Program." *North Carolina Historical Review* 36 (July 1959).

Born, Lester K. "The Archives and Libraries of Postwar Germany." *American Historical Review* 56 (Oct. 1950).

Boyd, Julian P. "In Memoriam: Philip May Hamer, 1891–1971." *American Archivist* 34 (July 1971).

―――. "These Precious Monuments of . . . Our History." *American Archivist* 22 (Apr. 1959).

Brand, Katherine E. "Developments in the Handling of Recent Manuscripts in the Library of Congress." *American Archivsit* 16 (July 1953).

Brayer, Herbert O. "Report on the Meeting of Professional Archivists Called by the United Nations Educational, Scientific, and Cultural Organization, June 9 to 11, 1948, Paris France." *American Archivist* 11 (Oct. 1948).

Brooks, Philip C., "The Archival Contributions of Ernst Posner." *Indian Archives* 18 (July–Dec. 1969).

————. "Archival Heritage Meets Modern Records in Panama." *American Archivist* 18 (Apr. 1955).

————. "Archives in the United States during World War II, 1939–1945," *Library Quarterly* 17 (Oct. 1947).

————. "The Harry S. Truman Library—Plans and Reality." *American Archivist* 25 (Jan. 1962).

————. "The Historians's Stake in Federal Records." *Mississippi Valley Historical Review* 43 (Sept. 1956).

————. *Public Records Management*. Chicago: Public Administration Service, 1949.

————. "The Selection of Archives for Preservation." *American Archivist* 3 (Oct. 1940).

Brubaker, Robert L. "The Publication of Historical Sources: Recent Projects in the United States." *Library Quarterly* 37 (Apr. 1967).

Bryan, Mary Givens. "Changing Times." *American Archivist* 24 (Jan. 1961).

Buck, Elizabeth H. "General Legislation for Presidential Libraries." *American Archivist* 18 (Oct. 1955).

Buck, Solon J. "The Archivist's One World." *American Archivist* 10 (Jan. 1947).

————. "Let's Look at the Record." *American Archivist* 8 (Apr. 1945).

————. "Essentials in Training for Work with Public Archives and Historical Manuscript Collections." In *Archives and Libraries 1940*. Edited by A. F. Kuhlman. Chicago: American Library Association, 1940.

Burke, E. E. "Some Archival Legislation of the British Commonwealth." *American Archivist* 22 (July 1959).

Burke, Frank G. "Automation in Bibliographical Control of Archives and Manuscript Collections." In *Bibliography and the Historian*. Edited by Dagmar Horna Perman. Santa Barbara, Calif.: Clio Press, 1968.

————. "SPINDEX II: An Aspect of Archival Information Retrieval." *Records Management Journal* 8 (Summer 1970).

Butterfield, Lyman H. "The Scholar's One World." *Archivum* 16 (1966).

Campbell, Edward G. "The National Archives Faces the Future." *American Historical Review* 49 (Apr. 1944).

————. "Old Records in a New War." *American Archivist* 5 (July 1942).

Cappon, Lester K. "The Archival Profession and the Society of American Archivists." *American Archivist* 15 (July 1952).

————. "Tardy Scholars among the Archives." *American Archivist* 21 (Jan. 1958).

Carter, Clarence E. "The Territorial Papers of the United States: A Review and a Commentary." *Mississippi Valley Historical Review* 42 (Dec. 1955).

Chatfield, Helen L. "The Problem of Records from the Standpoint of Management." *American Archivist* 3 (Apr. 1940).

———. "Records and the Administrator." *Public Administration Review* 10 (Spring 1950).

Church, Randolph W. "The Relationship Between Archival Agencies and Libraries." *American Archivist* 6 (July 1943).

Clarkson, Jesse Dunsmore. "Escape to the Present." *American Historical Review* 46 (Apr. 1941).

Claus, Robert. "The Archives Program of the United Nations." *American Archivist* 11 (July 1948).

———. "The Proposal for a United Nations Archival Agency." *American Archivist* 33 (Jan. 1970).

———. "The United Nations Archives." *American Archivist* 10 (Apr. 1947).

Collingridge, John H. "Implementing the Grigg Report." *Journal of the Society of Archivists* 1 (Apr. 1958).

Commager, Henry Steele. "Should Historians Write Contemporary History?" *Saturday Review* 49 (12 Feb. 1966).

Connor, Robert D. W. "Adventures of an Amateur Archivist." *American Archivist* 6 (Jan. 1943).

———. "FDR Visits the National Archives." *American Archivist* 12 (Oct. 1949).

———. "The National Archives: Objectives and Practices." *Bulletin of the American Library Association* 30 (Aug. 1936).

———. "The National Archives of the United States." *Military Engineer* 31 (Jan.–Feb. 1939).

Crittenden, Christopher. "The Archivist as a Public Servant" *American Archivist* 12 (Jan. 1949).

———. "The North Carolina Records Center." *American Archivist* 18 (Jan. 1955).

Drewry, Elizabeth B. "The Role of Presidential Libraries." *Midwest Quarterly* 7 (Autumn 1965).

Duniway, David C. "On the Use of Archives by Historians." *Pacific Historical Review* 28 (Aug. 1959).

East, Sherrod. "Archival Experience in a Prototype Intermediate Repository." *American Archivist* 27 (Jan. 1964).

Edmunds, Henry E. "The Ford Motor Company Archives." *American Archivist* 15 (Apr. 1952).

Edsall, Preston W. "The File Microcopy Program of the National Archives." *Journal of Documentary Reproduction* 4 (Mar. 1941).

Epstein, Fritz. "Archives Administration in the Soviet Union." *American Archivist* 20 (Apr. 1957).

Evans, Frank B. "Archivists and Records Managers: Variations on a Theme." *American Archivist* 30 (Jan. 1967).

———; Harrison, Donald F.; Thompson, Edwin A.; and Rofes, William L. "A Basic Glossary for Archivists, Manuscript Curators, and Records Managers." *American Archivist* 37 (July 1974).

———. "Educational Needs for Work in Archives and Manuscript Depositories." *Indian Archives* 21 (July–Dec. 1972).

———. "Modern Methods of Arrangement of Archives in the United States." *American Archivist* 29 (Apr. 1966).

———. "The National Archives and Records Service and Its Research Resources:

A Select Bibliography." *Prologue–The Journal of the National Archives* 3 (Fall 1971).

Feis, Herbert. "The Shackled Historian." *Foreign Affairs* 45 (Jan. 1967).

Fenyo, Mario D. "The Record Group Concept: A Critique." *American Archivist* 29 (Apr. 1966).

Final Report of the Joint AHA-OAH Ad Hoc Committee to Investigate the Charges against the Franklin D. Roosevelt Library and Related Matters. n.p.: American Historical Association and Organization of American Historians, 1970.

"The Fiftieth Annual Meeting." *American Historical Review* 40 (Apr. 1935).

"The First International Congress of Archivists." *Indian Archives* 5 (1951).

Fishbein, Meyer H. "A Viewpoint on Appraisal of National Records." *American Archivist* 33 (Apr. 1970).

Ford, Frederick W. "Some Legal Problems in Preserving Records for Public Use." *American Archivist* 20 (Jan. 1957).

Ford, Guy Stanton. "Your Business." *American Historical Review* 48 (Apr. 1943).

Frier, David A. *Conflict of Interest in the Eisenhower Administration.* Ames, Ia.: Iowa State University Press, 1969.

Gondos, Victor, Jr. "The Movement for a National Archives of the United States, 1906–1926." Ph.D. dissertation, The American University, 1971.

Griffin, Burt. "Lewis and Clark II, A Legal Analysis," *Manuscripts* 10 (Winter 1958).

Grover, Wayne C. "Archives: Society and Profession." *American Archivist* 18 (Jan. 1955).

———. "Federal Government Archives." *Library Trends* 5 (Jan. 1957).

———. "Government Records for Research." In *Responsible Freedom in the Americas.* Edited by Angel del Río. Garden City, N.Y.: Doubleday & Co., 1955.

———. "The National Archives at Age 20." *American Archivist* 17 (Apr. 1954).

———. "A Note on the Development of Records Centers in the United States." *Indian Archives* 4 (1950).

———. "Recent Developments in Federal Archival Activities." *American Archivist* 14 (Jan. 1951).

———. "Research Facilities and Materials at the National Archives." *American Political Science Review* 34 (Oct. 1940).

———. "The Role of the Archivist in the Preservation of Scientific Records." *Isis* 53 (Mar. 1962).

———. "Toward Equal Opportunities for Scholarship." *Journal of American History* 52 (Mar. 1966).

Gustafson, Milton O. "Archival Implications of State Department Recordkeeping." *Prologue: The Journal of the National Archives* 7 (Spring 1975).

———. "The Empty Shrine: The Transfer of the Declaration of Independence and the Constitution to the National Archives." *American Archivist* 39 (July 1976).

Gwam, Lloyd C. "The First Permanent Building of the Nigerian National Archives." *American Archivist* 26 (Jan. 1963).

Haines, Gerald K. "Who Gives a Damn about Medieval Walls." *Prologue—The Journal of the National Archives* 8 (Summer 1976).

Hamer, Philip M. " . . . authentic Documents tending to elucidate our History." *American Archivist* 25 (Jan. 1962).

_____. "Finding Mediums in the National Archives: An Appraisal of Six Years." *American Archivist* 5 (Apr. 1942).

_____. "The Records of Southern History." *Journal of Southern History* 5 (Feb. 1939).

Herbst, Jurgen. *The German Historical School in American Scholarship: A Study in the Transfer of Culture.* Ithaca, N.Y.: Cornell University Press, 1965.

Hesseltine, William B., and Kaplan, Louis. "Doctors of Philosophy in History." *American Historical Review* 47 (July 1942).

Higham, John; with Krieger, Leonard; and Gilbert, Felix. *History.* Englewood Cliffs, N.J.: Prentice-Hall, 1965.

Hill, Roscoe R. "Archival Terminology." *American Archivist* 6 (Oct. 1943).

_____. "Classification in the National Archives." In *Archives and Libraries 1940.* Edited by A. F. Kuhlman. Chicago: American Library Association, 1940.

Holmes, Oliver W. "Areas of Cooperation Between the National Archives and State Archives." *American Archivist* 14 (July 1951).

_____. "The National Archives and the Protection of Records in War Areas." *American Archivist* 9 (Apr. 1946).

_____. "The National Archives at a Turn in the Road." *American Archivist* 12 (Oct. 1949).

_____. "The Problem of Federal Field Office Records." *American Archivist* 6 (Apr. 1943).

_____. "Recent Writings Relating to Documentary Publication Programs." *American Archivist* 26 (Jan. 1963).

_____. "Territorial Government and the Records of Its Administration." In *The Frontier Reexamined.* Edited by John Francis McDermott. Urbana: University of Illinois Press, 1967.

_____. "Toward an International Archives Program and Council, 1945–1950." *American Archivist* 39 (July 1976).

Hull, Felix. "'Modern Records' Then and Now." *Journal of the Society of Archivists* 4 (Apr. 1972).

"In Memoriam: Theodore R. Schellenberg." *American Archivist* 33 (Apr. 1970).

Jackson, W. Turrentine. "Materials for Western History in the Department of the Interior Archives." *Mississippi Valley Historical Review* 35 (June 1948).

Jenkinson, Hilary. "An International Council on Archives." *Archives* 1 (1949–52).

Jennings, John Melville. "Archival Activity in American Colleges and Universities." *American Archivist* 12 (Apr. 1949).

Jernegan, Marcus W. "Productivity of Doctors of Philosophy in History." *American Historical Review* 33 (Oct. 1927).

Johnson, Edward N. "Trends in County Records Management." *American Archivist* 24 (July 1961).

Johnson, Mrs. Lyndon B. "Welcome to the LBJ Library." *Reader's Digest* 99 (July 1971).

Jones, H. G. "Archival Training in American Universities, 1938–1968." *American Archivist* 31 (Apr. 1968).

————. *The Records of a Nation, Their Management, Preservation, and Use.* New York: Atheneum, 1969.

Kahlenberg, Friedrich. *Deutsche Archive in West and Ost: Zur Entwicklung des Staatlichen Archivwesens seit 1945.* Düsseldorf: Droste Verlag, 1972.

Kahn, Herman. "Libraries and Archivists—Some Aspects of Their Partnership." *American Archivist* 7 (Oct. 1944).

————. "The Presidential Library—A New Institution." *Special Libraries* 50 (Mar. 1959).

————. "Records in the National Archives Relating to the Range Cattle Industry, 1865–1895." *Agricultural History* 20 (July 1946).

————. "World War II and Its Background: Research Materials at the Franklin D. Roosevelt Library and Policies Concerning Their Use." *American Archivist* 17 (Apr. 1954).

Kecskeméti, Charles. "The Spirit of Washington: ICA Congress of 1966." *American Archivist* 32 (Apr. 1969).

Kirkendall, Richard S. "Presidential Libraries—One Researcher's Point of View." *American Archivist* 25 (Oct. 1962).

————. "A Second Look at Presidential Libraries." *American Archivist* 29 (July 1966).

Knapp, William. "Death of a Document." *Reporter* 2 (28 Mar. 1950).

Krauskopf, Robert W. "The Hoover Commissions and Federal Recordkeeping." *American Archivist* 21 (Oct. 1958).

Lagerquist, Philip D. "The Harry S. Truman Library as a Center for Research on the American Presidency." *College and Research Libraries* 25 (Jan. 1964).

Lamb, W. Kaye. "The Fine Art of Destruction." In *Essays in Memory of Sir Hilary Jenkinson.* Edited by Albert E. J. Hollaender.

Leahy, Emmett J. "Records Administration and the War." *Military Affairs* 6 (Summer 1942).

————. "Reduction of Public Records." *American Archivist* 3 (Jan. 1940).

Lee, Charles E. "Documentary Reproduction: Letterpress Publication: Why? What? How?" *American Archivist* 28 (July 1965).

Lefler, Hugh T. "Robert Digges Wimberly Connor." In *Keepers of the Past.* Edited by Clifford L. Lord. Chapel Hill: University of North Carolina Press, 1965.

Leisinger, Albert H. "Microreproduction of Archives for Reference and Publication Purposes." *Archivum* 16 (1966).

Leland, Waldo G. "The Archivist in Times of Emergency." *American Archivist* 4 (Jan. 1941).

————. "Robert D. W. Connor, First Archivist of the United States." *American Archivist* 16 (Jan. 1953).

Lemisch, Jesse. "The American Revolution Bicentennial and the Papers of Great White Men." *AHA Newsletter* 9 (Nov. 1971).

Leopold, Richard W. "Crisis of Confidence: Foreign Policy Research and the Federal Government." *American Archivist* 34 (Apr. 1971).

Lloyd, David. "The Harry S. Truman Library." *American Archivist* 18 (Apr. 1955).

Lokke, Carl L. "The Continental Congress Papers: Their History, 1789–1952." *National Archives Accessions*, no. 51 (June 1954).

Lutz, Paul V. "Government Loses Suit for Documents." *Manuscripts* 19 (Fall 1967).

Maass, Richard. "Arguments Heard in the Clark Case." *Manuscripts* 8 (Winter 1956).

McCain, William D. "Some Suggestions for National Archives Cooperation with the State Archives." *American Archivist* 14 (July 1951).

McCool, Ollon. D. "The Metes and Bounds of Records Management." *American Archivist* 27 (Jan. 1964).

McCoy, Donald R. "The Beginnings of the Franklin D. Roosevelt Library." *Prologue: The Journal of the National Archives* 7 (Fall 1975).

———. "The Crucial Choice: The Appointment of R. D. W. Connor as Archivist of the United States." *American Archivist* 37 (July 1974).

McLean, Ian. "Australian Experience in Record and Archives Management." *American Archivist* 22 (Oct. 1959).

MacMillan, David S. "Archival Reform in Australia." *Journal of the Society of Archivists* 1 (Oct. 1958).

———. "Archives in New South Wales." *American Archivist* 20 (Jan. 1957).

———. "Business Archives." In *Essays in Memory of Sir Hilary Jenkinson*. Edited by Albert E. J. Hollaender.

Marx, Leo. "The American Scholar Today." *Commentary* 32 (July 1961).

Mason, Philip P. "Archival Security: New Solutions to an Old Problem." *American Archivist* 38 (Oct. 1975).

Mendenhall, Thomas C. "Carry On: Echoes from New York." *American Historical Review* 49 (Apr. 1944).

Metzdorf, Robert F. "Lewis and Clark I: A Librarian's Point of View." *Manuscripts* 9 (Fall 1957).

Mitchell, Thornton W. "The State of Records Management." *American Archivist* 24 (July 1961).

Mommsen, Wolfgang A. "Ernst Posner, Mittler zwischen deutschem und amerikanischem Archivwesen." *Der Archivar* 20 (July 1967).

Morris, Richard B. "The Federal Archives of New York City: Opportunities for Historical Research." *American Historical Review* 42 (Jan. 1937).

———. "The Need for Regional Repositories for Federal Records." *American Archivist* 6 (Apr. 1943).

Muller, S.; Feith, J.A.; and Fruin, R. *Manual for the Arrangement and Description of Archives*. Translated by Arthur H. Leavitt. New York: H. W. Wilson Co., 1940.

Munden, Ken. "Records Essential to the Continuity of State and Local Government." *American Archivist* 22 (Jan. 1959).

Noggle, Burl. "A Note on Historical Editing: The Wilson *Papers* in Perspective." *Louisiana History* 8 (Summer 1967).

Norton, Margaret C. "The First International Congress of Archivists, Paris, France, August 21–26, 1950." *American Archivist* 14 (Jan. 1951).

Oliver, Ben. "Records Management is Becoming International." *Records Management Journal* 8 (Winter 1970).

O'Neill, James E. "Secrecy and Disclosure: The Declassification Program of the National Archives and Records Service." *Prologue—The Journal of the National Archives* 5 (Spring 1973).

———. "Will Success Spoil the Presidential Libraries?" *American Archivist* 36 (July 1973).

Overman, William D. "The Pendulum Swings." *American Archivist* 22 (Jan. 1959).

Owen, Thomas M., Jr. "How the National Archives Can Aid Genealogists." *National Genealogical Society Quarterly* 36 (June 1948).

Page, Thaddeus. "R. D. W. Connor, 1878–1950." *American Archivist* 13 (Apr. 1950).

Perlman, Isadore. "General Schedules and Federal Records." *American Archivist* 15 (Jan. 1952).

Petrowski, William R. "Research, Anyone? A Look at the Federal Records Centers." *American Archivist* 30 (Oct. 1967).

Pinkett, Harold T. "Records in the National Archives Relating to the Social Purposes and Results of the Civilian Conservation Corps." *Social Service Review* 22 (Mar. 1948).

"Plans for the Historiography of the United States in World War II." *American Historical Review* 49 (Jan. 1944).

Porter, Charles W. III. "Documentary Research Methods Applied to Historic Sites and Buildings." *American Archivist* 14 (July 1951).

Posner, Ernst M. *Archives and the Public Interest: Selected Essays.* Edited by Ken Munden. Washington: Public Affairs Press, 1967.

———. *Archives in the Ancient World.* Cambridge, Mass.: Harvard University Press, 1972.

———. "The National Archives and the Archival Theorist." *American Archivist* 18 (July 1955).

———. "Public Records Under Military Occupation." *American Historical Review* 49 (Jan. 1944).

———. "Round Table on Archives—Warsaw, 1961." *American Archivist* 25 (Jan. 1962).

Reid, Warren R. "Public Papers of the Presidents." *American Archivist* 25 (Oct. 1962).

Rhoads, James B. "The Future of Hard Copy." *Records Management Journal* 8 (Spring 1970).

———. "One Man's Hopes for His Society, His Profession, His Country." *American Archivist* 39 (Jan. 1976).

Rieger, Morris. "Archives for Scholarship: The Washington Extraordinary Congress of the ICA." *American Archivist* 30 (Jan. 1967).

———. "The Regional Training Center Movement." *American Archivist* 35 (Apr. 1972).

Robertson, Walter, Jr. "NARS: The Politics of Placement." *American Archivist* 39 (Oct. 1976).

Rundell, Walter, Jr. "Clio's Ways and Means: A Preliminary Report on the Survey." *Historian* 30 (Nov. 1967).

———. *In Pursuit of American History.* Norman: University of Oklahoma Press, 1970.

_____. "Relations Between Researchers and Custodians of Source Materials." *College & Research Libraries* 29 (Nov. 1968).

_____. "Restricted Records: Suggestions from the Survey." *AHA Newsletter* 7 (June 1969).

_____. "Uncle Sam the Historian: Federal Historical Activities." *Historian* 33 (Nov. 1970).

Sabbe, Etienne. "Les Archives de l'État." *Archivum* 10 (1960).

Santovenia, Emerterio S. "El Archivo Nacional de Cuba." *Archivum* 7 (1957).

Schellenberg, Theodore R. "Applying American Archival Experience Abroad." *American Archivist* 19 (Jan. 1956).

_____. *Modern Archives: Principles and Techniques.* Chicago: University of Chicago Press, 1956.

Schlesinger, Arthur M., Jr. *The Imperial Presidency.* Boston: Houghton Mifflin, 1973.

Schiller, Irving P. "The Archival Profession in Eclipse." *American Archivist* 11 (July 1948).

Scott, Peter J. "The Record Group Concept: A Case for Abandonment." *American Archivist* 29 (Oct. 1966).

Shafer, Boyd C., ed. *Historical Study in the West.* New York: Appleton-Century-Crofts, 1968.

_____. "Lost and Found." *American Archivist* 18 (July 1955).

Shelley, Fred. "The Choice of a Medium for Documentary Publication." *American Archivist* 32 (Oct. 1969).

_____. "The Interest of J. Franklin Jameson in the National Archives." *American Archivist* 12 (Apr. 1949).

Simpson, Robert R. "Leland to Connors: An Early Survey of American State Archives." *American Archivist* 36 (Oct. 1973).

Smiley, David L. "The W. P. A. Historical Records Survey." In *In Support of Clio: Essays in Memory of Herbert A. Kellar.* Edited by William B. Hesseltine and Donald R. McNeil. Madison: State Historical Society of Wisconsin, 1958.

Smith, Wilfred I. "Archives in Developing Countries: A Contribution to National Development." *American Archivist* 35 (Apr. 1972).

_____. "The Public Archives of Canada." *Records Management Quarterly* 7 (Jan. 1973).

Society of American Archivists. *Proceedings, Providence, R.I., Dec. 29–30, 1936 and Washington, D.C., June 18–19, 1937.* Urbana, Ill.: Society of American Archivists, 1937.

Stender, Walter, and Walker, Evans. "The National Personnel Records Center Fire." *American Archivist* 37 (Oct. 1974).

Stewart, William J. "Opening Closed Material in the Roosevelt Library." *Prologue—The Journal of the National Archives* 7 (Winter 1975).

Stinnett, Caskie. "Lacking Wastebaskets, Bureaucrats Have to 'Downgrade' Their Debris." *Saturday Evening Post* 223 (15 July 1950).

Tate, Vernon D. "File Microcopy Project—The National Archives." *Journal of Documentary Reproduction* 5 (Dec. 1942).

_____. "Microphotography in Archives." In *Archives and Libraries 1939.* Edited by A. F. Kuhlman. Chicago: American Library Association, 1939.

Thomas, Lewis A. "Provincial Archives in Canada." *American Archivist* 19 (Oct. 1955).

Thompson, Edwin A. "Records Declassification in the National Archives." *Prologue—The Journal of the National Archives* 7 (Winter 1975).

Thurber, Evangeline. "Suggestions for a Code for Cataloging Archival Materials." In *Archives and Libraries 1939*. Edited by A. F. Kuhlman. Chicago: American Library Association, 1939.

Trever, Karl L. "Administrative History in Federal Archives." *American Archivist* 4 (July 1941).

————. "The Organization and Status of Archival Training in the United States." *American Archivist* 11 (Apr. 1948).

Turner, Robert W. S. "To Repair or Despair." *American Archivist* 20 (Oct. 1957).

Ulibarri, George S. "The Inter-American Technical Council on Archives." *American Archivist* 27 (Jan. 1964).

Van Schreeven, William J. "The International Congress on Archives, 1953." *American Archivist* 17 (Jan. 1954).

Van Tassel, David D. "John Franklin Jameson." In *Keepers of the Past*. Edited by Clifford L. Lord. Chapel Hill: University of North Carolina Press, 1965.

Waple, Gregory L. "Freedom of Information Act: A Seven Year Assessment." *Columbia Law Review* 74 (June 1974).

Wellbrenner, Bernard. "The Public Archives of Canada, 1871–1958." *Journal of the Society of Archivists* 2 (Apr. 1961).

White, Gerald T. "Government Archives Afield: The Federal Records Centers and the Historian." *Journal of American History* 55 (Mar. 1968).

Wright, Esmond. "The Papers of Great Men." *History Today* 12 (Mar. 1962).

Young, David R. "Secrecy and Disclosure: Braking the Classification Machine." *Prologue: The Journal of the National Archives* 5 (Spring 1973).

Zobrist, Benedict K., II. "Reform in the Classification and Declassification of National Security Information: Nixon Executive Order 11,652." *Iowa Law Review* 59 (Oct. 1973).

INDEX